July 1944

July 1944

Deportation of the Jews of Budapest Foiled

Edited by
Géza Jeszenszky

Copyright 2017 © Helena History Press LLC

All rights reserved

H P

Published in the United States by:

Helena History Press LLC

A division of KKL Publications LLC, Reno, Nevada USA

www.helenahistorypress.com

Publishing scholarship about and from Central and East Europe

ISBN: 978-1-943596-06-5

Distributed by IngramSpark and available through all major e-retail sites
Order: *info@helenahistorypress.com*

Publication support in part provided by the Hungary Initiatives Foundation (HIF) through the American Hungarian Federation.

Copy Editor: Jill Hannum

Graphic Designer: Sebastian Stachowski

German Translation: Jill Hannum, Joanna Cummings

French Translation: Lovice Ullein-Reviczky

English Translation: Thomas Cooper, Tamás Stark

Table of Contents

Foreword
Charles Fenyvesi: The Long Silence of a Heroic Hungarian   1

Introduction by the editor (Géza Jeszenszky)   7

Chapter 1
Tom Lantos: Ferenc Koszorús: A Hero of the Hungarian Holocaust   33
[from *The Congressional Record*]

Chapter 2
György Ránki: The Unwilling Satellite or the Last Satellite   37
[essay in *Hungarian history – World History*. ed. by György Ránki. Budapest: Akadémiai Kiadó, 1984.]

Chapter 3
Géza Jeszenszky: Hungary in the Second World War:
Tragic Blunders or Destiny   65

Chapter 4
Deborah Cornelius: From Occupation to Koszorús's Action   103
[from *Hungary in World War II* pp. 268–288, 292–314,]

Chapter 5
István Deák: The Holocaust in Hungary.   159
Reproduced from *The Hungarian Quarterly*, Vol. 45. Winter 2004.
pp. 50–70. (With the permission of *The Hungarian Quarterly*]

Chapter 6
Tamás Stark: Facts about the Number of Shoah Victims in Hungary   187

Chapter 7
Attila Bonhardt: The Role of Colonel F. Koszorús
in the Prevention of the Deportation of the Jews of Budapest   203

Chapter 8
Susanne Berger and Vadim Birstein: Raoul Wallenberg
– Not an Accidental Choice for Hungary in 1944   219

Chapter 9
Ferenc Koszorús, Jr: Colonel Ferenc Koszorús: Witness and Paragon   249

Appendix
Selected Documents Related to Hungary from the German
Foreign Office Archives   263

Index   307
List of Contributors   313
Photo Gallery

Foreword
The Long Silence of a Heroic Hungarian

Charles Fenyvesi

Unlike Ferenc Koszorús, whose heroic action in July 1944 forms the central theme of this volume, few individuals risked their lives in Nazi-occupied Europe by defying Adolf Hitler's maniacal campaign to hunt down every man, woman and child who had even a single close relative of Jewish descent. A far more common phenomenon was that an informer would alert state authorities to Jews hiding out a city block away ... or next door. In Hungary, as elsewhere on the continent, locals knew – or thought they knew – who was "of Jewish origin".

That every tenth person in Hungary had "some Jewish blood coursing in his veins" was a quip long shared at both the highest and the lowest levels of society. But more so than at any other time in history, one's percentage of Jewish blood had become a life-or-death issue because of the racist legal system imported from Nazi Germany, the superpower neighbor more feared than admired, but also endorsed by the Hungarian parliament. These new laws demanding that every citizen search local archives for proof that they had no Jewish ancestors. Tragically, synagogues throughout the country maintained extensive records of births reaching back to the eighteenth century, and those documents fell under state control.

Ferenc Koszorús, who traced his family's origins to Transylvania, is not known to have had Jews among his ancestors. Nor did he grow up in a neighborhood or live in an intellectual environment where he could have encountered many Jews. His father, his role model, was, like Ferenc himself, a career army officer. He had retired with the rank of lieutenant colonel and died in

1938. In the twentieth century, career army officers did not usually seek out Jewish friends – and vice versa.

Debrecen-born Koszorús's fellow Protestants of the Calvinist denomination, most of whom were church-going Hungarian patriots, were responsible for forming his *Weltanschauung*. Generations earlier, during the 1848 revolution, Koszorús's ancestors had resigned from the ranks of the nobility, and he took pride in that decision, thus earning a reputation as a liberal – at least one in the nineteenth century mode.

Throughout his life Koszorús was an enthusiastic student of Hungary's past. During the post-war decades he spent in the United States, he composed letters and essays almost daily, many of them dealing with the Trianon peace treaty* and World War II, which he singled out as the two catastrophes of recent Hungarian history. He also co-authored a book on the Hungarian military in World War II.

A little over six feet in height, slender and ramrod-straight, Colonel Koszorús walked and talked like a stereotypical Hungarian army officer. He offered a firm handshake and looked straight into the eyes of the people he spoke with. Those who knew him well called him "earnest" and "old fashioned". "Dignified" was another frequent characterization. Undeniably, he was also handsome.

However, he was not in the habit of discussing the one historic and heroic segment of his curriculum vitae: in July 1944 he thwarted a Nazi scheme to liquidate the remnant of Hungarian Jewry, itself the last significant Jewish community still functioning in Hitler's Europe. In a unique action, he ordered the armored division he commanded to take over strategic positions throughout Budapest and threaten to fight the pro-Nazi Hungarian gendarmerie, which was poised to carry out a roundup of all Jews in order to ship them to Auschwitz, despite the fact that Regent Horthy had been warned by the Allies and the King of Sweden to stop the deportation of Jews. Faced with tanks, the gendarmerie, which was cooperating with the pro-Nazi Arrow Cross, gave up without firing a shot and marched back to their local assignments throughout the countryside.[1]

---

* The Peace Treaty signed on 4 July 1920 at the Grand Trianon Palace at Versailles reduced Hungary to a third of its historic territory. Note by the editor.

1 This action forms the central theme of the present volume; it is described in detail in Attila Bonhardt's essay in Chapter 7 of this volume pp 203–218

German Nazi officials and their Hungarian cohorts were furious with Koszorús's maneuver against the gendarmerie. "They pursued me and tried to kill me like a rabid dog," he later wrote in a letter addressed to a relative.

Koszorús's old friend General Károly Lázár – the commander of Horthy's personal bodyguard – wanted to send him to the front, where the Germans would not find and kill him. Although Koszorús wanted to stay in Budapest and argued with Lázár, eventually he and his soldiers loyal to the Regent went off to fight the Russians, who were already in Hungary in September 1944.

In April 1945, the Wehrmacht retreated back to the Reich, along with much of the Hungarian officer corps. Koszorús ended his military career by surrendering to the Americans. After half a dozen difficult years in Displaced Persons' camps in the U.S. occupation zone, Koszorús was vetted and allowed to emigrate to the United States in 1951. He first worked as a day laborer on a farm in Watsonville, California. He also accepted part-time jobs, such as lubricating machinery for the Southern Pacific Railroad. He was a hard worker.

Next, Koszorús engaged briefly in émigré affairs in the hope that the United States might be amenable to liberating Hungary from Moscow's control. When he learned that the Hungarian war veterans' group organized in Western Europe included pro-Nazi officers, he quit it. He soon concluded that U.S. Secretary of State John Foster Dulles's call for a "rollback" of Soviet power in Eastern Europe was more a popular Republican campaign promise than a strategic commitment of the Eisenhower administration. Soon the Pentagon abandoned the idea that a Hungarian veteran's organization could serve as the base of a liberation force.

Koszorús's disappointment in U.S. policies and politicians might have contributed to his reluctance to explain his role in thwarting the July 1944 Nazi coup/deportation attempts.

In 1956 he became a U.S. citizen, and, cleared of any connections with Nazism or Communism, he found employment in classified government jobs that made use of his broad knowledge of mathematics, cartography and geography.

He remained a quiet figure. He was not active in the Washington area Hungarian community of some thousand souls, including leaders who were also Calvinists born in Debrecen. Nor did he seek out individuals in American Jewish institutions or historians of the Holocaust who would have been eager to hear from the army officer who saved – alas, in many cases only temporarily – the Jewish inhabitants of Budapest. His son, Frank Koszorús Junior, recalls that his father, "a strong personality", would neither "brag" about his wartime achievements nor talk about other aspects of his World War II military record. Like others who knew the colonel well, he describes his father as "a very modest person" though "friendly" and "cordial".

Perhaps his inadequate knowledge of the English language contributed to Koszorús's reluctance to lecture, to take part in scholarly conferences, or to write articles about his own historic role. As very private person, he was uncomfortable in that aspect of the American culture that demands full public disclosure and insists on debating complicated, sensitive issues such as Hungary's alliance with Germany in two world wars and the strength of the far right Arrow Cross. His family traditions and his military upbringing both made it natural for him to avoid and distrust public exposure. It would not have been correct for an army officer – and "correct" was an important adjective in the Hungarian value system – to raise the painful subject of why his colleagues did not follow his example.

Koszorús died in 1974, at the age of 74, never having returned to Hungary. He did not leave behind a clear, definitive answer to questions now being raised by some historians. His prolonged silence has made it difficult to determine a precise, unambiguous explanation of his reasons for preparing his division to confront an armed gendarmerie allied with the Germans. Strangely enough, Horthy did not once mention Koszorús in his memoirs. Did he not want to divulge that a little known colonel saved his job?

Koszorús's widow, Gabriella Fülöp, and their son, Frank Junior, broke at least part of the silence when in the 1980s they tracked down the private letters the colonel had written and interviewed witnesses to the events of the summer of 1944.

Based upon information from my acquaintances who knew Koszorús, I think his ideology was far from Horthy's lifelong polite anti-Semitism and from the Regent's coldly opportunistic approach to the *Judenfrage* – "the Jewish question", the official Nazi term connoting the extinction of "the Jewish race". Though Koszorús did not play cards once a week with Hungary's leading Jewish industrialists, as Horthy did, he was an egalitarian who did not believe in the existence of superior and inferior races and classes. He was able to persuade the soldiers in his division that his order to confront the gendarmerie and the Arrow Cross was "correct". He did not hold back the move, despite the likely reprisals by the well-armed and numerous German troops stationed in Hungary. Fortunately, at the time, the Germans were otherwise busy fighting on both the Eastern and the Western Fronts.

We will never know what made the tradition-bound army colonel volunteer his armored division. Was he protecting Horthy, to whom he had taken an oath of allegiance, from a coup? Or was his main intention to shield tens of thousands of Budapest Jews from the Nazi death camps?

The fact is, he was successful in averting both events. No one else would – or perhaps could – have done either.

I am sorry that I did not have an opportunity to interview Colonel Koszorús when we both lived in the Washington, D.C., metropolitan area. I had known several of the people his son lists as having been his close friends in the local Hungarian community. Unfortunately, they had not mentioned his name as a source I should rely on when writing about World War II.

Nevertheless, I think that the time has come to recognize Colonel Koszorús as a rare hero of the anti-Nazi resistance.

Introduction

Géza Jeszenszky

On 19 March 1944, with the German occupation of Hungary, 800,000 Hungarian Jews and a large number of Jewish refugees from Nazi-dominated neighboring lands, the last physically intact Jewish population in Europe, fell under total Nazi domination. Following that, in less than three months half a million of Hungary's Jews were deported to the German-run concentration camps, primarily to Auschwitz, where most of them were "liquidated," murdered. What should make that chapter of the Holocaust especially painful for all Hungarians is the shameful fact that the victims were removed from their homes and taken to makeshift camps, ghettos, and from there were sent to their death under most inhuman conditions *by their fellow Hungarians.*[1] [My italics.] Of course such a crime would have never taken place but for the presence of a quarter million German soldiers, who initiated and backed the deportations.

The Oscar-winning Hungarian film *Saul's Son* was a very special and dramatic presentation of that very process and the reactions of the inmates at Auschwitz. The deportation and murder of half a million Hungarian citizens in 1944 is often brought up in the world press, usually in connection with

---

[1] The most authoritative work on this subject is Randolph L. Braham, *The Politics of Genocide: The Holocaust in Hungary* (New York: Columbia University Press, 1981), 2 Vols.; condensed edition published by Wayne State University Press, 2000. Braham grew up in Transylvania and went through trying years before emigrating to the U.S.A. Cf. Randolph L. Braham and Attila Pók, eds., *The Holocaust in Hungary: Fifty Years Later* (New York: Distributed by Columbia University Press, 1997). The most recent collective and insightful publication is Randolph L. Braham and András Kovács, eds., *The Holocaust in Hungary: Seventy Years Later* (Budapest – New York: Central European University Press, 2016). For the background see: Deborah S. Cornelius, *Hungary in World War II: Caught in the Cauldron* (New York: Fordham University Press, 2011), part of which is reproduced in the present volume.

contemporary political developments in Hungary. Before the 2014 elections a monument planned in the center of Budapest to commemorate the German occupation of Hungary and its victims led to hot debates inside and outside Hungary. Most recently, Hungary's Prime Minister, Viktor Orbán, called Miklós Horthy, Hungary's head of state between 1920 and 1944, "an exceptional statesman," raising many voices in criticism. The issue that remains is the question of responsibility for the enormous tragedy that befell the Jews of Hungary. Does it fall exclusively on Germany, which occupied its nominal ally, and under the direction of Adolf Eichmann initiated "the final solution of the Jewish problem" in Hungary, too, where until then Jews had lived in relative safety? Or is the guilt more than shared by the collaborationist Hungarian government and its civil servants, who ordered and carried out the collection of the Jews and their transportation to Auschwitz in overcrowded cattle-cars? That also brings up the responsibility of head of state Admiral Horthy. He and his governments refused earlier German demands to surrender the Jews, but after the German occupation, he did not resign, and passively watched the deportations, allegedly not knowing what was in store for his fellow-citizens. At the end of June 1944, however, seeing the coming defeat of Germany and having received international protests for the deportations, he managed to halt the process just before the deportations from Budapest were to start. By 6 July, gendarmerie units that were loyal to the pro-Nazi puppet government and ready to carry out the deportation of the close to 300,000 Jewish Hungarians living in Budapest, were brought to Budapest – which by law they were not entitled to enter. (In Budapest the police force was responsible for keeping order; the gendarmerie looked after the countryside.)

There were rumors that the pro-Nazi and rabidly anti-Semitic under-secretary of the interior, László Baky, was in fact planning a coup to remove Horthy and to continue the deportations. Colonel Ferenc Koszorús volunteered to intervene, and having received the command from Horthy, entered Budapest with his 1st Armored Corps, ordered the withdrawal of the gendarmerie, and thus foiled both the planned coup (if that really had been planned) and the continuation of the deportations. The Jews of Budapest were thus temporarily saved and escaped the fate of the Jews in the countryside, who had already been sent off to their destiny. There were still terrible months ahead for

Introduction

them, especially when on 15 October an attempt by the regent to conclude an armistice was thwarted by the Germans and their Hungarian allies, the so-called Arrow Cross Movement. Having taken over the government, this rabble carried out mass murder, shooting thousands on the banks of the Danube, near the Parliament building, where today metal replicas of their shoes serve as a memorial. Nonetheless, Raoul Wallenberg, other diplomats and also brave Hungarians managed to save many Jews in Budapest, helping them to survive the war until, by mid-February 1945, the Soviet army occupied Budapest and expelled the Germans.

Should Horthy be praised for defying the Nazis or condemned for not having prevented the crime earlier? Or there is the larger controversy: as a result of the German occupation, did Hungarian sovereignty come to an end and so the responsibility for the ensuing horrors rests entirely with Nazi Germany? Or perhaps the whole Hungarian nation is guilty because of the active collaboration by many Hungarians? That is not so much a debate among historians as it is part of the political conflict between the government of Viktor Orbán and his opponents. But no political agenda should lead to overlooking the historical facts, either to whitewash or to blacken the record. This is an extremely hot subject, after all, it is about the deliberate murder of more than half a million innocent people. Here the attempt for historical accuracy runs parallel to understanding the sentiments of the survivors, those related to the victims, and indeed all decent people. The present collective volume cannot answer all the historical questions and settle the debates; its purpose is only to show what really happened in those crucial days in early July.

✶ ✶ ✶

Hungarians, like the Americans, are also a nation of immigrants. The seven Hungarian tribes, nomadic warriors who moved into the Carpathian Basin from the eastern steppe region at the end of the ninth century. They absorbed the Slavic and probably the Avar populations. Then the Hungarian settlement was followed by other waves of immigration: the Transylvanian Saxons and the German settlers in the north (in today's Slovakia) in the twelfth, Cumanians in the thirteenth century. The Kingdom was devastated by attacks by the Ottoman Turks in the sixteenth–seventeenth century, then it was repopulated by Germans ("Swabians"), Serbs and Romanians, especially in the south and east in the eighteenth century.

There were already Jews living on the territory of Hungary during the time of the Roman Empire, and also in the medieval kingdom, but they arrived in larger numbers in the eighteenth and especially in the nineteenth century. They escaped from persecution, *pogroms*, in the Russian Empire, but also arrived from the west as Hungary, with its rich natural resources, offered great opportunities. Jews settled all over the country. Although most of them spoke Yiddish, practically a dialect of German, they quickly learned the Hungarian language and came to identify themselves fully with the Hungarian people. The legal emancipation of the Jews was enacted as soon as Hungary became self-governing in 1867. There were Jewish members elected to the Hungarian Parliament beginning in 1865, and in the early twentieth century several Jews became government ministers. A minority converted to Christianity, but the vast majority kept Judaism, many in a modernized "Neolog" form. The integration and assimilation of the Jews in Hungary was more thorough than in any other country, including Germany and Austria, with the exception of the United States – but there only in the last decades. Immigrant Jews played an essential role in the remarkable development Hungary achieved during the fifty years of the Austro-Hungarian Dual Monarchy. They excelled in science and the arts, as attested by great works in literature, music, painting, and, later, in films. By the twentieth century their number had reached one million (5 percent of the population), and they constituted about 25 percent of the inhabitants of the capital, which the Austrian and German anti-Semites called "Judapest."

As several essays in the present volume point out, Hungary was most harshly and unfairly treated in the peace treaty following World War I. The generally shared hope and aim to reverse the enormous territorial losses of the historic kingdom compelled Hungary to draw close to whoever was ready and able to facilitate any change in the borders in Central Europe. The League of Nations did allow border changes under certain circumstances. Italy was the first to endorse Hungary's claim for treaty revision, but only Germany had the power to really press for that – for the sake of its own nationalist agenda. In his deservedly popular textbook Joseph Rotschild wrote: "Though the Hungarians are probably the most Anglophile nation of East Central Eu-

Introduction

rope, they served in World War II as one of Hitler's calculating satellites." The author's explanation is that Hungary's territorial truncation in 1920 was partly remedied by Hitler between 1938 and 1941.

> Supping with the devil proverbially requires a long spoon, and the spoon of the Anglophile, whiggish, old-fashioned, liberal-conservative Hungarian ruling classes was not long enough to avoid paying a price for Hitler's patronage of their territorial expansions, though they maneuvered resourcefully to try to hold that price down. [...] Hungary was virtually a neutral in the war between the Axis and the Western Allies. And in such noncombatant war efforts as industrial production, the export of food and raw materials to Germany, and the facilitation of the Wehrmacht's communication and supply systems, Hungary minimized its contribution to the Axis effort. [...] To the chagrin and rage of the Radical Rightists, domestic social and institutional coordination with the Nazi model was also diluted by the ruling conservatives. Parliamentary debate was vigorous, opposition parties were active, trade unions remained free, the press was lively – though overt criticism of Germany was taboo. Civil liberties endured. Escaping Poles and Allied war prisoners received shelter, and the Jews though economically and socially molested, were shielded from extermination. Finally, the exasperated Hitler occupied Hungary in mid-March 1944 and forced the replacement of the foot-dragging and peace-seeking conservative government with a more pro-German one though, still not within all-out Radical Right one.[2]

Anti-Semitism reared its ugly head in Hungary, too, after World War I, but it is unfair to say that Hungarians were instinctively intolerant towards the Jews. If that had been the case, Jewish assimilation would not have been so wide-spread and deep. The racist ideology of Hitler, however, found an echo in the 1930s, mainly among people who envied the success of the Jews, who saw in them rivals for jobs, and who were looking for scapegoats for the political and econom-

---

2   Joseph Rothschild, *Return to Diversity: A Political History of East Central Europe Since World War II* (New York – Oxford: Oxford University Press, 1993), 40–42.

ic miseries Hungary sustained after the Great War. Starting in 1938, several laws were passed by the Hungarian Parliament and decrees issued restricting the rights of the Jews. But despite those most deplorable and disgraceful laws, the life and liberty of the close to 800,000 Hungarian citizens of Jewish background were not in danger until the occupation by Germany. Hungary's Jews considered themselves (and indeed were) patriotic Hungarians; most were confident that the Hungarian State would protect them from Hitler.

Starting in 1942 the new prime minister, Miklós Kállay, initiated secret talks with British and American diplomats and intelligence officers about defecting from the German camp. A secret armistice was even signed on 9 September 1943 in Istanbul upon Hungary's surrender. It would have come into force when Allied forces reached the border of Hungary. Without that, a break with Germany would have been tantamount to suicide for the many anti-Nazi elements, above all for the Hungarian Jews and the Allied POWs and European Jews who found asylum in Hungary. Following the Wannsee Conference in January 1942, when Hitler decided on "the final solution" of "the Jewish question", the extermination of all, Germany demanded the implementation of the harshest anti-Jewish measures in Hungary. Specifically: legislation for the complete elimination of the Jews from cultural and economic life, marking of Jews with a yellow star, their evacuation from Hungary, and the confiscation of Jewish property.[3] The Hungarian Government flatly rejected the German request, explaining that meeting the demands would ruin the economy of Hungary. Prime Minister Kállay added that the peasants, who formed the majority of the population, did not have anti-Semitic feelings.[4] The German view was that the one million Jews Hungary sheltered were responsible for its "defeatist attitude" and for sabotaging the common war effort. Hitler was determined to remove all Jews from Europe while the war was on. SS Brigadier General Edmund Veesenmayer visited Hungary twice in 1943 and recommended a stick and carrot policy towards Hungary: forcing the replacement of Prime Minister Kállay by a loyal pro-

---

3   Memorandum from Staatssekretär Luther to Foreign Minister Ribbentrop, 6 October 1942. See Appendix, Doc.1.
4   Randolph L. Braham, *Eichmann and the Destruction of Hungarian Jewry* (World Federation of Hungarian Jews, distributed by Twayne Publishers, 1961).

Introduction

German, but keeping Horthy as a figurehead, isolating him from the aristocrats and the Jews, and encouraging his endeavors to create a Horthy dynasty. Veesenmayer considered it essential to "to take the *Judenfrage* in our hands."[5]

Angered by "the unrestricted presence of some one million Jews as a concrete menace to the safety of German arms in the Balkan Peninsula," by the defiance of Hungary, and also by the information about secret peace feelers extended to the Allies, Hitler decided to forestall the defection of a geopolitically very important ally, and on 12 March 1944 ordered the Margarethe Plan, the military invasion and occupation of Hungary, to be carried out. He invited head of state Admiral Horthy for talks on the Hungarian request to call back the Hungarian Army from the Russian Front. That was a simple trap: while Horthy was held practically captive in Schloss Klessheim near Salzburg, the German troops marched into Hungary. With much of the Hungarian Army on the Russian Front, and also having too many pro-German officers – both at the front and also in the ministry of defense – armed resistance was not offered; no preparations had been made for that.

The Gestapo immediately arrested several members of the Hungarian Parliament and hundreds of prominent citizens; Veesenmayer, appointed as Minister to Hungary and Plenipotentiary, demanded that Horthy install a government ready to meet all Germany's wishes. Having rejected two proposed candidates, Horthy appointed Döme Sztójay, Hungary's minister in Berlin, as prime minister. While most Hungarians watched passively, quite a few still believed in a German victory, and/or sympathized with the Nazi ideology, including its anti-Semitism. Others just preferred Nazi occupation to Soviet communist occupation.[6] The new, blindly pro-Nazi members of the

---

5 Veesenmayer's report to Staatssekretär Steengracht, 4 December 1943. Document 561 in *A Wilhelmstrasse és Magyarország. Német diplomáciai iratok Magyarországról 1933–1944* [Wilhelmstrasse and Hungary. German diplomatic papers on Hungary 1933–1944], György Ránki, Ervin Pamlényi, Loránt Tilkovszky, Gyula Juhász, eds. (Budapest: Kossuth Kiadó, 1968). (Hereafter, *Wilhelmstrasse*.)

6 Hungary had a brief experience of communism in 1919, when anger over social injustice and foreign occupation led to a Bolshevik coup, with disastrous internal and external consequences. See Rudolf Tőkés, *Béla Kun and the Hungarian Soviet Republic: The Origins and Role of the Communist Party of Hungary in the Revolutions of 1918–1919* (New York: F.A. Praeger, 1967); Andrew C. Janos and William Slottman, eds., *Revolution in Perspective: Essays on the Hungarian Soviet Republic of 1919* (Berkeley, CA: University of California Press, 1971); Bennet Kovrig, *Communism in Hungary: From Kun to Kádár* (Stanford, CA: Hoover Institution Press, 1979). The memory of the "Red Terror" and news about the Soviet Union led most Hungarians to abhor communism.

puppet government imposed on the country betrayed their Jewish compatriots and surrendered them to Nazi Germany. There are numerous accounts of what followed, including memoirs by survivors.[7] Adolf Eichmann arrived in Budapest with a special detachment of the SS, "experts" in mass deportation. The first order was that the yellow Star of David be worn by all people of Jewish origin, including those who had converted to Christianity. Then the Jews who lived outside of Budapest were gathered in temporary camps, where conditions were appalling. At the end of April, the transportation of the collected Jews to the extermination camps started. The Sztójay government, the Hungarian civil service and the Hungarian gendarmerie facilitated the deportations with decrees and with their merciless actions. The official explanation, accepted also by the victims, was that the Jews were to be taken to Germany to make up for the depleted workforce, and their families were to accompany them as a favor. The welcoming words at Auschwitz, "Arbeit macht frei", were to disguise that the aim was to liquidate the deported immediately or by working them to death.

Both Germans and Hungarians bear responsibility for the Holocaust in Hungary. One can only agree with Randolph Braham: "While the Germans were eager to solve the Jewish question, they could not have proceeded without the consent of the newly established puppet government and the cooperation of the Hungarian instrumentalities of power. ... The Hungarian ultra-rightists, in turn ... could not have achieved their ideologically defined objectives in the absence of the occupation [in March 1944]."[8] Those who were responsible for taking Hungary recklessly into the war, and who issued the orders for the deportations and carried those orders out, were tried in Hungary after the war. Between 1945 and 1949, 59,429 persons were tried by specially created "people's courts": 26,997 were found guilty, 477 were sentenced to death, and 189 were actually executed, including four heads of government and several ministers. Compare that to relevant figures in other

---

7   Randolph L. Braham, *Bibliography of the Holocaust in Hungary* (New York: Distributed by Columbia University Press, 2011).
8   Randolph L. Braham: "The Uniqueness of the Holocaust in Hungary", in Randolph Braham and Béla Vágó, eds., *The Holocaust in Hungary Forty Years Later* (New York: Columbia University Press, 1985), 186.

Introduction

countries occupied by Nazi Germany, or even to Germany itself – Hungary cannot be charged with having been lenient towards its war criminals. Those were indeed traitors to their nation, as they aided in the death of almost 5 percent of their compatriots and blackened the reputation of Hungary.

While I hold it to be self-evident that the guilty ones had to answer for their deeds, I disagree with those who deny that the sovereignty of Hungary was abolished with the Nazi German occupation. The new government installed was picked by Veesenmayer, Germany's Plenipotentiary. The Hungarian Army was placed under the command of the German Army. In addition to the arrest of hundreds of prominent politicians and other individuals, the majority of the mayors and the heads of local government were also replaced. There were massive dismissals of public servants. Can one say that Belgium, the Netherlands, Denmark or Norway remained sovereign states following their invasion by Hitler and the installation of obedient puppets to run those countries?[9] After 19 March, the real authority over all the affairs of Hungary was not the regent, nor the head of the puppet government, but Edmund Veesenmayer, the German Plenipotentiary. His letter of appointment, signed by Hitler, stated: "The Reich Plenipotentiary is responsible for all political developments in Hungary and receives his directives through the Reich Minister for Foreign Affairs."[10] On the other hand, it is a sad truth that "the majority of the officials in Hungary went about solving the 'Jewish question' with initiative, flexibility, and often even with enthusiasm."[11] Many Hungarians gave vent to their anti-Semitic prejudices and happily participated in stealing the properties of their deported or hiding Jewish compatriots, while the majority of the population just passively watched the cruel removal of their Jewish neighbors. (Just as, a few years later, they were paralyzed with fear as the terror imposed by the communists raged, persecuting hundreds of thousands of innocents.)

---

9   The diplomatic missions in Budapest of the neutral States considered that with the German occupation, Hungary ceased to be a sovereign country. They saw decisive proof for that in the arbitrary activities of the Gestapo and other German security organs. E.g., Veesenmayer's cable to Ribbentrop, 16 June 1944. Doc. 686 in *Wilhelmstrasse*.
10 *The Confidential Papers of Admiral Horthy*. Prepared for press and introd. by M. Szinai and L. Szűcs (Budapest: Corvina Press, 1965), 289. (Hereafter, *Horthy Papers*.)
11 Judit Molnár, "Nazi Perpetrators: Behavior of Hungarian Authorities during the Holocaust", http://www.jewishvirtuallibrary.org/behavior-of-hungarian-authorities-during-the-holocaust.

But it would be wrong to think that all Hungarians swallowed the anti-Semitic poison. In the fall of 1943 the parliamentary opposition demanded the revocation of the anti-Jewish laws, calling it "a disgrace for Hungary."[12] Following the occupation, a large number of Gentile Hungarians did their best to save the Jews by hiding them, giving them falsified documents etc., risking severe punishment or their own life.[13] The American Jewish Yearbook notes that "hundreds of people were arrested for hiding Jews and helping them to escape."[14] The exact number of such persons cannot be ascertained, but a proof of their bravery is the fact that close to a thousand received the recognition "Righteous among the Nations" from the Yad Vashem Institute.[15] The most honest and self-critical analysis of the behavior of the Hungarian people during and after the Holocaust was provided by the scholar (and politician in 1956) István Bibó.[16] So in my view, while all Hungarians must accept, woefully, responsibility for the death of their Jewish compatriots, György Ránki was right in his conclusion that "with all due regard to the major Hungarian component, upon examining the events, one must conclude that without the Germans, the Hungarian Holocaust would not have occurred in the same manner."[17]

When remembering the Shoah, one of the most painful questions is whether, by employing different policies, the annihilation of such a large part of Hungary's Jews could have been averted, or at least the number of victims substantially reduced. Traditional, mainly Marxist historiography blamed Hungary for the failure to break with Nazi Germany before the occupation. But contemporaries, like Lewis Namier of the Jewish Agency, warned that

---

12   Memorandum by the Independent Smallholders Party, 31 July 1943. See Cornelius, *Hungary in World War Two*, 253.
13   Fenyvesi, Charles: *When Angels Fooled the World: Rescuers of Jews in Wartime Hungary* (Madison: The University of Wisconsin Press, 2003).
14   Eugene Hevesi, in *The American Jewish Year Book*, Vol. 46 (1944–1945), 254–261.
15   The honored ones include Vilmos Nagybaconi Nagy, the minister of defence in 1942–43, other military officers, high-ranking civil servants like József Antall Sr., whose son was elected prime minister in 1990, following the collapse of communism.
16   István Bibó, "The Jewish Question in Hungary after 1944", in *Istvan Bibó: Democracy, Revolution, Self-determination. Selected Writings*, Károly Nagy, ed. (New York: Columbia University Press, 1991), 192–244.
17   György Ránki, "The Germans and the Destruction of Hungarian Jewry", in Randolph L. Braham and Béla Vágó, eds., *The Holocaust in Hungary Forty Years Later*, 77. Cf. Frank Koszorús, Jr., "Reflections on 19 March 1944 and its Aftermath: A Perfect Storm of Tragedy and Folly", *Hungarian Review*, Vol. V, No. 2 (2014).

Introduction

such a step would lead to Germany occupying Hungary and destroying its Jewish population on the pattern seen in the rest of German-controlled Europe. "The only hope, as far as the Jews are concerned, is that the Hungarians would choose not to move until it was practically certain that the Germans would not be able to react."[18] Hence Braham's tentative hypothesis:

> Had Hungary continued to remain a militarily passive but politically vocal ally of the Third Reich instead of provocatively engaging in diplomatic maneuvers that were essentially fruitless, if not merely aimed at establishing an alibi, the Jews of Hungary might possibly have survived the war relatively unscathed.[19]

That is indeed "a frightening conclusion."[20] This debate on alternatives cannot be answered and put to rest. But closely related to it is the question posed by András Kovács: "To what extent did cooperation [of the Hungarian authorities with the German occupiers] influence the outcome," the almost complete annihilation of the Jews who lived in the provinces, outside Budapest?[21] According to one school (Christian Gerlach, Götz Aly, Gábor Kádár, Zoltán Vági and Krisztián Ungváry) "a large part of the Jewish population might have survived the German occupation if the Hungarians had refused to collaborate with the country's occupiers." On the other hand, László Karsai has pointed out that "the order to destroy Hungarian Jewry came directly from Hitler, while its execution was assigned to Himmler and the SS. Only this can explain why such senior members of the SS as Kaltenbrunner, as well as Eichmann and his team of deportation experts, arrived in Hungary in the immediate aftermath of the occupation."[22] Actual histo-

---

18 "Note by Sir A.W.G. Randall on 14 October 1943", in Elizabeth Barker, *British Policy in South-East Europe in the Second World War* (London: Macmillan Press, 1976), 258. Cf. Gyula Juhász, ed., *Magyar-brit titkos tárgyalások 1943-ban* [The Secret Talks between Hungary and Britain in 1943] (Budapest: Kossuth, 1987), Doc. 82.
19 Braham, *The Politics of Genocide*, Vol. 1, 225–226.
20 István Deák, "Could the Hungarian Jews Have Survived?" *The New York Review of Books*, Vol. 24 (24 February 1982), 1.
21 András Kovács, "Hungarian Intentionalism: New Directions in the Historiography of the Hungarian Holocaust", in Braham and Kovacs, *The Holocaust in Hungary Seventy Years Later*, 9.
22 Ibid., 9–14.

ry should make it possible to draw close to a consensus. Anti-Semitic notions and tendencies were present in Hungary at least since 1919, the Hungarian Soviet Republic, where most of the leaders came from Jewish families, and due their blind faith in the communist utopia they employed terror against those whom they considered dangerous opponents, including Jewish capitalists. Red terror led to "white" terror following the fall of the communists. In the 1930s, influenced by Germany, anti-Semitism increased, but both the liberals and the genuine conservatives were opposed to discrimination based on religion or racial origin. The political leadership, with only a few exceptions, detested both the ideology and the practice of Nazi Germany and its Hungarian followers. The radical anti-Semitic Right was kept away from the government by Horthy and his closest advisers, and without the German takeover of the country, they would not have been able to carry out their program of "de-Judification" (*Entjudung*). Even among those on the Right, that aim did not necessarily mean the physical destruction of the Jews; many thought that emigration (to Palestine, or to an African country) might be a solution. But after the German occupation, they did not mind what happened to those who were deported; it was even welcome that the dirty work was done by others.

It is not true that Hungary has not faced up to those terrible crimes. Already in 1946 the Hungarian National Assembly passed Law XXV, expressing its mourning over the murder of so many of its citizens. But during the communist years there was hardly any mention of that great tragedy. Since 1990, however, many Hungarian leaders have admitted the responsibility of the Hungarian State for the enormous loss and the pain caused. Let me quote passages from a message sent on 24 June 1992 by the late prime minister of Hungary József Antall to the Paris Conference on Anti-Semitism organized by UNESCO and the Wiesenthal Centre.

> Several hundred thousands of our compatriots were ejected from the body of the nation at the time of the Second World War, were deprived of all their possessions, humiliated in their human dignity, deported, and robbed of their dearest treasure, their lives. All this bears down as a dreadful burden on the victims' contemporaries and pos-

Introduction

terity alike. A reckoning must be made not only for the survivors and the descendants of the victims, but for ourselves, that we may take part with cleansed souls in building the renewing Hungary of today. [...] The Hungarian government, motivated by its sense of historical responsibility and as a sincere advocate of democracy, gives its utmost support to preserving and fostering Jewish intellectual and cultural values, which belong to the common heritage of society. [...] My government considers it important that compensation for injustices perpetrated in past decades should extend also to individuals robbed of their freedom or lives between 1939 and 1945. We know that nothing can now replace a lost family member, but we wish to contribute to healing the painful wounds of the past and bringing about social redress. Hungary is so far the only country in our region to offer legal redress of this kind for injustices suffered during the Second World War. We cannot forget our innocently murdered compatriots and we keep in mind their deeds and their deaths. Our martyrs of 1944, like the fallen of the 1956 revolution or those executed after it, are symbols of the Hungarian will to live. The Hungarian government also intervenes in its international relations to combat discrimination against peoples or religious and ethnic groups. We are delighted that after a forced break of more than two decades, we can now build up flourishing relations with the State of Israel. It is our belief that both the Jewish community in Hungary and the Hungarian-speaking citizens of Israel as a whole can play the role of a bridge between the two countries.[23]

Modest compensation programs were introduced by Hungarian legislation after the system change. The Jewish Heritage of Hungary Public Endowment was created in 1997; it pays monthly pensions to approximately 18,000 Hungarian Holocaust survivors. All subsequent prime ministers, including the Socialist Gyula Horn and Viktor Orbán, the present one, admitted the guilt and offered apologies.

---

23 József Antall, *Selected Speeches and Interviews*, Géza Jeszenszky, ed. (Budapest: József Antall Foundation, 2008), 297–298.

Horthy's conduct

Hungary's head of state was clearly not a democrat, but neither was he a dictator. His ambition was to be like Emperor-King Francis Joseph, not to interfere in the daily business of politics, but to have the final say in selecting a prime minister as well as in foreign policy. As a naval officer Horthy admired the British, also for their role in selecting him as regent in 1920. He often expressed his conviction that the maritime powers would always prevail; nevertheless he had a decisive role both in Hungary joining Hitler's war against Yugoslavia and eventually against the Soviet Union. Hitler pretended to respect him, but in fact considered him "an old fool," and was very much aware of the regent's Anglophile proclivities.

Practically all professional historians agree that Horthy's call in the Crown Council of 26 June not to proceed with the deportation of the Jews of Budapest saved those living (or hiding) in the capital – at least for the time being. "It is an irony of fate that in saving the Jews of Budapest decisive credit belongs to Horthy."[24] Without that call, Wallenberg, Lutz, and the many Hungarian and non-Hungarian Righteous could not have found many to save. Why did Horthy do that then, and why he did not act earlier? Was he passive, despondent after 19 March? Was he powerless then, but found new strength in late June? Was his decision motivated by the Normandy landings and prompted by the protests he received from President Roosevelt, the Pope, the King of Sweden, and from many Hungarians, including church leaders? Was the Auschwitz Protocols being forwarded to him the decisive factor? Should Jews really be grateful to Horthy? Or should he be regarded a war criminal as half a million of his fellow-citizens were rounded up and sent to their death when he was head of state? There are elements of truth in all these questions.

It is beyond doubt that Horthy, like so many of his contemporaries, had anti-Semitic prejudices. He distinguished between the Jewish high bourgeoi-

---

24 György Ránki, in *Élet és Irodalom*, Vol. 26, No. 25 (1982). Republished in *A Harmadik Birodalom árnyékában* [In the shadow of the Third Reich] (Budapest: Magvető, 1988), 207. At the age of 14 Ránki survived Auschwitz.

Introduction

sie, many of whom had been ennobled by Emperor-King Francis Joseph,[25] and the more recent arrivals from the East, Galicia (Galizien). Horthy held that "those who have excelled themselves in science, in the industrialization of Hungary and in finance should be considered good patriots, and they should not be touched. He does not tolerate that those who received the title of nobility, those whom he appointed privy councilor, Member of the Upper House or university professor should be lumped together with the other Jews. Hungary owes them the great economic progress of the last decades."[26] Members of the Chorin, Vida, Goldberger and Weiss families, some of them his regular bridge partners, were close to Horthy, and in his exile in Portugal he received financial support from those very same Hungarian-Jewish families.[27] Horthy did sign the "Jewish laws" passed after 1938, which put serious economic and social constraints on a section of Hungarian society, violating the principle of equality before the law, but he refused to introduce the harsh measures used in all German-occupied Europe. In April 1943 in his talks with Hitler at Schloss Klessheim, when Hitler reproached him for his permissive policy towards the Jews, Horthy retorted that having deprived the Jews of nearly every means of getting a living, he could not "beat them to death". To this, foreign minister Joachim von Ribbentrop declared that the Jews must either be killed or sent to concentration camps. Wasn't that a clear indication of the Nazi policy? On 18 March 1944, on his second visit to Schloss Klessheim, Horthy was confronted with Hitler's decision to occupy Hungary lest it follow "the Italian treason." Horthy's protests were answered by accusations against Prime Minister Kállay's secret overtures and the anti-German mood of the Hungarian press and public. Another charge was that Hungary "was not prepared to settle accounts with the large Jewry in Hungary." Horthy was practically detained while he considered the terms

---

25 William O. McCagg, *Jewish Nobles and Geniuses in Modern Hungary* (New York: East European Quarterly, distributed by Columbia University Press, 1972).
26 Regent Horthy's behavior in the Jewish question. Doc. 506-1 in *Wilhelmstrasse*.
27 When Horthy was a penniless exile in Portugal regular financial support was provided for him and his family by a foundation initiated by J.F. Montgomery, the US minister to Hungary in 1933–1941. Contributions to the Fund came from the Chorin, Weiss and other Hungarian-Jewish families. Péter Gosztonyi, *A kormányzó Horthy Miklós és az emigráció* [Regent Miklós Horthy and the emigration] (Budapest: Százszorszép, 1992), 148. Cf. Ilona Edelsheim Gyulay, *Becsület és kötelesség* [Honor and Duty] 2 Vols. (Budapest: Európa Könyvkiadó, 2001), Vol. 2., 219.

of Hitler's ultimatum, which included the threat to use also Romanian, Slovak and Croat troops in the occupation. Finally, pressed by his entourage, he gave in and agreed to remain at his post against Hitler's promise that if he appointed a government acceptable to the Germans, the occupying forces would be promptly withdrawn. But he refused "to sign a proclamation according to which the German troops entered Hungary in agreement with him and with his consent."[28] No reliable source on that meeting suggests that Horthy agreed to the deportation of the Jews from Hungary. But he may have accepted that a substantial number of them would be sent to Germany in order to ease the shortage in the workforce in the Reich.[29]

Arriving back in Budapest on 19 March in the late morning, Horthy called for a Crown Council (a meeting of the cabinet chaired by the regent) where he told his ministers what had happened at Klessheim. Prime minister Kállay in his memoirs wrote that he begged Horthy to abdicate. "I cannot," Horthy said, striking his chair, "leave this chair empty ... I have sworn to this country not to forsake it ... Who will defend the Jews or our refugees if I leave my post? I may not be able to defend everything, but I believe that I can still be of great, very great, help to our people."[30] The minutes of the Crown Council show, however, and Horthy himself states in his memoirs, that Kállay and all the ministers insisted that the regent should hold on so as to be able to restrain the effects of the occupation. "The Regent should preferably retire from the actual management of the various affairs. Yet this position, the Regency, he should abandon neither from his own free will, nor under duress."[31] Horthy was right in saying that it would have been far more comfortable for him and would have saved him from many recriminations if, with a firm gesture, he had relieved himself from all further responsibility by resigning.[32]

---

28 Minutes of the Crown Council dealing with the talks of Miklós Horthy and his suite at Klessheim and the situation brought about by the German occupation, *Horthy Papers,* Doc. 59, 278–290.
29 C.A. Macartney, *October fifteenth: a history of modern Hungary, 1929–1945,* 2 Vols. (Edinburgh: Edinburgh University Press, 1956–1957), Vol. 2, 239; Bryan Cartledge, *The Will to Survive. A History of Hungary,* 2nd ed. (London: Hurst & Company, 2011), 396. No serious Hungarian historian believes that at Klessheim Horthy agreed to the deportation of all the Jews of Hungary against a promise that once *Judenfrei,* Hungary's sovereignty would be restored.
30 *Nicholas [Miklós] Kállay, Hungarian Premier. A Personal Account of a Nation's Struggle in the Second World War* (New York: Columbia University Press, 1954), 433.
31 Minutes of the Crown Council, *Horthy Papers,* 287.
32 Miklós Horthy, *Emlékirataim* [My Memoirs] (Budapest: Európa, 1990), 284.

Introduction

This is the crux of the matter: had Horthy abdicated, he could not be blamed for the crimes and tragedies which followed, and his personal reputation would be far better today. But would life have become easier for both Jews and non-Jews in Hungary if he had done so? Hardly. What cannot be given an answer to, however, is whether, by making it clear to all that with the regent's departure the constitutional and legal order in Hungary had come to an end, at least passive resistance to the German occupation would have been stronger. What would have been the reaction of the army, the officers and the rank and file with the commander-in-chief gone? Would all the Jews have obeyed the order of an obviously illegal puppet administration to move into ghettos and walk to the trains which took them to a very suspicious destination? Some of those dilemmas are illuminated by István Deák's essay in the present book. And of course much would have been very different if the world have known what the real aim of the deportations was, and at least after the revelations of the Auschwitz Protocols had been publicized. Braham is right in denouncing "the conspiracy of silence."[33]

Having refused two candidates proposed by the Germans, Horthy, under another ultimatum (now from Veesenmayer), appointed as prime minister Döme Sztójay, the minister to Germany, a narrow-minded pro-German military officer. Horthy presumed that a soldier would show respect for the commander-in-chief, but Sztójay turned out to be loyal not to Horthy but to Hitler. The regent, an admiral, thought that he should not abandon the sinking ship by resigning and hoped to preserve enough influence to prevent complete subservience to Germany. But he should not have acquiesced to the measures introduced by the puppet regime. Was Horthy really so gullible as to believe in Hitler's promise that if he appointed a government acceptable to the Germans, the military occupation would end? Seeing that the Gestapo had arrested hundreds of prominent politicians, including his friends, and he was unable to have them released, he should have stepped down at least then. In that case, however, nobody would have prevented the deportation of the Jews nof Budapest.

Immediately upon being formed on 23 March, Hungary's Quisling-government started to issue drastic decrees which deprived all persons of Jewish

---

33 Braham, *The Politics of Genocide*, Vol. 2, Ch. 23.

extraction of the most basic necessities for survival. Instead of signing those decrees, Horthy just washed his hands. "According to the Prime Minister's statement, His Highness has granted full powers to the government under his [Sztójay's] leadership in respect of all [anti-]Jewish regulations, and in this matter he wants to exercise no influence whatever."[34] Did Horthy know what the decrees and the ensuing deportations meant? Could he believe that families with old people and children were just taken to Germany to work in fortifications and factories? Surely he did not know exactly what went on at Auschwitz, but he should not have watched passively the systematic mass deportation of Hungarian citizens, starting on 15 May. Although his public functions became rare, amounting to passive resistance, to all appearances Horthy continued to function as head of state. He signed new appointments to state functions, including the nomination of László Endre and László Baky, well-known for their hatred of Jews, as under-secretaries in the Ministry of the Interior. Still the Germans did not trust him. Veesenmayer was instructed to keep the regent "more and more at a distance from the business of the government, pushed into the background and gradually completely isolated in the castle."[35]

Isolated or not, Horthy, too, learned about the brutalities of the collection, the ghettoization and the transportation of the Jews. Some of the leaders of the Christian churches protested, most notably Catholic Bishop Áron Márton of Gyulafehérvár/Alba Iulia in Southern (Romanian) Transylvania. In a sermon in Kolozsvár/Cluj (Hungarian Northern Transylvania) he warned as early as 22 May that "we should not bring the wrath of God to ourselves by committing crimes which the catechism lists among the unpardonable sins. Experience tells that their punishment usually takes place even in this world."[36] He sent a letter to Primate Jusztinián Serédi and Papal Nuncio Angelo Rotta, as well as to Prime Minister Sztójay and Minister of the Interior Jaross. Unlike the latter two, Horthy felt compelled to speak out. He called upon the prime minister to mitigate the methods, to stop "the exagger-

---

34 Protocol of the Council of Ministers, 29 March 1944, Dávid Turbucz, "Horthy Miklós antiszemitizmusa" [Miklós Horthy's anti-Semitism], *Kommentár* No.5 (2012), Note 59.
35 Document 5 in the present volume.
36 Lőwy Dániel, *A Kálváriától a tragédiáig. Kolozsvár zsidó lakosságának története* [From the Calvary to the tragedy. The history of the Jewish inhabitants of Kolozsvár] (Kolozsvár: Koinónia, 2005), 233–235.

Introduction

ations." In a letter (a "rescript") the regent explained that following the German occupation, "after short deliberation" he decided not to abdicate so as to be able to mitigate conditions.

> I was aware of the fact that in the given emergency the government would have to enact a number of measures which I do not consider right and for which I cannot accept any responsibility. Among these measures is the treatment of the Jewish problem in a manner of not conforming to the Hungarian mind, nor corresponding to conditions in Hungary, and in turn to Hungarian interests.

Horthy went on to say that he was not in a position to prevent anything the Germans demanded, but lately he had received information about such "brutal, and sometimes inhuman" measures and "unreasonable cruelty," which had not even been done in Germany. "I consider it necessary that appropriate measures should be taken without delay in putting an end to the exaggerations." In particular in the professions such as engineering or medical work, in trade "or in occupations where special learning or experience is required [...] the Jews concerned should not be removed from their domiciles, nor should measures taken against them hampering them in their work. [...] I also desire that fair distinction be made among the Jews in favor of those belonging to a Christian denomination." Horthy also insisted on the recognition of his prerogative of pardon and exemptions from regulations applying to certain individuals. Finally he expressed his wish that "the administration of the affairs of Jews in the Royal Ministry of Home Affairs should be taken away from Under-secretaries Endre and Baky."[37] On 21 June Veesenmayer informed Ribbentrop of Horthy's "secret" letter to Sztójay blaming the government for the harsh treatment of the Jews. The plenipotentiary ascribed the letter to the intrigues of former prime minister Bethlen and Horthy's son Miklós, also to the activities of the churches.[38] It is true that the letter did not

---

37 Miklós Horthy to Prime Minister Döme Sztójay, early June 1944, Doc. 62, *Horthy Papers*. It cannot be ascertained when this letter reached Sztójay, but at the latest it was handed over at the Crown Council held on 26 June.
38 *Wilhelmstrasse*, Doc. 687.

order a stop to the deportations, and Horthy continued to show a sympathetic interest only in the well-educated, "useful" professional Jews, and wanted to protect those who converted to Christianity, but nevertheless the intention was to radically curtail "the final solution".

By June it must have been obvious to Horthy that Hitler had no intention to restore the sovereignty of Hungary, even with a totally subservient government. The regent composed a letter to Hitler complaining that "innocent and upright persons are still under arrest ... in vermin-infested rooms, on bread and water," and that the economic resources of the country were utilized by Germany without any payment, even the costs the German occupation were borne by Hungary. A large number of Hungarian soldiers fought on the Russian front while there were "about 250,000 German troops in Hungary, who would certainly render good service at the front".[39]

Whether intentional or not, Horthy's stern letter to Sztójay largely coincided with the date when the deportation of the Jews from the provinces was due to come to an end and the turn of the largest and most influential group, those living in Budapest, has come. With the successful landing of the Allies in Normandy and the quick advance of the Soviet Army towards the Carpathian border of Hungary, the defeat of Germany was impending. Hungary's foreign image was at an historical ebb even in the neutral European countries, due to the news about the atrocities committed. Even Hitler's staunchest allies, like Slovakia and Romania, stopped mistreating the Jews and were seeking contacts with the winning side. Protests addressed to the regent were pouring in, from former prime minister Bethlen in hiding to the Pope, President Roosevelt and the King of Sweden. On 26 June Horthy called for a Crown Council at which he was visibly upset and stated: "I shall not tolerate this any further! I shall not permit the deportations to bring further shame on the Hungarians! Let the Government take measures for the removal of Baky and Endre! The deportation of the Jews of Budapest must cease! The Government must take the necessary steps!"[40]

As the renowned Hungarian-American historian, István Deák wrote,

---

39   Miklós Horthy to Adolf Hitler, 6 June 1944, Doc. 63, *Horthy Papers*.
40   Braham, *The Politics of Genocide*, Vol. 2, 873.

Introduction

When Adolf Eichmann and the Hungarian government wanted to deport two hundred thousand Budapest Jews, the hitherto cooperative Horthy suddenly used his power as Regent to veto their plans, whether because of his awakening conscience, the Allied landing in Normandy, his fear of postwar punishment, his sympathy, however limited, for the generally assimilated and educated Jews of the capital, the threat of Allied bombing attacks on the capital, or vigorous protests by President Roosevelt, Pope Pius XII, and other foreign statesmen. Former Prime Minister István Bethlen, his trusted friend, who was hiding in the countryside, sent him a letter arguing that the deportations had "soiled the name of Hungary," and with the looting of Jewish property "the whole Christian Hungarian society will soon be contaminated irreversibly." Whatever the reason, some of Hungary's radical right-wing leaders were outraged by the Regent's slackening interest in ridding Hungary of Jews. Deputy Minister of the Interior László Baky conspired with the fanatically anti-Semitic officers of the Hungarian gendarmerie to take matters in hand. They sent thousands of gendarmes, theoretically confined to the countryside, into the Hungarian capital with the aim of deporting the Jews. But Horthy worried that the gendarmes also intended to throw him out of office and used his still considerable prestige as well as a hastily gathered armored brigade to persuade the gendarmes to leave the capital. As a result, the Jews of the city were safe, at least until after a Nazi coup d'état in October. Thus Horthy, an avowedly anti-Semitic statesman, used the threat of military force to prevent most of "his" Jews from being deported, a unique event in the annals of the Holocaust.[41]

The German reactions to Horthy's interference with the deportations can be followed in Veesenmayer's telegrams, reproduced in the Appendix. Although the "Auschwitz Protocols", the testimony of two escaped prisoners drawn up at the end of April, probably reached Horthy only in early July, it should have contributed to making his stand stronger. It was against this background that Col-

---

41 István Deák, "*Fateless* by Imre Kertész", *The New York Review of Books*, Vol. 50, No. 14 (25 September 2003).

onel Koszorús offered his services to the regent to prevent the rumored coup by Baky and the gendarmerie. The details of this action are to be found in the studies in the present volume and in the German documents published here, for the first time in English.[42] They show that contrary to Horthy's wishes the deportation of the Jews who lived in the suburbs of Budapest did take place in early July. The advance of the Allies both from the east and west, and Horthy's inability to influence the government led him to decide on the removal of Sztójay and the formation of a government made up of generals and civil servants. Obviously he had in mind the renewal of the efforts to conclude an armistice. Veesenmayer used threatening language in trying to dissuade the regent from such a step and reminded him of the 19th of March.[43] This blackmailing compelled Horthy to recall a letter written to Hitler in which he urged the Führer to end the occupation "in accordance with your valuable promise to withdraw the occupying forces in the country, the special staff of the SS, and above all the Gestapo which day after day, in a quite senseless manner, creates martyrs and transports Hungarian property by the wagon-load from the country." He indicated his intention to replace the Sztójay government with a more competent caretaking military administration, which, however, would not depart from the line required by Germany. (The real aim of Horthy was, of course, to prepare for a break with Germany.) In order to allay German opposition, Horthy added that "the further solution of the Jewish problem will be realized without the often unnecessary brutal and inhuman methods."[44]

Veesenmayer immediately informed Ribbentrop about Horthy's plan on the telephone. As a result, on the following day, 17 July, Veesenmayer gave Horthy an ultimatum which "had been read out to him by Ribbentrop at the command of Hitler, and whose essence was that if the regent made the slightest change in the Sztójay administration he would have to reckon with the gravest reprisals."[45] Consequently, Horthy did not send this letter, but it was

---

42 The dramatic events surrounding the alleged coup, the attempt on Under-secretary Bárczy's life, the stoppage of the deportations and the military action against the gendarmerie are recounted by Braham, but without mentioning even the name of Koszorús. Braham, *The Politics of Genocide*, Vol. 2, 878–887.
43 *Wilhelmstrasse*, Doc. 699.
44 Miklós Horthy to Adolf Hitler, draft, 17 July 1944, Doc. 65, *Horthy Papers*, 316–317.
45 *Wilhelmstrasse*, Doc. 700.

eventually delivered by General Béla Miklós on 21 July, when the commander of Hungary's First Army was received by Hitler just one day after the unsuccessful attempt to kill the German dictator. On 17 July, however, Veesenmayer had an almost two-hour-long conversation with Horthy. The plenipotentiary tried to counter all the Hungarian complaints reiterated by the regent, reaffirmed that Sztójay enjoyed the full confidence of Hitler and the German government, condemned Bethlen and the alleged bad influences on Horthy, and warned him that there would always be enough German forces left "to put things in order" in Hungary. "Our negotiation utterly exhausted him [Horthy], his whole body was trembling, and he gave the impression of an old, broken man."[46] On the very same day, Veesenmayer also saw both Sztójay and Bárdossy. The latter advised him to make a clear distinction between the regent and the circle close to him. Sztójay was resolved to cleanse Horthy of the bad influences in his entourage and expected that the regent would give up the plans for a government composed of soldiers and civil servants.[47]

Interestingly, recently an article in a periodical founded by Elie Wiesel came to the defense of Hungary's regent:

> That Horthy was very difficult for the Germans to deal with we see from the German ambassador Edmund Veesenmayer's telegram to Ribbentrop where he described the Regent as "a liar, physically incapable of discharging his responsibilities, constantly repeating and contradicting himself, and at times speaking haltingly." But he was mistaken: Horthy's biographer Thomas Sakmyster wrote that Horthy knew how to deceive and to create an impression described by Veesenmayer if he wanted to avoid a discussion; he could even bring up his poor hearing. [...] we may say that nobody in the world saved as many Jews as he did. In Sakmyster's words: "Horthy's action was unprecedented in the history of the Holocaust: never before had a leader successfully used the threat of military force to halt the deportation of Jews to the death camps." Wallenberg arrived in the city on July 9. If not for Horthy's actions, he would have had

---

46 Ibid., Doc. 701.
47 Ibid., Doc. 702, also Doc. 16 in the present volume.

nothing to do: all the Jews would have already been deported by that time. He understood it well, and on July 29, 1944, reported to his government: Horthy's "position is illustrated by the very real fact that the deportations were canceled per his order, but also by a number of smaller interventions. Among them, two verified instances of trains loaded with prisoners being ordered to turn back just before reaching the border."[48]

By holding on to his office Horthy unquestionably had a decisive role in preventing the deportation of the Jewish population of Budapest, but before that he passively watched the roundup and deportation of half a million Jewish Hungarian citizens. He, nominally still head of state, had a responsibility for their fate. On 29 August 1944 Horthy at last dismissed Sztójay and appointed General Lakatos as premier. The regent assured Samuel Stern, president of the Jewish Council, that there would be no deportations from Budapest. What a tragedy that he did not (could not?) act earlier!

Was Horthy a war criminal?

With the Russians approaching the borders of Hungary, Horthy, in great secrecy, not revealed even to the government, sent a team to Moscow seeking an armistice. There was no alternative, its harsh terms had to be accepted, and it was signed on 11 October. Tragically, the execution of the armistice was hardly prepared; some high-ranking officers, breaking their oath to the regent, did not carry out and pass on the order to cease fighting, and Germany helped the Hungarian Arrow Cross Party, mostly the rabble, to take over the government, to continue fighting on the side of Nazi Germany, and to resume the persecution of the remaining Jewish population. In all, "76,209 Jews were deported from the capital during the Arrow Cross era, while 21,744 people lost their lives in acts of terror."[49] Horthy and his close family, too, were deported by the Nazis – not to a death factory but to a castle in Bavaria, where they were under house arrest until liberated by the U.S. Army.

---

48 Eliezer M. Rabinovich, "How 'Anti-Semite' Miklos Horthy Saved the Jews of Budapest", *Moment Magazine*, http://www.momentmag.com/horthy-jews-budapest/
49 See T. Stark's essay in the present volume.

Introduction

The 77-year-old former head of the Hungarian State was detained as a possible war criminal and was questioned extensively, but based upon investigations by the United Nations War Criminal Committee and Robert Jackson, the American prosecutor general of the Nuremberg Trials, it was decided not to raise charges against him. His written testimony was used in the Nuremberg trial of the German leaders, and he was called as a witness in the trial of Edmund Veesenmayer in 1948. Josip Tito, then Yugoslavia's minister of defense, asked for Horthy's extradition in connection with the 1942 massacre in Novi Sad/Újvidék, but it was refused by the Allies, sensing that Horthy would not receive a fair trial. Stalin knew that putting Horthy in the dock would only make the imposition of communism in Hungary more difficult.[50]

It is worth reflecting on the fact that while many Hungarian participants in the deportations leading to the death of over half a million Hungarian Jews were tried and executed in Hungary, the German plenipotentiary who urged Hitler to occupy Hungary and was personally responsible for so many crimes and so much destruction in Hungary, was sentenced in 1949 to only 20 years imprisonment and was released in 1951. Veesenmayer died in 1977 as a well-to-do businessman.

What happened in Hungary in 1944 is both a Jewish and a Hungarian tragedy. Israel and a Jewish nation did not exist yet. Most of the murdered half a million considered themselves Hungarians of Jewish faith. They rightly felt themselves betrayed by their homeland, by their fellow Hungarians, and let down by its head of state, Regent Horthy. No amount of penitence and remorse, let alone financial compensation can undo what happened. Mourning for all the human losses of the war should be common, while making a clear distinction between those who fell on the frontlines or died in Soviet captivity and those who vanished due to gas and fire. Whole nations are never guilty, but, shamefully, there were many guilty Hungarians – and many more guilty Germans. The early 1940s were dreadful times in Hungary, and few suspected what dreadful times were still to come.

* * *

---

50 Éva Haraszti-Taylor, "Why was Admiral Horthy not considered a war criminal?" *The New Hungarian Quarterly*, 113 (Spring 1989), 133–143. Idem, *Horthy Miklós dokumentumok tükrében* [Documents related to Miklós Horthy] (Budapest: Balassi, 1993).

This book starts with the late Congressman Tom Lantos's entry in the Congressional Record recording the role of Koszorús in saving the Jewish population of Budapest, including himself. A historical overview, the summary of Hungary's conduct during the Second World War is given by György Ránki (1930–1988), himself a survivor of Auschwitz. Then the editor of the present volume attempts to answer whether Hungary's foreign policy ran on a set course, predetermined by the unfair 1920 Trianon Peace Treaty, or, despite the most difficult circumstances, there were better but missed alternatives. Extracts from Deborah Cornelius's book *Hungary in World War II* (New York: Fordham University Press, 2011) present a detailed account of the German occupation up to Koszorús's action. We republish an essay by István Deák, emeritus professor of Columbia University and a foremost scholar on the Second World War, on the Austro-Hungarian Monarchy and on military and Jewish history. His piece summarizes the history of the Jews of Hungary, with emphasis on the Holocaust. The paper by Hungarian military historian Attila Bonhardt tells the most important story, the actions of Col. Koszorús; while an essay by two specialists on Raoul Wallenberg, Susanne Berger and Vadim Birstein, proves that the brave Swede had extensive connections to Hungary even before his heroic humanitarian actions. The book includes two personal pieces: the Preface, written by the noted Hungarian-American journalist Charles Fenyvesi, on the personality of Koszorús, and the concluding piece, written by the son of the colonel himself, Frank Koszorus Jr.

The Appendix contains documents which first appeared in a collection published in Hungarian, *A Wilhelmstrasse és Magyarország. Német diplomáciai iratok Magyarországról 1933–1944* [The Wilhelmstrasse and Hungary. German diplomatic papers on Hungary], edited and introduced by György Ránki et al. (Budapest: Kossuth, 1968). Our translation is directly from the German originals.

Chapter I
Ferenc Koszorus: a Hero of the Hungarian Holocaust

Hon. Tom Lantos of California
in the House of Representatives
Thursday, May 26, 1994

Mr. LANTOS: Mr. Speaker, this year marks the 50th anniversary of the Hungarian holocaust. I rise today to recognize one of the great heroes of the Hungarian holocaust. Ferenc Koszorus, who at great personal sacrifice to his own life, saved thousands of Hungarian Jews from deportation to Nazi death camps.

During the turbulent time in the summer of 1944, advancing Allied forces were closing in on Berlin while Hitler was racing to implement the final solution, the destruction of the Jewish race. There were many acts of heroic compassion and humanitarianism during this period. I would like to recount the story of Col. Ferenc Koszorus, one of the most remarkable examples of bravery and courage of the time.

By June 1944, the Nazis had incarcerated and liquidated most of the Jewish population of Europe. In the capital of Hungary, Budapest, there remained approximately 250,000 Jews still alive. Budapest was still under control of the Hungarian police force. The Nazis believed that this force was not ruthless and brutal enough to deal adequately with the complete destruction of the large remaining Jewish population of Budapest.

---

* Source: Reprinted from the Congressional Record Volume 140, Number 68 (Thursday, May 26, 1994) Extensions of Remarks: Page E
From the Congressional Record Online through the Government Printing Office <www.gpo.gov>
https://www.gpo.gov/fdsys/pkg/CREC-1994-05-26/html/CREC-1994-05-26-pt1-PgE94.htm
Accessed 1.29.2018

Ferenc Koszorus was a colonel in the Hungarian Army in charge of the First Magyar Armored Division stationed in and around Budapest. He learned that Laszlo Baky, Secretary of State and director of all security forces, with the exception of the army, had planned a coup d'état to install a police force completely subservient to the Nazis. They would see to it that Hungary was purged of all remaining Jews.

With the help of the Gestapo, Baky formed several battalions of "gendarmerie" forces loyal to him. Orders from the Regent to disband the gendarmerie went unheeded. Colonel Koszorus controlled the last remaining active army unit in Hungary. At a time when few others would stand up to the Nazi occupation, Colonel Koszorus took the initiative to resist.

Realizing the severity of the situation, Colonel Koszorus consulted with the Regent and began preparations on his own to stop Baky and the gendarmerie battalions. On July 5, 1944 at 11:30 p.m., Colonel Koszorus ordered the units of the 1st Armored Division to take up positions at strategic points in Budapest, sealing off all road leading into the city. By 7:00 a.m. on July 6, 1944 all the units were in place and Colonel Koszorus informed Baky that if his gendarmerie did not leave and disband they would be destroyed. On July 7, 1944 Baky capitulated and evacuated his forces.

Colonel Koszorus' unparalleled action was the only case known in which an Axis power used military force for the purpose of preventing the deportation of the Jews. As a result of his extraordinarily brave efforts, taken at great risk in an extremely volatile situation, the eventual takeover of Budapest by the Nazis was delayed by three and a half months. This hiatus allowed thousands of Jews to seek safety in Budapest, thus sparing them from certain execution. It also permitted the famous Raoul Wallenberg, who arrived in Budapest on July 9, 1994, to coordinate his successful and effective rescue mission.

In October 1944, after the Germans had taken Budapest, Colonel Koszorus was forced into hiding to avoid certain execution by the Gestapo. While alive, Colonel Koszorus never received recognition of his actions. In 1991, Ferenc Koszorus was posthumously promoted to the rank of general by the Hungarian Government. His memory is honored with a plaque placed in the famous Dohany Street Synagogue in Budapest. Therefore, it is with great honor and pride that I rise today in recognition valiant, patriotic efforts of

Ferenc Koszorus

Ferenc Koszorus. Many thousands of families are alive today as a result of the heroic actions of one man who stood up for his beliefs in a very uncertain and dangerous time. His loyalty to his country and love of humanity are an inspiration to all who struggle against oppression and the vile bigotry of racism.

Too often the efforts of those who struggle against the Nazi oppression go unrecognized. This year, the 50th anniversary of the Hungarian holocaust, the world reflects on the lessons learned. I am proud to honor Colonel Koszorus, a patriot, a humanitarian, and a hero.

Chapter 2
"Unwilling Satellite" or "Last Satellite"— Some Problems of Hungarian-German Relations

György Ránki

The title of the book of the former American ambassador[1] and the epithet echoed so often in the years immediately following World War II express the two possible poles of evaluating Hungary's role in the Second World War. Needless to say, *in gross modo,* most of the memoirs written by the former politicians of the Horthy regime and its supporters took positions while, though they differed in some substantial matters, were nearer to the former formulation. On the other hand, the books and articles written by historians in postwar Hungary—even if they never accepted the brand "last satellite"— focused on the circumstances that had caused Hungary to become that, a German satellite which was unable to disengage itself from the war up to the very last minute. This dichotomy, however, cannot be regarded as merely expressing different approaches, intentions and judgments. These poles were not created after the war for purposes of self-justification or for casting blame on the regime which fell in with the Germans. In some sense, these poles characterized Hungary and her foreign policy from 1933 to 1944, and expressed

---

*   Originally published in: *Hungarian History – World History*: Edited by György Ránki,(Budapest, Akadémiai Kiadó, Budapest, 1984 pp 261–288.
1   J.F. Montgomery, *Hungary, the Unwilling Satellite* (New York, 1947). Editor's Note: J.F. Montgomery (1878–1954) was U.S. Minister to Hungary in June 1933 - March 1941. His memoir, *Hungary: The Unwilling Satellite,* is a valuable source on a critical period of Hungary's history. Cf. Tibor Frank, *Discussing Hitler. Advisers of U.S. Diplomacy in Central Europe, 1934–41,* Budapest–New York: Central European University Press, 2003

the play between things as they were and things as they were wishfully perceived to be, expressed the various foreign policy trends in Hungary, and the different ideas as to how to carry these out. These were the poles of the Hungarian reality.

According to Macartney, after "Hitler had become chancellor of the Reich, and... after fifteen years, a power was at last in the field which seemed both willing and able to smash the chains of the peace settlement. Many people expected Hungary at ones to throw herself into Germany's arms."[2] If this was not really the case Macartney found four different reasons for it:

1. Hitler was far from being ready to help Hungary to integral revision.
2. Genuine fear for Hungary's independence, awakened by the reemergence of a great united Germany standing on Hungary's very frontier for the first time in modern history.
3. Simple calculation. While the army officers, almost to a man, were convinced of the invincibility of the German arms, many of the influential politicians believed that the West would win.
4. The nation was sharply divided by ideological questions, particularly the Jewish problem.

In the same foreword Macartney described Hungary's position after 1938, "as a succession of short downward slides, in each case due to very strong propulsion from outside, in each case followed by prolonged efforts, if not to regain the lost ground, at least to avoid further loss."[3]

I agree with Macartney's statements so far that there was a succession of downward slides with the perpetual attempt to control it. However, if we regard the whole story from the beginning (1933) to the sad end (1944), then I would put it in the slightly different and probably more complex way. Kossuth's definition of politics as the science of exigencies is true of foreign policy as well. Exigencies may not, however, be regarded as just the potentialities of a given situation. I would regard a government's freedom of action as a function of its own aims and means combined with the possibilities of action left to it by force of circumstance, or the pressure put on it by more

---

2   C.A. Macartney, "Foreword" in N. Kállay, *Hungarian Premier, A Personal Account of a Nation's Struggle in the Second World War* (here after: Hungarian Premier) (New York, 1954), p. xxi.
3   C.A. Macartney, *op. cit.,* p. xxiii

major powers, or the great powers. According to these premises, German-Hungarian relations are to be examined in the context of this combination of forces, and although, undoubtedly, the force of circumstances (German pressure) became more and more the decisive factor in this relationship, we ought not to forget that the Hungarian government always had a stake in the relationship, almost to the bitter end. The Hungarian interest in that alliance was focused on three main considerations. The first, which had a particularly great influence on the relationship with the Third Reich in the first few years after the Great Depression, was the economy. The second is almost too obvious to speak of. Hungary strove for the revision of the treaty of Trianon which – *nolens-volens* – under the given international circumstances could not be achieved but with German help. This was an issue already at the beginning of closer German - Hungarian cooperation, and became a dominant factor in Hungarian foreign policy from 1938 to 1942, the years of Germany's successes.

Last but not least, in spite of substantial differences in the political, ideological and power structures of the two systems, they had certain affinities: both regimes were anti-liberal and anti-democratic; only Germany was Fascist, but Hungary was authoritarian. How far this affinity helped build up the alliance in the 1930s is a moot point. I myself do not regard it as a decisive element; however, I would allow it a certain degree of importance. But by the end, roughly from 1942 to 1944, nothing else—neither economic interest nor the prospect of revision—would have tied Hungary to Nazi Germany. German pressure was certainly the decisive factor at this period of the war. In spite of the tremendous differences which became more and more explicit in the course of the war. The features common to the two regimes—the anti-liberal, retrograde political and social structure of both—contributed greatly to the paralysis of important Hungarian political forces, and contributed to the country's downward slide from the position of an unwilling satellite to that of those satellites which were unable to successfully extricate themselves from the war. The dilemma of the unwilling or the last satellite was her need to maneuver in the permanent crossfire of the force of circumstance, i.e. the power of Germany, and the need to assert her own foreign policy aims. These two were compatible from time to time, though finally they proved to be contradictory. Still, occasionally, even the attempts to preserve an independent foreign policy line reinforced Hungarian-German collaboration. As the war progressed, external pressures on Hungary came to dominate, and unwillingness to follow the German line came to characterize her. It was, in the final analysis, the force of circumstances that was decisive in Hungary's moving from her position in 1942 as the most unwilling satellite to her position in the fall of 1944 of being the last one.[4] But Hungary's political aims had been such that a large number of army officers and politicians - who had a great influence on public opinion - continued as late as all that to consider this her only real option.

In my short paper, I wish to show the three different periods in the history of German (Nazi)-Hungarian relations, the parts played by three main considerations (economic, foreign-policy, and domestic power structure) in shaping this relationship, and the effect on it of the growth of German power. In addition, I would like to show the effect that this relationship had on the possibility of Hungary's actually conducting her own foreign policy during the war. It is well known that after World War I the political reorganization of Southeastern Europe was accompanied by the attempt on the part of the victorious Allied powers to gain economic hegemony over the countries of the area. However, the Anglo-French hegemony that developed at the beginning of the 1920s contained numerous contradictions. From 1928–29 onward, Anglo-French economic hegemony was in a state of continuous crisis, partly because of the conflicts between British and French interests, and partly because of the objective demands of economic development, expressed in the difference between the related credit and market systems. The international economic crisis further undermined the unity of the Anglo-French hegemony, and when the attempts to resolve the economic difficulties of the countries of the Danube Valley by uniting them in some kind of economic block under French leadership failed, the initiative was seized by Germany. It took almost a year for Germany to take the first real opportunity that presented itself. This year, decisive in the building of Hitler's totalitarian system,

---

4   Editor's note: In fact the two puppet states of Germany, Slovakia and Croatia, remained the satellites of Germany longer than Hungary, not only because of Hungary's earlier liberation, but also as a Provisional Hungarian Government was formed in Debrecen on 22 December 1944.

was significant also for Hungary's economy, which became more shaky during 1933, one of the reasons being that the volume of her agricultural export to Germany reached rock bottom. (The fall in the value of exports to Germany was roughly 14 percent.)

On April 22, 1933, Gömbös, Prime Minister of Hungary, wrote a letter to Hitler in which we read the following: "Nationalist Hungary, now governed with a strong hand, has always looked to Berlin with some expectation and sympathy. It is, I believe, also in Germany's interest to prevent unstable economic relations from undermining this sympathy ...

I would therefore request urgently that the German government take a decision to come to our assistance in matters of agricultural export. I am convinced that Your Excellency's strong will be obeyed over this issue as well, all the more so as I know that Your Excellency holds views that are identical with mine, *viz.* that politics and economic policy should be coordinated as far as possible.

Agricultural export, as I view it, is not merely an economic problem but one which has a bearing upon politics; and ... my political line would be strengthened, if this were appreciated on the part of Germany ..." [5]

Early in 1934, on the occasion of a conversation with Mackensen, the German Ambassador, Gömbös expressed himself bluntly: "The necessity of maintaining Hungarian-German friendship is too obvious to require emphasis. The further development of these—at present very good—relations depends on the attitude to be taken by Germany regarding German imports of Hungarian farm products."[6] Formally, at this point, Hungary was supposed to choose between Italian or German political orientation and economic help. In spite of Italian pressure Gömbös was reluctant to opt for Italy; and though there was a sort of balancing between the two countries, his preferences, for economic, political and military reasons as well, were increasingly for Germany. Germany, aware of the situation, made up her mind to profit from Hungary's economic needs and political retribution and to manipu-

---

5   Quoted by: I. Berend and Gy. Ránki, "German-Hungarian Relations Following Hitler's Rise to Power (1933–34)," *Acta Historica* (Budapest, 1961), p. 321.
6   Országos Levéltár (National Archives) KÜM (Ministry of Foreign Affairs) File 195, 29/34 Political Department.

late circumstances so as to acquire Hungary as her first helper in the Danube Valley. The twenty-page memorandum prepared by Counselor Schnurre of the German Foreign Ministry briefly summarized Hungarian foreign policies, emphasizing that Gömbös was working with Germany and Italy and was not bound by Italian-Austrian cooperation. He was strongly anti-French and anti-Little Entente, and he rejected all plans for a Danubian Confederation, whether an Austrian-Czech-Hungarian tariff union, or some wider cooperation as envisioned by the Tardieu Plan. "This Hungarian policy corresponds to the demands of German foreign policy and guarantees that they will not enter into any kind of Southeastern European combination without us."[7] Conclusion: we need to support Hungarian foreign policy and must tie the country to Germany economically, "which can be done by assuring a sufficient market for Hungarian products."

So, by early 1934, the Germans thought the situation ripe enough to move to prevent the deepening of the Italian-Austrian-Hungarian connection, and to start to stake Hungary out as a definite economic territory. On January 19, 1934, there as a conference with the participation of Foreign Minister Neurath, Finance Minister Schwerin von Krosigk, and the President of the Reichsbank, Schacht. By then, the decision "that from the political point of view a new form of special treatment are needed when regulating relations with Hungary" had been made. Foreign minister Neurath addressed a letter to Hungary's foreign minister Kánya[8] on January 13, 1934.[9] In it he explained that the improved German economic situation made it possible to begin discussions, in the spirit of the Hitler-Gömbös talks, about deepening German-Hungarian economic ties. A German economic delegation was to travel to Budapest for the purpose of detailed discussions.

It was clear to the German ruling circles that concessions would have to be made in favor of Hungarian agricultural exports during the discussions. This, however, no longer created much of a problem. The newly evolving German

---

7   National Archives Microfilm, German Foreign Ministry 10945/E479975, Schnurre's note, September 1933.
8   Editors note: Kálmán Kánya (1869–1945), an experienced professional diplomat, was foreign minister in 1933–1938.
9   National Archives, German Foreign Ministry 10945/E 674981.

economic policy wished to place its agricultural point of gravity in Southeastern Europe anyway. These points of view emerged at the January 17 meeting of the Economic Ministry, where it was stated that discussions with the Hungarians were justified for the following reasons:

"1. In the course of our exchange of letters last summer, the Reich Chancellor made a promise to Hungarian Prime Minister Gömbös that he would consider the Hungarian request regarding trade policy. 2. The Italian government, as it is well known, is experimenting with the creation of an Italian, Austrian and Hungarian tariff union.

It is in our interest to create a strong position for ourselves in Hungary to counterbalance these aspirations."[10]

The meaning of the German decision was clear: "Germany's purpose in the treaty about to be concluded consisted of tying the Hungarian economy closely and inseparably to the German economy by means of increased exchange of goods."

The Trade Treaty of 1934 is too well known to be dealt with here. It is clear that it was extremely important for Hungary to establish close ties with a larger economic unit. Viewed from this perspective, German economic penetration appears to have brought temporary advantages for Hungary because it created favorable circumstances for overcoming the effects of the Great Depression, and satisfied the demands of Hungarian agriculture for markets.

After the signing of the treaty, German foreign policy makers expressed their satisfaction. "It may be expected that Hungary will not lightly risk the very considerable advantages granted her by Germany and will be mindful of this in her political attitude and also with respect to commercial policy."[11] Nevertheless, whatever the advantages of the Treaty for Hungary's economy might have been in the short run, in the long run these connections brought political as well as economic dangers. Could Hungary have pursued any other kind of foreign economic policy under the given circumstances? After the total failure of the Danubian block of any kind - to which Hungarian foreign policy contributed as well - and after her total neglect by the Western pow-

---

10   Deutsche Zentralarchiv, Potsdam, Auswärtiges Amt, Abt II 41228
11   Documents on German Foreign Policy, Series C. Vol. II, Washington, 1959, Bulow's note of March 13, 1934.

ers, her freedom was very limited. A drowning man will not refuse the hand stretched out to help him for fear of blackmail in the future. However, one may ask if it would not have been better to grasp the Italian hand instead. Was turning to Germany just an economic decision, or was it more of a political one, as Gömbös said: "we, long standing fellow defenders of our race, who hold a common ideology, shall understand and back each other on economic policy as well."[12] Anyway, there is no doubt that in this very early period of the history of Nazi Germany, Hungary opened her door to German penetration (as was to be done a few months later by Yugoslavia, and in 1935, by Romania), and she became a basic element of German foreign policy in frustrating any plans and possibilities which did not coincide with German foreign policy aims. German-Hungarian relation in that phase was still based on a community of interest (which, of course, is never of equal weight when the partners are a great power and a small nation).

As the time was approaching for the second element of the community of interest (i.e foreign policy aims) to yield fruit, the built-in dangers of economic cooperation came more and more in to view. However, even at this stage, material interests made a rather large and important part of the Hungarian land-owning class a strong supporter of strengthening German economic ties, and of selling more and more goods on her markets. (Naturally, the entire agricultural sector had a stake in this but the peasants did not have any influence to speak of in shaping foreign policy decisions.) After 1938, of course, foreign policy issues became more important than economic ones due to the changes in the international agricultural market. The Hungarian politicians of the interwar period never shared the views of Gambetta, who, after the annexation of Alsace in 1871, had declared: always think of reannexation, but never speak about it.

Hungary's foreign policy aims, i.e., the complete revision of the Treaty of Trianon, had never been concealed. Let us disregard for now the very important issue of to what extent this foreign policy aim might have been justified by the absolutely anti-Hungarian territorial stipulations of the Peace Treaty.

---

12 Gömbös's letters: April 22, 1933. Deutsches Zentralarchiv, Potsdam, Auswärtiges Amt, Abt. II 41288.

"Unwilling Satellite" or "Last Satellite"

Nowadays, it is almost a commonplace that the victorious powers in general, and French politicians in particular, sowed the seeds of a new conflict, when, for a variety of reasons, they showed complete disregard for the ethnic lines of demarcation in the case of Hungary and a population of almost 3.5 million ethnic Hungarians (Magyars), roughly 35 percent of Hungary's population, were ceded to the successor states. Just as obviously, Hungarian foreign policy aims were not confined to a revision along ethnic lines—which might, in the long run, have brought some kind of understanding among the Danubian countries—but proposed to restore the Kingdom of Saint Stephen, i.e. all the old territories along with almost 8 million non-Magyars. There were some very characteristic (but absolutely unrealistic) plans for revision nurtured already in the early 1920s by Horthy and his government; but the first foreign policy program that was in the realm of possibilities was the one that regarded Germany as the likely ally in any revision. Bethlen had attempted already in the late 20's to forge closer links with Germany. He believed that any well-founded foreign policy left to the Italo-German military alliance was still far in the future; and Germany was not willing as much to associate herself with Hungary for either foreign or domestic policy reasons.[13] Things changed after Hitler's seizure of power. One cannot regard a matter of chance the fact that Gömbös was the first foreign statesman who paid Hitler a visit. In spite of the fact that some Hungarian politicians, among them Bethlen, quickly realized that Hitler's Germany was not the Germany they were looking for, Gömbös was obliged to write clearly in a letter (which Hitler never answered) that Germany had to acknowledge Hungary's leading role in the Carpatho-Danubian basin.[14]

Nevertheless, the formation of the German-Italian axis had been extremely well-received by the Hungarian government and by the Hungarian press. "Dès lors 'l' axe Rome-Berlin est devenu pour les Hongrois la baguette magique dont on peut attendre tous les miracles, bientôt, pour ces gens toujours pénétrés d'esprit troubadours, la connivance politique, d'une atmosphère Ro-

---

13 As a sentence of a letter Horthy addressed to Hitler in 1939 put it: "Even at the time when during the period of the social democratic régime a whole world separated us from the German government, we always entertained close relations to the Reichswehr." *The Confidential Papers of Admiral Horthy*, (hereafter: Admiral Horthy's Papers), eds. Miklós Szinai and László Szücs (Budapest, 1965), p. 126.
14 Documents on German Foreign Policy, Series C. Vol II. Gömbös's letter of Feb. 4, 1934.

manesque (sic). Défenseurs attirés de l'Europe chrétienne éteint á une croisade qu'ils marchaient avec l'Italie et l'Allemagne. Ils enrolaient certes avec un enthousiasme sincère au service de la bonne cause mais un élément de calcul entrait pourtant dans leur geste." (From then on, the Rome-Berlin axis became for the Hungarians the magic wand from which one can expect all miracles, for these people, always permeated with the spirit of wandering troubadours, the political connivance of a Romanesque atmosphere (sic). Defenders drawn from Christian Europe were on a crusade marching together with Italy and Germany. They certainly enlisted with sincere enthusiasm in the service of the good cause, but an element of calculations nevertheless entered into their gesture.)

This is how Maugras, the French Ambassador, characterized Hungarian foreign policy in one of his reports.[15]

I would like to emphasize the last sentence of his report concerning the element of calculation. It is not my intention to blame the policy-makers for this element of calculation. One of the things in which Hungarian foreign policy was always at fault was its lack of the certain necessary amount of calculation. The *élément de calcul* is connected with a few further remarks in this report by the French Ambassador. As he saw it, the enthusiastic voice of the press was directed mainly by Gömbös. Kánya, the Foreign Minister, was much more cautious. As to the questions of whether the ambassador was really expecting any results from this new Holy Alliance, he answered: "Attendez vous de moi, que je desavoue nos espérances nationales?" ("Do you expect from me, that I disown our national aspirations?")

Kánya reiterated the formal Hungarian statement that revision was to be achieved by peaceful means; nevertheless he also acknowledged that even he doubted that it would be possible without waging war.

As Germany regained her former strength, built up her military forces, and won diplomatic successes, the two trends in Hungarian foreign policy became more and more recognizable. These two trends had always been connected with different social and political forces, with different politicians,

---

15 Documents diplomatiques français 1932–39, Second Series Tome III, Paris, 1966, report of Sept. 4, 1936. François Gustave Gaston Maugras (1884–1965), was France's Minister to Hungary in December 1934–November 1938.

and with different personalities. Nevertheless, the position which came more and more to gain the upper hand was that Hungary had to march along with Germany, which was proving very successful in her foreign affairs. According to this view, the element of *calcul* dictated support for a foreign policy based mainly on an alliance with Germany.

Doubts were certainly raised. Opposition politicians, themselves warm supporters of a foreign policy aimed at the revision of Trianon, urged more caution. Eckhardt[16] stressed that Hungary had to leave open which camp she would join in case of war.

"Il faut que la Hongrie garde la faculté en cas de conflagration de marchander avec l'un et l'autre parti. Nous ne voulons pas nous asseoir encore une fois á la table des negotiations parmi les vaincus."[17] ("It is necessary that Hungary retains the ability, in case of conflict to haggle with one or the other party. We do not want to sit at the bargaining table again among the vanquished.")

Even French diplomats who, for obvious reasons, were not very fond of Hungarian foreign policy aims and methods, acknowledged that the relationship between Germany and Hungary was far from being as good as it had been declared.

"La féte de Saint-Étienne a d'ailleurs elle-méme mis en relief les differences que séparent les théses politiques de l'Allemagne nationale socialiste de la tradition magyare ... 'l'idée stéphanistienne' apparait comme essentiellement humaniste et chrétienne par consequent trés éloignée des theories étroites et materialists de la race... L'évolution des rapports germane-magyars est donc assez complexe. Il y a outre, à côté des facteurs purement doctrinaux, des considerations de politque extérieure proprement dites. La Hongrie ne croit pas pouvoir se presser de l'appui de l'Allemagne mais elle ne veut pas laisser dominer ni manoeuvrer."[18] ("The celebrations of St. Stephen Day has highlighted the differences that separate the political theses of German National

---

16 Editors note: Tibor Eckhardt (1888–1972) was then the leader of the oppositional Smallholders' Party. He clearly saw the danger on reliance on Hitler; in 1941 he left for the United States in the hope of being recognized as the leader of anti-Nazi Hungary.
17 Documents diplomatiques français 1932–1939, Second Series, Tome VII, Paris, 1972, report of Nov. 13, 1937.
18 *Idem*, Tome VI, Paris, 1970, Chargé d'Affairs' Report of Sept. 1939

Socialism from Hungarian tradition... 'the idea of Stéphanistienne'[19] appears as essentially humanist and Christian, consequently quite distant from the narrow and materialistic theories of race ... the evolution of German-Hungarian relations is therefore quite complex. In addition to purely academic factors, there are also strategic foreign policy considerations. Hungary does not think she can hurry to Germany's support, but she does not want to be dominated or manipulated."

Of course, the report was signed in 1937 when, theoretically, Hungary was still able to defend herself against attempts by Germany to rule over her, but not against being maneuvered. A few months after November 1937, when Hitler held out a glimmer of hope for real revision at the expense of Czechoslovakia, Darányi,[20] who was certainly regarded as more moderate than his predecessor, Gömbös, gave his consent to Hungary's participation in a scheme for an attack aimed at dismembering Czechoslovakia.

The possibilities of maneuvering deteriorated after the *Anschluss* and Munich. Top Hungarian politicians, who, a few months earlier, their revisionist aims notwithstanding, had been cautious enough not to give their unconditional support to an attack on Czechoslovakia, made a sudden *volte-face*. Others were either not willing to do this, or saw best to refrain from such gestures, for having led to foreign policy not entirely trusted by Hitler, their *volte-face* would have lacked credibility. They were dismissed from the government (Kánya, for example).

From 1938 on, when the possibility of revision was at hand, the basic element of Hungarian-German relations was given. Yet even during this honeymoon period, when Hungarian Foreign Minister Csáky[21] took for granted that "the leading role of the Axis was assured for the next twenty-five years in Europe", there were several occasions when Hungarian foreign policy refused to follow the German lead unquestionably. Hitler made it quite clear to Csáky in January 1939 that he would not set the restoration of the Empire of Saint

---

19 Editor's note: Hungary's first king, István (Stephen), 1000–1038, canonized in 1083, advised his son to welcome foreign settlers and to respect all the languages used in his realm. After the 1920 Peace it became customary to refer to St. Stephen's multi-lingual kingdom as the model for the would-be Hungary, once the historic borders would be restored.
20 Editors note: Kálmán Darányi (1886–1939) was Prime Minister of Hungary in 1936–1938.
21 Editors note: István Csáky (1894–1941) was Foreign Minister in 1938–1941.

"Unwilling Satellite" or "Last Satellite"

Stephen as the aim of the Great German Empire. The most courageous act of the Hungarian leaders was the famous letter Teleki[22] addressed to Hitler in July, 1939, which, after declaring that his government was on the side of the Axis in every respect, stated that, for moral reasons, they did not wish to be a party to the attack on Poland.[23] Hitler was certainly infuriated, and, after two weeks, Csáky declared that this letter had never been written. After that declaration, Hitler stated that he was not requiring Hungary's military assistance against Poland; her withdrawal had become more or less a formal act. But still, the obvious question remains to be answered: How was Hitler able to press for the repudiation of Teleki's letter in July of 1939? I would say that at this time, Hungary did not yet fear German military intervention. The most important element of the pressure Hitler brought to bear on the Hungarians was the threat of their losing German support for their revision plans.

In the years of Paul Teleki's government, clashes of interest on many secondary questions were a permanent feature of German-Hungarian relations. The attempt to maintain a relatively independent foreign policy course was coupled with the intention of continuing to go along with Hitler as far as revision was concerned. During the first part of the Second World War, the balance of power between the two states shifted much more in favor of Germany. I would not attribute too much importance to Hungary's refusing to grant the German request to use a Hungarian railway line against Poland[24] because this was a second rate issue more to test Hungary and to apply diplomatic pressure. Germany certainly was not pleased by Hungary's granting asylum to almost 150,000 Polish refugees[25] and still trying to keep two irons in the fire. However, Hungarian foreign policy had to maneuver between the Scylla of maintaining a relative independence and the Charybdis of further revision at the expense of Romania. As a matter of fact, the two aims were

---

22 Editors note: Pál Teleki, a Hungarian statesman from Transylvania, was Prime Minister in 1920–1921, and in 1938–1941. He committed suicide rather than joining the German war against Yugoslavia.
23 *Magyarország és a második világháború* (Hungary and the Second World War) eds. László Zsigmond, Magda Ádám, Gyula Juhász, Lajos Kerekes (Budapest, 1959).
24 Ciano in his diary was of a different opinion. He wrote: "The Germans will not forget the refusal, the Hungarians will have to pay for this one day …" *The Ciano Diaries*, ed. Hugh Gibson, (New York, Doubleday & Co. 1946) p. 142. Entry of September 11, 1939
25 Editors note: Most of the Polish refugees were soldiers, and about 50,000 of them were tacitly allowed to escape and join the Polish forces fighting on in France and later joined to the British Army.

not reconcilable. Hungary failed more and more to maintain a certain degree of independence on the one hand because Germany had won the war in the West and had almost become the master of Europe; on the other hand, Hungary's revisionist aims provided the opportunity for further German interference in Danubian affairs, and allowed Germany to become the supreme judge in political disputes among the countries neighboring Hungary. The sheer contradiction of her foreign policy became more and more perceptible. Hungary's most important foreign policy success, the return to Hungary of the northern part of Transylvania with two and a half million inhabitants, became *eo ipso* the reward for limiting Hungary's independence from Germany, for putting Hungary in a kind of (willing and unwilling) satellite position.

Teleki saw quite clearly that Hungary would have to pay a high price for the Second Vienna Award. It was not mere coincidence that he handed his resignation to the Regent on the day following the award. In his letter, he referred mainly to domestic policy issues and to his government's disputes with the Chief of Staff and with the army; but there were many direct and indirect references to the main issue, which was, in fact, the main aspect of his political method and ideology, his relations to Germany. Part of the payment was stipulated already in the separate provisions of the Vienna award: the German ethnic groups in Hungary to be represented by the Volksbund as their sole party. Germany soon made the rest of the cost known to the Hungarian government through the Hungarian Ambassador at Berlin.[26] Hungary was to integrate more fully into the new German economic order (*Großraumwirtschaft*). This was the purpose of the new agreement concluded on October 10, 1940, according to which Hungarian agricultural production was to be suited more closely to the German requirements.

On the domestic scene, a lot was happening: the remission of Szálasi's remaining prison sentence;[27] the retraction of Decree 3400, which prohibited civil servants from joining the Arrow Cross Party; the proclamation of

---

26 Editor's note: From 1936 until the occupation of Hungary by Germany in March 1944 Hungary's Minister to Germany was Döme Sztójay (1883–1946). Sztójay, "the Quisling of Hungary" was executed as a war criminal in 1946 in Budapest.
27 Editor's note: Ferenc Szálasi (1897–1946) was the leader of the Hungarian Nazi party, the so-called Arrow Cross Party. He was imprisoned in 1938, was released in 1940 after a general amnesty. In 1946 he was tried and executed as a war criminal.

"Unwilling Satellite" or "Last Satellite"

the Third Anti-Jewish Law; the formation of a new party strongly adhering to the German platform (Imrédy's Hungarian Revival Party); and last but not least, Hungary's joining the Tripartite Pact. But, in spite of the cost, the Vienna award can still be regarded as the last act in the history of German-Hungarian relations when Hungarian interests still prevailed (at least at the foreign policy level), when Hungary's aims and her decisions were still the decisive factors, and not her fear of German power. Nineteen forty-one can be established as the end of the second period in the history of German-Hungarian relations between 1933 and 1944. This year marked the transition into a new period when decisions came to be determined partly with an eye to German power, and partly by fear of the political and social transformations which were envisioned as possible after the war. The increasing subordination of Hungarian interests is well illustrated by the three major foreign policy decisions made in 1941. The first of these, the plan for a joint attack on Yugoslavia, can still, in theory, be seen as a part of Hungary's own revisionist program. However, there is no doubt that Teleki's agreeing to the German proposal of a common attack, or to the German troops attacking from Hungarian territory was much more due to his fear of German military force than to his eagerness for a new response to his revisionist foreign policy aims. (There is no doubt that Horthy was influenced by different considerations; and the army leaders might as well have had different priorities, too. I am not trying to pass judgment on to what extent Teleki's decision was influenced by domestic policy components; but it is important to mention that the opposite decision might not have been supported by a large segment of his party and of his followers.)

The declaration of war against the Soviet Union, which was to prove so fatal a step, was overwhelmingly a response to German pressure, and a policy flight forward, i.e. the decision to enter the war at a phase when this step could still be said to bear certain elements of voluntariness, at a time when German pressure, which was sure to be forthcoming, was not yet acute. Hungary had no territorial claims against the Soviet Union, and her basic foreign policy from the outset of her friendship with Germany involved no belligerence against her, unless we take into consideration that after Romania and Slovakia were already involved in the war, Hungary's continued aloofness would serve to deprecate her in the eyes of the German leaders. Of course, with regard to political systems, or sheer ideology, Hungary was much closer to Germany than to the Soviet Union; nevertheless, I don't regard that similarity as a decisive factor in leading Hungary into war; German pressure was what predominated.[28]

Finally, the third act, the declaration of war against the United States in December of 1941, was merely obedience to Germany's will, and proof of Hungary's trustworthiness as an ally.[29] This act, which according to Kállay[30] was the gravest error committed by the government,[31] marked the end of the process of transition. The relationship between Germany and Hungary entered into its third and final stage. Though a large percentage of Hungarians probably still believed that there was some community of interest, this was already the stage when the salient feature of German policy, even when it clearly contradicted the interest of the Hungarian government, was coercion.

Ribbentrop and Keitel visited Hungary after the German defeat in the battle for Moscow, demanding that the Hungarian army send a large number of well-equipped troops to the Soviet Union. These acts were plain evidence that the basic element in the relationship was, by that time, German force, and that the phase when Hungary had been a mere German satellite was over. She had become a satellite without any kind of privilege 14 months earlier, when she signed the Tripartite Pact, the pact that Germany referred

---

28 This is not to underestimate the anti-Soviet ideological elements in Hungarian foreign policy. According to the report of the German ambassador, when he informed Horthy of the German invasion, "the old champion of the struggle against Bolshevism welcomed it with jubilation." Documents of German Foreign Policy, 1918–1945 D XII, Washington 1962, report of June 22, 1941. A possible attack against the Soviet Union was a favored topic of Horthy's in his letters addressed to Hitler. "Russian Bolshevism and Pan-Slavism are one and the same, as far as their military and political objectives are concerned," he wrote in 1936. "There is no rest, security and happiness for mankind until the Soviets have been knocked down." *Admiral Horthy's Papers*, p. 82. "After November 11, 1918, Marshal Foch made the official proposal that France, England, Italy, Germany and Austro-Hungary should all immediately march against Moscow," Horthy wrote in a letter of Nov. 3, 1939, "establish order there, break up into its component parts that gigantic empire composed of 118 nationalities which was a threat to all; then they were to return, sit down at the green table, and as comrades in arms conclude an eternal peace … this would have been the only practical way to save Europe." *Admiral Horthy's Papers*, pp. 127–128; also in Documents on German Foreign Policy, D VIII, Washington, 1954.
29 Britain declared war on Hungary. Some ideological elements in the official anti-democratic anti-liberal ideology of the Horthy regime certainly might have contributed to this declaration of war, but I think we can regard this element a negligible part of the actual process.
30 Editors note: Miklós Kállay (1887–1967) was Prime Minister in 1941–1944.
31 N. Kállay, *Hungarian Premier*, p. 64.

to in demanding her declaration of war on the United States. We might find it ironic that Csáky had tried to express the hopes Hungary had attached to this pact with the formula *primus inter pares* i.e. the first German satellite in the Danube Basin.

The third period of German-Hungarian relations may be dated from 1942. It is certainly open to discussion to what extent the change of government and the replacement of Bárdossy with Kállay was a sign of a proper change. Kállay's instructions when he was appointed by the regent were to reverse Bárdossy's policy: Bárdossy's had been to move further to the right domestically in the interest of retaining Germany's good will.

Many of Kállay's acts show that in the beginning he really was following the second route. Many of his words, even a lot of his actions, certainly showed no clear signs of attempt to dissociate from Germany, even if you admit, and one must admit, that under the given circumstances any top Hungarian politician had to operate with a large degree of dissimulation. I wonder whether the real turning point was not the spring of 1942 rather than the end of the year after El Alamein and Stalingrad. No doubt, during the period of discussion, Kállay refused Hitler's demands for new measures against the Jews (including yellow stars, ghettos and a certain amount of deportation). But in 1942, he still had not ruled out the possibility of the war ending at least in a draw; as a consequence, his policy was quite different after the turning point, when he no longer had any doubts about Germany losing the war. "Hungary began to appreciate more promptly than the others ... what may happen"—we read in *The Times* of June 4, 1943.[32] "Hungary was the first satellite that already felt the lash of the German whip," said Cordell Hull in his statement after the German occupation of Hungary.[33]

No doubt, Hungary was the first satellite to look for a way out after the hopes of a German victory faded. Certainly, Kállay's main concern was to give in as little as possible, and to find an opportunity for disengaging the unwilling satellite as soon as possible. And yet he did not succeed. He not only failed, but Hungary was the last to leave the wrecked ship of the Axis coali-

---

32 *The Times*, June 4, 1943.
33 *The Times*, March 29, 1944.

tion. What were the reasons for the missed opportunities: her geopolitical situation, awkward leadership, military force, betrayal by the West, fear of Bolshevism or just bad luck? Probably all of these, plus one more component to which I would attribute very great significance in any explanation of Hungary's remaining in the Axis camp. After the German occupation of Hungary, two letters were published in the appropriate section of *The Times*. The first one was written by Judy Listowel, who supported her thesis of Hungary's complete surrender to Germany by asserting that the ministers in the new government were mainly of German origin. In one of the next issues, an answer bearing the signature *"Times* correspondent" was published. In this letter reference was made to the overall continuity of government personnel even after the occupation; in fact, the majority of the government was made up of politicians who had served in different capacities in several governments and during the previous ten years, and had become part of the top Hungarian political elite.[34] In short, even in this last period of German-Hungarian relations, when the main features were sheer German force and Hungarian loss of interest in cooperation, a sufficient number of Hungarians with significant political influence were willing to stay on the side of the Germans for various reasons. Fear of the Soviets was one, but certainly not the only reason against dissociation. A great many people were willing to stay on the German side even when the German idea of Hungary's role was best expressed in the famous sentences of Veesemayer: "Every Hungarian, whether a peasant, a worker, or a soldier, who by this activity reduces our burdens, strengthens the Führer's reserves within the Reich. Every Hungarian who bleeds for us, reduces our own losses and reinforces our own reserves for further military efforts..."[35]

There is no question that there were large and influential political forces in Hungary whose activity is very important to an understanding of Hungary's permanent move from the position of unwilling to last satellite. Of course, the resistance of these forces might have been overcome under circumstances which Kállay had expected but which had not ensued. Were these expecta-

---

34 *The Times*, March 25–29, 1944.
35 Gy. Ránki, "The German Occupation of Hungary," *Acta Historica*, (Budapest, 1965), p. 261.

tions merely a case of entirely unrealistic wishful thinking, or were they based on realistic assumptions? Neither the one, nor the other.

Until, the end of 1943 there was a certain element of realistic calculation in Kállay's plans. Since the beginning of that year, Hungary slowly moved in the direction of disassociating herself from Germany. No more troops were sent to the Russian Front (except of course, for the remainder of the Second Army, which returned to Hungary during the summer of 1943; the Hungarian troops which were involved as security forces were not withdrawn).[36] Preparations were made to give more freedom of expression and of organization to left-wing opposition parties. Even the peace feelers that were put out seemed to be successful; a preliminary agreement in Istanbul was signed to the effect that Hungary would change sides if the Allied (Anglo-American) troops in Southern Italy made that kind of probability likely.

In early September of 1943 the Soviet troops were fighting farther from Hungary's borders than the British troops. The same day that Allied troops landed in Italy, Kállay refused a German demand to send Hungarian troops as security forces to the Balkans. The background of this German demand was that they wanted to disperse their troops along the coastlines in the effort to ward off an invasion. Hitler and his military advisers were almost convinced by the end of 1942 that they would have to face an allied landing on the Balkan Peninsula in the not too distant future.

According to Hitler's directive issued on December 28, 1942, the situation in the Mediterranean was such that an attack on Crete was likely in the near future, and consequently, also on German and Italian bases in the Aegean Sea and on the Balkan Peninsula. "It must be expected that this attack will be supported by uprisings in the Western Balkan countries. If the worst comes to worst, the Italian Peninsula can be sealed off Europe somehow. Above all, it is of decisive importance for us to hold the Balkan oil, copper, bauxite and chrome securely."[37]

During the last months of 1942, after the Allied landings in North Africa, the top political (Hitler and Mussolini at the meeting of 18 December, 1942)

---

36 According to Himmler in 1943, "Sie haben anständig mitgemacht:" *Hitler's Lagebesprechungen. Die Protokollfragmente seiner militärischen Konferenzen,* ed. Helmut Heiber (Stuttgart, 1962)
37 H. Hubatsch, *Hitlers Weisungen* (Stuttgart, 1960), Dec. 28, 1942.

and military axis leadership considered this territory as the next possible Allied target, and tried to take all the necessary measures to prevent a successful attack. The landing was expected in the spring of 1943, "after the Tunisian battle had been brought to certain conclusion."

According to a memorandum of Warlimont's written in captivity after 1945, "In May 1943, Hitler's fear of an attack on the Balkans took concrete form." At a conference on May 19, Hitler declared that "an attack on the Balkan Peninsula was even more dangerous than the problem of Italy." Even after the fall of Mussolini, and after the landing in Sicily and on the Italian Peninsula, he was afraid that the attack may have been just a camouflage, a diversion with the main offensive coming later on the Balkan Peninsula.[38] If Hitler was almost sure of a landing on the Balkans, why should Kállay have thought differently? After all, it was his only hope of a possible relief. General Szombathelyi, Chief of Staff of the Hungarian army, in a memorandum submitted to Kállay in February of 1943, stated that since the end of 1942, "We have had to reckon with a landing in the Balkans," "A landing is likely already from the end of March."[39] However, even at this time, Kállay was overconfident, and in making his calculations he disregarded some important factors which could interfere with the carrying out of his plans. One such factor was domestic, and it was referred to in the memorandum sent to Kállay by the Smallholders and the Social Democrats in August 1943: They warned him of the strong influence of right-wing ideas, of the unreliability of the army, and called his attention to the tone of the press, to the belief that Hungary had no choice but to go along with Germany, an idea that Kállay, too, had often paid lipservice to in his first year of office, if only by way of dissimulation.

The other factor which Kállay did not sufficiently take in to consideration was the strategic role assigned to Hungary in Germany's military plans, and Hitler's suspicion of Hungary's political moves. As far as I know, historians so far have failed to note a remark made by Hitler on the very day of Mussolini's

---

38 F.W. Deakin, "The Germans and Allied Plans for a Balkan Landing" In *The Third Reich and Yugoslavia 1933–1945*, (Belgrade, 1977), p. 478.
39 *Admiral Horthy's Papers*, pp. 213–214. Szombathelyi's conclusion was not quite Kállay's: the general was counting on the defection of Romania; in his view, intervention against Romania was the first step to "preparing" the complete occupation of Transylvania and her defense.

"Unwilling Satellite" or "Last Satellite"

fall. According to his *Lagebesprechungen*, at the first meeting with his chief military advisers after having received the bad news concerning Mussolini, Hitler had the following to say: "Wir müssen nur aufpassen, daß nicht hier bei den Ungarn noch irgendwelche Schweinereien passieren. Welche Verbände können wir unter Umständen kurzerhand da hereinjagen... Panther Abteilungen mag da noch irgend etwas herimprovisieren? Wenn da eine Schweinerei wäre..."[40] (We need to make sure that no such mess happens among the Hungarians. What associations can we hunt up there on short notice? Maybe Panther divisions can improvise something? If there were to be a mess there [in Hungary].)

It was not accidental that when faced with the first attempt by Italy to change sides, Hitler referred to Hungary as the next possible candidate. He was suspicious enough of Hungarian policy from the beginning of 1943 (it may not be an exaggeration to say that he was the *most* suspicious of Hungary of all his allies or satellites) to express his doubts during a meeting with Horthy in April of 1943 concerning the reliability of the Hungarian alliance.

"Die Hoffnung Kállays durch einen Stellungswechsel über die Türkei and England eine Lösung herbeizuführen sei natürlich Kállay trügerisch. Deutschland und seine Verbündeten, in einem Schiff saßen, der sich auf stürmischem Meere befinde. Es sei klar, daß bei dieser Lage jeder, der etwa aussteigen wolle, sofort ertrinken würde."[41] (Kállay's hope to effect a solution via a change of position regarding Turkey and England was, of course, Kállay being deceptive. Germany and its allies were in a ship on a stormy sea. Clearly, in this situation anyone who might want to get out would drown immediately.)

This reproach for Hungary's peace-feelers, and particularly for the negotiations conducted by Professor Szent-Györgyi, on which he had quite accurate reports, let Hitler go on with a long series of complaints, particularly against Kállay, which concluded with the remark: "Kállay durch sein Verhalten den Eindruck erweckt habe, daß Ungarn nicht mehr an den Sieg Deutschlands und Seiner Verbündeten glaube." ("Kállay, by his behavior,

---

40 *Hitlers Lagebesprechungen*, p. 332.
41 *Staatsmänner und Diplomaten bei Hitler*, ed. Andreas Hillgruber (Frankfurt, 1970), April 16, 1943, p. 238–259.

gave the impression that Hungary no longer believed in the victory of Germany and its allies.")

Horthy defended his premier during the conversation and repudiated the German charges a few weeks later in written form.[42] However, the German intelligence was so much better, and the Hungarians' conspiracy and peace-feelers were so badly organized, that German suspicions did not abate, and in the summer of 1943, it came to the point that the German Ambassador to Hungary, von Jagow, received secret instructions to terminate all personal contact with Kállay.[43]

It is not the purpose of this paper to trace the events which led to the German occupation of Hungary; the story has been told in different books, and one of mine in particular, was devoted exclusively to this topic.[44] This paper is concerned to find a proper explanation for Hungary's disassociating herself from Germany only later in the war, in spite of efforts to do so earlier. And in this respect, it is extremely important that from the German point of view, Hungary had a very important strategic role and was regarded, from the economic point of view, as of vital interest. For this very reason, Hitler was even less prepared to leave Hungary alone than his other satellites. Immediately after the defection of Italy, the Wehrmacht was requested to elaborate a plan for the occupation of Hungary. And the project proper was submitted to Hitler by the Wehrmacht Führungstab on September 30, 1943.[45] But while Germany was prepared to carry out such a withdrawal plan. Hitler was able to frustrate Kállay's plan through the occupation of the country on March 19, and he was able to do the same on the 15th of October. In a conversation with General Jodl on July 31, 1944, Hitler made it clear once again that he was attributing special importance to the control of Hungary: ""Die notwendigste Sicherung ist und bleibt für uns zunächst die Sicherung des ungarischen Raums, ernährungsmäßig ein einziger möglicher Ersatz für das, was wir

---

42 *Admiral Horthy's papers*, p. 249.
43 *A Wilhelmstraße és Magyarország (Wilhelmstraße and Hungary)*, eds. Gy. Ránki, Gy. Juhász, E. Pamlényi, L. Tilkovszky (Budapest, 1968).
44 Gy. Ránki, *1944 Március 19. Magyarország német megszállása* (March 19, 1944. The German occupation of Hungary) (Budapest, 1978).
45 *Kriegstagebuch des Oberkommandos der Wehrmacht* (Frankfurt, 1961), Vol. IV, p. 181, January 1944, May 22, 1945.

sonst verlieren; rohstoffmäßig eine Quelle für eine ganze Menge: Bauxit, Mangan usw ... Aber vor allem verkehrsmäßig überhaupt die Voraussetzung für den südosten, (ist) die Sicherung des ungarischen Raums von einer lebenswichtigen Bedeutung für, so wichtig, daß man sie überhaupt nicht überschätzen kann. Man muß also sehr überlegen, was wir an neuaufstellungen gleich entweder hineingeben können oder dort aufbauen, um jederzeit in der Lage zu sein, wenn notwendig, einem ungarischen Staatsstreich des Herrn Horthy vorzubeugen oder zuvorzukommen.[46] ("For us, the first and most necessary safeguard is and will remain securing the Hungarian arena, regarding nutrition, a single possible substitute for that which we would otherwise lose; regarding raw materials, a source for bauxite, manganese, and so on. But above all, regarding transport, securing the Hungarian territory is of vital importance, [is] an absolute prerequisite for the south-east, so important that it cannot be overvalued. We must, therefore, seriously consider what realignments we can either enter into, or build upon in order to be able at any time, if necessary, to prevent or forestall a Hungarian treason by Mr. Horthy.")

Any judgment concerning the opportunities open to Hungary's policymakers must bear in mind the special strategic position of the country, the fine possibilities this gave Germany to intervene, and her firm decision to do just that if intervention seemed to be necessary.

Last but not least, there is one more important point to be mentioned in connection with Hungary's attachment to Germany even during this final period, when German-Hungarian relations were based entirely on German interests. This is Hungary's relations with her neighbors, and the issue of the Trianon frontier. It is a well-known fact that one of the pillars of the Nazi foreign policy was the exploitation of the controversies between the Danubian countries. Ribbentrop did not even try to conceal this, as is shown by the cynical remark he made to the Bulgarian Foreign Minister in "proof" of the fairness of the second Vienna award: "Der Schiedsspruch sei beider Parteien gerecht werden. Dies habe sich bei seiner Verkündung ergeben, bei der rumänische Außenminister in Ohnmacht fiel und der ungarische Außen-

---

46 *Hitlers Lagebesprechungen*, p. 589.

minister seinen Rucktritt erklären wollte ..."[47] ("The arbitration award would be fair to both parties. This was revealed at the time of its announcement, when the Romanian Foreign Minister fainted and the Hungarian Foreign Minister wanted to explain his resignation...")

If in the first period of the Second World War this controversy helped the Germans to lure both countries into the war,[48] then in the second period it may have helped to keep them on Germany's side.

On November 19, 1943, Hitler, reflecting on a report presented by Keitel that the Allies had allegedly concluded negotiations with both Hungary and Romania, and that both of them were going to ask for armistice within a few days, had the following to say: "Beiden zusammen werden es auf gar keinen Fall Machen. Einer wird es Machen, und der andere wird auf Grund dieser Unruhen sofort einmarschieren. Wenn in Ungarn Unruhen kommen sollten, worauf uns die rumänen aufmerksam Machen, dann müßten sie uns bitten daß wir und sie gemeinsam die Ruhe in Ungarn wiederherstellen."[49] ("The two of them won't do it together under any circumstances. One will do it, and the other will invade immediately because of the unrest. If unrest should come to Hungary, and the Romanians make us aware of it, then they would have to ask us to restore the peace in Hungary jointly with them.")

These rivalries were well reflected by the fact that the Czechoslovak and the Yugoslav ambassadors to London were constantly expressing their concern lest British foreign policy make any concessions to Hungary.[50] This sort of policy also was reflected in the conversation of Beneš with Stalin concerning the future of Hungary and Romania.[51] Though the Hungarian government was the first to explore the possibilities of peace negotiations, and though her preliminary armistice of September, 1943 was more far-reaching than any diplomatic step of any other Nazi satellite country, the definitive relapse or retreat in Kállay's policy (which occurred between November 1943

---

47 Quoted in Gy. Ránki's "East Central Europe and World War II," *Acta Historica,* 1974, pp. 199–200.
48 The *Times* argues in an article of July 13, 1941 that one of the reasons Hungary joined the campaign against the Soviet Union was her rivalry with Romania for Transylvania.
49 *Hitlers Lagebesprechungen,* p. 424.
50 Public Record Office, Foreign Office 371/349956681.
51 V. Mastny, "The Benes-Stalin-Molotov Conversation in December 1943," *Jahrbücher für Geschichte Osteuropas,* September, 1972.

"Unwilling Satellite" or "Last Satellite"

and February 1944, when Hungary did not meet the obligations agreed to in September) was to a great extent due to concern over the fate of Transylvania, to the fact that, unlike Romania, Hungary was promised no territorial reward in case of disalignment.[52]

Playing off Romania against Hungary had a very important part in Hitler's successful occupation of Hungary, and in the failure of Kállay's attempts to preserve Hungary's relative independence and to dissociate her from Germany. Hitler's allusion to an eventual German-Romanian intervention to prevent Hungary's exit from the war became a built-in element of German military plans for Hungary's occupation. One of the versions of the so-called Margharete Plan was based on the assumption that Romanian, Slovakian and Croatian troops would join the German army in carrying out the military campaign. Hitler proved to be not a bad prophet. In a conversation with Marshall Antonescu on February 26, 1944, he made a seemingly unusual remark at the close of the discussion, relating that he had received a letter from Horthy demanding the withdrawal of Hungarian troops from the Soviet front.[53]

During the rest of the day, the Romanian Prime Minister returned to Hungarian affairs:

"Eine Million rumänischer Soldaten für den kampf zur Verfügung standen, wenn erst einmal die ungarische Gefahr beseitigt sei." (A million Romanian soldiers were available for the fight when the Hungarian danger had been eliminated.) He went further when he asked Hitler to deal seriously with the question of Hungary: "Müsse man gegen Ungarn einschreiten, und zwar möglichst bald, da bei einer etwaigen Verschlimmerung der Lage an der Ostfront ein unsicheres Ungarn im Rücken zu einer außerordentlichen Gefahr werden könne."[54] (One ought to intervene in Hungary, and as soon as possible, for in the event of a worsening of the situation on the eastern front, an uncertain Hungary at the rear could be an extraordinary danger.)

---

52 I want to refer to the differences in British and Soviet armistice terms. The British demanded the evacuation of the Allied territories (Czechoslovakia and Yugoslavia), the latter demanded the evacuation of all *occupied territories* (Transylvania as well). Public Record Office F.O. 371/ 34495C16684.
53 Hillgruber, *op. cit.* p. 354. Actually Horthy's letter was addressed to Hitler on Feb. 12, 1944.
54 Quoted in Gy. Ránki, "East Central Europe and World War II," *Acta Historica*, 1974, p. 199.

To avoid the German occupation of Hungary was a permanent feature of Kállay's policy during his attempts to dissociate Hungary from Germany. If there was a genuine fear of a German occupation, then the possibility of a German occupation in alliance with the Romanians was regarded as a nightmare. Another reason for apprehension of a German occupation was the fear that it might strengthen the role of the radical elements in the event of a resistance. Horthy's final decision at Klessheim on March 18, 1944 to stay on even though the Germans were occupying the country, was made in the hope that he could prevent Romania's participation in the campaign. A few days after the occupation of Hungary Hitler told Antonescu, who was again paying him a visit: "Nach der illoyalen Haltung der ungarischen Regierung und nachdem sowohl Rumänien als auch Ungarn sich den Wiener Schiedsspruch innerlich nie zu eigen gemacht hätten und nachdem Italien jetzt ausgefallen sei, halte es Deutschland nicht für angebracht, weiterhin als Signatar des Wiener Schiedsspruchs zu fungieren. Er (der Führer) bäte Antonescu, die vorgenannte Erklärung zunächst niemandem gegenüber zu erwähnen; im gegebenen Augenblick würde er (der Führer) sie öffentlich abgeben. Zunächst aber liege es im deutschen wie im rumänischen Interesse zu versuchen, einen Partisanenkrieg in Ungarn zu vermeiden; den es sei jede deutsche Division wertvoll, die in Ungarn nicht gebraucht wurde und an die Front geschickt werden könne."[55] (After the disloyal attitude of the Hungarian government, and after both Romania and Hungary never really took the Vienna arbitration to heart, and after Italy has now fallen away, Germany no longer considers it appropriate to continue to function as a signatory of the Vienna Accord. He (the Fuhrer) would ask Antonescu not to mention the above explanation [statement or announcement] to any one; at the appropriate moment, he (the Fuhrer) would make this public. First, however, it is in both Germany's and Romania's interest to try to avoid a partisan war in Hungary, because every German division that is not needed in Hungary and could be sent to the front is valuable.)

Antonescu was very pleased with Hitler's communication and warned Hitler not to trust the Hungarians. The next day Hitler told him that North Transylvania would be declared an operations zone ("Operationszone") and

---

55   Hillgruber, *op. cit.,* pp. 391–2.

that the Hungarian troops would be withdrawn ("von ungarischen Truppen geräumt werden müsse"). Antonescu proposed to let the Romanian refugees from North Transylvania return; if the Hungarians started any kind of partisan war, they could be used to fight against them ("gegen ungarische Partisanenbanden eingesetzt werden könnten").[56]

Actually, the troops sent to Galicia in April and May 1944 were mainly from Transylvania; however, not all the Hungarian troops were withdrawn, for the Hungarian army was ready to compromise, and to amass again at the Eastern Front.

The German occupation of the country put an end to the story of Hungary as the unwilling satellite. The event came after it was already on the road to becoming the last to stay in the Axis camp. What followed was the horror story of the deportation of the Jews at Germany's wishes by the Hungarian gendarmerie; the story of the annihilation of the First Army; and the story of the Nazification of Hungary. In the five months which passed between March 19 and August 25, Hungarian foreign policy was almost non-existent, negotiations with the Allies ceased, Horthy practically withdrew from politics and public life and was entirely passive. During this five-month period Hungary's international credit deteriorated tremendously; the military situation changed completely, and all the other German satellites came close to switching sides. Horthy started his secret negotiations again only after the Romanian upheaval, proceeding along his old premises as if nothing had happened during the last months. But the very event that had inspired Horthy to get in touch secretly again with the Western Powers entailed significant changes in the military and political situation of the Danube Valley. The Romanian upheaval altered the situation: "The turning over of Romania to the Allied cause has given the Russians a great advantage and it may well be that they will enter Belgrade and Budapest and possibly Vienna before the Western Allies succeed in piercing the Siegfried line. However desirable such a Russian incursion may be, its political effect upon Central and Southern Europe may be formidable in the last degree."[57]

---

56   Hillgruber, *op. cit.*, p. 405.
57   J. Ehrman, *Grand Strategy* vol. V., (Aug. 1943–Sept. 1944) (London, 1956), p. 402.

Romania, Bulgaria and Finland were already out when Horthy finally turned to the Soviet Union for an armistice. But due to bad preparation, due to German unwillingness to leave Hungary alone, and due to internal forces which either were still most ready to fight for Germany or were not ready to draw the necessary lessons from what had transpired, even this attempt failed. Horthy was obliged to cede power to the Arrow Cross, and the armistice was signed with Hungary only in January 1945, when the others had already long been on the winners' side.

Chapter 3
Hungary in World War II: Tragic Blunders or Destiny?[1]

Géza Jeszenszky

Many historians have written fair and balanced accounts of Hungary's conduct in World War II, but there are also one-sided, prejudiced, or apologetic works on the subject. Public perception (both in Hungary and outside it) is dominated by two equally fallacious tendencies: whitewashing or blackening. Though flawed, it is understandable that many Hungarians believe that their country was basically innocent in becoming an ally, a satellite of Nazi Germany, because it was a kind of set course, doom, inevitable destiny, caused by the 1920 Peace Treaty signed at the Greater Trianon Palace at Versailles. The summary of this version is as follows: the Paris Peace Conference reduced the historic kingdom to one third of its territory and transferred close to 3.5 million Hungarians (including those of Jewish origin), against their will, to Czechoslovakia, Romania and Yugoslavia respectively.[2]

---

[1] This is a modified and expanded version of my essay with the same title, which appeared in *Hungarian Review* V, No. 2 (March 2014), 7–21. Until today the most thorough account of Hungary's road to and conduct during World War II in any language is by the British scholar C.A. Macartney, *October fifteenth: a history of modern Hungary, 1929–1945*, Vols. I, II (Edinburgh: Edinburgh University Press, 1956–1957). Among the vast literature on the same subject in English, Mario D. Fenyo's *Hitler, Horthy and Hungary. German-Hungarian Relations, 1941–1944* (New Haven and London: Yale University Press, 1972) is still a solid, reliable account. The newest, thorough work is Deborah S. Cornelius, *Hungary in World War II. Caught in the Cauldron* (New York: Fordham University Press, 2011). Three authors stand out among the scholarly publications in Hungarian: Antal Czettler, *Teleki Pál és a magyar külpolitika 1939–1941* [Pál Teleki and Hungarian foreign policy] (Budapest: Kairosz, 1997); idem, *A mi kis élethalál kérdéseink. A magyar külpolitika a hadba lépéstől a német megszállásig.* [Our little life or death problems. Hungarian foreign policy from the entry into the war to occupation by Germany] (Budapest: Magvető, 2000); and András Joó, *Kállay Miklós külpolitikája. Magyarország és a háborús diplomácia, 1942_1944* [The Foreign Policy of Miklós Kállay. Hungary and War-Time Diplomacy] (Budapest: Napvilág Kiadó, 2008); but several studies by Pál Pritz are also outstanding.
[2] The first detailed and objective work on that treaty in any language is Francis Deak, *Hungary at the Paris Peace Conference. The Diplomatic History of the Treaty of Trianon* (New York: Columbia

Those Hungarians became ill-treated minorities, longing to be returned to Hungary. It was only Mussolini and later Hitler who gave (at first only verbal) support to the unanimous wish and claim of the Hungarians for revising the borders in line with ethnic realities, honoring the principle of self-determination. In addition, having experienced 133 days of Bolshevik misrule in 1919, Hungary could not but welcome a "crusade" against the Soviet Union, especially as unidentified airplanes, assumed to have been Soviet, bombarded a Hungarian town on 26 June 1941. Despite becoming a formal ally of Germany in 1940, Hungary tried to limit its participation in the war effort to the minimum. The multi-party political system, a free press and opposition parties were preserved; about a hundred thousand Polish refugees were warmly welcomed, and many were helped to join the Allied forces. Hungary gave asylum to escaped allied POWs, and the lives of its large Jewish population were not in danger. Finally, from March 1942 the Hungarian Government did its best to prepare for leaving the German camp, and in September 1943 it even concluded a secret armistice with the British to surrender as soon as Allied (Anglo-American) forces reached the border of Hungary. In order to prevent Hungary's defection, Hitler ordered the invasion of Hungary in March 1944 and imposed upon it a puppet government. Adolf Eichmann arrived in Hungary and directed the deportation and murder of over half a million Hungarian Jews. In this interpretation Nazi Germany is to blame for all the crimes committed during the occupation. The above story was first presented in English by the former US Minister to Hungary.[3]

The alternative version of the story differs mainly in the conclusion. Although Hungary had a large, assimilated and highly patriotic Jewish community, the first law restricting Jews (limiting their admission to universi-

---

University Press, 1942). A good – and still not outdated – collection of essays: Bela K Kiraly, Peter Pastor, Ivan Sanders, eds., *Essays on World War I: Total War and Peacemaking: A Case Study of Trianon* (New York and Boulder, CO:. East European Monographs, Columbia University Press, 1982). A succinct and balanced account is Ignác Romsics, *The Dismantling of Historic Hungary: the Peace Treaty of Trianon, 1920* (New York: East European Monographs, Columbia University Press, 2002).

3 John Flournoy Montgomery, *Hungary, the Unwilling Satellite* (New York: Devin Adair Co, 1947). Cf. Tibor Frank, ed., *Discussing Hitler. Advisers of U.S. Diplomacy in Central Europe, 1934–41,* Budapest - New York: Central European University Press, 2003 C.A. Macartney was not far from that interpretation.

ties) was passed in 1920. Anti-Semitism grew in the 1930s, and after 1939 it culminated in several laws limiting the rights and livelihood of those who were at least half Jewish by origin. Admiral Horthy, the head of state (regent) from 1920 to 1944, introduced and maintained an authoritarian political system, had anti-Semitic prejudices, was ready to pay any price for border changes and thus became an ally of Nazi Germany. With Hitler's help, Hungary annexed territories from the neighbors, and, following the German occupation, the Hungarian civil service and the gendarmerie collected and deported more than half a million Jewish Hungarians to be transported to the German-run death camps. So the Hungarians themselves were responsible for the calamities of the early 1940s.[4]

The controversy about Hungary's role in World War II is much more than an academic debate. It is a moral issue and seeks an explanation for what probably is the greatest human tragedy of Hungary's thousand-year-old history, the decimation of the nation.[5] Is it true that Hungary was an eager and effective ally of Nazi Germany? It is beyond doubt that Hungary, or more properly its legal governments, had to make very hard decisions in the twentieth century, and many were bad ones with tragic consequences. But what were the alternatives for the decision-makers? Nothing is further from my intentions than to exonerate those Hungarians, – politicians, civil servants and opportunists, –who accepted and endorsed the Nazi ideology (or just Nazi Germany's foreign policy) and committed terrible crimes against their fellow Hungarians. The guilty ones were duly punished by Hungarian courts after the war. What is needed, however, is a dispassionate analysis of the causes, the precursors

---

[4] That was the official Marxist version taught at school and propagated during the days of communism in Hungary. Labeled "a guilty nation" and "the last satellite" of Germany, the over-simplified and biased history of Hungary was happily abandoned after the collapse of communism, but it is still propagated by the nationalists of Hungary's neighbors and it survived in much of the Western media.

[5] Almost one tenth of the Hungarian nation perished during and due to World War II. In 1941 the number of Hungarians (those who identified themselves as such in and around Hungary) was about 12 million. Out of that around 160,000 died in action, on the Russian front; 280,000 perished in Soviet captivity, as POWs in "the Gulag Archipelago." The number of civilian casualties when Hungary became a war theatre ran to 130,000. More than 450,000 Jews, who were Hungarian speakers and considered themselves Hungarian, were killed in the Holocaust. Tamás Stark, *Magyarország második világháborús embervesztesége* [Hungary's Human Losses in the Second World War] (Budapest: MTA Történettudományi Intézet, 1989); Tamás Stark, *Zsidóság a vészkorszakban és a felszabadulás után* [Hungarian Jews in the Shoa and after Liberation] (Budapest: MTA Történettudományi Intézet, 1995). Cf. Stark's essay in the present volume.

of the fateful decisions that brought Hungary into World War II. Then one must also ponder whether there was any way to break with Germany before 19 March 1944, the occupation of the nominal ally? What would have been the consequences of defying Hitler? By showing more loyalty to Nazi Germany and meeting its political demands, including harsher measures against the Jews, could the German occupation have been avoided? Was Hungary's liaison with Germany indeed "a Faustian Pact" with first a glowing prize (territorial readjustment in Hungary's favor), and a terrible price to be paid after?[6]

* * *

Eighteen years after Hungary lost its war for independence from Austrian Habsburg rule (due to the intervention of the Russian Czar) a compromise or settlement was reached with Emperor Francis Joseph in 1867 and the dual Austro-Hungarian Monarchy was established. It entered into a defensive alliance with Germany in 1879, and 35 years later the latter's rivalry with the Entente Powers led to a world war, ending in the break-up of the Monarchy and the partition of Hungary. The exodus or expulsion of half a million Hungarians from the territories detached by the 1920 treaty did not eliminate the tensions between Hungary and its neighbors, it rather added to them. "In each of the new states there prevailed a narrow official nationalism," and the oppressive policy pursued against the national, religious and political minorities led to internal and external tensions and conflicts.[7]

In the 1920s Hungarians, from communists to conservatives and right radicals, were unanimous in denouncing "Trianon" as an unfair deal. "No, no, never" (shall we accept the unjust borders) was a catchphrase practically all Hungarians agreed upon. The answer of "the successor States" was that "not a furrow" will be given back. Given the harshness of the terms of the Trianon Treaty (in addition to the unfair borders, a high amount of war reparation was imposed upon Hungary, and very serious restrictions were placed

---

6   Byran Cartledge in his remarkable *The Will to Survive. A History of Hungary*. 2nd ed. (London: Hurst & Company, 2011), Chapters 15–16.
7   Hugh and Christoper Seton-Watson, *The Making of a New Europe: R.W. Seton-Watson and the Last Years of Austria-Hungary* (London: Methuen, 1981), 435.

on the size of its army and its armaments), it is unreasonable to blame Hungary for advocating peaceful territorial revision throughout the inter-war period. A number of prominent European politicians, from Lloyd George and Churchill to former Italian Prime Minister Nitti, and many journalists agreed that Hungary's borders were unfair and should be changed. The craving to revise the treaty peacefully was the leitmotif of Hungary's foreign policy. The Covenant of the League of Nations made that theoretically possible. But Czechoslovakia, Romania and Yugoslavia, now with millions of unhappy national minorities (not only Hungarians but also a large numbers of Germans, Ukrainians, Albanians, Bulgarians, etc.), formed the so-called "Little Entente" with the aim of preventing Hungary from gaining back any territory. That dashed the hopes that the League would be instrumental in convincing or compelling Hungary's neighbors to cede back their overwhelmingly Hungarian-inhabited regions. "This state of generalized and mutual hostility provided opportunities for any great power intent on disturbing the peace," was the conclusion of the sons of the British historian who was one of the makers of the Trianon Treaty.[8] The only hope left for Hungary was that one or more of the Great Powers might endorse Hungary's claims. Memories of the brief Hungarian Soviet Republic of 1919 meant that Hungary was also on bad terms with the Soviet Union, the other opponent of the post-war borders. Britain was instrumental in Hungary's admission to the League of Nations in 1922, but stood by the borders drawn in 1919/20. So did France. It was only ambitious Italy under Mussolini that supported the Hungarian claims. Having come to power in Germany, Hitler started to expand eastward, first swallowing Austria. The desire not to have another world war and also their limited resources and lack of direct interests in Central Europe induced Britain and France to pursue a policy of appeasing Hitler. At the Munich Conference (September 1938) they gave up Czechoslovakia by consenting to the transfer of its German-inhabited western rim to Germany and proposing bilateral negotiations over the territorial claims of Poland and Hungary. The message sent to Central Europe was that each state was left to the mercy of Germany.

---

8   Ibid.

Admiral Horthy (a well-deserved rank earned in World War I in the Adriatic) as regent and his governments were not unaware of the danger presented by Nazism and were not enthusiastic supporters of Hitler. The sentiments of the Hungarians were divided. The upper class was largely Anglophile, and so were most of the professionals and the artists. (The also strong Francophile tradition almost disappeared, due to the French role at the Paris Peace Conference.) In the army and among the civil servants sympathy was strong for Germany, but not necessarily for Nazism. The majority of the diplomatic service was conservative-leaning and feared Germany. The Third Reich, however, was rather popular with the lower middle class, and in general among those who were ignorant of world affairs. The annexation of Austria rang some alarm bells in Hungary, too, and it increased the importance of Hungary's behavior in the eyes of the West. That was reflected in the increased attention Britain paid to Hungary.[9] The regent, "the ancient Mariner," was equally convinced of the invincibility of the maritime powers and the might of the German army. Count Pál Teleki, appointed prime minister in February 1939, based his foreign policy on keeping Hungary out of a new world war at all costs, so that at the next peace an intact army would give weight to Hungary's territorial claims. He sent the following message to London: "although Hungary's geographical and political situation compelled her to co-operate loyally with Germany up to a point, he [Teleki] was already determined that such co-operation should never go so far as to impair, much less sacrifice, Hungary's sovereignty, independence or honour. The Government attached great importance to the understanding and support of the British Government, and would never do anything to injure the interests of Great Britain."[10] That line was known and appreciated by such experts as Arnold Toynbee, the director of the Royal Institute of International Affairs; while in the Foreign Office, Lord Vansit-

---

9   András D. Bán, *Illúziók és csalódások : Nagy-Britannia és Magyarország, 1938–1941* [Illusions and disappointments] (Budapest: Osiris, 1998), 33–63. (The expanded English edition: *Hungarian-British Diplomacy 1938–1941: The Attempt to Maintain Relations* (London–Portland, OR: Frank Cass, 2004).) Lajos Arday: "Magyarország és Nagy-Britannia diplomáciai kapcsolatai– 1931–1941" [Diplomatic relations between Hungary and Great Britain], in Lajos Arday, *Az Egyesült Királyság és Magyarország* [The United Kingdom and Hungary] (Budapest: Mundus Magyar Egyetemi Kiadó, 2005), 47–148, esp. 123–127.
10 Macartney, *October Fifteenth*, 331–332. Cf. György Barcza, *Diplomataemlékeim* [Diplomatic Memoirs], Vol. I (Budapest: Európa Kiadó, 1994), 403.

tart, the permanent under-secretary (1930–1938), and Sir Orme Sargent, the assistant under-secretary, rather sympathized with the Little Entente. Sargent thought that in Hungary the game was already lost and there was no point in wasting money and energy trying to change it.[11]

At the end of the 1930s there were some attempts to put up a common Central European front against Hitler. In August 1938 Hungary normalized its relations with the Little Entente, and (to Hitler's fury) Horthy rejected Hitler's proposal that Hungary, backed by Germany, should attack Czechoslovakia. With that rejection, Hungary "prevented Hitler from starting his adventurous plan."[12] That and other Hungarian diplomatic attempts at the end of the 1930s to keep a distance from Germany received little recognition and no assistance whatever from the Western governments. They did not give real support even to their actual friends and allies, Poland and Czechoslovakia. To be more exact, verbal exhortations and encouragements were abundant, but when Hitler broke his promise to respect the post-Munich borders of Czechoslovakia, occupied the Czech lands and made Slovakia a Nazi puppet state, no action was taken. Finally, however, when the German attack on Poland was imminent, Britain concluded an alliance with the Poles in the hope that it would be sufficient to dissuade Germany from starting a war. It did not deter Hitler from invading his eastern neighbor, so on 3 September Britain and France declared war on Germany as an act of solidarity with Poland, without giving it any military help whatsoever. Hungary, an old and staunch friend of the Poles, feared a similar fate.

Hungary did receive a few encouraging words in the summer of 1939 from the British side:

> Please take note, if you persist in defending your independence, if you resist German pressure and in case of war you strive with Poland and the small nations around you to prevent Germany from bringing Central

---

11 Tamás Magyarics, "Nagy-Britannia Közép-Európa-politikája 1918-tól napjainkig" [Great Britain's policy on Central Europe since 1918], *Pro Minoritate*,. (Summer and Fall 2002), 29.
12 Pál Pritz, "Magyarország és a nagyhatalmak 1938-ban" [Hungary and the Great Powers in 1938], in *Az objektivitás mítosza? Hazánk és a nagyvilág. 20. századi metszetek* [The Myth of Objectivness. Hungary and the World in 20th Century Sketches] (Budapest: Magyar Történelmi Társulat, 2011), 104.

and Eastern Europe under its control, Hungary's claims for border adjustment will be met generously. When the time comes, please remind me of my statement. But if Hungary fights again on the side of Germany, don't be surprised if the consequences will be the worst.

These were the words of Winston Churchill, uttered on 9 July 1939 to Tibor Eckhardt, then leader of the opposition Smallholders' Party, and Pál Auer, a Hungarian expert in international law.[13] Throughout the 1930s Churchill was seen as a Tory die-hard, a relentless critic of appeasing Germany, but after the destruction of Czechoslovakia his star was again rising. Churchill accepted that Hungary could not join an anti-German coalition but thought that it should stick to neutrality. He spoke in the same vein to György Barcza, Hungary's minister at the Court of St. James: "The time will come ... when the endangered small nations in Central-Eastern Europe will have to make their choice. After Allied victory, their wartime stand will be the only criterion by which they will be judged."[14] Unfortunately Hungary did not follow Churchill's advice. If it had, the price would have been very high, but worth its while.

All the governments of Central Europe tried to avoid conflict with Germany; it was Hitler who decided who to destroy and who to make a satellite. Sir Owen O'Malley, the last British minister to Hungary before the war, made the point: Hungary had the "sombre [...] choice between being victim or accomplice of Germany."[15] Austria, Czechoslovakia and then Poland became victims, but their conduct was far from similar. Most Austrians were

---

13   Bán, *Illúziók és csalódások*, 76–79. The quotation is from *idem*, "Az összeköttetés megszakad. Brit-magyar kapcsolatok [The connection is broken. British–Hungarian relations] 1938–1941", Rubiconline, 1997/1. http://www.rubicon.hu/magyar/oldalak/az_osszekottetes_megszakad_brit_magyar_kapcsolatok_1938_1941/. The quotation is from Auer's memoirs, *Fél évszázad* [Half a century] (Washington, D.C.: Occidental Press, 1971). A slightly different version of that important statement is: "Let me assure you ... that if you succeed this time to defend your independence and collaborate in case of war with Poland and the other small nations friendly to us, Hungary's claim for treaty revision will be fully satisfied. When the time comes for it, remind me of this statement." Katalin Kadar Lynn, ed., *Tibor Eckhardt in His Own Words: An Autobiography* (Boulder, CO: East European Monographs, 2005), 64.
14   Lynn, *Tibor Eckhardt*, 65.
15   O'Malley to Eden, 2 April 1941, FO 371/26603/3247/123/21, quoted by Miklós Lojkó in László Péter and Martin Rady, eds., *British–Hungarian Relations Since 1848* (London: Hungarian Cultural Centre and School of Slavonic and East European Studies, University College London, 2004), 223.

elated with the *Anschluss,* the Czechs shook their fists and then worked hard manufacturing weapons for the *Wehrmacht,* while the Poles created an underground state and an army (Armija Krajowa) to fight the aggressor, until it was crushed. There was also a tremendous difference between Finland, Slovakia, Croatia, Romania, Bulgaria and Hungary in their degree of collaboration with Germany.[16]

Albeit for his own selfish interests, Hitler was instrumental in Hungary getting back some of the territories lost in 1920 which had an overwhelmingly Hungarian population. In the so-called First Vienna Award on 2 November 1938, the Hungarian-inhabited region of Slovakia was ceded back to Hungary by way of German–Italian arbitration. (Hungary's grave mistake was not to insist upon the four-power conference involving Britain and France, too, envisaged at the Munich Conference.) On 14 March 1939, one day before Germany marched into Prague, the Slovak parliament passed a declaration of independence and set up a typical pro-German puppet state with a Catholic priest as head of state. Seeing a good opportunity, Hungary occupied Ruthenia, the sub-Carpathian region of historic Hungary. Hitler, who had categorically rejected Hungary's claim earlier, now accepted it, while both the United States and Britain preferred this re-annexation to German (or Soviet) control.[17]

It has become customary to say that becoming a satellite of Nazi Germany was Hungary's inevitable destiny, a course predetermined by the Trianon Treaty and the desire to revise its terms. If Hungary had defied Hitler, it is certain that sooner or later Germany would have managed to replace its leaders with a pro-German Quisling government. The Anglophile wing of Hungary's political and economic elite hoped to avoid what happened at the end of World War I, when the country lay prostrate at the mercy of the victorious

---

16   This is corroborated by István Deák, *Europe on Trial. The Story of Collaboration, Resistance and Retribution During World War II* (Boulder, CO: Westview Press, 2015). Documentary evidence is to be found in György Ránki, ed., *Hitler 68 tárgyalása kelet-európai államférfiakkal 1939–1944* [Hitler's 68 talks with East European statesmen] (Budapest: Magvető, 1983). The original documents are to be found in Andreas Hillgruber, ed., *Staatsmänner und Diplomaten bei Hitler* (Frankfurt am Main: Bernard & Graefe Verlag, 1967).

17   Macartney, *October Fifteenth,* Vol. I, 329–332; Ablonczy Balázs, *Teleki Pál* (Budapest: Osiris Kiadó, 2005), 397–398. Cf. Domokos Szent-Iványi, *The Hungarian Independence Movement, 1936–1946* (Budapest: Hungarian Review Books, 2013, 189–190; Cornelius, *Hungary in World War II,* 104.

Great Powers and they treated it very harshly. It was thought that by engaging in limited collaboration with Germany, Hungary could remain outside of the looming war. The conundrum faced by Hungary in this dreadful period was what diplomat and historian George Kennan has described as "one of humanity's oldest and most recalcitrant dilemmas: the dilemma of a *limited collaboration* with evil, in the interests of its ultimate mitigation, as opposed to an uncompromising, heroic but suicidal resistance to it, at the expense of the ultimate weakening of the forces capable of acting against it."[18]

The Molotov–Ribbentrop Pact of 23 August 1939 made the Soviet Union a partner in the partition of Central Europe. It was a courageous step by Hungary under Teleki to refuse participation in the rape of Poland (unlike Slovakia and, of course, the Soviet Union). Hungary accepted well over a hundred thousand Polish (including Jewish) refugees, many of whom eventually left Hungary to continue fighting Germany on the side of the British. The Soviet annexation of eastern Poland did not make it more attractive to get close to the Soviet Union, although an opportunity for that soon presented itself. Following Poland's fall, the Soviet Union became Hungary's neighbor, and the two countries restored their diplomatic relations, broken after Hungary joined the Anti-Comintern Pact in March 1939. Now it was the Soviet Union which seemed to be keener on improving relations with Hungary. When Stalin annexed Moldavia (Bessarabia), the easternmost part of Romania, in June, Hungary did not move. On 3 July 1940 Commissar for Foreign Affairs Molotov told József Kristóffy, Hungary's minister in Moscow, that in the view of the Soviet Union, Hungary's territorial claims against Romania were well-founded and in case of a war between Hungary and Romania, it would behave accordingly. Rather than involving the Soviet Union in its subsequent diplomatic efforts to get back at least part of Transylvania from Romania, Hungary sought the support only of Germany and Italy, finally accepting their arbitration, and the smaller, northern part of Transylvania (having a slight majority of Hungarians over Romanians) was ceded back to Hungary on 30 August 1940. That was called the Second Vienna Award.

---

18 George F. Kennan, *From Prague after Munich. Diplomatic Papers, 1938–1940* (Princeton, NJ: Princeton University Press, 1968), x.

Hungary in World War II

The return of parts of the lost territories was received most enthusiastically in Hungary and by the returned Hungarian population. The circumstances of the long-hoped-for border revisions were, however, most unfortunate. Britain and France declined to participate in the arbitration over the borders of Hungary, so the changes were linked to Germany's aggressive schemes. Thus, the Hungarian claims for fairer borders became compromised in the eyes of Germany's adversaries. Hungary as well as its neighbors became economically and politically ever more dependent on Germany – which was exactly Hitler's aim. Those affected most closely, the Hungarians of the re-attached territories, did not realize how questionable the future of the new borders was, and could not foresee how high a price they were to pay for the few happy years. (In fact, they were not so happy, due to the narrow-minded and haughty behavior of many Hungarian carpet-bagger officials. The Jews in those territories also rejoiced, only to be gravely disappointed by the anti-Jewish laws of Hungary, which were immediately imposed.)

It is easy to pass judgment in hindsight on Hungary's ill-advised steps leading to the war. But as my brilliant, one-time tutor, Péter Hanák, warned: we must play an honest game with the dead. The leaders of the past could not see the outcome of their decisions. While in 1939 Germany's victory in a world war was far from certain, in 1941, following Hitler's victories and before the entry of the United States into the war, it was not at all unrealistic to believe that the *Neue Ordnung* would be the fate of Europe.[19] Nevertheless, it was most unwise and it was not due to any German pressure that Hungary (together with Romania, Slovakia and Bulgaria) joined the Tripartite Pact of Germany, Italy and Japan concluded on 20 November 1940. The Pact did not oblige the signatories to join in a war involving the other members of the alliance, nevertheless it was an inexcusable mistake to adhere to it. True, when most of Europe was conquered by Germany and the Soviets went out of their way to please Hitler and to share the spoils, most Hungarians, not only the pro-Nazis, thought that the only course for a small nation was to go along with the new master of the continent.[20]

---

19 How close Germany was to defeating the Soviet Union is shown by, among others, John Lukacs, *The Last European War* (New York: Anchor Press/Doubleday, 1976), 151–153; 389.
20 How so many in western and northern Europe collaborated with Nazi Germany during „Europe's Honeymoon with Hitler" is shown by István Deák, *Europe on Trial*, esp. 41–66.

The treaty of "eternal friendship" Hungary signed with Yugoslavia in December 1940 could be interpreted (as was really meant by Prime Minister Teleki) as an alliance between two neutrals facing German pressure; while Hitler welcomed it as bringing another state closer to the German camp. When in March 1941 Yugoslavia, too, signed the Tripartite Pact, its government was immediately overthrown in a military coup. That led to Hitler's decision to attack and destroy the southern Slav state. Hungary's position became impossible: Germany needed Hungary's roads and railway lines for the attack and offered the return of the formerly Hungarian regions of Yugoslavia. Teleki thought up an ingenious-looking plan: not to join in the German military action until Yugoslavia disintegrated (with the likely separation of Croatia), and then to occupy only the territory which used to be part of Hungary. It did not work. Barcza, the Hungarian minister in London, cabled the British position on 2 April: if Hungary allowed German troops to use Hungarian territory for the attack, His Majesty's government would break off diplomatic relations, and Hungarian participation in the invasion would be met by a declaration of war. That was the end of the road for Teleki. His policy of staying out of the war by all means became impossible. Now came the time to realize his contingency plan, setting up a Hungarian government-in-exile if Germany's pressure became unbearable. The prime minister had even deposited five million US dollars to the US to be used by that government, but after the defeat of France he gave up the idea.[21] By this time the Czechoslovak government-in-exile led by Edvard Beneš had been recognized by the British, and the Czech nationalist did all in his power to denounce Hungary as a hopelessly reactionary pro-Nazi state. Nevertheless given Teleki's good reputation in London, he or former Prime Minister Bethlen most probably would have been accepted as the true representative of the Hungarian nation. Teleki, however, did not want to deliver Hungary to the mercy of Germany via the pro-German rightist Hungarian politicians who would have certainly been installed if he had fled, and they would have put all Hungary's resources at the disposal of Germany, while eliminating the "Anglophile" section of

---

21   John Pelényi: "The Secret Plan for a Hungarian Government in the West at the Outbreak of World War II", *Journal of Modern History*, Vol. 36, No. 2 (June 1964), 170–177. Cf. Cornelius, *Hungary in World War II*, 122–123; Szent-Iványi, *The Hungarian Independence Movement*, 203–204.

the traditional elite. The fate of the Jewish Hungarians would have also been in jeopardy.

The regent ultimately could not resist the temptation of marching into another part of historical Hungary detached in the Trianon Treaty, and most Hungarians were of the same mind. There was also the very real danger that if Hungary refrained from joining in the attack, all of formerly-Hungarian Bánát and Bácska (today's Vojvodina in Serbia) would be given to Romania. Or a small German puppet state might be set up, based on the considerable number of Germans who had moved into the southern region of Hungary depopulated in the wars again the Ottomans in the eighteenth century. Teleki thought that if Hungary refrained from moving into Yugoslavia until it fell apart as Croatia declared its independence, that would save face for Hungary, which would be seen as acting only to protect the half million Hungarians of the Yugoslav state. However, neither Britain nor posterity fell for that legal loophole. When Hungary's minister in London made that clear in a dispatch, Teleki saw no way out. With the prevailing mood in Hungary and lacking the support of Horthy, also with his wife fatally ill, he felt he could not just leave as head of a government-in-exile. On the night of 3 April, he shot himself, thus assuming responsibility for Hungary's breach of faith. In his farewell letter addressed to Horthy he wrote: "We have broken our word – out of cowardice. [...] The nation feels it, and we have thrown away its honor. We have placed ourselves at the side of the scoundrels [...] We shall be corpse snatchers! the most abominable nation. I did not hold you back. I am guilty."[22] Churchill was moved to say: "His suicide was a sacrifice to absolve himself and his people from guilt in the German attack on Yugoslavia. It clears his name before history."[23]

A break with Hitler at that time and having a government-in-exile recognized by the Allies would have certainly served Hungary well at the end of the war; and given Slovakia's and Romania's whole-hearted support of Nazi Germany, Hungary would have had a good chance to retain the Hungarian-inhabited territories gained with Hitler's help, but in March 1941 Ger-

---

22 Macartney, *October Fifteenth*, Vol. I, 488–489; Cornelius, *Hungary in World War II*, 140–144. My own translation of Teleki's letter.
23 Winston S. Churchill, *The Second World War*, Vol. 5 (London: Cassel, 1948–1954), 148.

many was at the height of its power, and it would have required a prophet to accept the certain costs of resisting Hitler, whose total defeat then looked most unlikely. Teleki's successor, former Foreign Minister Bárdossy, was certainly not a prophet, neither was he a good choice for leading the country in such difficult times. He, too, did not sympathize with the Nazi system but thought that only Germany's victory, of which he was almost certain, would give Hungary advantageous peace terms.

On 6 April Germany attacked Yugoslavia, with the collaboration of Bulgaria and Romania, using also Hungary's territory. On 10 April Zagreb fell, and the leader of the pro-Nazi Right, the Ustashi, proclaimed the independence of Croatia. Interpreting that as the termination of the Yugoslav state, the next morning Hungary's army invaded and occupied the formerly Hungarian region north of Belgrade. Until that move, Hungary had already taken several inopportune foreign political steps, but joining the German war against Yugoslavia was not only morally reprehensible, it was undoubtedly a blunder. Thanks to Teleki's sacrifice and Churchill appreciating it, Britain refrained from declaring war on Hungary and only broke diplomatic relations. Nevertheless with that step Hungary – to use the words of Teleki – joined the scoundrels, eventually the losers.

A consequence of the plan to establish a Hungarian government-in-exile was the mission of Tibor Eckhardt to the United States. The leader of the opposition Smallholders' Party, with the approval of Teleki, left Hungary to arrive in the U.S.A. in August 1941, where he established a Movement for Independent Hungary, relying heavily on Hungary's former minister to the U.S.A., János Pelényi, and the American Hungarian Federation, an umbrella organization of Hungarian Americans created in 1906. After initial success, Eckhardt came under vicious attack from the Czecho-Slovak emigration and leftist Hungarian exiles led by Rusztem Vámbéry. They recalled Eckhardt's rightist past in the 1920s and charged that he stood for a feudal and reactionary Hungary. Eckhardt was compelled to resign from the Movement for Independent Hungary, but it could not be effective even when world-renowned composer Béla Bartók became its head. A similar fate awaited the Free Hungarians of England, organized by the diplomat Antal Zsilinszky, which was denounced by Mihály Károlyi, the exiled president of

Hungary (1918–19), in association with the Czechoslovak government-in-exile, led by Edvard Beneš.[24]

In March 1941, in a clever gesture, the Soviets returned the flags of the Hungarian Homeland Defense Army, captured in 1849, when Czar Nicholas intervened to suppress Hungary's War for Independence against the Habsburgs. It was not enough to keep Hungary out of the war. With signs that a German–Russian war was imminent, the chief of the General Staff, General Werth, submitted several memoranda arguing that Germany would obtain victory very quickly, and by joining in that war Hungary would get back all its lost territories. On 15 June the council of ministers turned down Werth's proposal. When on 22 June Germany attacked the Soviet Union, and Romania and Slovakia (as well as Italy and Finland) joined in, Hungary did not follow suit. Immediately after the German attack, Molotov summoned Hungarian Minister Kristóffy to enquire if Hungary planned to remain neutral. He told Kristóffy that the Soviet Union had found the realization of Hungary's territorial claims against Romania justifiable and would not object to such claims in the future. Hungary did not even bother to give an answer. Another blunder. The silence was taken as an affront, and most probably it contributed to the Soviet's decision at the end of the war to refuse to consider even the modest rectification of Hungary's borders, as proposed by the United States and Britain. Although at first Hungary tried to convince Germany of the usefulness of keeping the Hungarian Legation in Moscow open, but having received a strongly negative German reaction to the proposal, Bárdossy duly broke diplomatic relations with the Soviet Union.[25] Once more a blunder. But of course the biggest blunder was joining the war against the Soviet Union.

Originally Germany did not request Hungary's participation, but General Bartha, the minister of defense and General Werth urged it, consider-

---

24 Macartney, *October Fifteenth*, Vol. II, 120–121; Fenyo, *Hitler, Horthy, Hungary*, 111–114; Gyula Juhász, ed., *Magyar-brit titkos tárgyalások 1943-ban* [The Secret Talks Between Hungary and Britain in 1943] (Budapest: Kossuth, 1987), 29; Béla Várdy, *Magyarok az Újvilágban* [Hungarians in the New World] (Budapest: A Magyar Nyelv és Kultúra Nemzetközi Társasága, 2000), 376–382; Katalin Kadar Lynn, *Tibor Eckhardt: His American Years 1941–1972* (New York: Columbia University Press, 2007).

25 The Head of the Government Press Section, Antal Ullein-Reviczky, tells in his memoirs how Bárdossy caved in to German pressure on maintaining diplomatic relations. Antal Ullein-Reviczky, *German War Russian Peace. The Hungarian Tragedy* (Reno, NV: Helena History Press, 2014), 73–75.

ing that Germany would defeat the Soviets in six weeks.[26] On 26 June three unidentified planes dropped several bombs on the north-eastern Hungarian town of Kassa (Košice in today's Slovakia). The identity of the attackers remains a mystery to this very day, but the Hungarian military authorities assumed and declared that the planes were Soviet. (Not very likely under the circumstances, unless it was a mistake due to bad navigation.)[27] Regent Horthy was appalled and welcomed the opportunity to participate in the crushing of his old enemy, Bolshevism. He ordered immediate retaliation, which couldn't but mean war. His prime minister accepted that, and a hastily summoned cabinet meeting gave its assent with one dissent. (According to another source, four ministers – the majority of those present - did not agree with declaring a state of war, but Bárdossy avoided taking a vote.) Next day the prime minister announced in Parliament that in view of the Soviet attack, "the Royal Hungarian Government concluded that a state of war has come to exist between Hungary and the Soviet Union."[28]

One cannot but condemn Hungary's decision to join the war against the Soviet Union – ostensibly in retaliation. But one should consider that in 1941 Germany was in effective control of the European continent from the Atlantic to the Soviet border, and Stalin's army had made a very poor showing in 1938 in attacking Finland. Most people in Hungary, including the regent, thought that Soviet Russia would not be able to resist the power of the Wehrmacht. Hungarians feared that after a German victory Hitler would reward its faithful satellites Romania and Slovakia by rescinding the two Vienna Awards and would return to them the coveted territories – the Hungarian-inhabited region of the former Czechoslovakia and northern Transylvania. Whoever carried out the bombing of Kassa, it was used as a justification for

---

26 Szent-Iványi, *Hungarian Independence Movement*, 334–336.
27 The mystery about the bombing is likely to remain unsolved forever. A feasible explanation is that Soviet planes mistook Kassa for the nearby Slovak town Presov/Eperjes: Nandor F. *Dreisziger*, "New Twist to an Old Riddle: The Bombing of Kassa (Košice) June 26, 1941," *Journal of Modern History*, 44, No. 2 (June 1972), 232–242. Another possibility is that on the 1941 Soviet maps the cession of Kassa to Hungary in 1938 was not indicated. Sándor Szakály, "Kassa bombázása és a hadba lépés" [The bombing of Kassa and Hungary's entry into the war], *Rubicon* No. 6 (2011), 52–56. Cf. Tamás Tarján M., http://www.rubicon.hu/magyar/oldalak/1941_junius_26_ismeretlen_repulogepek_bombazzak_kassat/
28 A good summary of the fateful decision, based on the research of several noted historians: Cornelius, *Hungary in World War II*, 148–151.

entering what promised to be a quick and successful war against the evil Bolshevik Empire. Regent Horthy was always proud to have been the first to stand up to Bolshevism in 1919. Only a relatively small number of sensible people – some members of the cabinet, opposition MPs like Bajcsy-Zsilinszky, and government officials like Domokos Szent-Iványi – opposed the precipitate step. Bárdossy banked on German victory in the new world war, or at the very least a stalemate. (A negotiated peace was found unacceptable in World War I; in World War II, given the ideological differences and the brutality of Germany, it was inconceivable.) According to Prime Minister Bárdossy, Hungary had "no real choice; for she was not master of her own will. Sooner or later she would have to yield, and the wisest and cheapest policy for her was to give the minimum; not to arouse suspicion and mistrust, not to provoke [Germany] to trample us down, destroy us, crush everything dear to us, reshape us irretrievably in her own image."[29]

The first weeks following the German attack appeared to justify Hungary's decision. Horthy thought that the Soviets were practically beaten and Germany unbeatable, so the hoped for negotiated peace would be difficult to attain, but he assumed that because of its arrogance Germany would not be able to control Europe for long.[30] Upon the urging of Moscow, Britain demanded that Finland, Hungary and Romania leave the war or face a declaration of war. None of those countries felt it possible to comply. The head of Hungary's Press Section, Ullein-Reviczky, the husband of an Englishwoman who was the daughter of a British diplomat, tried through the good offices of the Pope to avoid war with England, a country so many Hungarians admired. Naturally it did not work.[31] US Minister Herbert Claiborne Pell Jr., representing British interests since the rupture of diplomatic relations in April, visited Bárdossy on 7 December informing him that from 6 December a state of war existed between Britain and Hungary. That announcement

---

29 Macartney, *October Fifteenth*, Vol. II, 26–27, quoted and discussed by Szent-Iványi, *Hungarian Independence Movement*, 337–339, 344–346. Szent-Iványi puts the blame for taking Hungary into the war mainly on the head of the General Staff, General Werth, and other officers of German descent, but also on Bárdossy. Pál Pritz, based on his painstaking research, considers that the utmost responsibility rests with Horthy. Pál Pritz, *Bárdossy László* (Budapest: Elektra Kiadóház, 2001), 93–99.
30 Horthy's talk with Herbert Pell, the U.S. Minister to Hungary, on 22 August 1941. Fenyo, *Hitler, Horthy*, 48–50.
31 Ullein-Reviczky, *German War Russian Peace*, 81–82.

was communicated by the prime minister to the Chamber of Deputies that very evening and was received "in deathly silence," followed by the singing of the national anthem.[32] At war with the Soviet Union and Great Britain, Hungary stood completely alone, and was now actually near-surrounded by a double ring of ill-wishers: the one consisting of the existing Slovak, Romanian, Serb and Croat States – not mutually allied, and indeed, often mutually hostile, but all anti-Hungarian; the other composed of the former Little Entente Governments, now established in London. From the latter the Romanian link was still technically missing, but her friends represented Romania so effectively that her absence was hardly noticed.

By now Italy, the former supporter, was also totally dependent on Germany, and showed indifference to the plight of Hungary.[33]

The next blunder followed the Japanese attack on Pearl Harbor on 7 December. Four days later, Germany declared war on the U.S.A. The Tripartite Pact was theoretically a defensive alliance, and it did not oblige Hungary to join in that war. Bárdossy first tried to avoid such a step by expressing only solidarity with the Axis powers, calling back Hungary's minister from Washington, and advising the latter's counterpart to leave. When Pell asked Bárdossy if that was meant as a declaration of war, the answer was "No". The next day, however, Germany and Italy made strong representations demanding that Hungary declare war, and Bárdossy, overruling the advice of his colleagues in his ministry, complied. He did not have the courage to face Pell, so he told him on the phone that, contrary to his previous statement, solidarity meant a state of war. The American, a good friend of Hungary, helpfully remarked, "You must have been subjected to the most terrible German pressure to end up like this." The prime minister, who also held the foreign affairs portfolio, retorted, very unwisely and undiplomatically, "Hungary is an independent State, who will allow itself to be commanded by no one."[34] The U.S.A. did not immediately answer with a declaration of war, because it con-

---

32 Ibid., 82.
33 Macartney, *October Fifteenth*, Vol. II, 57–58.
34 Ullein-Reviczky, *German War Russian Peace*, 84–88; Macartney, *October Fifteenth*, Vol. II, 63–65. These differ only in the exact wording.

sidered Hitler's allies as mere puppets,[35] but on 5 June 1942 President Roosevelt signed the war declarations on Bulgaria, Hungary and Romania. On his visit to Washington in May, Molotov had already indicated that such a declaration was desirable.[36] Notwithstanding the American decision, one can see a slight but not insignificant difference between the attitudes of the two Western allies towards Hungary. Whereas the British held Hungary unequivocally responsible for siding with Germany, the United States considered that Hitler's ruthless policies made his satellites mere puppets, not expressing the will of the (whole) population.

By the time of the entry of the United States into the war it could already be seen that a quick German victory over Russia was not going to happen.[37] If only Hungary had held out as a non-belligerent until Pearl Harbor, it would have been much easier to reckon with the eventual defeat of Germany, and thus to stiffen its resistance to German demands. But Bárdossy, with his frail health and weak nerves, and basically a civil servant and not a politician, was not the man to stand up to such a task. True, Germany might not have acquiesced in Hungary's abstention from the war effort, especially when the war began to go badly, but an overt German intervention (military or political) would have placed Hungary in a different light at the end of the war.

In January 1946, still before the Communist takeover, Bárdossy was tried for his role in taking Hungary into the war, even overriding some of the stipulations of the laws of the country. In his trial he maintained that he had believed that Hungary's future hinged upon a German victory, otherwise it would lose its independence and fall under Soviet domination. But as we have seen, in the critical days in June 1941 he was aware that a German victory would lead to total control over Hungary by Nazi Germany. Today we know what Hitler thought about Hungary, and that a German victory would have resulted in the loss of more than some territories, most likely in the total disappearance of independence, including the mass deportation of Hungarians

---

35   Fenyo, *Hitler, Horthy,* 52–53.
36   Ibid., 55.
37   John Lukacs showed how close the Germans were in mid-October to taking Moscow, and how by 7 December the attempt failed, and with that, all chances for a German victory practically evaporated. Lukacs, *Last European War,* 151–160.

to former Soviet territories.[38] Bárdossy was sentenced to death and was shot. Today there is a debate about whether he really deserved that penalty.

Not questioning the responsibility of Horthy, Bárdossy and many others in taking Hungary into the war, one must note that before 1941 Hungary received very little encouragement from the West to move away from the Axis, and there was no indication that more fair borders could be expected as a return for the sacrifices. After the entry of the Soviet Union (and Hungary) into the war, the prospects for Hungary became alarming. The *Times* of London – the same paper that was notorious for advocating accommodation with Nazi Germany in the 1930s – on 1 August 1941 called for the appeasing of Stalin and admitted that in Central and Eastern Europe the Soviet Union had special interests. It was undoubtedly right for Britain and later the United States to make an alliance with Stalin: the West had a strong interest in helping the Soviet Union to survive and to fight Nazi Germany. In my opinion, however, it was a grave mistake to give Stalin a kind of unconditional support and to acquiesce to the annexation of the Baltic States and eastern Poland as early as December 1941, during British Foreign Secretary Anthony Eden's talks in Moscow.[39] The entire tenor of the British–American–Soviet discussions from 1941 on led Stalin to believe that he had a free hand at least to retain the Soviet borders he agreed with Hitler before 1941. But whereas Britain and the U.S.A. did not assume that Soviet "special interests" would mean turning all of Central Europe communist, Hungary (as well as Poland and Romania) was increasingly afraid of such a fate. Then (as today) it was beyond the grasp of Central Europeans to understand why the British and the Americans, having resisted the totalitarian and inhuman Nazi system, did not foresee that the similarly aggressive, expansionist and inhuman Soviet great power was about to subjugate the eastern half of Europe. It was within the reach of the Western

---

38   Pritz Pál, *Pax Germanica. Német elképzelések Európa jövőjéről a második világháborúban* [German ideas about the future of Europe in the Second World War] (Budapest: Osiris, 1999). For Hungary pages 122–127 are most revealing. Evidence for some of the most extreme German Nazi ideas can be found in Stephen G. Fritz. *Ostkrieg: Hitler's War of Extermination in the East* (Lexington, KY: The University Press of Kentucky, 2011).
39   Sir Llewellyn Woodward, *British Foreign Policy in the Second World War,* Vol. 3 (London: H.M.S.O., 1962), 564–5; Anthony Eden, *The Reckoning* (Boston: Houghton Mifflin Company, 1965), 269; Bennet Kovrig, *The Myth of Liberation. East-Central Europe in U.S. Diplomacy and Politics since 1941* (Baltimore and London: Johns Hopkins University Press, 1973), 7.

democracies, with their economic and strategic strength and deliveries of essential war materiel for the Soviet Union (certainly until the battle of Stalingrad) to prevent that and to make sure that the Atlantic Charter, with its high-sounding phrases, did not become a dead letter.

After the German Blitzkrieg was halted before Moscow and America entered the war, Horthy realized that the Western Allies were more likely to become victorious.[40] He and the strong "Anglophile" wing of the Hungarian middle and upper classes started their efforts to take Hungary out of the war. On 12 February 1942 Horthy managed to have his son István, an upright and sensible man and a well-know Anglophile (strongly disliked by the Nazis), elected deputy regent by the Parliament. The hope was not only to have a strong man beside the ageing regent, but also to move away from Germany. In March 1942 Horthy told Bárdossy that he no longer enjoyed his confidence, and upon the latter's resignation appointed Miklós Kállay prime minister. It was indeed "a superhuman task" to "convince the leaders of the great powers allied against Germany that Hungary was sincere in its efforts to leave the war and to take the side where it ought to belong by its culture and historical traditions."[41] The task was more than superhuman; it was unattainable. Having joined the war, Hungary was indeed on a set course, no longer master of its fate. That was, however, not obvious to Horthy and Kállay. The latter, the calm, phlegmatic, robust scion of one of the oldest Hungarian noble families, started a subtle game named after a dance the "Kállay double". In his public speeches he paid lip-service to the common anti-Bolshevik cause, and he could not avoid sending a large part of Hungary's army to the Eastern Front, as agreed (under very strong German pressure) by his predecessor. At the same time, he tried to reduce Hungary's contribution to the war effort and soon started sending out peace feelers towards the British and the Americans.[42]

---

40 The so far most authoritative biography of Horthy questions the regent's determination to abandon Germany, thinking that he was simply an opportunist biding his time to see which side would prevail: Thomas Sakmyster, *Hungary's Admiral on Horseback: Miklos Horthy, 1918–1944* (Boulder, New York: Columbia University Press, 1994).
41 Czettler, *Teleki Pál*, 602.
42 Nicholas [Miklós] Kállay, *Hungarian Premier. A Personal Account of a Nation's Struggle in the Second World War* (New York: Columbia University Press, 1954; Macartney, *October Fifteenth*, Vol. II, 139–144. Juhász's *Magyar-brit titkos tárgyalások* and its hundred documents bear testimony to the seriousness of the Hungarian efforts, but also to their undeservedly cold reception.

Kállay wasted no time in launching peace feelers. His secret emissaries ventured out in the early summer of 1942 and targeted Britain, the one great power with which Hungary's leaders – most of them upper-class men with English manners – felt an affinity. But the emissaries could gain access only to junior officials who proved unresponsive, sloughing off the plea that British rather than Russian soldiers occupy Hungary. They hectored the Hungarians, who requested a reconsideration of the borders drawn by the post-World War I peace treaties, which often ignored large ethnic Hungarian populations. After each secret meeting in neutral Turkey, Portugal, and Sweden, the British informed the Soviets who demurred, demanding Hungary's immediate unconditional surrender first, and then negotiations. Shrugging off Hungarian fears of Joseph Stalin's Red Army, British representatives clung to their high imperial ground: as long as Hungary had soldiers fighting any member of the Grand Alliance, it could expect "neither sympathy nor mercy".[43]

Anthony Eden, the British foreign secretary, used that harsh expression in a cable to Ambassador Sir Knatchbull-Hugessen in Ankara, and that became the official line of H.M. government.[44]

The debacle of the Hungarian army's annihilation at the River Don in January 1943 led to the doubling of the Hungarian efforts to leave the war. New, hitherto unknown details of those efforts, using declassified American documents, reinforce the documents published by Gyula Juhász and show how earnest and serious were Kállay's peace feelers. Eventually, they found some echo in London. Following a conference convened in the Foreign Office by Deputy Under-Secretary Sir Orme Sargent on 24 February 1943, which assessed the behavior of Hitler's satellites, it was admitted that

Hungary has succeeded in preserving a greater degree of independence than any other satellite in South Eastern Europe. [...] There have been not unsuccessful efforts in Hungary to moderate the persecution of the Jews [...]

---

43 Charles Fenyvesi, "Official Enemies, Secret Allies," *Hungarian Review*, Vol. II, No. 5.(2011). The author is an American journalist who escaped from his native Hungary after the suppression of Hungary's uprising in 1956. The best summary of the peace feelers is Joó, *Kállay Miklós*, 50–65.
44 15 January 1943. Juhász, *Magyar-brit titkos tárgyalások*, 84.

Although His Majesty's Government do not consider that any early and decisive change in Hungarian policy is likely, the general background seems favourable for some slight modification of the rigid attitude which His Majesty's Government have hitherto adopted towards Hungary.[45]

The conclusion was to welcome the promising tendencies and to judge the country by the practical measures it adopted in order to disentangle itself from Axis domination. An aide-mémoire along those lines was sent to Washington and Moscow, and its attachment listed the various Hungarian attempts in Stockholm, Lisbon and Ankara to start talks about leaving the war and achieving fair post-war borders. While dismissing the efforts of the regime which allied with Germany and attacked Great Britain's allies, the Foreign Office saw more hope in following up the contacts with Professor Albert Szent-Györgyi, a 1937 Nobel Laureate in Physiology or Medicine, who represented circles independent from the government.[46]

Kállay was eager to coordinate his efforts with Italy. Visiting Mussolini in early April 1943, he predicted that Hitler would lose the war and proposed that Hungary and Italy together bolt from the German camp and co-ordinate their approaches to the Western Allies. Kállay thought that if the Allies could ally themselves with a Bolshevik dictator they could also collaborate with the much milder Italian one. Mussolini answered that he still believed in Hitler's assurances that he would achieve victory over Russia in 1943. But at least he did not denounce Kállay by revealing the plan to Hitler.[47]

It did not take long for the Germans to see through Kállay's rhetoric, his sham loyalty to the Axis. Hitler invited, or rather summoned Horthy to his Klessheim castle near Salzburg, and on 17–18 April 1943 vehemently confronted his guest with accusations on account of Hungary's many contacts with the enemy. The German chancellor spoke very critically about the Hungarian army's performance at the Don-Voronezh catastrophe, then heatedly complained that Hungary's prime minister sent Professor Szent-Györgyi to

---

45 Fenyo, *Hitler, Horthy*, 121; Juhász, *Magyar-brit titkos tárgyalások*, 36–38.
46 Document 14, dated 10 March 1943, Juhász, *Magyar-brit titkos tárgyalások*, 100–107.
47 For a detailed analysis of Kállay's initiatives, including his talks in Italy in April 1943, as well as the Klessheim meeting of Hitler with Horthy, see: Czettler, *Teleki Pál*, Chapter 4. Cf. Kállay, *Hungarian Premier*, esp. 147–203.

Istanbul in order to inform the Allies of his country's intention to break with Germany. A large number of Hungarians were on probably similar missions at the neutral countries, Switzerland,[48] Portugal and Sweden, he added.[49] In his encounters with Hitler, Horthy never shared the servile admiration the leaders of Hungary's neighbors showed towards the Führer. He refuted the charges that the Hungarian soldiers had not fought valiantly; it was Germany that failed to keep its promises to provide the weapons and other equipment needed. He dismissed the accusations about Kállay, saying that those were merely gossip collected by the German Legation in Budapest. Then Hitler presented the regent with intercepted and decoded telegrams from Allied missions, proving the charges. His conclusion, repeated several times, was that he had lost all confidence in Kállay but still believed in the loyalty of the regent.[50] In the communiqué published after the meeting, Hungary refused to include a reference to continuing the war against Bolshevism's "Anglo-Saxon allies," a phrase accepted by the Romanian leader, Ion Antonescu, after his meeting with Hitler.[51]

It is painful to observe that while Hitler was fully aware of the real feelings of the Hungarian government about the likely outcome of the war and their intention to quit the German alliance, Britain and the United States were reluctant to take the secret approaches seriously. Not appreciating that the Hungarian government deliberately kept its contribution to the war effort much lower than Hitler's other allies, they demanded actions rather than words, without promising any reward for what would have involved very serious sacrifices on the part of Hungary. The Foreign Office swallowed

---

48 György Barcza, the last Hungarian minister to the Court of St. James, arrived in Bern in April 1943, trying to catch the ear of British and American officials. Barcza, *Diplomataemlékeim,* Vol. II, 67–124. Barcza in his memoirs was very critical of the too many uncoordinated peace feelers carried out mainly by amateurs, as they only alerted the Germans. Szent-Iványi is even more critical, but mainly due to his personal animosities and antipathies towards both the amateurs and the professional diplomats. Neither does he give due credit to Kállay's actions.
49 Aladár Szegedy-Maszák, deputy head of the Political Department at the Foreign Ministry travelled to Stockholm in March as a courier. Juhász, *Magyar-brit titkos tárgyalások,* 38–39, and Doc. 16.
50 Ránki, *Hitler 68 tárgyalása,* Docs. 41–43, 67–113, esp. 77–87. Fenyo, *Hitler, Horthy,* 125–130. The text of a memorandum prepared by the Hungarian Foreign Ministry for the meeting, the German written complaints and also Horthy's written answer are published by Szent-Iványi, *Hungarian Independence Movement,* 409–422.
51 Macartney, *October Fifteenth,* Vol. II, 151–152.

the charges by émigré politicians Beneš and Károlyi that Horthy and Kállay only wanted "reinsurance" for the survival of a reactionary, feudal regime in Hungary.[52] Were those in London not aware of the fact that the Hungarian opposition, the Smallholders and the Social Democrats gave their full support for the peace feelers?[53] One must admit, however, that practically all the Hungarian anti-Nazis were mistaken to think that London and Washington would be receptive to the Hungarian fears about Soviet expansion, would understand and accept that Hungary could not disengage from Germany until the Allies re-entered Europe, and that the Anglo-Americans would be ready to discuss conditions for Hungary's defection from the Axis. Two detailed Hungarian memoranda, one presented in April 1943 to the British ambassador to Turkey by Károly Schreker, a banker,[54] the other by Szegedy-Maszák written in the summer of 1943, drew rather negative reactions from the British. The latter memorandum was a long explanation of how and why Hungary could not avoid having ended up in the Axis camp, what its present predicament was, and what were its ideas about a just and lasting peace in Central Europe. Ethnic-based borders, retaining Sub-Carpathia and Transylvania as a Hungarian–Romanian condominium[55] (i.e. under the joint control of the two states) did not appeal to the Foreign Office.[56]

Today most historians admit that the demand for unconditional surrender was a most serious mistake which considerably extended the duration of the war. It did not make it easier for Hungary to carry out an open break with Germany while the troops of the Allies were in Africa only, and the end of the war, the defeat of Germany, was still not in sight. What would have brought it closer, perhaps already in 1943, was the overthrow of Hitler by his generals. Many Prussian officers, including the head of Germany's military intelligence, Ad-

---

52 Szent-Iványi, *Hungarian Independence Movement,* 402.
53 Macartney,*October Fifteenth,* Vol. II, 131–133.
54 Juhász, *Magyar-brit titkos tárgyalások,* 38–40, and Doc. 21.
55 In international law, a condominimum is a political territory (state or border area) in or over which multiple sovereign powers formally agree to share equal *dominium* (in the sense of sovereignty) and exercise their rights jointly, without dividing it into „national" zones. Lake Constance is a triple condominium.
56 Ibid., 50–51, and Doc. 46. Szegedy-Maszák published the text of his memorandum in his memoirs and gave an explanation and an answer for the criticism it drew in the British Foreign Office and at the hands of later Hungarian historians. Aladár Szegedy-Maszák, *Az ember ősszel visszanéz...* [At Twilight One Looks Back], Vols. I, II (Budapest: Európa, 1996), Vol. II, 230–282.

miral Canaris, were ready, and may have been able to do that, were it not for the unfortunate "unconditional surrender" formula and the refusal of President Roosevelt to pursue any secret talks with the anti-Hitler German officers.[57]

It was the unexpected overthrow of Mussolini in August and the surrender of Italy which, at least for a few days in September 1943, held out the hope for Hungary to be able to leave the war immediately and even to join the Allies. Having sent a number of unofficial emissaries abroad with the task of making contact with British and American diplomats and agents, and trying to obtain acceptable terms (mainly on Hungary's post-war borders), on 9 September 1943 the Hungarian government's official representative, foreign service officer László Veress, signed a secret preliminary agreement on unconditional surrender with the British ambassador to Turkey (or his deputy) in Istanbul, more exactly on a ship in the Sea of Marmara. According to the agreement Hungary would reduce military and economic co-operation with Germany, including withdrawing her troops from the Soviet Union, would allow allied aircraft to fly over Hungary, and would resist Germany's attempt to occupy her, and at a given moment would "place all her resources at the disposal of the Allies for the continuation of the fight against Germany." It was to be announced "at a suitable moment," i.e., when Allied forces reached or approached the borders of Hungary so that the government were capable to honor it.[58] It was still hoped that Italy's surrender (signed on 3 September) would soon bring the Anglo-American forces into Central Europe, reaching Hungary. The plan was thwarted by the clumsy American military and the Italian political leadership, which allowed German forces to overrun Italy and to check the advance of the Allies.

But there is an interesting sub-chapter to the blunder committed by the Allies in (mis)handling the great opportunity presented by the Italian

---

57 Charles Fenyvesi, *Három összeesküvés. Rundstedt tábornagy, Canaris tengernagy és a zsidó mérnök, aki megmenthette volna Európát* [Three conspiracies. General Rundstedt, Admiral Canaris and the Jewish engineer who could have saved Europe] (Budapest: Európa Könyvkiadó, 2007). For the events related to Hungary see the author's three installments in the *Hungarian Review*, Vol. II, Nos. 5, 6 (2011), Vol. III, No. 1 (2011).
58 For the text and the fate of the agreement: Macartney, *October Fifteenth*, 185–188; Fenyo, *Hitler, Horthy*, 143–147; Juhász, *Magyar-brit titkos tárgyalások*, 61–65. It is of little importance whether the agreement was signed by Ambassador Sir Hughe Knathbull-Hugessen or, as Juhász thought, by his deputy, J.C. Sterndale Bennet.

switch. Parallel with Kállay's diplomatic efforts for a "jump-out", the chief of staff of the army, General Szombathelyi, came close to an agreement which could have led to Hungary's defection from the German alliance and to the military occupation of the country by Anglo-American forces. In mid-summer, with Horthy's approval (probably encouraged by Canaris), Kállay called upon the chief of staff, General Ferenc Szombathelyi, to turn to the Americans and seek a military and political agreement. Szombathelyi assigned the task to his director of intelligence, Colonel Gyula Kádár. Otto Hatz, the military attaché in Sofia, managed to get into contact with agents of the Office of Strategic Services (OSS) in Smyrna and Istanbul, who came up with a "Proposed Agreement with Representatives of Hungarian General Staff Concerning Cooperation in the Sphere of Intelligence". The document began with a reference to Hungary's repeated "unofficial overtures" to the British and the "failure" of its attempts to secure political assurances as to the future borders and on the occupying power. It recognized "the effort of the supreme military authorities in Hungary to enter into contact with the Allies" as evidence of "a firm and sincere determination to collaborate." Hungary's delegate promised "detailed military intelligence concerning the German Army and German operations" and pledged "active military aid" to an Allied landing on Hungarian territory. Alas, with the hopes about Italy coming under the control of Anglo-American forces dashed, and because of the futile efforts of the Hungarian negotiators (using coded messages transmitted in ordinary radio programs) to receive some encouragement about Hungary's future borders and assurance of a three-power occupation, no more action was taken than Szombathelyi sending information. As historian Charles Fenyvesi writes:

> Much of the intelligence the Hungarians sent to OSS-Istanbul was accurate and important, including the locations and the production figures of Hungarian military industries working for the Germans, assessments of German morale on the Russian front, and the details of German plans to send planes to Bulgaria. Regardless of the failure to prepare military units for a resolute stand for independence and the tragic helplessness in face of the German invasion, official Hungarian resistance to German power was sincere. [...] Had there been a quick accord following the

September 1943 meeting in Istanbul, events might have taken a different turn. Momentum might have gathered for closer cooperation, and Donovan [Director of the OSS] might have found support in the US Army and the White House for his proposal to land an airborne division or two in Hungary at a time when Wehrmacht troops in the country numbered only a few thousand. Another step would have been to line up Hungarian military units loyal to Horthy and Szombathelyi to receive and protect the Americans. The arrival of additional US forces from nearby Italy could have turned a token presence into a bridgehead.[59]

And Fenyvesi's conclusion: "The agreement launched in September 1943 constituted the only accord of its kind that the United States is known to have reached with a government formally allied with Nazi Germany.[60]

One may add that in Hungary the most effective acts of resistance to Nazi Germany were performed by some officials of the government, initiated by the prime minister, often even with the connivance of the head of the state.

The position of Hungary in late 1943 was worse than its leaders thought. The Hungarian leaders and the anti-Nazi opposition could not believe that the Anglo-American leaders would not be opposed to the Soviet domination of Central Europe. Hungarians remembered the anti-communist stance of pre-war Britain, but they overlooked the radical change of mood, the "sudden and, in retrospect, exaggeratedly sentimental admiration for the Russians," whipped up by the press.[61] Exactly the same phenomenon occurred in the U.S.A.[62] People in Hungary regarded the Anglo-American alliance with the Soviet Union as only a marriage of convenience, and certainly not a vehicle of Soviet expansion.[63] In London and Washington, however, the majority of the establishment and the opinion-makers had illusions about the Soviet Union and forgot the

---

59   Charles Fenyvesi, *Hungarian Review*, Vol. II, Nos. 5–6 (2012).
60   Charles Fenyvesi, *Hungarian Review*, Vol. III, No. 1 (2012). More details on the contacts of Hungarian and American intelligence are in Fenyvesi's book, which has so far appeared only in a Hungarian translation: *Három összeesküvés* [Three conspiracies], Chapters 6–7. The account of this American–Hungarian secret collaboration is based on the recently declassified documents of the US National Records and Archives Administration (NARA), RG 226, Entry 210.
61   Lukacs, *Last European War*, 411–413.
62   John Lukacs, *Year Zero. The Shaping of the Modern Age* (Garden City, NJ: Doubleday, 1978).
63   Kállay, *Hungarian Premier*, 11.

past, the dictatorship, the persecution of the old upper and middle classes, the purges; they only planned post-war co-operation with the reborn Great Power. Stalin, "Uncle Joe", duped Roosevelt and to a lesser degree even Churchill. All other considerations were subordinated to victory, in the case of the U.S.A. also to Stalin joining the war against Japan. The Allied governments as well as the public and the press understandably favored the governments-in-exile of Czechoslovakia and Yugoslavia (from 1943 the communist Tito) to the Hungarian enemy. Many felt a moral obligation to support Czechoslovakia just because it was abandoned at Munich, and also to reward those Yugoslavs who carried on a guerilla war against the Germans.[64] (On the other hand, the heroic Poles were let down in their conflict with Stalin, although their escaped soldiers formed the fourth largest allied military force, while the underground Home Army carried out very effective resistance at home.[65]) The British Foreign Office considered Horthy and his system reactionary. That is how the leaders of the Allies came to support the restoration of the unfair pre-1938 Trianon borders. But the idea of making Transylvania an independent state was not unrealistic, the British were ready to support it; it was Stalin who vetoed that. On the level of the British and American experts, however, proposals were made for modifying those borders in favor of Hungary, in line with the ethnic principle. Some of those advisers naively thought that after the War the governments of Hungary's neighbors would be ready to do that.[66] The most thought out plan was drawn up by the British scholar C.A. Macartney, who worked for the Foreign Research and Press Service section of the Foreign Office as well as for the Political Warfare Executive of British intelligence. Rather than punishing some and rewarding others he proposed the equal and just

---

64 Géza Hercegh, *A szarajevói merénylettől a potsdami konferenciáig. Magyarország a világháborús Európában 1914–1945* [From the Outrage at Sarajevo to the Potsdam Conference. Hungary in the Europe of the World Wars] (Budapest: Magyar Szemle Könyvek, 1999), 425–426.
65 One of the many testimonies to that is J.K. Zawadny, *Nothing but Honour: The Story of the Warsaw Uprising, 1944* (London: Macmillan, 1978).
66 Ignác Romsics, ed., *Wartime American Plans for a New Hungary* (Boulder, CO: East European Monographs, distributed by Columbia University Press, 1992); András D. Bán, ed., *Pax Britannica. Brit külügyi iratok a második világháború utáni Kelet-Közép-Európáról 1942–1943* [British foreign policy documents on post-Second World War East Central Europe] (Budapest: Osiris Kiadó, 1996); Ágnes Beretzky, *Scotus Viator és Macartney Elemér: Magyarország-kép változó előjelekkel (1905–1945)* [Scotus Viator and Elemér Macartney. The Varying Image of Hungary] (Budapest: Akadémiai Kiadó, 2005), Chapter VI; Hercegh, *A szarajevói merénylettől*, 426–429.

treatment of all the peoples of Central Europe, with borders based on the ethnic principle, preferably within a confederation.[67] Otto von Habsburg, the son of the last king of Hungary, also did his best to win President F.D. Roosevelt over to the idea of a democratic Central European federation, but Stalin's veto destined all federation plans to be discarded.[68]

The Teheran Conference – unwittingly for Churchill and Roosevelt – settled the fate of Central Europe for half a century. For political and (questionable) military reasons, a landing in the Balkans was abandoned in favor of the invasion of France, thus making it almost inevitable that the Soviet Red Army would eventually liberate Central Europe. Neither Roosevelt nor Churchill imagined that liberation everywhere, even in their heroic ally, Poland, would become a cruel invasion leading to the imposition of Soviet communist imperialism. Stalin's promise to enter the war against Japan once Germany was defeated also compelled the U.S.A. to be even more accommodating to the Soviets, to swallow the annexation of eastern Poland (and pushing the entire country westward) and of the Baltic States.

The main lines of the decisions made at the Teheran conference became known or at least suspected in Budapest, thanks to the Hungarian diplomats stationed in the neutral countries. It was devastating news for the Anglophiles, while giving the pro-Germans an additional argument that Hungary had no choice but to stick with Germany through thick and thin. The anti-Nazi factions in governing circles, supported by the leftist opposition (the Smallholders and the Social Democrats, joined also by the "Legitimists" (who were hoping for the restoration of the Habsburg dynasty), increased their pressure on Kállay to bring the Hungarian troops home from the eastern war theatre in preparation for a "jump-out", a break with Germany. It was easier said than done. The more the Hungarians insisted on withdrawing their forces (claiming a military threat from Romania), the more suspicious Hitler became of Hungary's intentions and the more determined he was to

---

67 Beretzky, *Scotus Viator*, 118–122. While Arnold Toynbee and other scholars agreed with Macartney, R.W. Seton-Watson in his *Transylvania: a Key Problem* (Oxford: Oxford University Press, 1943) argued for returning to the Trianon borders.
68 Szent-Iványi, *Hungarian Independence Movement*, 398; S. Bela Vardy, "Archduke Otto Von Habsburg and American Hungarian Emigrés during and after World War II", *East European Quarterly*, Vol. 36, No. 4 (Winter 2002), 441–163. Cf. Juhász, *Magyar-brit titkos tárgyalások*, Doc. 76.

prevent such a defection. Hungarians still hoped that the advance of the Allies in Italy would bring them to the southern border of Hungary before the Red Army reached the Carpathians. In early 1944 that still looked possible.

Nobody feared a "too early" break with Germany more than the close to a million Jews in Hungary, as well as the international Jewish associations, because Hungary's occupation by Germany, however temporary it would be, was likely to put their lives in grave danger.[69] It is a mistake to think that the fate of the Jews of Hungary was an important consideration for the leaders of the Western democracies. Professor Lewis Namier of the Jewish Agency told a British Foreign Office official that "his people were most seriously concerned at the possible consequences to the 800,000 Jews, who now enjoy comparative security in Hungary, of any premature desertion of Germany by the Hungarian Government. [...] The only hope, as far as the Jews are concerned, was that the Hungarians would choose not to move until it was practically certain that the Germans would not be able to react."[70] So Kállay's options were extremely narrow: an early breakaway from Germany, most likely at a very high cost (the anti- Nazi elements and particularly the Jews would have to pay dearly), or continue the "wait and see" attitude to the displeasure of the Allies, while even the modest "good points" earned by Hungary's limited cooperation with Germany (being "the unwilling satellite") and preserving a parliamentary system would fade away. Hungary's leaders would have been ready even to suffer the consequences of the break with Germany if acceptable terms had been offered, mainly on the issue of the future borders. But – as we have seen – the Western democracies were bound by their morally unavoidable support for Czechoslovakia and Yugoslavia, while the Soviet Union was determined to dominate its Polish and Romanian neighbors. For the latter the most obvious way to befriend those two traditionally anti-Russian nations was to take their side against their respective old adversaries, Germany and Hungary. Most probably Stalin had already decided to give the whole of Transylvania to Romania in December

---

69 Juhász, *Magyar-brit titkos tárgyalások.*, Doc. 82; Czettler, *Teleki Pál*, 312–313.
70 Note by Sir A.W.G. Randall on 14 October 1943 in Elizabeth Barker, *British Policy in South-East Europe in the Second World War* (London: Macmillan Press, 1976), 258. Cf. Juhász, *Magyar-brit titkos tárgyalások,* Doc. 82.

1941 (during his talks with Eden), and after Teheran it was in his power to carry that out.

The offensive by the Soviet Red Army in January 1944 and the snail's-pace advance of the Allies in Italy shattered all the hopes that the Anglo-American forces would forestall the Russians in Hungary. It was now inevitable to heed the long-time advice of London and Washington to turn to Moscow. Earlier schemes like defending the Eastern Carpathian passes and the Soviets bypassing rather than forcing them were irrational, and Kállay understood that. Early in 1944 he instructed Minister Ullein-Reviczky in Stockholm to approach Madame Alexandra Kollontay, his Soviet counterpart there. She was accommodating,[71] but winning over Romania, much closer to the frontline, was more important for Moscow. For the very same reason, keeping Hungary in the German orbit was essential for Hitler, so on 12 March he ordered that the Margarethe-Plan, the military invasion and occupation of Hungary, should be implemented starting on Sunday, 19 March. That was exactly what the Allies wanted. The British and the American intelligence services managed to make the Germans think that an invasion of the Balkans was in the offing, thus misleading them about the preparations for Overlord, the invasion of France at Normandy. So it was not only Kállay's many steps for the "jump-out" but also the covert actions of the Allies which practically provoked the German invasion of Hungary on 19 March 1944.

Hungary's policy (which was in fact Kállay's) in 1942–44 has seldom been given much understanding let alone credit in the many writings which appeared on that subject, with the exception of C. A. Macartney's seminal work, and recently by Deborah Cornelius. Based on Macartney and on András Joó, who used new material from Hungarian archives,[72] my conclusion on those efforts is the following:

Kállay was not a double dealer stepping once to the right, once to the left, he was carefully but seriously moving towards extricating Hungary from the German bond. He was the opposite of an anti-Semitic and was strongly opposed to the Nazi ideology. His statements about loyalty to Germany or on

---

71 Joó, *Kállay Miklós*, 239–244. Ullein-Reviczky's memoirs, written during the hottest period of the Cold War, are silent about those last-minute attempts.
72 Joó, *Kállay Miklós*, esp. Ch. 1.

the Jewish issue were meant only to dispel suspicions. His diplomatic efforts to break away from Germany were not amateurish, and the Germans were far from knowing all about them. Kállay was sincere in his determination to protect the Jewish citizens of Hungary, and he succeeded while several hundred thousand Jews were being persecuted, deported and murdered in Romania and Slovakia. He did his best to improve relations with Hungary's neighbors, too.[73] Miklós Bánffy, the great Transylvanian author and successful foreign minister in 1921–22, with the approval of Kállay, went to Bucharest in June 1943 with the offer to break with Germany simultaneously. He was turned down even in the pro-Ally circles. Kállay brought the high-ranking Hungarian officers who were responsible for the massacre in Újvidék/Novi Sad in January 1942 to court. He refused the German proposal to use Hungarian troops for occupation and peace-keeping in the Balkans. His army chief of staff, General Szombathelyi (executed as a "war criminal" by Yugoslavia in 1946), made a serious attempt in November 1943 to call back all the Hungarian forces from the Soviet theatre of war; the German answer was that in case of such a step they would attack those units.

I think that the facts as well as an impartial analysis of the conduct of Hungary after March 1942 substantiate the epithet that Hungary was the unwilling satellite of Nazi Germany. The distinguished Hungarian historian György Ránki, himself a Holocaust survivor, came to support that view in his later writings, particularly in his essay in the present volume, and in more detail in his introduction to his published collection of Hitler's talks with the leaders of Central and Eastern Europe.[74]

Notwithstanding the short-sightedness of the Western leaders about the danger presented by Stalin's ambitions, it would be a mistake to think that they lacked any understanding for Hungary, and that the tragic fate of Hungary was due to their ill-will, while Hungary was an innocent victim. Churchill felt a kind of personal sympathy for the Hungarians,[75] and

---

73   Ibid., Ch. 7.
74   Ránki, *Hitler 68 tárgyalása*, 5–101.
75   John Lukacs, "Churchill és Magyarország" [Churchill and Hungary] and "Egy nagy államférfi érdeklődése Magyarország iránt" [A great statesman's interest in Hungary], in *Magyar írások* [Writings concerning Hungary] (Budapest: Európa Könyvkiadó, 2007), 29–36, 154–164.

more superficially even Roosevelt was not unsympathetic, but their subordinates and even more so the historical-political setup determined the unfavorable decisions about Hungary. In his often misinterpreted "percentage agreement" with Stalin in October 1944 Churchill tried to save some Western influence in the countries threatened by Soviet domination. If 50 percent British influence (as it was first agreed) had really been the fate of Hungary, the coming decades would have been very different. Alas, Foreign Secretary Anthony Eden immediately gave in to Molotov's pressure and agreed to change the percentage to 75 per cent Russian influence over Hungary.[76]

Is there then nothing to blame in the conduct of Kállay and the Anglophile Hungarian circles prior to the German occupation? Certainly there is. Although the opposition, in effect the agrarian Smallholders' Party led by Bajcsy-Zsilinszky and Peyer's Social Democrats came closer together, they were thinking more of the future, when they would run the country, than preparing for a confrontation with Germany in the last phase of the war. Following the arrest of Mussolini and Italy's invasion by Germany, Hungary might have surrendered, and it was open to an airborne Allied occupation. That, in combination with the Greek and the Yugoslav partisans, could have led to the collapse of German control in south-eastern Europe, as Romania would have surely turned against Germany. But responsibility must be shared. As I see it, the biggest mistake committed after the blunders of 1941 was that early in 1944 Kállay and the leaders of the army made no preparations for resisting a potential German invasion, although they received much information about suspicious military movements close to the western border of Hungary, and even direct information about an impending invasion.[77] By accepting Hitler's invitation to visit him at Klessheim Castle in March 1944, Horthy walked into a trap which should have been avoided at all costs. Horthy in his *Memoirs* wrote that when Hitler told him that Germany would occupy Hungary, he should have shot the dictator. Why did he not do that? A pistol

---

76 András D. Bán, "A 'százalékegyezmény'. Európa megmentése vagy Kelet-Európa 'elárulása'?" [The percentage agreement. The saving of Europe or the betrayal of Eastern Europe?] *Európai utas* 38 (2000), 38–42.
77 This is much emphasized by Szent-Iványi, *The Hungarian Independence Movement*, 473–476. Macartney pointed out that a decision to resist the Germans could have been taken until 15 March 1944 at the latest.

was part of his Admiral's uniform, but he deliberately left it in his train when he dressed for his tête-à-tête with Hitler.[78] He did have a dagger on him, but it was politely taken from him before that meeting.[79] Although in the absence of the regent and the chief of the general staff Kállay was not entitled to give an order for military resistance to the German invasion, but Horthy was cut off from all communications, and the prime minister should have disregarded legal considerations. Military resistance could not have been effective and would have cost lives, but it would have turned Hungary from a German ally into a victim of German aggression. It would have awakened many in Hungary to who their enemy was, and would have alerted the Jews. Morally it would have counted for much internationally, and politically, too, since it was well before Romania's break with Germany on 23 August and the Slovak uprising on 29 August.

It is beyond the scope of the present essay to discuss in detail what happened after Hungary lost its sovereignty on 19 March 1944. It could not carry out any foreign policy of its own. Despite the most deplorable and disgraceful anti-Jewish laws passed by the Hungarian Parliament after 1938 the life and liberty of the close to 800,000 Hungarian citizens of Jewish background were not in danger until the occupation of the country by Germany. With the forceful removal of the legitimate Kállay government, and by Germany installing a puppet regime, the new leaders of the country betrayed their Jewish compatriots, and with the active participation of the authorities surrendered them to Nazi Germany, where most of them were murdered. The grave responsibility of the Nazis' Hungarian collaborators is beyond doubt; their guilt blackened the reputation of Hungary. The most detailed account of that fateful period is by Randolph Braham,[80] and an insightful one is by Charles Fenyvesi.[81]

---

78 Miklós Horthy, *Emlékirataim* [My memoirs] (Budapest: Európa, 1990), 281.
79 I am grateful for that information to Professor Pál Pritz.
80 Randolph L. Braham, *The Politics of Genocide: The Holocaust in Hungary*, Vols. I, II (New York: Columbia University Press, 1981).
81 Charles Fenyvesi, *When Angels Fooled The World: Rescuers of Jews in Wartime Hungary* (Madison, WI: The University of Wisconsin Press, 2003).

Epilogue

By the end of summer 1944 Germany had lost the war beyond any doubt, and it needed the utmost credulousness to believe that with some miraculous weapons Hitler could turn the tide. The bombardment of Hungary, which started only after the German occupation (before that there was an unwritten agreement that the Allies would not bomb the country but would be allowed to fly over it unhindered), brought that home even to the ignorant and uninformed, but not to the members and supporters of the extreme right, the Arrow Cross Party. Their blindness is incomprehensible; but what was catastrophic was the conduct of so many officers of the army. At the end of August, after the successful Allied landing in Normandy, Horthy recovered some of his mental and political strength, replaced Sztójay with one of his loyal (but as it turned out, overcautious) generals, Géza Lakatos, who released many of the political prisoners. By that time the Soviet Red Army, making use of the Romanian turnaround on 23 August, reached the Great Plain and in mid-September entered Hungary. Horthy decided to turn personally to Stalin, asking for an armistice, and sent a three-member team to Moscow to negotiate it. That had to be done in utmost secrecy, as the cabinet included at least two blindly pro-German members, in effect spies of Hitler. The small staff of the "breakaway" group (its strongest member was the widow of Horthy's son István, who in 1942 died in action on the Russian front) did not succeed in preparing sufficiently for the showdown with Germany, partly because the regent, the commander of the army, decided not to leave the Buda castle to join the army, which was commanded by officers loyal to him, at its headquarters at Huszt (in Subcarpathia, today in Ukraine). The (preliminary) armistice, with its very harsh terms, was signed in Moscow on 11 October. In it Hungary accepted the obligation to evacuate its civilian and military authorities from the territories gained since 1937 and to declare war on Germany. After some unnecessary delay, while the Germans prepared to arrest Horthy and to install the Hungarian Nazis, the Arrow Cross, and finally kidnapped Horthy's surviving son Miklós, the regent had his proclamation read on the radio on 15 October, announcing that he was asking for an armistice and ordered the army to cease fighting. He did not announce that his representatives had already signed the preliminary armistice, and did not declare war on Germany. He hoped that the German army would voluntarily evacuate Hungary without fighting, as it did in Finland. That was an unfounded and fateful delusion, which a soldier should not have held.

The story of how this half-blundered attempt was foiled by the Germans and their Hungarian accomplices, and of how so many military officers broke their oath to the regent, need not be told here. Nor how the war dragged on for half a year on the territory of Hungary, largely due to the traitorous behavior of the Arrow Cross, causing terrible suffering and enormous damage to lives and property. In the Peace Treaty signed again in Paris in 1947, Hungary had to cede back all the territories it gained in 1938–41. Unlike after World War I, now there was not even the consolation of international guarantees for the protection of the Hungarian minorities.

The gradual communist takeover was not the consequence of the conduct of Hungary during the war; the example of Poland shows it beyond doubt. There is, however, a very important lesson to be drawn from the final blunder of 15 October, which was rightly called by C. A. Macartney "the end of a world", the death of traditional Hungary. How important it would have been in 1944 for the population of Hungary to be sufficiently aware of the real military, political and economic position of their country! In critical times, on essential issues, party, class and personal interests should all be set aside and the national interest should prevail. As to what is the national interest in a given situation, it should be obvious to all well-informed people, whatever their social and political position. If that is not the case, the responsibility lies with the leaders of the country.

Chapter 4
The Road to Occupation
Deborah Cornelius

For a time Kállay and his supporters thought that by contacting the Western Allies they had achieved their aims; they would only have to wait for the end of the war, which seemed to be very close. They believed that they would be able to avoid negotiating with the Soviet Union and by making some reforms be able to establish a government after the war. Antipathy to Bolshevism was almost universal, intensified by the deeds of the Soviet Union under Stalin: the famine in the Ukraine, the show trials, the purge of the military.[1] The spirit of optimism began to dim with the slow progress of the Allies in Italy and the steady advance of the Russians. Coalition armies with their mixed command advanced slowly and the front remained static from October 1943 until May 1944. The government plan based on surrendering to the allies at the border became ever less plausible; yet the government held fast to its resolve to avoid negotiations with the Russians.

While Kállay had counted on the Allies to enable him to collaborate with them, the British were more interested in sending secret service members to organize underground activities and sabotage, a form of resistance that made no sense to the Hungarians. Former Ambassador Barcza criticized Radio London, which kept urging Hungary to open opposition. Only someone who had no idea of their situation could think that Hungary could openly take up weapons against the Germans—surrounded and infiltrated as they were.[2]

---

* Excerpts pp 268–288 From Chapter 7: Efforts to Exit the War: pp 292–314 Chapter 8: German Occupation
Hungary in World War II: Caught in the Cauldron New York, Fordham University Press, 2011
(With the permission of Fordham University Press and the author)

1 There was even knowledge of the Katyn massacres in the officer corps and also in the medical community; one of the experts taken to the site was the Hungarian professor of pathology, Dr. Ferenc Orsós.
2 Barcza, *Diplomataemlékeim*, 2:126.

At the end of November at the Teheran Conference, Roosevelt and Churchill had given in to Stalin's demands, allowing Russia hegemony over Central and Eastern Europe. The British then urged Kállay to seek contact with the Soviets before their army reached Hungary's borders. The Americans also urged an immediate bailout and urgent negotiations with the Soviet Union. Yet Horthy's intense anti-Bolshevism and the pro German stance of the military made it next to impossible for Kállay to act on their suggestions. Responding to a question posed by Barcza in February 1944, Kállay answered if they had to choose between a Germany of the defensive or an expansive Russia, they had no choice other than to stick with the Germans; Hungarian politicians had long considered Russia the greater danger.

The Hungarians did not have exact information on the diplomatic agreements at Teheran, but the Beneš trip to Moscow and the ensuing Czech-Soviet alliance, as well as a Soviet mission to Tito and Allied assistance to Tito's partisans, made the general terms of the agreement clear. A report came from Ullein-Reviczky, now in Stockholm, that he had learned from Japanese colleagues that 1944 would start the British offensive in the West and that there would be no serious attack in the Balkans.[3]

At the time of the Italian armistice in the fall of 1943, Hitler had decided that to prepare against another betrayal it would be necessary to plan for a possible occupation first of Hungary and then of Romania. The OKW completed a plan for a Hungarian invasion, code-named Margarethe I, on September 30. The plan included the use of Romanian and Slovak troops, although at the time Hitler had no actual intention of occupying Hungary, having decided that as long as things remained calm he would leave the regent in charge.

The situation changed early in 1944 with the spectacular victories of the Red Army and rapid Soviet advances in the Ukraine. As Soviet armies drew nearer to the Carpathians the importance of the lines of communication across Hungary increased enormously. Besides, if the Russians reached the Carpathians there would be direct contact with the Hungarians who might use the opportunity to defect. In light of Hungary's strategic position it was

---

3 István Páva, *Ország a hadak útján: Magyarország és a második világháború*, [Country on the march: Hungary and World War II] (Budapest: Pannónia, 1996), 229.

clear that Hitler could not leave Hungary in the hands of a government whose loyalties were suspect, while the Hungarian economy had become of even more crucial importance to Germany. With the retreat of German troops and the advance of the red Army, Hungary was almost the only significant foreign territory under German control. Hitler was especially anxious to hold out in western Hungary, the source of Hungarian oil.[4]

The Germans also lacked trust in the Hungarian military. Their view was colored by the fact that the military had been unable to push through the measure for Hungarian troops to join the Wehrmacht in the occupation of the Balkans—exactly as Szombathelyi had feared.[5] Hitler had also been angered by the attempts of the Hungarian military to secure the return of the Hungarian units remaining on the eastern front. During his visit to Hitler's headquarters in January 1944, Szombathelyi again requested the return of the Hungarian occupation units, explaining to Wilhelm Keitel that Hungary intended to defend the border on the Carpathians with Hungarian troops alone. Keitel found the idea ludicrous, partly because he found it inconceivable that the German lines should have to withdraw so far west; Hitler as well considered there was no possibility that the Russians would push forward to the Carpathians. When Horthy repeated the request in a letter to Hitler on February 12, 1944, Hitler was furious and did not answer Horthy or Szombathelyi.[6]

Operation Margarethe

It is difficult to determine when Hitler made his decision to order the execution of Operation Margarethe. The plans for the occupation had been changed several times depending on the political and military situation. His decision may have been precipitated by Horthy's letter requesting the return of the Hungarian troops, as well as a report from the German espionage service that Horthy and his son were attempting to make contact with the allies. The timing of the invasion may well have been influenced by the Allies' deceptive strategy to hide their plans for the Normandy invasion, Operation

---

4 Fenyo, *Hitler, Horthy, and Hungary*, 99; Macartney, *October fifteenth*, 2:222.
5 Szombathelyi, *Visszaemlékezései*, 22—23.
6 Fenyo, *Hitler, Horthy, and Hungary*, 155, Géza Lakatos, *Ahogy én láttam*, 74.

Overlord. At Teheran, Roosevelt, Stalin, and Churchill had agreed on the strategy code-named Operation Bodyguard to deceive the Germans about the planned Normandy landing, leading them to expect an invasion of Norway, an invasion at Calais, or a landing in the Balkans, Operation Zeppelin, was intended to take advantage of Hitler's obsession over the vulnerability of his southern flank and tie down German troops in preparing for the attack. The deception probably misled Hitler, whose fears would have been confirmed when he received the report at the end of February that Hungary was expecting an American mission.[7]

The deception was also intended to fool the Hungarians. Since the Allied invasion in Normandy required that German troops be removed from the Western theater of war, it would be an advantage if Germany's allies should attempt to change sides, bringing on a German occupation. In Hungary's case these policies were somewhat contradictory since a German invasion was likely to destroy the democratic elements of the Allies needed for democratic reconstruction, as well as the last intact Jewish community in Europe.[8]

For Hitler the question became not whether to occupy Hungary, but if there were enough German troops available, or whether he should allow Romanian, Slovak, and Croat troops to take part—and then to allow the neighboring countries to take over parts of the country. He even considered the idea that Hungary should disappear from the map. Romania and Slovakia would be rewarded by cancellation of the two Vienna awards; Croatia would get the Muraköz. By March 7, when the Red Army was only about a one hundred sixty kilometers from the Hungarian borders, Hitler could delay no longer.[9]

The German secret service in Hungary got wind of Hitler's plans to use troops from the hostile neighboring countries. Dr. Wilhelm Höttl recalled: "When Hitler found out that Horthy, in spite of every warning, was continuing negotiations with the English, he decided in his choleric manner: 'Occupation!

---

[7] Major Jon S. Wendell, United States Air Force, "Strategic Deception Behind the Normandy Invasion," CSC 1997. http://www.globalsecurity.org/military/library/ report/1997/Wendell.htm (accessed September 1, 2010); Gyula Juhász, "Some Aspects of Relations Between Hungary and Germany During the Second World War," in *Hungarian History/World History*, ed. Gy. Ránki (Budapest: Akadémiai Kiadó, 1984), 217–218.

[8] László Borhi, *Hungary in the Cold War 1945—1956*, 18.

[9] Fenyo, Hitler, Horthy, and Hungary, 159.

The Road to Occupation

And with the cooperation of Romanian and Slovak troops! I already arranged it with Antonescu!' Probably with Tiso as well."[10] According to this plan the Hungarian army would have been disarmed, divided up, and put into work brigades. At the most Hungarian battalions would have been mixed in with German units. "This is how the original order went out. And you have to know that an order from the Führer could not be reversed. There was no precedent."[11]

In what he termed perhaps the greatest success in his secret service career, Höttl explained: "Knowing Hungarian traditions, I saw that if they carried out this order there would be big trouble. If we carried out an open military action against Hungary, at least several garrisons would oppose us."[12]

Höttl wrote a memorandum recommending a political solution with military force, but without Romanian and Slovak troops. Most important, the solution needed to be carried out to give the appearance that everything happened with Horthy's knowledge and consent! This would result in a Hungary friendly to Germany with Horthy still at his post and the army and police collaborating. Hungary's economic resources would be at the full disposal of the Reich. Romania would be free to send her troops to the front.

Getting the memo to Hitler was the most difficult part, since both Himmler and Ribbentrop were in favor of Hitler's drastic occupation plan, Margarethe II. Schellenberg, chief of the SS secret service, sent the memo to a minister assigned to Hitler's staff, who then gave it to the Führer's aide-de-camp, telling him to put in on Hitler's night table. It was Hitler's custom before he went to bed to read the most recent messages. Höttl was certain that Hitler had read his memo. "Clearly he read my memorandum too, because the next morning he arranged that they invite Horthy for negotiations."[13]

Hitler agreed to make a last attempt with Horthy, but it was clear that the

---

10 Péter Bokor, „A nagy politikai naivitás: Nem számítottak Magyarország megszállására: Bokor interview with Pál Lieszkovszky, Gyula Kádár, and Wilhelm Höttle" [Political naivety: they didn't count on the occupation of Hungary], Magyar Hírlap, March 19, 1996. (Although Höttl, who worked for the U.S. Office of Strategic Services (OSS) became known as a notorious liar, his account of how the memo got to Hitler's bedside table is generally accepted by all branches of Hungarian historians, including the eminent historian Gyula Juhász.)
11 Ibid.
12 Péter Bokor, *Végjáték a Duna mentén*: Ausztriai beszélgetés [End game along the Danube: conversation in Austria (with Wilhelm Höttl)] Budapest: RTV-Minerva- Kossuth, 1982, 187.
13 Ibid., 187.

occupation would take place. The concession was only that it would be restricted and the country would not be dismembered immediately—everything would depend on Horthy. The restricted occupation was to be carried out while Horthy was with Hitler so he would be confronted with a *fait accompli*. If he could put a good face on it, order the Hungarians to accept it, pretend to the outer world that it had his consent and would guarantee Hungary's full cooperation, then Hitler would also pretend it had all been a transaction between friends. He would even let the occupying troops leave the country when the situation stabilized. If not, total occupation, using satellite troops, would be put into effect. The orders for Operation Margarethe I were issued March 12, signed by Hitler.[14]

In early March 1944, unrealistic optimism prevailed in Hungary. Despite the spectacular Soviet victories with their armies within one hundred sixty kilometers of the Hungarian border, there was no move for a general Hungarian mobilization. Only two divisions were given definite orders to mobilize. The Second Armored Division was warned, but left at peace strength. The remaining troops in the country were given no orders at all. Horthy still hoped to persuade the Germans to let Hungary defend the Carpathians, thus motivating the Russians to go around through the flat Polish plain.

It was carnival season. Life in Hungary went on as if there was no cloud in the sky. The former minister to London, Barcza, writes that never "was the season so filled with dinners, déjeuners, teas and cocktail parties."[15] Streets were still crowded, shops with ridiculously expensive luxury goods still found buyers. "Jews occupied the best tables in the restaurants and the best seats in the theatres."[16] Moderate politicians, the Independent Smallholders, and even the Social Democrats, addressed the largest audiences of their lives and made promises of a democratic world around the corner. Much of the public was under the illusion that the most difficult parts of war were behind them. Although German troops had been moving up to the Hungarian borders since early March, no one believed in the danger of German occupation.[17]

---

14 Juhász, "Some Aspects of Relations Between Hungary and Germany," 217; István Csicsery-Rónay, "Új tények az ország megszállásáról: 1944. március 19.—ahogy Macartney látta" [New facts on the occupation of the country: March 19, 1944—as Macartney saw it], *Magyar Nemzet*, March 21, 1995. 13.
15 Quoted in Macartney, *October Fifteenth*, 2:221.
16 Macartney, *October Fifteenth*, 2:221.
17 Páva, *Ország a hadak útján*, 236.

The Road to Occupation

Along with plans for the traditional celebration of March 15, the Hungarian national holiday of independence, a special celebration of the fiftieth anniversary of the death of Kossuth, the great Hungarian patriot, was to be held on March 20. Expectations were high for the speech Kállay was to give in Parliament. People thought he might proclaim a Hungarian surrender and perhaps the arrival of Allied air-borne divisions.

A three-member American mission, code named Mission Sparrow, actually landed March 15 close to the Yugoslav border near a village named Podturen.* The landing had to take place during the full moon from March 10–15, and a storm had delayed their takeoff from Bari, Italy. Their long-planned mission originated in OSS headquarters with Allen W. Dulles in Bern. The idea was to help the Hungarians break with Hitler's Germany and join the Allies. They chose a village close to the Yugoslav border for the landing so if captured, the men could say they had landed in Hungary by mistake. After burying their parachutes and supplies they met a Hungarian, a former waiter in France, who introduced them to the villagers. In celebration, the women brought quantities of food to the village hall - eggs, ham, butter, rolls, dumplings. They toasted with slivovitz. To the Americans it was like an operetta. Where was the war?[18]

After some questioning by the Hungarian military, they were taken to Budapest where they expected to be received immediately by Kállay. They had no way of knowing that at the moment Horthy and Szombathelyi were meeting with Hitler.

Meeting at Klessheim, March 18, 1944

On March 15 Admiral Horthy and his wife attended the gala premiere of the opera "Petőfi," arranged by students at the university, along with government officials, diplomats, and other dignitaries. It was the first time that the regent's wife, Magda, had appeared in public since the death of her son István. During the intermission a member of the German legation interrupted

---

* A village inhabited by Croatians, between 1941 and 1945 it was attached to Hungary as Bottornya. Note by the editor.

18 The mission consisted of commanding officer Colonel F. Duke, Major Alfred M. Suarez, and Captain Guy T. Nunn, who was fluent in French and German. See Florimond Duke, *Name, Rank, and Serial Number* (New York: Meredith Press, 1969), 11–17.

them, saying that Minister von Jagow requested an urgent audience to deliver a personal letter from Hitler. The letter turned out to be a belated response to Horthy's request in February for the immediate withdrawal of Hungarian forces from the eastern front. Now Hitler was prepared to discuss the matter personally and asked that Horthy kindly meet him at Klessheim Castle before March 20. Hitler asked him to bring Chief of Staff Szombathelyi and Foreign Minister Csatay, but not the prime minister, Miklós Kállay, nor the minister of the interior Keresztes-Fischer whom he also distrusted.

On the morning of March 16 Horthy met with Kállay, Foreign Minister Ghyczy, Csatay, and Szombathelyi to discuss his response. Kállay urged him not to go, arguing that his absence from the country could lead to disorder and arbitrary actions by Germany and her Hungarian sympathizers: "I warned Horthy it would be extremely dangerous to leave Hungary before it was clear what the Germans meant to do with the troops they had lined up on our frontiers." No important decisions could be made in his absence, and the country as well as the army "would remain without the supreme leadership at the mercy of the arbitrary will of the Germans."[19] Kállay of course knew of the landing of Mission Sparrow and its ramifications.

Horthy seemed to accept these arguments and to agree that Chief of the General Staff Szombathelyi be sent instead, but Szombathelyi— although willing to take on the assignment if necessary—argued that if Hitler was finally willing to discuss the withdrawal of Hungarian troops, only the regent himself would be able to achieve the desired result. In the past Hitler had only been willing to give in to Horthy. For twenty-five years the regent "had shouldered every burden for the nation's sake," and could not now refuse to undertake this difficult task. Szombathelyi did not consider a German occupation likely—as he told his adjutant, Pál Lieszkovszky, "for Hitler it would be madness: such an aggressive move would make it impossible for Hungarian and German soldiers to continue to fight together as allies."[20] Horthy could not resist this call to his patriotism.[21]

---

19 Kállay, *Hungarian Premier*, 413.
20 Péter Bokor, „A *nagy* politikai naivitás," Bokor interview with Pál Lieszkovszky, *Magyar Hirlap*, March 19, 1996.
21 Sakmyster, *Admiral on Horseback*, 325—6; Kállay, *Hungarian Premier*, 414–415.

The Road to Occupation

Horthy and his party—Csatay, Szombathelyi, and Ghyczy—left Budapest secretly on the evening of March 17, arriving at Klessheim Castle the morning of March 18. Greeted by Hitler, Ribbentrop, and Keitel, they found the atmosphere frigid. Hitler asked Horthy for a private conversation, and since Horthy who spoke fluent German objected to the presence of Hitler's interpreter the two were strictly alone, thus there was no exact record made of their discussion.[22] The Fuhrer said that in light of the terrible catastrophe of the Italian surrender he had to prevent Hungarian betrayal. He knew that Hungary planned to double-cross Germany and he would not allow it. He had to defend himself and therefore would take necessary measures. Horthy was furious at the charge of betrayal. In its thousand-year history Hungary had never betrayed an ally, and if it should be in the national interest to ask for a ceasefire, he considered it a matter of honor to first tell the Germans.

At the end of the hour-and-a-half meeting, Hitler announced that he had already decided on a military occupation of Hungary. Horthy now became really furious. As he told the historian C. A. Macartney later, "If I had had my revolver with me, I would have shot the scoundrel; all my life I'll regret that I didn't do it."[23] He jumped up and ran out of the room. According to witnesses, Horthy, with a face red with fury, ran toward his rooms. Hitler came after him at the door, also furious. He tried to talk Horthy into coming back, but Horthy shook him off and shut himself in his room. Hitler turned around and went back to his own room, calling Ribbentrop to him. Not long afterward he asked that the regent join him for lunch. Members of Horthy's entourage assembled to hear the regent's account of the meeting but he was so agitated he was unable to give a lucid account. When the invitation to lunch was delivered Horthy replied he would attend only if the talks were to continue. The lunch took place in icy silence.

In their second conversation, the regent took the offensive, telling Hitler he should reconsider, that the Hungarians were the only people still friendly to Germany. The Germans had behaved so badly that even the Hottentots and

---

22 A circumstantial account exists from Ambassador Paul Schmidt, the inter- on by Horthy. Horthy gave various accounts, first to his Crown Council is return to Budapest as well as at the Nuremberg Trials. He recounted their conversation several times to the historian, C. A. Macartney, who attempted to reconstruct the interview. See Macartney. *October Fifteenth*, 2:234.

23 Personal statement to C A. Macartney. Horthy was in Admirals uniform—no revolver with this uniform. Macartney, *October Fifteenth*, 2:234–5.

Laplanders hated them. Hitler rehashed the accusations made at the earlier meeting at Klessheim and handed Horthy a protocol, which listed the objectives of the German occupation. It called for the appointment of a new Hungarian government with Imrédy as prime minister and General Jenő Rátz as minister of defense, as well as a German minister plenipotentiary to be sent in with the occupation army. The regent was to issue a proclamation instructing the Hungarian people and army to receive the Wehrmacht in a friendly way.[24]

Horthy indignantly refused to sign the proposed protocol, declaring that never in his life had he told a lie and he would not do so now. In desperation Horthy told Hitler that if he refrained from attacking Hungary he would give his solemn promise that Hungary would not defect to the enemy, and if the promise were broken he would commit suicide. Hitler replied, "But what good would that do me?"[25] On this bizarre note the conversation ended in deadlock. Horthy changed into travel clothes and announced his intention of departing immediately. To delay him Ribbentrop staged a fake air raid with a smoke screen over the castle.

Szombathelyi, convinced that any resistance would have disastrous consequences, seems to have persuaded Horthy to make one final effort with Hitler. Both Hitler and Ribbentrop had hinted that some compromise was possible—if Horthy agreed he could return to Budapest and appoint a new government acceptable to Germany. Once the guarantees were achieved Hitler told Szombathelyi that he would withdraw his troops from Hungary. This promise may have begun to tip the balance. Around 8 p.m. Ribbentrop appeared to tell Horthy that Hitler was prepared for further discussion. Making an effort to appear conciliatory Hitler implored Horthy to remain at his post and promised "that the German troops shall be withdrawn as soon as a new Hungarian government that has my confidence has been formed."[26] There is controversy over just what Horthy agreed to at Klessheim, but there definitely was some kind of agreement.[27]

---

24 Sakmyster, *Admiral on Horseback*, 329–330.
25 Quoted in Sakmyster, *Admiral on Horseback*, 330.
26 Horthy *Memoirs*, 260
27 Fenyo, *Hitler, Horthy, and Hungary*, 164–165; Horthy *Memoirs*, 260; Sakmyster, *Admiral on Horseback*, 332.

The Road to Occupation

Horthy would not resign; he would dismiss Kállay and appoint a government that had the Germans' trust. But Hitler had promised that he would withdraw the troops as soon as Horthy named an acceptable government, and Horthy later affirmed that this was the most important point on which he made his decision. It seems that the regent did not continue to request that the Hungarian troops be brought home but would send the whole Hungarian army to the Russian front, and of course the massive deliveries of foodstuffs and war material to Germany would continue. At their departure, Hitler accompanied the Hungarian party to their train to send them off.[28]

Evidently, Horthy's assurances were enough to convince Hitler that the occupation could be accomplished without major complications. He ordered certain changes in Operation Margarethe, calling off plans for a military seizure of the castle. The number of units to be used to occupy the country was somewhat reduced, and Hungarian troops were to be confined to their barracks but their weapons were not to be confiscated.

As he left Klessheim Castle, Horthy had little idea of the seriousness of the situation. He could hardly have imagined that the German occupation would put an end to what has been called the most remarkable accomplishment of the so-called Horthy era—the preservation of a degree of political freedom and pluralism in face of repeated attempts by the radical Right to introduce one-party dictatorship.[29] Until the German occupation Hungary was one of the three islands of cultural and intellectual freedom in Europe, along with Sweden and Switzerland. Book publishing flourished, with a great and increasing interest shown in foreign literature; especially English. Even a few Jewish authors were published at a time when elsewhere in Europe Jewish books were being burned.[30] Although civil and political rights had been eroded, Hungary had remained one of the few countries on the Continent and the only one

---

28   Horthy, *Memoirs*, 261; Sakmyster, *Admiral on Horseback*, 332–333.
29   Andrew C. Janos, *The Politics of Backwardness in Hungary* : 1825–1945 (Princeton, N.J.: Princeton University Press, 1982), 306.
30   In the first three months of 1944 before the German occupation, English and American authors published included Willa Cather, Joseph Conrad, Charles Dickens, Aldous Huxley, Sinclair Lewis, Jack London, and Upton Sinclair. See Rezső Szíj, "Magyar könyvművészet és könyvkiadás 1920–1940/1944 között" [Hungarian typographic art and book publishing between 1920–1940/1944] in *Erővonalak a két világháború közti magyar szellemi* életben, 228.

in Eastern Europe that permitted the functioning of a multiparty system and some freedom of assembly and the press.[31]

The regent's train left Klessheim around 9:30 p.m. and arrived in Vienna at 1 a.m. There it was held up until at least four in the morning, the moment when German troops began their advance into Hungary. When Horthy awoke on March 19 he was surprised to find himself still several hours from Budapest. By the time his train crossed the Hungarian border, German troops were near the capital, and when he reached the railroad station in Budapest he was greeted by a German honor guard. The troops marched into Hungary unopposed.[32]

German Occupation

German troops occupied Hungary on Sunday morning, March 19, 1944, virtually without resistance. The occupation took the inhabitants of Budapest completely by surprise. It was a beautiful early spring day, and the cafés, beer gardens, and terraces of Budapest were crowded. The occupation troops entered Hungary ceremonially as if on parade, with bands playing—they were the cream of the German army, the elite, good looking and well educated. As they drove through the streets of Budapest, their disciplined, motorized convoy provided an impressive display to those on the streets and cafe terraces, who may not have understood the true meaning of the occupation. A young Budapest woman and her friends, leaving the pastry shop after their usual Sunday outing, were not surprised to see them; Babi explained that they were used to seeing German military around.[33] By midday, German officers were sitting in the finest restaurants and cafes enjoying their Sunday dinner. Yet there was no cheering in Budapest as there had been in Vienna. The population looked on passively as the Germans entered.

Sándor Kiss, a student leader, recalled: "I happened to go up to the castle on that... Sunday morning.... I hiked up from the streetcar stop on the Széll

---

31 As late as March 1944 the Hungarian press offered a choice among conservative, liberal, socialist, monarchist, Catholic, fascist, and national socialist points of view.
32 Fenyo, *Hitler, Horthy, and Hungary*, 167–171; Sakmyster, *Admiral on Horseback*, 332–333.
33 Mrs. László Bakonyi, interview with the author, Budapest, November 6, 2001.

The Road to Occupation

Kálman square. When I reached the gate, I was surprised to see two soldiers standing on either side, their weapons at the ready—the camions on either side of the gate. So this was it. I got cold shivers up my spine.... I knew that there was big trouble, and it suddenly hit me: the Germans."[34]

Hungary-Enemy Country

Very few knew of the circumstances surrounding Admiral Horthy's visit to Klessheim. Because the Germans delayed his return, sidetracking his train and keeping his company incommunicado, Prime Minister Kállay received no instructions. He had been waiting for news from the regent since March 17 and had gone to bed at midnight after taking a strong dose of sleeping medicine. "I was hardly in my bed when my direct phone with the ministry of the interior rang. Keresztes-Fischer... told me only to get dressed and that he would be with me very quickly because serious events were under way. A few minutes later he arrived to tell me that the frontier guards had reported that the Germans had crossed the border in trains, tanks, and armored cars, the various units evidently heading towards Budapest."[35]

Reports from the army then began to come in. "According to the general staff the following forces had been concentrated against us: on the western frontier, five German divisions; in the north and around Kassa, one German and one Slovak division; along the southeaster frontier, ten Rumanian divisions; in the Belgrade area, four to five German divisions; westward of this, important Croatian forces had been disposed against us. The only forces that we had ready for action were those in the Carpathians."[36]

Kállay called in the three army commanders who were in Budapest— István Náday, Károly Beregffy, and János Vörös. At that moment two telegrams arrived, one addressed by Foreign Minister Ghyczy to his deputy, Szentmiklóssy, which ran: "Please Let My Wife Know That I Am Well."[37] Accord-

---

34 Two weeks before the occupation, at the national student meeting to determine how Hungary should leave the war, the final statement read that the country should leave the war honorably, and afterward carry out the long awaited social reforms (Sándor Kiss, *A magyar demokráciáért*, 33).
35 Kállay, Hungarian Premier, 419.
36 Ibid, 419–420.
37 Ibid, 420.

ing to the agreed code, this meant military occupation to be expected, but the Germans had purposely delayed transmission of the telegram. The second telegram from Chief of Staff Szombathelyi to his deputy Chief of Staff, General József Bajnóczy, stated that nothing should be done until the regent returned, and that German troops were to be received as friends. The German military attaché, General Greiffenberg, then arrived with a long telegram from Keitel saying that the German troops were going to occupy Budapest in accordance with an agreement reached between the Fuhrer and the regent. The regent and the new German minister plenipotentiary would arrive the next morning. The Germans would act in a restrained manner but would relentlessly crush any resistance, and if Hungary resisted, the armies of the neighboring countries which were standing in readiness on the borders would march on Budapest

Kállay faced the dilemma whether to act independently or wait for the regent. When he asked the army commanders if they were prepared to accept his instruction to order resistance in the absence of the regent, all three immediately replied that resistance against the Germans was absolutely impossible. Kállay pointed out that the issue was not one of relative strength but of showing that the Hungarians were prepared to defend their independence. Both Beregffy and Vörös refused, adding that they would forbid their subordinates to carry out orders to resist in the absence of the regent. Náday was willing but believed resistance would be dangerous if the army was not united. It was finally agreed that if the Germans attacked any Hungarian military unit they were to be resisted. Army commanders were to issue orders that officers and other ranks be concentrated in barracks, the gates to be bolted, ammunition to be distributed, and guns made ready for action; then to await the regent's orders.[38]

During the next three hours, Kállay ordered the burning of the secret archives of the ministries of foreign affairs, the interior, defense, and other more important offices, including his own. Kállay's son, Kristóf (Christopher), sat at the telephone all night calling individuals to warn them of the imminent danger, beginning with the members of the left-wing parties, prominent An-

---

38 Ibid, 422.

The Road to Occupation

glophiles, and Jewish representatives. The commanders of the refugee camps were warned and given orders that the internees were free to leave if they wished and were to be given a month's wages in advance.[39]

When German troops began appearing the military was in a quandary—the Germans were their allies, yet German troops were invading Hungary—a sovereign nation. Their dilemma was partially solved by the telegram from Chief of the General Staff Szombathelyi, instructing them to receive the German troops in a friendly manner. Thus armed resistance took place only in a few pockets that had not received the command.

At the Ludovika Military Academy the cadets had been looking forward to a Sunday cross-country race, then perhaps Sunday afternoon leave. Instead, in the early morning hours they received the news that the Germans had occupied Hungary. One of the cadets, Tibor Petrusz, summed up their reaction: "I have to say honestly we didn't know how we should react, what we should feel. The Germans were our military comrades, we were allies. But this, that they should occupy Hungary, offended our national pride. At the Ludovika we got the order to 'hold together' (*együtt-tartást*), but we didn't understand what that command meant. That we should stand against the Germans?—or perhaps that we were to carry out something with the Germans? They handed out ammunition, so that if there actually should be a skirmish with the Germans, they could bring in the Ludovika classes trained to carry out policing actions."[40]

General Jenő Major, commander of the First Armored Army Corps, awaited information on how they should conduct themselves. In his memoirs he recalled: Only around noon a directive came from Budapest through the 1st army corps command that German troops were marching into our country. We were instructed not to resist but to protest against being disarmed. Troops were to remain in their barracks, but still no explanation....

German troops moved into all our barracks—set up guards. In some places they didn't allow them to leave the barracks—in other words held them prisoner. In others had complete freedom. Our officers in many places greet-

---

39 Ibid., 425.
40 Tibor Petrusz, interview with the author, July 20, 2001.

ed and entertained the German officers in friendship. Over white tablecloths and wine the sad truth came out—Hitler had really given the command to occupy Hungary during the time that the country's regent and chief of staff were his guests. Over wine the German officers explained that the written command began: *Ungarn Feindesland*, [Hungary—enemy country] They themselves were the most surprised when they got the command to occupy a friendly allied country and were ashamed to carry it out.[41]

The occupation did not take place smoothly everywhere. At several border locations there was firing on German troops and several airports also fired on the occupiers. At Bicske railroad workers tried to oppose them. But in German military documents of the time, there is hardly a word about Hungarian opposition. In his diary from March 19, 1944, commanding general of the occupying forces, Field Marshall Baron Maximilian von Weichs, who had been transferred from Belgrade to carry out the occupation, noted: "Morning: the occupation is going according to plan. Only one place where Hungarian troop disarmament took place. And only because my command did not arrive in time. But we took care of it. In Budapest everything quiet. Nowhere any opposition.... Evening: we achieved all of our goals. Parts of the army received us ceremonially. In other places some resistance—but by mistake.... In Budapest there is quiet."[42]

Next day, after meeting with Hitler's new minister and Reich Plenipotentiary, Edmund Veesenmayer, and discussing the Hungarian domestic situation, he wrote: "The situation is quiet. The Hungarian troops accept us loyally. The population is in general neutral."[43] 11 Veesenmayer later said that in Hungary he felt completely safe, one year in Hungary was less dangerous than one day in Yugoslavia. The regent's train approached at a snail's pace, finally arriving at the Kelenföld station at 11 a.m. When Kállay arrived at the station he found a large German honor guard drawn up and German staff officers led by Field Marshall

---

41 Jenő Major, Emléktöredékek: *Visszaemlékezés az 1944. március és 1945. július közötti háborús eseményekre* [Fragments of a memoir: memoirs of the military events between March 1944 and July 1945 (Budapest: Hadtörténelmi levéltári kiadványok, n.d), 12–13.
42 Von Weichs diary, quoted in Péter Gosztonyi, "The Hungarian Resistance" Movement and Reaction in Mirror of German Writing;" in *Magyarország 1944: fejezetek az ellenállás történetéből* (Hungary 1944: chapters from the history of the resistance], ED. M. Kiss Sándor(Budapest: Nemzeti Tankönyvkiadó, 1994), 10–11.
43 Ibid., 11.

The Road to Occupation

Weichs. When the regent's special train opened its doors, "at every door an armed SS soldier appeared instead of the usual Hungarian bodyguard."[44] Kállay reported that the regent was deathly pale, "and he looked worn out but still master of himself."[45] The regent presented Veesenmayer, the new German minister to Budapest; following him was Döme Sztójay, the Hungarian minister in Berlin, with whom Kállay avoided shaking hands.

At the crown council, ordered by the regent for one o'clock, Horthy told of his conversations at Klessheim, including Hitler's threat to invite Romanian, Croatian, and Slovak troops to join in the attack. He asked the cabinet to continue in office until new decisions were made, but both Kállay and Keresztes-Fischer argued that all such actions were legally null and void since they were taken under foreign duress. Kállay offered his resignation and would not sign the notes of the sitting or the resignation document. He recommended that either Keresztes-Fischer or an administrative government take over the cabinet, but from the beginning it was clear that a government acceptable for the Germans had to be found. In the midst of the meeting Keresztes-Fischer gave the alarming report that the Gestapo had already arrested forty-five prominent Hungarians—including some members of Parliament. Severe measures against the Jews were apparently being planned; not a single Jew was being permitted to leave Budapest. Ilona Horthy, István Horthy's widow, who had been in Szolnok for an unveiling of a statue to the regent's son, was only able to pass through the roadblocks and return to the city in the company of a German officer.[46]

Throughout the afternoon Horthy agonized over critical decisions, snuggling with conflicting advice. A Jewish delegation, headed by Ferenc Chorin and Móric Kornfeld, implored him not to abdicate but to appease the Germans by appointing a new government. Otherwise the Jews would face certain extermination.[47] In the evening, Kállay, who had been shocked by the reports of brutal Gestapo actions, tried to persuade him to resign. According to Kállay, it "was the only way we could refute the story which the Germans

---

44 Péter Bokor interview with Pál Lieszkovszky, *Magyar Hírlap*, March 19, 199
45 Kállay, *Hungarian Premier*, 428.
46 Kállay, *Hungarian Premier*, 431–432; Sakymyster, *Admiral on Horseback*, 335–336; Ilona Gyulai, *Becsület és Kötelesség*, 228–229.
47 Sakmyster, *Admiral on Horseback*, 337.

were spreading that he had consented to the military occupation."[48] Horthy answered: "The captain cannot leave his sinking ship; he must remain on the bridge to the last. Whom will it serve if Imrédy sits here? Who will defend the army? Who will save a million Magyar lads from being dragged away to the Russian shambles? Who will defend the honorable men and women in this country who have trusted me blindly? Who will defend the Jews or our refugees if I leave my post?"[49] Kállay then suggested that he follow the example of King Christian X of Denmark—retire to Kenderes, withdraw from all state business, and adopt a completely passive attitude, but Horthy insisted he could not abandon his people in the time of extreme emergency.

István Bethlen, Horthy's trusted advisor, had made his way to the Royal Castle through an underground passage and was waiting for the regent on his return. He advised him not to appoint a prime minister or to form a government. Forced to leave March 22, since Magda Horthy feared the consequences if he was discovered, Bethlen again warned Horthy: "If there is no government the Germans have no one with which to negotiate. Public opinion at home and abroad will see that there has been an end to legitimate government"[50] He gave Horthy two lists of names—those trusted anti-Nazis and those who might be traitors or too weak to hold up against the Germans. Early on the morning of March 19, the Gestapo began to arrest all of the possible opposition leaders according to a carefully prepared list. Those arrested were the elite of traditional political, economic, and diplomatic life, leaders of the opposition parties, known anglophiles, industrial leaders and bankers. Among those arrested were thirteen members of the lower house of Parliament and nine of the upper house members. Parliament met on the March 22 as scheduled but only to be adjourned indefinitely. Only one deputy, József Közi-Horváth of the Christian Party, protested the violation of the Hungarian constitution and arrest of members of the house by a foreign power, but he was stopped by the speaker of the house and shouted down by other members.[51]

---

48 Kállay, *Hungarian Premier*, 433.
49 Ibid, 433.
50 Count István Bethlen, *Hungarian Politics during World War Two: Treatise and Indictment*, ed. Countess Ilona Bolza (München: Dr. Dr. Rudolf Trofenik, 1985), 2.
51 Macartney, *October Fifteenth*, 2:248.

The Road to Occupation

One civilian put up armed resistance, Endre Bajcsy-Zsilinsky, the vehement leader of the opposition for Hungarian independence. When the SS rang the doorbell his unsuspecting wife said he was sleeping, to call again at 11 a.m. While they continued to ring the doorbell, Bajcsy-Zsilinsky called the captain of police, asking for protection as a free Hungarian parliamentary representative, but the police had been occupied themselves. Meanwhile the Germans kept knocking on the apartment door. Then there was quiet. The SS, who had not expected any resistance, sent for help. When they returned they succeeded in shooting out the lock, pushing their way into the hallway. Bajcsy-Zsilinsky's widow recalled the dramatic encounter:

Holding his pistol ready to shoot, my husband stood in front of the bedroom door. One of the armed SS.... shouted, „Hinaus! Hinaus!"... That's when Endre took his first shot. The SS answered with a machine gun round. Again Endre shot and the Germans returned it with another round. Pieces of the glass from the glass door, the window, the mirror flew around the flat. They also hit the radio.... In the middle of the shooting I heard Endre say: 'A shot in the stomach... one in the shoulder ...' I thought he wanted to tell me of the targets he had hit, but it turned out that he spoke of his own wounds.... After he had shot the last bullet from his pistol. Endre then threw the pistol through the door into the living room, at which the SS rushed into the room, tied his hands behind him and took him away bleeding from several wounds.[52]

The arrest of Károly Rassay, leader of the Budapest liberal opposition, was typical of the morning arrests. At 6 a.m. Chorin telephoned him, warning that the Germans were detraining at the Kelenföld station near Budapest. Then came the news that Bajcsy-Zsiliszky had been arrested. Soon afterward two German soldiers arrived at his home accompanied by a young Hungarian, probably an Arrow Cross member. With only his overcoat and glasses he was taken to a cell already filled with about five prisoners, where a file for him had been prepared with the number 18, a number he had noticed on his villa some weeks before.[53]

---

52 Mrs. Endré Bajcsy-Zsilinszky [widow of Endre Bajcsy-Zsilinszky], "1944- Március 19-e egy budai lakásban" [March 19, 1944 in a Budapest apartment], *Kortársak Bajcsy-Zsilinszky Endréről*, Budapest: Magvető könyvkiadó, *1984, 413–415*.
53 Zsuzsa L Nagy, *Egy Politikus Polgár Portréja Rassay Károly* (1886–1958) [Portrait of a political citizen Rassay Károly (1886–1958)] Budapest: Napvilág Kiadó, 2006, 169.

Some prominent individuals managed to escape. Kállay and his family escaped to the castle and the Turkish minister, Şevket Fuat Keçeci, offered Kállay refuge, while his family remained in the castle.[54] Chorin and István Bethlen fled to the countryside. Bethlen, disguised as a colonel of the Hussars, found refuge in Transylvania at the headquarters of General Veress. Social Democrat leaders, Szakasits and Mme Kéthly, and Smallholders Tildy and Varga had been at political meetings outside of Budapest and were warned not to return. Peyer gave himself up when the Germans threatened his family but Szakasits managed to remain free. The German police took over the Royal Hotel where they kept prisoners in the basement. By April 28, 8,240 individuals were being held. Those arrested included the Allied prisoners of war: 812 French, 5,450 Polish, 39 English, 11 American, 16 Belgian, 12 Dutch, 180 Soviet, as well as members of the Royal Italian Legation.[55]

On Sunday, Budapest Radio made no announcement and many people were not aware that the occupation had taken place. That evening the radio began to broadcast news solely of German origin in contrast to the usual practice of news based on the British radio. The head of the Magyar Távirati Iroda és Rádió [Hungarian telegraphic news agency and radio], Antal Náray, bewailed the fact that on Monday, April 20, Ferenc Schaub, who had been empowered to control the radio, dictated the news, "using a tone against the Jews which was unworthy of the Radio's serious and objective tone before March 19."[56]

For three days the Hungarian press made no mention of the German occupation. Papers published news of the war and the home news as if nothing had happened, although only news from German sources appeared. The only indication of the German occupation was the announcement in all morning papers on March 20 that the minister for internal affairs had prohibited all theater and cinema performances as well as dancing and public meetings. Morning papers on the March 21 carried the item that the Kossuth anniversary celebrations, to have been held the morning of March 20, had not tak-

---

54 Ilona Gyulai, *Becsület és Kötelesség*, 234–235.
55 Fenyo, *Hitler, Horthy, and Hungary*, 175.
56 Sándor Szakály, ed., *Náray Anted visszaemlékezése 1945* [Antal Náray memoirs 1945] (Budapest: Zrínyi, 1988), 97–100.

en place because of the ban on public meetings. At the time that Kállay was scheduled to deliver his long awaited speech to the Hungarian population the radio played a philology lecture.

In London, émigrés who followed events in Hungary closely got their first indication of the occupation by the change in tone of the radio broadcasts. Actual news of the occupation arrived on Monday afternoon in a message from the Bucharest correspondent of the Agence Anatolique and broadcast by Ankara radio. The same day news was received from all neutral capitals that telephone and telegraph communications with Hungary had been cut. Since Germany dominated all the surrounding countries it was impossible to get news of the occupation. Hungary was now completely sealed off from the outside world.[57]

Formation of the Sztójay Government

Horthy soon discovered how difficult it was to navigate without the aid of his advisors and fellow officers. He had to rely increasingly on his dwindling entourage at the castle and close family members—his wife, Magda, his daughter-in-law, Ilona, and his son, Nicky. Veesenmayer, although relatively moderate and pragmatic, was a formidable opponent. He had been given three days by Hitler for the formation of the new government, but if the negotiations were not successful a total occupation would be put into force. Thus Veesenmayer put all his efforts into persuading Horthy to cooperate, believing that his subordinates would then obey orders. The prevailing atmosphere was tense, the Gestapo was rounding up victims and all public events were canceled. Negotiations moved slowly and threatened to break down.

Horthy rejected out of hand the idea of naming Imrédy prime minister; he favored a caretaker government, but Veesenmayer demanded Horthy appoint a government from the radical right-wing parties, excluding the Arrow Cross. An ultimatum arrived that if the new government was not formed by 6 p.m., the Germans under Field Marshall von Weichs would occupy the

---

57 *Hungarian News Survey,* ed. Andrew Révai and Béla Iványi-Grünwald in London (for private circulation only) XIX-J-i-a.II-18—1945~47, box 11.

castle and take over complete power.⁵⁸ Weichs, who had received instructions to prepare to occupy the Palace and disarm the army, expressed his reservations about such a base policy: "A step like this on our part would immediately line up against us the various circles of the Hungarian opposition ... The government just established would resign, along with the regent. A general Hungarian uprising would take place. Instead of gaining new troops for the eastern front with the Hungarians, we would have to withdraw troops from there in order to keep order."⁵⁹ The Red Army had advanced 265 kilometers between March and April on the southern front and inflicted irreparable damage on Army Groups A, South, and Center.⁶⁰ Weichs concluded that the radical measure would achieve exactly the opposite of the object of the occupation.

Horthy finally prevailed upon Sztójay, a professional soldier and longtime Hungarian minister in Berlin, to take the position of prime minister. Although Horthy did not like Sztójay, he believed that as a professional soldier he would be honorable and loyal. He had participated in the regent's Crown Council meeting, but he was a sick man, a diabetic, and felt himself unfit mentally and physically.⁶¹ Horthy finally convinced him, promising that if they succeeded in winning the Germans' trust, they would erect a statue to him in one of the most beautiful places in Budapest.

On March 22 at 3:45 a.m., an agreement was reached, with a final slate including rightist ministers from the government party and several followers of Imrédy. It was a compromise solution but Reményi-Schneller, Szász, and Jurcsek were specialists in their respective fields, and Horthy had succeeded in keeping General Csatay as minister of defense.⁶² Since one half of the ministers had already held office and a number were members of the traditional government party, the new government had credibility. But of most importance was that Horthy had appointed it as a legal government, which satisfied

---

58 Ilona Gyulai, *Becsület és Kötelesség*, 235.
59 Von Weichs diary, quoted in Gosztonyi, "The Hungarian Resistance Movement," 11.
60 Keegan, *The Second World War*, 478–479.
61 Péter Bokor, interview with Lieszkovszky Pál, *Magyar Hírlap*. March 19, 1996.
62 Döme Sztójay, Prime Minister and also Minister of Foreign Affairs; Jenő Rátz, Deputy Prime Minister without Portfolio; Andor Jaross, Interior; Lajos Csatay, Defense; Reményi-Schneller, Finance; Béla Jurcsek, Supply and Agriculture; Lajos Szász, Industry; Antal Kunder, Commerce and Communications; István Antal, Education and Cults.

the German desire to have a constitutional government still under the regent. On March 23 at 6 p.m., shortly before the ultimatum would have expired, the Sztójay ministry took the oath in the auditorium of the Royal Castle.

The change of government was announced as if nothing untoward had happened; the population learned about it only after the new government had been sworn in. The official notice read: "In order to assist Hungary in the common war… against the common enemy, and in particular in effectively combating Bolshevism.… German troops have arrived in Hungary as the result of a mutual agreement.… The two allied Governments have agreed that the measures which have been taken will contribute towards Hungary's throwing into the scale every resource calculated to help on the final victory of the common cause, in the spirit of the old friendship and comradeship in arms between the Hungarian and German peoples."[63]

While much of the population greeted the German presence passively, there were many who welcomed the Germans as friends and allies against the much-feared Russians, whom the all-pervasive propaganda depicted as brutes and rapists. Judit Stúr, the daughter of an upper-middle-class family in Kőszeg, made friends with a German soldier with her family's blessing. Her father, a mid-level government official, was right-wing and anti-Semitic, believing the Jews were too intelligent and had too much power for their numbers. He would not allow the family to shop in Jewish stores, but—rather typically of the attitude of many so-called anti-Semites—her mother went to a Jewish hairdresser because she was good, while Judit's best friend in school was a Jewish girl.[64]

Horthy removed himself from day-to-day affairs, living in relative isolation, although his name was given to all measures taken by the new government. His way of protesting was to remain secluded in the castle, asserting that he was a prisoner of the Germans. Through his self-imposed isolation he wished to disassociate himself as much as possible from decisions by the Sztójay govern-

---

63 Quoted in Macartney, *October Fifteenth*, 2:252.
64 Later she saw groups of Jews walking on the road but didn't think much about it, since as students they had to go out to dig trenches. The Yellow Star didn't seem so bad. At first she didn't believe in the Holocaust; thought it was communist propaganda (Dr. Judit Stúr, interview with the author, June 12, 2003).

ment, but this also served German interests. Ribbentrop had instructed that the Hungarian political role be reduced to the barest minimum.⁶⁵

With his earlier contacts broken, surrounded by a foreign army, it appeared that the regent had decided he could do nothing more for the time being than try to collect some trustworthy people around him, settle down and bide his time. The government leaders and heads of the political parties were in prison or concentration camps and most of the officers with whom he had worked up to then were either under arrest or scattered, with the exception of his minister of defense, Csatay. At the same time the officers who had been sentenced for their roles in the Újvidék massacre and had escaped to Germany returned and were reinstated and promoted. His suspicion of General János Vörös, whom he had been forced to appoint as chief of the general staff, replacing Szombathelyi, proved correct since Vörös began to press to reactivate pro-German officers who had been retired.⁶⁶

Horthy's decision to remain as regent has been one of the most intensely debated questions among Hungarians ever since. Would Hungary have been better off if Horthy had resigned—or if he had removed himself from all government affairs as had the king of Denmark? The country would have received more brutal treatment from the Germans but perhaps have gained more at the peace settlement. In an audience with Szálasi, whom he received reluctantly, Horthy told him that he would have nothing to do with the government—his sole concern was to keep the army in his own hands. In Horthy's view, Hungary needed to have a powerful army at the end of the war in order to avoid a similar fate that had befallen Hungary after World War I. He later said that Hitler's promise at Klessheim that he would withdraw German troops as soon as a Hungarian government was formed that enjoyed his confidence was the most important factor in his decision to maintain a semblance of legal continuity and to remain as regent. Unfortunately, because he retained his position as regent, the Allied powers regarded Hungary as a Nazi vassal state and not as an occupied country.⁶⁷

---

65   Sakmyster, *Admiral on Horseback*, 339.
66   Sakmyster, *Admired on Horseback*, 341–342; Fenyő, *Hitler, Horthy, and Hungary*, 180.
67   Considering the circumstances when the peace treaty was signed in early 1947 at the time of the start of the Cold War, it is questionable whether Hungary could have gained any better terms.

The Road to Occupation

In the days after March 19, the German occupiers and the Gestapo basically transformed the domestic situation, replacing officials loyal to Horthy with those loyal to the Germans. Veesenmayer, who had visited Hungary in the spring and fall of 1943 as a private person, had decided then that it was necessary to reorganize the Hungarian government. His impression was that most of the political leaders were ready to collaborate and cooperate with the Germans; it was only necessary to replace the highest leadership, the so-called "castle clique" which he proceeded to do.[68]

In one of his frequent telegrams to Ribbentrop, Veesenmayer informed him on April 28 that he had succeeded in exchanging nineteen of the Lord Lieutenants who ruled the government of the counties. In all out of forty-one Lord Lieutenants twenty-nine were removed. He replaced many high government and administrative officials, including the mayor of Budapest and two-thirds of the mayors of other cities, men who would probably have been loyal to Horthy.[69] The opposition parties were banned, including the Social Democrats, as well as their newspapers, trade unions, and worker associations. The press and radio were tightly controlled, and it was forbidden to listen to foreign newscasts.

Until this point German-Hungarian relations could have been referred to as "equal" but now they clearly became hierarchical. Though the Hungarian army kept its formal independence, and restrictions imposed in March were lifted, subordination of its operations became final. Even Hungarian troops not destined for operational tasks were now used in the front lines. The Germans replaced military leaders whom they disliked and some were even arrested. István Náday and Ferenc Szombathelyi were relieved of their duties, while Major General István Újszászy, Staff Colonel Gyula Kádár and Staff Major Károly Kern were arrested by the Gestapo.[70]

Soon after the German occupation the full horrors of war descended on the Hungarian population. There had been no Allied bombing raids against Hungarian targets in the time of the Kállay government but now they became a reg-

---

68 Ungváry, *The Hungarian Army in World War II*, 230.
69 Gosztonyi, "The Hungarian Resistance Movement," 14, Ungváry, *Hungarian Army*, 232.
70 Sándor Szakály, "Hungarian-German Military Cooperation during World War II" in *20th Century Hungary and the Great Powers,* ed. Ignáz Romsics (New York: Columbia University, 1995), 152.

ular event. Allied bombing began April 2 with a daylight attack by American aircraft and on April 3 a nighttime attack by the British. Both attacks involved several hundred airplanes, inflicting extensive damage, and from then on blanket bombing hit the factories on Csepel, the airplane factory, the oil fields and railroad centers, but also population centers. For the first time the population had to black out windows, cease using car headlights, make use of the air raid shelters and shelters in the cellars of large apartment blocks. The start of the bombing had a powerful effect on public opinion—the sirens and radio alerts heightened the atmosphere of fear and destroyed the German legend of invincibility. Rather than rallying the population in support of the fighting, as it had in Great Britain, the bombing increased the desire to get out of the war.[71]

The new Hungarian government proceeded to carry out the measures urged on them by the Germans. Despite the fact that the occupying force was small—many troops had been withdrawn soon after the occupation—members of the military and government agreed to German demands even when aware that they could not be fulfilled. Mobilization was speeded up. The Germans began the reorganization of the Hungarian economy with the aim of subordinating war and weapons production and the delivery of raw materials completely to their interests. And the solution to the Jewish question in Hungary—so long demanded by the Germans—was immediately begun under the supervision of Adolf Eichmann, the *Schutzstaffe* [SS] commander in charge of deportations.

Measures Against the Jewish Population

Although Jews were not the reason for the German occupation, they became a primary concern once the decision to launch Operation Margarethe had been made. The preparations for the occupation included plans for the deportation and eradication of the Hungarian Jews. Adolf Eichmann arrived shortly after the occupying troops at the head of the Eichmann Kommando, consisting of not more than 200 to 300 people. He had received the command from Himmler, the leader of the SS, to "sweep out the Jews from the

---

71 L. Nagy, *Magyarország története*, 240–242.

country in the direction from east to west, and deport every Jew to Auschwitz as quickly as possible. To start in the eastern counties which the Russians are approaching, and to take care that no event similar to the Warsaw ghetto uprising takes place."[72]

The Germans' task was facilitated by the fact that they had destroyed the traditional Hungarian political leadership; the anti-German groups of the Hungarian economic, diplomatic, and military elite had been removed from positions of influence. The conservative-liberals, leftist liberals, and social democrats who had protested against the Jewish laws had either been taken into German prison or concentration camps or had gone into hiding. Veesenmayer's replacement of the Lord Lieutenants and other county officials lessened the chance of any possible protest against the deportations from the provinces. Jewish leaders hoped that with the worsening military situation and scarcity of transportation, the Germans would not be able to remove the 825,000 Jews in the few remaining months of the war, but they did not reckon on the breakneck speed with which the deportations were carried out.

Relying on the model developed through deportation of the Jews elsewhere in Europe, the Germans accomplished their goal in an amazingly short time with the full cooperation of the Hungarian authorities. The fact that Horthy remained in office, giving the new government the appearance of legitimacy, increased the assurance that commands would be followed. The SS followed the pattern used in other countries; first isolation laws and the confiscation of Jewish wealth, then the gathering of Jews into ghettos, afterward deportation, then annihilation. Veesenmayer wrote to Berlin that the Hungarian government took the job seriously— and carried it out in a praiseworthy fashion. In the space of a few weeks after the occupation, Jews were confined to ghettos, internment camps and "yellow-star houses." Then, in only fifty-six days starting with May 16, all 437,402 people from the countryside were deported to Auschwitz-Birkenau, except for some 15,000 who were taken to Strasshof, Austria.[73]

---

72 Gyurgyak, *A zsidókérdés magyarországon,* 173; Tamás Stark, Zsidóság a vészkorszakban, 20.
73 Gábor Kádár and Zoltán Vági, "The economic Annihilation of the Hungarian Jews, 1944–1945," in *The Holocaust in Hungary: Sixty Years Later,* eds. Randolf L. Braham and Brewster S. Chamberlin (New York: Columbia University Press, 2006), 79–80.

Establishment of the Jewish Council

On the day following the occupation the Gestapo demanded the establishment of a so-called Jewish Council with the goal of providing the means by which they would round up the Jews. The majority of the Budapest Jewish community lived on the Pest side of Budapest.[74] On the morning of May 20, leading members of the Jewish community were commanded to report to the main office of the Pest Israelite congregation. Hastily gathering the evening of May 19, the leaders, who were all good law-abiding citizens, called the Hungarian government's Ministry of Culture to ask what their attitude to the Germans should be. After repeated calls and evasive answers they were told the next morning only that they should follow all of the Germans' orders.

At the Pest Israelite headquarters at 12 Síp Street, they were greeted by SS officers, the Gestapo's infamous Jewish Division, accompanied by machine-gun carrying soldiers. The officers of the Eichmann Kommando issued the order to establish the Central Council of Hungarian Jews. The leaders of the congregation were to prepare reports on the structure, organizations, property, and associations of the Jewish religious community.[75] The SS informed them that the Gestapo alone was to be responsible for Jewish affairs; anyone who did not follow their orders would be executed. Reassuringly they added that if the Jewish population complied with their orders they would come to no harm. Although there would be certain restrictions, individuals and property would be safe and there would be no deportations. They emphasized that Jewish religious ceremonies should continue as usual. The council was to represent the Jewish community and receive and carry out all orders given them by the SS. As president they chose the seventy-year-old Samu Stern, a culturally assimilated Hungarian and long-time president of the Pest Israelite Religious Community, who had made a brilliant career in economic

---

74 For the first time in 1849 Buda and Pest were joined by the Széchenyi lánchíd (Széchenyi Chain Bridge] across the Danube, the first permanent bridge to connect the western and eastern sides of Budapest. In 1873 Budapest became a single city occupying both banks of the Danube, with unification of the right (west) bank, Buda and Óbuda, with the left (east) bank Pest.

75 J. Molnár, "The Foundation and Activities of the Hungarian Jewish Council, March 20–July 7, 1944." Shoah Resource Center. The International School for Holocaust Studies, Yad Vashem Studies, XXX, Jerusalem 2002, 2–3. http://wwwi.yadvas- hem.org/odot_pdf/Microsoft%20Word%20-%205417.pdf (accessed August 12, 2010).

life.⁷⁶ Eichmann met with the Jewish representatives on March 31 and repeated the assurances that Jews as such were not going to be harmed.⁷⁷

It was vitally important for the Germans that the Jewish communities throughout the country accept the Central Jewish Council as legitimate leader of the Jewish community, thus ensuring compliance with Nazi demands. On March 24 the chairmen of Jewish congregation districts throughout the country were invited to Budapest to attend a meeting to organize a national committee. The leaders, who had traveled on permits issued by the German authorities, resolved to establish a unified national organization under the leadership of the Jewish Council and adopted a foundation document in the first days of April. The founding of a national organization gave the impression of a longer-term operation; yet there is no document to prove that any council other than the Jewish Council actually functioned. Existing data mentions only the above-noted meeting of March 28. Even the Central Council did not hold regular sessions. Many of the meetings were held in the office of the chairman and often in the presence of others than the chief officials.⁷⁸

On April 6, the Jewish Council sent a circular letter to the provincial religious leaders in Hungary informing them of the establishment and powers of the council, and that by order of higher authorities Hungarian Jews were to be organized all over the country under the direction of the Jewish Council. The circular called on the provincial religious communities to organize and lead local Jewish councils. From documents recovered it appears that in some places local organizations were set up by the Jewish Council itself. In others, leaders representing the interests of the Jewish population were appointed by local administrative authorities, while in some places local Jewish councils were never organized.⁷⁹

---

76   Samu Stern memoirs, in Maria Schmidt, *Kollaboráció vagy kooperáció? A Budapesti Zsidó Tanács* [Collaboration or cooperation? The Budapest Jewish Council] (Budapest; Minerva, 1990), 57–59.
77   The council was to be faced with the most outrageous demands. Late one afternoon an SS officer barged into their office to demand that 300 mattresses and 600 blankets be delivered to the Royal Hotel in one and a half hours. When told that his request was completely impossible he shouted that in ten minutes it was possible to kill 10,000 Jews; therefore it would be possible to meet his demand in an hour and a half. "So we went to the hospitals, where the doctors and nurses pulled out the mattresses from under the patients and took their blankets." See Stern, 64.
78   J. Molnár, "The Hungarian Jewish Council," 6–7.
79   The provincial Jewish councils functioned for a few weeks or at most a couple of months (Ibid., 19).

On the same day as the circular was issued the readers of the Magyar *Zsidók Lapja* were informed that the Jewish Council had been established. The paper, heavily censored by the Germans, continued to call on the Jewish population to remain calm, be disciplined, and execute orders unconditionally. In the early weeks the Hungarian authorities effectively ignored the existence of the Jewish Council, which remained entirely under German command. It was not until April 19 that Minister of the Interior Jaross submitted a proposal that would establish a self-governing organization of Hungarian Jews—the already existing council—to be supervised by the Ministry of the Interior.[80]

Proclamation of Anti-Jewish Decrees

The first decrees to isolate the Jewish population were published at the end of March. Jews were instructed to wear the six-cornered star which was to be made to specific directions: ten by ten centimeters in size, of silk or velvet, in canary yellow, a color that was easy to see. The Jews were removed from their jobs and workshops, and their businesses were to be turned over to Christians. Jews were forbidden to travel, except on urgent business when they might get a special permit on payment of a fee. They were not allowed to use cars, taxis, trains, ships, or other vehicles except trams or omnibuses in towns. Jews also were not to use public baths, restaurants, or places of amusement. Radios, telephones, and cars, if they had them, were confiscated.[81] Tamás Gábor had just received a bicycle for his sixteenth birthday, and now he had to give it up. Up to this time, anti-Semitism had not affected him, but now students in his Lutheran secondary school began to taunt him.[82]

Jewish assets, estimated to make up 20 to 25 percent of the nation's wealth, were impounded. Ironically, this measure affecting the Jews was to be used by the communists a few years later to nationalize the wealth of all Hungarians. One result was that the Weiss-Manfréd Works, essential to the nation's war production, was sold to the Germans. Competition had begun

---

80 Ibid., 6–7, 14–15.
81 Gyuigyák, A zsidókérdés, 173–174; Fenyo, *Hitler, Horthy, and Hungary*,
82 Tamás Gábor, interview with the author, Santa Fe, October 31, 2001.

among the German political groups over the plundering of the country, with the Weiss-Manfréd complex a sought-after prize. The Hungarian government had agreed to a proposal that some factories be turned over to a Göring Works subsidiary, but through a startling move the SS was able to take over the works. The SS representative Kurt Becher carried out secret negotiations with Ferenc Chorin, the head of the Weiss family, after securing his release from an internment camp and threatening him, as well as his two brothers-in-law, Baron Móric Kornfeld and Baron Jenő Weiss, with a return to the camps if he did not sign. He succeeded in getting Chorin to sign an agreement essentially giving over the whole fortune into the hands of Himmler's SS in exchange for allowing the extended family to escape to Portugal with much of their portable wealth.[83]

Chorin, a member of Horthy's close circle, felt obliged to write a letter to the regent explaining the decision, although there was little to prevent German agents from taking over the Weiss-Manfréd complex without consulting the owners. Chorin commented that the regent had surely learned that he had been arrested, during which time, "unfortunately and surely under pressure, under the serene highness's aegis the Jewish question was regulated, and a whole series of illegal decrees were put through. These decrees blocked, but actually expropriated Jewish wealth and created a terrible precedent, the consequences of which we can already foretell."[84] Chorin took pains to emphasize that the family had not betrayed the country's interests, but—as he believed—he had ensured that the factory would remain in Hungarian hands. He concluded: "In saying farewell to your serene highness ... I especially thank you for the kind disposition which accompanied my activities in service to Hungarian industry throughout twenty years. And to me personally for which I am and will always be sincerely thankful."[85] The loss of the Weiss-Manfréd Works was such a dramatic blow to the independence of the country that even the rightist Imrédy protested against it. The SS ac-

---

83 Chorin was one of the most significant personages of Hungarian capitalism in the interwar period.
84 "Chorin Ferenc Levele Horthy Miklóshoz a Weiss Manfréd-konszernnek az SS-sel kötött szerződéséről" [Ferenc Chorin letter to Miklós Horthy on the Weiss Manfréckoncern and contract made with the SS] in *Horthy Miklós titkos iratai*, [Miklós Horthy secret papers] 1944. May 17, 441–442.
85 Ibid, 442–443.

tion alarmed Hungarian leading circles, and led Horthy a few days after the agreement was signed on May 22, 1944 to agree to name Imrédy minister of economics, although he had rejected the idea up to then. The hope was that because of his German connections Imrédy would be better able to protect Hungarian capital.

Establishment of Ghettos

The ghettoization of the Jews outside of Budapest began in mid-April in the larger towns and cities according to an order of the Hungarian Ministry of Interior. In the provinces, the Jewish population was to be collected in designated camps; in the cities and larger towns in designated Jewish houses or ghettos. According to these regulations, ghettos were to be established in all towns and cities with populations of more than 10,000. However decisions about which streets were to be used were left to local officials. In practice, county officials decided which towns and cities would have ghettos and to which of these ghettos smaller towns and villages would send their Jews. In Vas county, for example, it was in early May that the deputy prefect decided that seven ghettos were to be established in the county, one of them in the town of Körmend. The Jews from the town and surrounding villages were ordered to move into the planned ghetto area by May 12, and the chief administrative officer ordered the local Jewish council to erect a fence around the ghetto by May 20.[86]

In accord with Himmler's instructions, Eichmann divided Hungary into six geographical zones, starting in the east. The areas in northeastern Hungary were considered particularly critical; military commanders of the operational zones insisted that the Jews constituted an element of military insecurity and must be cleared out of those areas completely. The process took place by gendarme districts, beginning April 16 in Ruthenia and northeast Hungary, followed by northern Transylvania. Afterward, the process was to continue from east to west—Miskolc, Debrecen, Szeged, Pécs, Szombathely, Szé-

---

86   Tim Cole, "Building and Breaching the Ghetto Boundary: A Brief History of the Ghetto Fence in Körmend, Hungary 1944" *Holocaust and Genocide Studies* 23, no. 1 (Spring 2009): 54–56.

kesfehérvár, and finally Budapest. It appears that local Jews in the Bácska had already been rounded up and put in camps.[87]

The rounding up of Jews in northeastern Hungary was accompanied by extreme brutality. Usually they would be collected from the village by early dawn, taken to the local synagogue, and a few days later moved to a nearby city, to lumber yards, brick factories, tobacco sheds, or empty factory yards, often under the open sky with inhuman conditions. The Jews were often beaten, humiliated, and robbed of their valuables. The possessions left at home were either distributed by the army or simply carted off by the local population. In a letter smuggled out from a brickyard at Kassa/Kosice, one Jew wrote: "We lie in the dust, have neither straw mattresses nor covers, and will freeze to death.... We are so neglected, that we do not look human anymore."[88]

The brutality accompanying the collections and inhumanity of the conditions under which they were confined—when they first became known—brought forth protests from the Jewish Council and from official leaders and prominent individuals among all the Christian churches. The two officers placed in charge of the campaign, State Secretary László Endre in the Ministry of the Interior with special responsibility for Jewish affairs, and State Secretary László Baky, reported to Horthy that for reasons of national security the Jews were to be removed from possible combat zones since they were all procommunist. The two had been former officers under Horthy at Szeged and Horthy tended to trust them.[89]

In the meantime in early April, in a separate move, the German government requested a Jewish labor contingent of 100,000 men from the Hungarian government. Since Horthy had agreed to supply the Reich with Jewish labor at his meeting with Hitler at Klessheim, the Hungarian authorities saw no problem in granting the request. Sztójay promised 50,000 Jews by the end of April and another 50,000 in May. Hungarian military authorities informed Veesenmayer that 5,000 men could be made available immediately

---

87   Stark, *Zsidósága vészkorszakban*, 20; Fenyő, *Hitler, Horthy, and Hungary*, 183; Macartney, *October Fifteenth*, 2:281.
88   David S. Wyman, *The Abandonment of the Jews: America and the Holocaust, 1941–1945* (Mew York: The New Press, 2007), 236.
89   Sakmyster, *Admiral on Horseback*, 343–344.

and another 5,000 every three to four days until the quota was fulfilled; on April 14 he reported to his superiors that both the government and the regent had approved dispatch of more than 100,000 Jews to carry out forced labor in the *Reich*. According to Macartney the agreement to send the Jewish laborers, as well as the frightful conditions in the camps where Jews had been collected, provided Eichmann with the excuse to offer to transport the entire Jewish population to Auschwitz and other camps.[90]

Already on April 20, Baky received a report that the conditions in the large camps in northeastern Hungary were intolerable. The inmates could not be fed or housed and there was a danger of epidemics. Eichmann suggested that he would see that these Jews were transported to Auschwitz and other camps, although he insisted on receiving a request from the Hungarian government, a request that was submitted by Baky. On April 25, Veesenmayer cabled Berlin and Eichmann that beginning in mid-May it would be possible to transport 3,000 Jews daily from northeastern Hungary, and if transport allowed, from other ghettos as well to the final destination, Auschwitz.[91]

The process began on May 15, when the original inmates of the Kassa camp were entrained, and ended on July 9. Veesenmayer's notes, which appear to be the most accurate, report that from May 14 to June 7 – 289,357 Jews were deported from Ruthenia and northern Transylvania. The next stop was in northern Hungary, where from June 14–16, another 50,805 were taken, From June 25–28, 41,400 were taken from southeast Hungary. Veesenmayer's notes sent from the western parts of Hungary were abbreviated. The total number of deported was 437,402. Since the number of trains the Germans could provide was limited, the usual capacity per wagon, forty soldiers per wagon, was increased to seventy persons. Thus the operation could be completed in sixty days. The deportations themselves were carried out with sickening brutality—during summer heat, gross overcrowding, hardly any food or water, doors padlocked, and windows boarded.[92]

---

90   See Macartney, *October Fifteenth*, 2:279–282.
91   Fenyo, *Hitler, Horthy, and Hungary*, 186–187; Macartney, *October Fifteenth*, 2:281
92   Gyurgyák, *A zsidókérdés*, 180–181; Stark, *Zsidóság a vészkorszakban*, 21; Macartney, *October Fifteenth*, 2:286.

The Road to Occupation

In his testimony at the Nuremberg Trials, Veesenmayer said that if the Hungarians had refused to meet German demands the deportations would not have taken place, since the Germans did nót have a sufficient force available, but his statement was only partially true. Although some were enthusiastic in carrying out the deportations, like Baky and Endre, Hungary was under German occupation; the German shadow government was everywhere and supervised the measures against the Jews. Yet there seems no doubt that Horthy consented to the deportation of at least the Jews from the northeast and probably of all Jews outside Budapest, and that the majority of the population supported measures to remove the Jews. Even the churches hardly moved against the decrees.[93]

Why Did Jews Not Try to Resist?

The question has often been asked, why did the Jewish population not resist? Why were there relatively few attempts to escape? Jewish leaders in Hungary must have known that Jews had been or were being deported from countries occupied by Germany. Yet they were prepared to cooperate with the Germans. In fact the rounding up of Jews for deportation was carried out not by the German SS or even by the Hungarian gendarmerie but in much of the country by the local administration, with the cooperation of Jewish representatives who executed the orders they received.[94]

In recriminations against the Jewish Council after the war, the question was often asked why the members had accepted membership in the council—the charge being that they had done so to protect themselves, their own families and relatives, and to gain extra privileges. Samu Stern explained that with his connections it would have been quite possible for him to escape to the United States or elsewhere. However, he "considered that to be cowardly, unmanly, irresponsible conduct, a selfish flight and desertion." He believed that

---

93 Fenyo, *Hitler, Horthy, and Hungary*, 184; Macartney, *October Fifteenth*, 2:275–276.
94 The local Jewish council in Szeged told Jews "to immediately move into the designated apartments." The local Jewish council of Kecskemét sternly reminded the Jewish population that "neither sickness nor the Sabbath could be used as an excuse for failing to move into the ghetto." See Molnár, *Hungarian Jewish Council*, 21,26.

perhaps with his long experience of leadership he would be able to help. He also hoped that he might be able to win over the regent, whom he had known for twenty years, in the interest of saving the Jews. He added that the other assigned members of the council, who had also served the Jewish community for a long time, must have felt the same way.[95]

The Jewish leaders have been criticized for not informing the Jewish population earlier about what was transpiring in the neighboring countries and for advising them to keep calm after the occupation. Randolph L Braham claims that by not informing the Jewish masses before the German occupation Jewish leaders gave them a false sense of security. By telling the masses to remain calm after the occupation and to obey and execute orders, Braham holds the Jewish leadership, along with the Nazis and their Hungarian accomplices, responsible for the murder of over half a million Hungarian Jews. Yet, Judit Molnár points out that before the occupation there was plenty of information available to the population from various sources, including Jewish forced laborers home on leave; the numerous Jewish refugees from Austria, Poland, and Slovakia; as well as radio broadcasts from neutral and antifascist countries. After the occupation it was a question of how the council could have informed the Jewish population. The Magyar *Zsidók Lapja* was under tight military censorship, as were all forms of publication.[96]

Yehuda Bauer comments that those who addressed the question of whether the Jews knew what was in store from them sometimes seem to have "mistaken information for knowledge or understanding." Even when members of Zionist youth movements tried to warn local Jewish councils that they were going to be "deported to their deaths" they were not listened to. "Until the very last, Hungarian Jews chose to believe they were being transported to labor camps within Hungary."[97]

Those who heard of the horrors from the radio or from refugees simply could not—or refused to—believe the inconceivable. One survivor who had been deported from the city of Pécs wrote decades later, "I was unable to com-

---

[95] Samu Stern memoirs, in Maria Schmidt, *Kollaboráció vagy kooperáció?*, 60–62.
[96] Molnár, *Hungarian Jewish Council*, 10–11.
[97] Yehuda Bauer, *American Jewry and the Holocaust: the Amerian Jewish Joint Distribution Committee, 1939–1945* (Detroit: Wayne State University Press, 1981), 388–389.

prehend reality, it seemed too unreal to me." Later he added. "What curse was it that inflicted complete blindness upon us?"[98] During the 1961 Eichmann trial in Jerusalem one survivor commented: "If I had known what Auschwitz was, then no power on Earth would have forced me onto that train. But there was no power on Earth that would have made me believe that such a place as Auschwitz existed."[99]

As late as spring 1944, when they were locked up in ghettos and collecting camps, Jews still did not believe the young Zionists who traveled illegally to provinces trying to encourage people to escape. In many cases the identification papers they had smuggled into a particular ghetto were not used. Those who did not believe the warnings—a majority of the Jews—could not see the logic of breaking up a family in the hour of need. Some warned the youth not to spread panic and create confusion at a time when the reputable leadership of the entire Jewish community was announcing in the official press that no harm would come to anyone if they would only maintain law and order. They could not imagine that the Jewish press was being censored, with the contents at times dictated by Gestapo.[100]

In his history of the Jewish population of Csorna, a town in western Hungary, Endre Berecz comments on the lack of attempts at rescue among the Hungarian Jewish population. People simply could not imagine that in Hungary the things they had heard of could happen. As an exception he mentions one successful rescue, when the Weiner couple managed to escape from the Csorna ghetto with the help of Kálmán Dreisziger, the man whose near-miraculous escape at the time of the disaster at the Don is mentioned in Chapter 6. Records indicate that it was common practice for local non-Jewish inhabitants to request Jewish labor from the ghettos. In the town of Körmend, groups of Jewish men, women, and children were mobilized from the ghetto into makeshift labor units largely to satisfy local requests for labor.

---

98 Quoted in Molnár, *Hungarian Jewish Council*, 11.
99 Recollectons on the Holocaust—The world's most extensive testimonial site. http://www.degob.hu/english/index.php?showarticle = 2021 (accessed January 25, 2010).
100 Asher Cohen, *The Halutz Resistance in Hungary 1942–1944* (Social Science Monographs, Columbia University Press, 1986), 78; Randolph L. Braham, "Rescue Operations in Hungary: Myths and Realities," *East European Quarterly*, XXXVIII, no. 2 (June 2004): 179–180.

Children were taken out to carry out minor tasks such as rag collection, and women were often called on to do gardening or farm work.[101]

In Csorna as well the inhabitants were sometimes called on to perform labor for non-Jews. The Dreiszigers declared that they needed the help of Sándor and Kati Weiner for an evening. Kati Weiner was working in the fields for someone else, and Kálmán fetched her by bicycle, a trip of six kilometers, and brought her back to Csorna. There a truck came for the couple to take them to Budapest under cover of darkness. Afterward Dreisziger was severely criticized by the Jewish leaders for helping the Weiners escape.[102]

It was primarily women and children who were called on for local labor, since Jewish men between the ages of eighteen and forty-eight were being mobilized for service in labor companies. In a decree issued at the end of April 1944, Jewish labor battalion members on active service were explicitly exempted from the ghetto, illustrating a degree of conflict between the Hungarian army and the German security police. The army had ordered mass conscription despite the claim by the security police that according to the Ministry of Defense agreement Jews could not be called up in areas where the Jewish population was being rounded up. Those who were with the army's labor battalions escaped deportation to Auschwitz and thus had a greater chance of survival.[103]

The Jewish Council agonized over whether to refuse to carry out the Germans' command to notify those who were to report to detention barracks. They faced a moral dilemma, with no acceptable alternative. They knew they would be condemned for helping with the internment but decided that it was better that the people receive some notification, giving them the opportunity to flee, hide, or procure a medical excuse. At least they would have time to prepare belongings to take with them. "Thus we felt we had to accept, even if we would be criticized. The text we sent out stated that we sent the no-

---

101 In the last week of the ghetto's existence over one-sixth of the female population were leaving early each morning to do gardening, agricultural work, and leaf collecting. See Cole, "Breaching the Ghetto Boundary," 64.
102 Endre Berecz, „Emlékezés a csornai zsidóság történetére." [Memoir of the Csorna Jews history] http:///www.hontar.hu/hely/berecz.htm, 11; Personal communication with Nándor Dreisziger, son of Kálmán, December 4, 2006.
103 Cole, "Breaching the Ghetto Boundary," 62.

tice on the order of higher command, and that they should take their things with them. In this way everyone would know what it was about. They could choose whether to hide or report. There were many who got a doctor's certificate which they sent instead of reporting themselves, or went to a hospital—perhaps for a long-considered operation—and thus saved themselves. Or simply hid with false papers. But there were many more, sadly, who reported."[104]

Reaction of the Christian Churches

The German occupation had taken the leaders of the Christian churches as much by surprise as it had the ordinary citizen, and they were just as much at a loss as to what course of action to follow. At first the leaders of the Protestant churches decided on a policy of passive resistance, to avoid all contact with the puppet government and the occupiers, but this proved completely unrealistic because of the tremendous number of requests for assistance which forced them to intervene with the government and administration.[105]

The Jewish Council appealed to church leaders but they were slow to respond. In the first weeks the main efforts of the leaders—Prince Primate Cardinal Jusztinian Serédi for the Catholic Church, Bishop Ravasz, head of the Calvinist Synod and Convent, and Béla Kapi of the Lutherans—were to have their own converts exempted from the new regulations, for example, wearing the Star of David, and they met with some success. On April 3 Bishop Ravasz submitted his first protest in writing to the Sztójay administration, requesting that converts be spared from wearing the yellow star, and on April 6 the Lutheran and Calvinist Convent joined in the request.

On April 5 Prime Minister Sztójay informed Cardinal Serédi that priests, nuns, and lay church official converts would be exempted from the anti-Jewish measures. Converted Protestant civil functionaries, Presbyters (elders in the Presbyterian church) and their families were also exempted. But when the Prince Primate visited Sztójay on April 13 and 23, handing over a written memorandum stating the position of the Church against government viola-

---
104 Stern memoirs, 66–67.
105 Leslie László, *Church and State in Hungary 1919–1945*, published dissertation (Columbia University, Faculty of Political Science, 1973), 381.

tion of human rights and protesting the cruel treatment in the internments of Jews in the northeastern provinces Sztójay told him that the Church should concentrate its energies on the struggle against communism instead.[106]

Despite censorship news of atrocities began to reach the capital, but the prime minister and other ministers feigned ignorance or denied everything. On April 12, Bishop Ravasz rose from his sickbed to warn Horthy, who summoned Andor Jaross, minister of the interior and Nazi sympathizer, and told him to conduct an investigation. Jaross sent State Secretary Endre on an inspection tour with Eichmann. The ghetto Endre visited had atrocious conditions—not enough water or food, and the Jews were often beaten, humiliated, and robbed of their valuables. But the report Endre brought back was filled with outlandish lies—that the provincial ghettoes were like sanatoria—healthy life in open air. Horthy was able to convince himself the alleged atrocities were only the "usual gossip of cowardly Jewish sensation-mongers."[107]

Ravasz, who had never before intervened in such a direct way in government affairs, was so alarmed that he requested a second audience with the regent. At their meeting on April 28, he implored the regent to ensure that his name not be associated with atrocities against the Jews. Horthy, irritated by clerical meddling, explained that he had responded to the first reports by making a commotion and ordering an investigation, but he was now convinced that any scandalous treatment had ended. Those Jews who could not be in the military were pressed into labor service, and they would work as did several hundred thousand Hungarian workers in Germany. Their families would accompany them. Ravasz was shocked at how Horthy was being misled by his ministers and generals.[108]

From the end of March to early April desperate appeals came to Cardinal Serédi from those calling for the Church to raise its voice against the persecutions. Bishop Ravasz proposed a plan for a united action by all the

---

106 Jenő Gergely, „A magyarországi egyházak és a Holocaust" [Hungarian churches and the holocaust], in Braham and Pók, *The Holocaust in Hungary 50 years later* (New York: Columbia University Press, 1997), 446–47; László, *Church and State*, 382–383.
107 Gyurgyák, *A zsidókérdés*, 180; Stern memoirs, 70; Sakmyster, *Admiral on Horseback*, 344–345.
108 László, *Church and State*, 303–384; Sakmyster, *Admiral on Horseback*, 344–346. (The official position was the same. When Dr. Ernő Pető of the Jewish Council went to the Minister of Finance to protest, Reményi-Schneller told him that he had investigated and there were no deportations. See Stern, 70–71.)

The Road to Occupation

Christian churches, which would be more effective than single actions, but the cautious Cardinal Serédi rejected the plan for a joint proclamation. As the persecutions continued some members of the Catholics Bishops' Council became impatient, urging the Prince Primate to take stronger steps and publicly protest. They judged that further discussions with the government were futile and demanded that Cardinal Serédi publicly and openly denounce the government. The retired Count János Mikes, former Bishop of Szombathely, made a concrete proposal for a joint pastoral letter, and on April 12, 1944, Vilmos Apor, bishop of Győr, wrote to Serédi that it was necessary to take action, but the cardinal did not believe it expedient. According to Serédi's reasoning, such open condemnation—which the censorship then in effect would prevent from reaching the public—would also not alleviate the fate of the persecuted. He felt it would do nothing to help the persecuted Jews but would enrage Hitler and merely worsen their situation. This was the same consideration that prevented Pope Pius XII from publicly denouncing Hitler.[109] Serédi feared incurring the wrath of the Germans, and also counted on the knowledge that some in the government did not agree with the bestial measures.[110]

Serédi's reluctance can be partially explained by the anti-Semitism of the population. Anti-Church propaganda raised the perception that the Hungarian churches offered sanctuary to Jews, which angered many on the radical right. State Secretary László complained in a public speech that the pastors of all kinds and ranks of the Christian confessions were in first place in the saving of Jews. Even after the deportations ceased, the director of Catholic Action reported to Serédi that the mass baptism of Jews had resulted in waves of anti-priest and anti-Catholic agitation in Budapest.[111]

---

109 Perhaps Serédi's caution can be partly explained by his background. In 1927 he was chosen by the Papal seat to succeed the former Archbishop, partially as a reward for the years he had spent codifying the Corpus Juri Canonici. Serédi came from a simple background; his father had been an agrarian worker and he had never aimed for such a high post, but he was trusted implicitly by the Vatican who knew he would hold true to strict dogma and follow the will of the church faithfully. See György Barcza, *Diplomataemlékeim*, 1:217–226; Jenő Gergely, *A Katolikus egyház története Magyarországon*, 61–62.
110 Both Sztójay and Imrédy spoke up in the Council of Ministers against the cruelties. See Laszlo, Church and State, 384–386.
111 Paul A. Hanebrink, *In Defense of Christian Hungary: Religion, Nationalism, and Antisemitism, 1890–1944* (Ithaca, N.Y.: Cornell University Press, 2006), 203.

In a pastoral letter of May 17 to the bishops, Cardinal Serédi summarized the measures taken by the church on behalf of the converts and admitted the results achieved were meager, but explained the reason for keeping negotiations secret and not publicly opposing the grievous regulations. "We did not wish to furnish anybody with a pretext for launching, parallel to our official negotiations, attacks upon our Catholic brethren—- not yet affected by the regulations—and upon the rights and institutions of our Church, which might have resulted in the curtailing of its rights or the withdrawal of the concessions granted. We had neither abandoned nor betrayed the true cause or our Catholic brethren, but under the prevailing circumstances we could achieve no more."[112]

After the order for mass deportations on May 15, 1944, officials in the Vatican, speaking through the nunciate in Budapest, Angelo Rotta, began urging the Prince Primate to take a more vigorous stand. The day after the deportations began on May 18, the Bishop of Transylvania, Áron Márton, in a sermon in Kolozsvár stated bluntly that the church rejected differentiating between one human being and another. On May 27, Bishop Vilmos Apor, after witnessing the brutal cruelty with which the deportation of captives of the ghetto of Győr was carried out, appealed again to the Cardinal's conscience. He deplored his resolution not to publicize the violations of human rights and pleaded with the cardinal that as head of the Hungarian Catholic Church he issue a pastoral letter on the religious and moral implications of the situation, or give the bishops a free hand to inform and guide their parishioners.

Horthy's Reaction to the Deportations

Meanwhile in late May, Regent Horthy began to become aware of the reality of the atrocities taking place. He received a detailed memorandum from Ernő Pető, a longtime friend of the family, and other members of the Jewish Council, which gave a graphic account of the brutal deportations and warned that unless countermeasures were taken the entire Jewish community would

---

112 His letter was officially addressed to the bishops, but he asked them to convey the message to members of the church of Jewish descent, to inform them by word of mouth of his interest in their protection. See László, *Church and State*, 389–390.

be destroyed. Through the compelling personal stories and graphic detail—of Jews crammed into railroad cars with only one bucket of water to drink, the deportation of the sick, the aged, even of war heroes—Horthy was finally convinced that there was inhuman treatment, but he still did not grasp the purpose of the deportations. He was slow to move, fearing confrontation with the Germans. The Final Solution was beyond his imagination, as well as that of many others. At this time the true fate of European Jewry was not universally known. Although Jewish leaders passed warnings on to the Allies, the Department of State and the British Foreign Office, for various reasons suppressed this information.[113]

At some point, realizing that he was not actually a prisoner of the Germans, Horthy began to regain some of his old self-confidence and attempted to take action to stop the excessive brutality and inhuman treatment of the Jews. He wrote a letter to Sztójay in early June, saying that recently things had been brought to his attention of which he had not been aware, especially over brutal and inhuman treatment of Jews and measures taken interfering with the essential contributions of the Jewish population. He considered it necessary to carry out immediately measures to prevent the excesses of brutality and to provide exemptions to baptized Jews and those of special merit, especially engineers, leaders in the economy, and particularly doctors, whose services were needed in wartime. In order to stop any continuation of uncalled-for merciless and inhuman measures, direction of Jewish matters should be taken out of the hands of State Secretary László Endre, and State Secretary László Baky should be removed from his position. He asked Sztójay to see that his ministers take action on his memorandum without delay. Angry that Hitler had not answered his letter in which he reminded him of his promise to end the occupation after a satisfactory Hungarian government had been formed, he asked Sztójay to deliver a second letter on his trip to Berlin June 6.[114]

In the last week of June an unprecedented international campaign was launched on behalf of the Hungarian Jews after a copy of the Auschwitz Pro-

---

113 Sakmyster, *Admiral on Horseback*, 347–349; Fenyo, *Hitler, Horthy, and Hungary*, 187–188.
114 *Horthy Miklós titkos iratai*, 450–453.

tocols was smuggled into Switzerland. The Protocols contained the report by two prisoners, Rudolf Vrba and Alfred Wetzler, who had escaped from Auschwitz on April 7, 1944, and made contact with the Jewish Council in Slovakia fourteen days later when they wrote down their report. Their report for the first time gave a precise description of the geography of the camp and an account of the mass murders in the gas chambers in Auschwitz. They also reported on preparations being made in Auschwitz for the impending reception of the Hungarian Jews which had started as early as January 15, 1944. Slovak Jewish leaders sent the report to the Jewish Council in Hungary, as well as to other key people in Hungary including church leaders, although— for reasons still debated— they did not release the information to the Jewish community at large.[115]

It has been debated exactly when the Auschwitz Protocols reached Hungary and when they were passed on to key leaders. It appears that the German language document reached the Jewish Council in early June. In a letter to Tsvi Erez, dated March 30, 1974, from Fülöp Freudiger, a member of the Jewish Council, Freudiger writes that the Protocols were brought on the eighth or tenth of June by courier from the Hungarian mission in Bratislava. Yet they were not passed on to either Horthy's circle or to other diplomats until the second half of June. The reason for the delay is unclear except that Freudiger was having the nearly forty- page text translated by his assistants. Then, on June 19, the protocols were sent out of Hungary. Freudiger personally handed the protocols to the head of the Magyar Quartermasters Corps, and the general was shocked by the descriptions of the atrocities.[116] Sándor Török, the Christian member of the Jewish Council, mentioned in regard to the documents: "I visited various leading people with our documentary material, such as the highly important secret reports we had about the Auschwitz camp; most had the opinion that they were not true, merely 'Jewish exaggerations.'"[117]

---

115 The Nazis had changed previous procedures by building a new railway ramp which provided direct access to the gas chambers and crematoria, allowing for increasingly rapid and efficient mass murder of the hundreds of thousands of victims scheduled to be transported from Hungary. See Rudolf Vrba, "The preparations for the Holocaust in Hungary: an eyewitness account," in *The Nazis' Last Victims. The Holocaust in Hungary*, ed. Braham (Detroit: Wayne State University Press, 1999), 55–57.
116 Recollections on the Holocaust, 11–12; Tsvi Erez, "Hungary—Six Days in July 1944" *Holocaust and Genocide Studies* 3, no. 1 (1988): 50.
117 Quoted in Recollections on the Holocaust.

The Road to Occupation

According to Vrba, none of the 437,000 Hungarian Jews deported to Auschwitz between May 15 and July 9 were ever given the information from the protocols. Failure of the official Jewish representatives in Hungary to inform the Jewish population contributed to Eichmann's stunning success in so rapidly organizing the deportation of the majority of the Hungarian Jews. "It is my contention that this tragedy could have been greatly impeded if our warning had been effectively and swiftly communicated to the intended victims."[118]

When the news about Auschwitz was published in Switzerland, although in an abridged form, it led to an extensive newspaper campaign, which eventually caused an international chain reaction. It triggered a major grass roots protest in Switzerland with glaring headlines protesting against Europe's barbarism and its dark age in the twentieth century. Publication of the report also triggered Sunday sermons in Swiss churches expressing deep concern over the fate of Jews. In addition there were various street protests.

Perhaps to counter the effect the Germans prepared a German propaganda film, which was shown in various Western countries. The film demonstrated the brutal conduct of the Hungarian gendarmes, showing them beating women with their gunstocks, hounding children with blackjacks, packing people like cattle into the railroad cars—with nary a German in sight. Only after crossing the Hungarian border did the humane Germans appear, arriving with Red Cross nurses, bringing fresh water, food, and aid to the suffering. Through his son, Nicky, Horthy received a report of the film from the Swiss Hungarian Ministry, and even more damning, an article in a Swiss paper mocking the Hungarians who claimed to be "the chivalrous nation" yet were involved in such shameful acts that would remain a dark stain on the nation's honor forever. Horthy, who had always been fiercely proud of Hungary's reputation for honor and chivalry, was appalled.[119]

Then, on June 23, the Jewish Council through Nicky sent a memo to the regent warning that the Germans intended to deport the Jews of Budapest in the near future and imploring him to halt the deportations. Near the end of June he received a long memorandum from Bethlen condemning the "inhuman and

---
118 Vrba, "The preparations for the Holocaust in Hungary," 56.
119 Stern memoirs, 82.

stupid persecution of the Jews with which the present government stain the Hungarian name."[120] He urged the regent to get rid of the present cabinet, appoint a new government of nonpolitical experts, and sue for armistice. On June 25 a personal letter arrived from Pope Pius XII, asking Horthy for his personal intervention, although not mentioning the Jews by name. He received a message from President Roosevelt, with remonstrances in a threatening tone, and a personal cable from the King of Sweden, requesting him in the "name of humanity" to take all steps to rescue all who can yet be saved. As an additional blow Horthy discovered that in the meetings on June 21 and June 23 his cabinet had failed to carry out his directives to Sztójay. Through the letters, messages, and the cabinet's failure to follow his orders, he was stirred to action.[121]

On June 26, Horthy summoned a meeting of the Crown Council—the first such meeting to be held since the early days of the German occupation. He spoke of the deportations and that he had received messages from all the Protestant bishops, from the Pope, from the Swedish king and also Roosevelt, making him responsible for the fate of the Jews in Budapest. Eden, the British foreign minister had spoken in Parliament. Horthy denounced the two state secretaries in charge of the anti-Jewish campaign, László Baky and László Endre, as sadistic scoundrels, demanded their resignation again, and insisted that the Hungarian administration and gendarmes take no part in the deportations. If the Germans wanted it at all costs, they should do it themselves.[122]

Despite his directive to stop the deportation of the Jews of Budapest, freight trains crammed with Jews continued to depart from Szeged, Sopron, and other cities in southern and western Hungary in the last days of June and early July. As a concession, Baky and Endre were temporarily relieved of their duties, but this was only for the sake of appearances, and the date for the beginning of deportations from Budapest was postponed from June 30. Horthy was allowed to exempt a small number of favored Jews from the anti-Jewish laws. Veesenmayer believed these concessions would satisfy Horthy.[123]

---

120 „Bethlen István gróf emlékirata a Sztójay-Kormány leváltásának szükségességéről és a Végrehajtás" [Count István Bethlen's memorandum on the necessity of the replacement of the Sztójay government and its fulfillment] in *Horthy Miklós titkos iratai*, 457–466.
121 Cohen, *The Halutz Resistance*, 131; Sakmyster, *Admiral on Horseback*, 358–359.
122 Cohen, *The Halutz Resistance*, 131; Sakmyster, *Admiral on Horseback*, 351.
123 Sakmyster, *Admiral on Horseback*, 352.

The Road to Occupation

Following the Pope's letter to Horthy, the Papal nunciate in Budapest, Angelo Rotta, again urged Cardinal Serédi to act, recommending he take action publicly to protest the deportations in a pastoral letter from the pulpit. At the same time, on June 15, Bishop Ravasz, head of the Reformed Convent, again attempted to initiate an action by all the Christian churches, suggesting in a letter to Serédi that they meet personally and formulate a common standpoint. But the cardinal, who had been reluctant to take any public action, continued to reject a public denunciation of the deportations in unity with the Protestant churches. The Protestant leaders decided to go ahead on their own and act in unison. A memorandum, formulated by Bishop Ravasz and signed by nine Bishops, was handed over to Prime Minister Sztójay on June 23; the protest received no answer.[124]

In late June, under pressure from his own bishops as well as the Papal Nuncio, the cardinal began to draft a pastoral letter to the faithful to be read in parishes throughout Hungary, although his assistant, Archbishop Gyula Czapik of Eger, reminded him of the popular reaction that any statement on behalf of the Hungarian Jews would arouse. The church had been virtually accused of treason by the radical right, even for insisting on certain minimal exemptions for its converts. Czapik suggested that the text give "as little unnecessary pretext as possible to the expected anti-Church attacks..."[125] The letter also reflected the Primate's ambiguity. Serédi declared that the Church deplored the new anti-Jewish measures as an affront to divine law, but still made accusations that some Hungarian Jews were guilty of a harmful influence in the economic, social, and moral life of the nation, and there was no doubt that the Jewish question must be regulated by law.[126]

The pastoral letter, dated June 29, was brought to the attention of István Antal, minister of justice, religious affairs and education, who promptly stopped its distribution, although some archdioceses did receive the letter and it was reportedly read out in some churches. Prime Minister Sztójay, accompanied by Antal and Imrédy, met with the cardinal, who was by this time seriously ill, and warned him of an Arrow Cross coup if the legitimacy of the government

---

124 Gergely, „A 'Magyarországi egyházak," 448–449? Hanebrink, *In Defense of Christian Hungary,* 208.
125 Hanebrink, *In Defense of Christian Hungary,* 209.
126 Gergely, „A magyarországi egyházak," 448–449; Hanebrink, *In Defense of Christian Hungary,* 209.

should be undermined. The government promised to investigate the atrocities, punish those involved, and stop the deportations. After negotiations, an agreement was finally reached by which the pastoral letter would be retracted if the Hungarian government would not permit further deportations.

The Hungarian-American historian, István Deák remarked: "The tragedy is that the Prince Primate kept discreetly protesting the atrocities in the ghettoes at a time when hundreds of thousands were already on their way to the gas chambers. One cannot help feeling that timely protestations in public... would have slowed down the deportation process. They would not have stopped Eichmann but they would have thrown confusion in the ranks of the allegedly Christian gendarmes and civil servants without whose assistance the deportations were impossible. The Prince primate's pastoral letter of June 29 came far too late."[127]

A pastoral letter of protest by Bishop Ravasz in the name of the Reformed Church was sent out on the last Sunday of June to be read July 9. 'There was no mention of Jewish individual or collective guilt or of the necessity of solving the Jewish question. On the suggestion of other bishops, the letter mentioned that the Jews had not been guilty—as had been charged—for the start of Allied bombing. But under similar circumstances this letter was also not read. On July 16 leaders from both churches told their congregations that they had taken steps on behalf of the Jews—especially the converted.[128] By this time the deportations had been halted through actions by Horthy. The prime minister declared that the deportations had been stopped at the request of the church.[129]

The question of when Horthy knew of the actual fate awaiting the Jewish deportees is still debated.[130] After the occupation Horthy spoke of him-

---

127 Cited in László, *Church and State*, 392.
128 Gergely, „A magyarországi egyházak," 449–450; Hanebrink, *In Defense of Christian Hungary*, 209.
129 László, *Church and State*, 404.
130 According to Randolph L. Braham, already at the time of his meeting with Hitler at Klessheim in March 1944, Horthy—as well as the top governmental and political leaders of Hungary—was well informed about the realities of Auschwitz. Later, he asserts, "The evidence is overwhelming that Horthy, like the other top leaders of Hungary, was fully informed about the barbaric treatment of the Jews, including their isolation, marking, expropriation, ghettoization, concentration, and deportation. See "Rescue Operations in Hungary: Myths and Realities," *East European Quarterly* XXXVIII, no. 2 (June 2004): 178–180.

self as a prisoner of the Germans, and removed himself from the actions taken by the government. By having the cabinet pass decrees rather than laws Horthy did not need to countersign the decrees, thus—to his thinking—absolving himself from responsibility. In his letter to Sztójay he acknowledged that he was out of touch with recent measures taken. Various dates have been given for the time when Sándor Török, a well-known writer and member of the Jewish Council, delivered a copy of the Auschwitz Protocols to the regent's daughter-in-law, Ilona, who then took it to Horthy's wife, Magda. Mme. Horthy then showed the report to Horthy which convinced him the reports were not mere exaggeration.[131]

Ilona Horthy, in her memoirs published in 2000, tells of receiving the Auschwitz Protocols from Török on July 3 and taking them to Horthy. Commenting on the dispute about "when Horthy knew," she points out, "I am the only one with a record of when the Hungarian translation of the Protocols were brought to Horthy,"[132] since she had recorded the date in her diary, while other accounts relied on memory. She recorded that on July 3, after she had completed her nursing duties, Török came up to her apartment in the castle and gave her the Auschwitz Protocols, which she read in his presence, and—confessing that she was utterly shocked— took them down to her mother-in-law, Magda Horthy, since Horthy was busy in his study. Ilona recalled: "I gave the protocol to her without saying anything, I only asked that she read it immediately. In tears, Magda-mama read it to the end, and promised that she would give it to Miklóspapa when he came out of his study. ... I wasn't there when my father-in-law read them. But Magda said afterwards how deeply he was affected—that such horrible things couldn't be true. He said then that the deportations must be stopped."[133] Three days later, on July 6, the Hungarian government stopped the Jewish deportations. Prime Minister Sztójay informed the Germans, who accepted the decision only because their military situation was so perilous.[134]

---

131 Thomas Sakmyster gives the date as June 19 or 20; his source is Tsvi Erez, "Hungary. Six Days in July, 1944," (Kibbutz Dvir, Israel) published in 1988.
132 Ilona Gyulai, *Becsület és kötelesség*, 263.
133 Ibid., 264.
134 For Hungarian historians the main debate regarding the Holocaust is still the question of who was responsible and to what extent—the Germans or the Hungarian government, Horthy, Hungarian society? Personal communication to the author from historian Tamás Stark, November 25, 2009.

If Horthy had attempted to intervene earlier, it is quite possible that he would have been removed or silenced, but by the end of June the general military situation for the Germans was desperate. The Normandy landings of the Western Allies had begun on June 6 and by the end of the month it was obvious that they could not be thrown back into the sea, despite the reinforcements Hitler sent to the new front, troops he could hardly afford to send. Much worse was the situation on the eastern front. On June 22, the Soviets had started Operation Bagration in which 166 Soviet divisions launched an all-out attack on the 3,200-kilometer front. The Soviets had not only numerical superiority—166 divisions versus some 30-odd German ones—but had superiority in heavy armor, artillery, even air power. Within ten days they inflicted enormous losses on the Germans. One historian calls the Red Army's success in destroying the German Army Group Center the "most spectacular single military success of the war."[135] For the Germans it was a catastrophe greater than that of Stalingrad or Kursk. The three German armies lost more than 196,000 men—over 130,000 were killed and 66,000 were taken as prisoners of war.

László Baky's Coup Attempt

In early July the regent learned of a plan by László Baky to carry out the rapid liquidation of the Jews of Budapest through a government coup, using the gendarme brigades which had served in his anti-Jewish operations. By early July several thousand gendarmes armed with bayonets were patrolling the streets of the capital in groups of two and three, breaking with the very strict division maintained between the police who served in the cities, and the gendarmerie, which was in charge of the countryside. Gendarmes were not supposed to be in the city except when they were off duty, and certainly not when armed.[136] An attempt by Baky to assassinate Horthy's friend, István Bárczy, state secretary and keeper of the minutes, on June 29 galvanized the regent to action.

---

135 M. K, Dziewanowski, *War at Any Price: World War II in Europe, 1939–1945* (Upper Saddle River, N.J.: Prentice Hall, 1991), 309.
136 Péter Bokor, „Az elvetélt csendőrpuccs ismeretlen története" [The unknown history of the aborted gendarme putsch], *Magyar Hírlap,* July 5, 1993. The excuse for their being in Budapest was the gendarme training school in Buda, thus circumventing the legal issue.

The Road to Occupation

Acting quickly, with uncharacteristic boldness and discretion, Horthy bypassed his Chief of Staff Vörös, and authorized Lt. Gen. Károly Lázár, the commander of his personal bodyguard, to assume military command in Budapest and take measures to prevent both the coup d'état and deportation of the Jews.[137] Concerned that there was not an armed force on hand, Lázár happened to meet his friend, Colonel Ferenc Koszorús, on the banks of the Danube on July 2. Through a trick of fate the Germans did not know of Koszorús' First Armored Division, which was stationed north of Budapest. When the remnants of the First Armored Division returned from the Don in March 1943/ they were not divided up among other units but dispersed to prevent the Germans from sending the army to the front. Since they were not placed within the order of battle the Germans did not know of their existence. On hearing of Baky's plan and the danger involved since the regent lacked an armed force, Koszorús asked Lázár: "... to tell the regent that if I received the command I would get rid of the gendarme units with force!"[138]

On July 5 around 11 p.m. Koszorús received the order from the regent to remove the gendarmerie from the capital—that Baky was planning the putsch for July 6. Koszorús had determined that the Germans had only three police battalions in the capital, motorized with excellent weapons, but Koszorús commanded a larger force: "On July 6 at 7 a.m. I sent an officers' patrol to László Baky.... I ordered that within twenty-four hours the gendarme units should evacuate Budapest, otherwise I would carry out the evacuation by force."[139]

Although a crisis atmosphere prevailed in the capital on July 7 and 8, with rumors of an imminent entry of German military units, by late July 7 the gamble was succeeding. Vörös had warned Horthy that the Germans would never stand for a unilateral action to stop the deportations, but General Faragho, the gendarmerie commander, was unwilling to disobey a direct command from the regent, and Sztójay felt compelled to carry out Horthy's orders. The Ger-

---

137 Sakmyster, *Admiral on Horseback*, 352.
138 Ferenc Koszorús, volt M.Kir.Vk.Ezredes—Az 1. Páncélos hadosztály parancsnokának. *Emlékiratai és tanulmányainak gyűteménye* [Ferenc Koszorús, former Hungarian Royal Staff Colonel, commander of the First Armored Division. Memoirs and collected papers], ed. Mrs. István Varsa. (Universe Publishing Company, 1987), 56–58.
139 Quoted in Bokor, „Az elvetélt csendorpuccs," 9.

mans, caught off guard, were not prepared to risk a direct confrontation. On July 7 at 9 A.M., Baky informed Koszorús that the gendarmes would evacuate within 24 hours. The gendarmes began an orderly withdrawal and Baky and Endre were relieved of their duties. According to an account by Endre, there were 170,000 Jews registered in Budapest and at least another 130,000 hiding with false papers, who were saved for the time being.[140]

Veesenmayer, who was often successful in persuading or threatening the regent, was convinced that he could resume the deportations later, but Eichmann was more alarmed; "In all my long practice this is the first time such a thing has happened to me; this won't do at all. It is contrary to all agreements."[141] It was the first time that a leader had succeeded in halting deportations of Jews through the threat of military force. Eichmann moved quickly to test the regent; with the cooperation of Andor Jaross he organized a rapid action to deport a group of 1,500 Jews held in a camp on the outskirts of Budapest, but Horthy, alerted by the Jewish Council, dispatched troops in time to intercept the train and return the transport safely back to camp. By subterfuge Eichmann succeeded in a second maneuver. While holding the members of the Jewish Council incommunicado in an all-day conference, Eichmann kidnapped the 1,500 Jews with an SS detachment and spirited them out of the country.[142]

There is ongoing debate about the numbers of Jews who were deported from Hungary, the number killed at Auschwitz, and the total number of survivors. István Deák comments: "Let me note here that statistical data on such things as the number of Second Army soldiers and forced laborers, ... or the number of Hungarian Jews gassed at Auschwitz, or the total number of wartime Jewish dead, are not much better than guesses. There exists no reliable information on these subjects."[143] According to Tamás Stark, who has ex-

---

140 Bokor, „Az elvetélt csenddrpuccs," 9; Sakmyster, *Admiral on Horseback,* 352–353.
141 Quoted in Sakmyster, *Admiral on Horseback,* 354. According to Randolph L. Braham one can only give Horthy credit for saving most of the Budapest Jews if one assigns him a significant share of blame for the deportations. See Braham, "Rescue Operations in Hungary," 179.
142 Stern Memoir, 86.
143 István Deák, "A Fatal Compromise? The Debate over Collaboration and Resistance in Hungary," in *The Politics of Retribution in Europe: World War II and Its Aftemath,* ed. István Deák, Jan T. Gross, and Tony Judt (Princeton, N.J.: Princeton University Press, 2000), 72, n. 22.

tensively analyzed statistics concerning Hungarian Jews, what is generally agreed is that 437,000 Jews were deported from Hungary in the summer of 1944; most of them were sent to Auschwitz. Those who were not fit for work were killed. In the fall of 1944, another estimated fifty thousand Jews were force-marched to the Austro-Hungarian border for fortification work, and many didn't survive the experience. The greater part of Jews in Budapest survived and tens of thousands of Jews in labor battalions also survived the persecution.[144]

Horthy Regains The Initiative

After his success in preventing the putsch and deportations, Horthy began to realize that he did have some room to maneuver and considered the appointment of a new government. In times past he had considered the possibility of appointing a government of military officers loyal to him, and once he had told Barcza in conversation that if ever he could not find a suitable prime minister he would just name a military government.[145] Yet still hesitant, he delayed his decision a number of times.

At the end of May, Horthy had told General Lakatos that he planned to name him prime minister sometime soon.[146] Now, incensed at how the treatment of the Jews had endangered the Hungarian reputation, he called Lakatos to his residence on July 7, telling him that he intended to force the Sztójay government to resign and appoint an apolitical government. Lakatos asked for twenty-four hours to consider the situation, and in a meeting with Bethlen, who was often smuggled into the castle to advise the regent, Lakatos referred to his complete lack of experience in domestic politics. Bethlen, who had recommended him to the regent, said that was exactly why he was suit-

---

144 Tamás Stark, personal communication to the author, February 5, 2010. Stark deals with the subject in his book, *Zsidóság a vészkorszakban és a felszabadulás után 1939–1955,* as well as in the English version, *Hungarian Jews During the Holocaust and After the Second World War, 1939–1949: A Statistical Review* (Boulder, Colo.: East-European Monographs, 2000).
145 Barcza, *Diplomataemlékeim,* 1:208.
146 In April of 1944 he had wanted to appoint Lakatos chief of staff, but had been pressured by Veesenmayer to appoint Lt. Gen. János Vörös, a careerist, who was appointed over many older and higher ranked officers. Since there was no position open for someone with Lakatos's rank and experience he retired to his wife's estate to wait for the regent's command.

able. Lakatos, hesitant whether the Germans would tolerate the change of government, conferred with Vörös, who emphasized that the Germans were still strong enough to resist. It was decided to wait.[147]

About two weeks later, Horthy again attempted to replace the Sztójay government, calling Lakatos to Budapest and demanding the resignation of Sztójay, but he was foiled by Veesenmayer and his own military officers. He felt it necessary to inform Veesenmayer, who said he must first notify Hitler. Veesenmayer immediately telephoned Ribbentrop and the next day, July 17, he called on Horthy to deliver Ribbentrop's message from Hitler. Hitler had reacted with extreme displeasure to the intention to replace Sztójay, which he regarded as nothing less than treason, and warned that any departure from the ways decided at Klessheim might jeopardize the very existence of the Hungarian nation. In his telegram to Ribbentrop, Veesenmayer wrote; "After the conclusion of this conversation Horthy was completely finished, his whole body trembled, and he was an old broken man."[148]

But evidently Horthy quickly pulled himself together. On July 17 he called in his generals, Csatay and Vörös, and without mentioning the conversation with Veesenmayer, asked, "what would happen if we were to undertake armed resistance against the Germans here?"[149] Vörös answered that it would mean the end of Hungary's national existence; thus the decision to replace the Sztójay government was again postponed. Afterward Vörös briefed his officers staff at headquarters, and they unanimously agreed that Hungary must avoid fighting against the Germans, and restore smooth relations with them at the earliest opportunity, a reaction that was to resonate during the armistice attempt on October 15.[150]

The effects of Horthy's new stance soon began to be felt. In summer the situation of the Jews was alleviated in many ways. Through negotiations opened up by the Red Cross with various neutral countries a few thousand

---

147 When asked why the regent had chosen him, Lakatos supposed that it was partially because of his pure Hungarian origins, but also that during his one year command on the battle field he had gone against the German command, once ordering the weakly armed Seventh Army Corps out of the zone where the Germans wanted to place them against Russian regular troops. See Lakatos testimony at trial of Szálasi, 1946, February 19, in Lakatos, *Ahogyan én láttam*, 361.
148 Quoted in Fenyo, *Hitler, Horthy, and Hungary,* 209.
149 Ibid., 210.
150 Ibid., 210.

The Road to Occupation

Jews, mainly children, were allowed to leave for Palestine, Sweden, or Switzerland, and hundreds of Jews bought their way out through complex financial negotiations with Himmler's men in Germany.[151] On July 18 Horthy made an offer through the International Red Cross to the United States and Britain to permit the emigration of Jewish children under ten with visas to other countries and of all Jews who had Palestine certificates. The overture put pressure on the United States and Britain, and within ten days the War Refugee Board in the United States assured that it would find havens for all the Jews released, but not wanting to act alone, informed the British that it would wait until August 7 for them to join in accepting the offer. The British stalled, alarmed at the pressure Horthy's proposal would place on their Palestine policy but unwilling to be the ones to reject the offer. It wasn't until August 17 that the two governments publicly issued a statement accepting the responsibility for finding havens for all the Jews allowed out, but they had delayed too long. While they were negotiating the Nazis who controlled the borders made it clear that they would bar any Jewish emigration.[152]

During the summer the Allied air raids were remorseless, devastating cities and disrupting communications. The stream of refugees fleeing before the Red Army began to swell, and public security was deteriorating rapidly. In Budapest itself the police were authorized to use firearms against anyone who refused to halt when challenged. Growing discontent among the workers became evident with the increase of resistance in the war industries, the reduced output of the harvest, and workers more openly agitating against the system. At the end of summer, bathing in the unusual heat, the majority of the Hungarian population waited in helpless passivity, expecting the country soon to become a battleground.

---

151 Macartney, *October Fifteenth*, 2:309.
152 Wyman, *The Ambandonment of the Jews*, 238–240.

Chapter 5
The Holocaust in Hungary*
István Deák

The Final Solution of the Jewish Question, as the Nazis called their genocidal programme, evoked widespread collaboration. With the admirable exception of Denmark and Finland, all the governments, national administrations and local authorities in Hitler's Europe participated in the execution of the Nazi programme. There was, however, a fundamental difference between the Nazi leadership, which aimed at a truly "final" solution, and the collaborationists, who were satisfied with partial extermination, trying to distinguish between "our Jews," and "their Jews," "good Jews" and "bad Jews," the wealthy and the poor, the assimilated and the non-assimilated. In other words, according to German Nazi standards, the collaborationist leaders of Italy, France, the Netherlands, Belgium, Norway, the Baltic countries, Hungary, Romania, Bulgaria[1], Slovakia, Serbia and Greece lacked the necessary dedication and toughness. But then what else to expect from people who were, after all, not Germans?

The extent to which other Europeans assisted or sabotaged German intentions depended on such factors as the number, the proportion and the relative wealth of the Jewish population; the domestic tradition of anti-Semitism; the strength of the local fascistic parties; and the diligence and reliability of the bureaucratic machinery. Nor was it immaterial whether the country was an ally of Germany or had been conquered during the war. Finally, there was the

---

* Reproduced from the *The Hungarian Quarterly* 2004 Winter, Vol 45. 50–70. No. 176. (With the permission of *The Hungarian Quarterly*).
1 Please note that whereas the Bulgarian government refused to surrender its 50,000 odd Jews to the Nazi death machine, it readily deported to Treblinka in Poland the 11,000 odd Jews who lived in Macedonia and Thrace, territories in Yugoslavia and Greece, respectively, which the Bulgarians administered during the war. Almost none of the deportees survived the war. For an illuminating analysis of this subject, see Tzvetan Todorov, *The Fragility of Goodness: Why Bulgaria's Jews Survived the Holocaust* (Princeton, N.J.: Princeton University Press, 1999).

crucial question of the apparent chances of a final German military victory when the time came for the Final Solution. The Netherlands, for instance, had scarcely any anti-Semitic tradition; its Nazi parties remained weak even under German occupation and most of the Dutch loathed the German occupiers; still, the Netherlands allowed nearly all of its Jewish citizens to be deported to the East. This was, in part, because the German army occupied the Netherlands as early as 1940, when final German victory seemed inevitable, and, in part, because the country's queen and government had fled to London, so that there was no central authority to negotiate the terms of collaboration with the Germans. No less significantly, the Dutch bureaucrats were zealous enough in the performance of their duties to make deportation a success; for example, they issued identity cards that were virtually impossible to forge. In Romania, on the other hand, hatred and contempt for the Jews had long permeated every stratum of society and, as early as 1941, Field Marshal Ion Antonescu's pro-Nazi government, the army, and the gendarmes perpetrated their own Holocaust in Bessarabia as well as in southern Bukovina and such regions of the Ukraine that the Romanian army occupied during the war. Moreover, a huge Romanian army fought on the side of Germany in the anti-Bolshevik campaign. But Romania had a king and a strong central government enabling it to determine when and to what degree it would participate in the Final Solution. Thus when it seemed to Antonescu and his colleagues that Germany might not, after all, win the war, they made sure that the lives of Romania's remaining Jews would be spared. The situation for the Jews was also considerably alleviated by the corruption and sloth that characterised the country's bureaucracy. Thus it came about that non-anti-Semitic Netherlands lost a much higher proportion, over seventy per cent, of its Jews than anti-Semitic Romania which protected the lives of over half of its Jews.[2]

How did Hungary fit into this complex picture? To this there is no easy answer because of the extremes of Hungarian governmental policy at the

---

2   The Holocaust in general, as well as in its specific aspects, boasts an enormous literature, yet information on individual countries is still hard to find, especially in English. For events in the Netherlands, see Jacob Presser, *The Destruction of the Dutch Jews* (New York: Dutton, 1969), and on Romania, Radu Ioanid, *The Holocaust in Romania: Destruction of Jews and Gypsies Under the Antonescu Regime* (Ivan R. Dee, 2000).

time, varying between decency and evil, relatively mild and murderous anti-Semitism, pro-Nazi and anti-German behaviour. And what applies to the government, applies also to a great many of the country's inhabitants, although, as it happened in all countries, the vast majority of the population just stood by. From a Jewish point of view, what counts is that on March 19, 1944, the day the German army occupied Hungary, that is, at a time when millions of Polish and other Jews had long been shot or gassed, there were still approximately 760,000 such persons in Hungary whom the law regarded as of the Jewish race. These people lived in their own homes, went to work daily, wore no discriminatory marks, and were free to move around in the country. Three months later, however, at least half of them were dead, in part because of the actions of the German occupation forces, but to an even greater part because of the actions of the same Hungarian authorities that, until March of that year, had protected the country's Jewish population.³ Altogether about two-thirds of such Jews died who lived within Hungary's 1944 boundaries, but while we must assign responsibility for their death mainly to the government and people of Hungary, we must also credit the government and the people for the survival of the remaining one-third. The fact is that the two to three hundred thousand survivors were not simply those who would have been killed, had there been time to do so, but were mostly persons whom government officials, army officers, clergymen and nuns as well as scores of individual Gentiles had saved at some risk to their own lives. Thus the balance sheet is mixed, which explains why some Jewish survivors would not hear of

---

3   By far the most important general work on the Hungarian Holocaust, in any language, is Randolph L. Braham, *The Politics of Genocide: The Holocaust in Hungary*, 2 volumes (Third Revised and Enlarged edition; New York: Columbia University Press, 2016). Professor Braham is the author of a dozens other books on the destruction of Hungarian and, specifically, Transylvanian Jews. For other works on the Hungarian Genocide, see T.D, Kramer, *From Emancipation to Catastrophe: The Rise and Holocaust of Hungarian Jewry* (Lanham, Md.: University Press of America, 2000, and Vera Ránki, *The Politics of Inclusion and Exclusion: Jews and Nationalism in Hungary* (New York: Holmes and Meier, 1999). Please note that statistical data on Jewish losses are always approximations for such reasons as, for instance, that at least ten per cent of those of the "Jewish race" were Christians by religious affiliation and therefore did not figure in the statistics on the Jewish population. Furthermore, more than one third of the Jews lived in lands that belonged to Hungary only during the war; therefore, survivors from those lands may or may not figure in the postwar Hungarian statistics. In addition, many Jews did not report their survival after the war or simply remained abroad, meaning that official statistics could not account for them. Finally, the postwar regime deliberately and rightly ignored religious affiliation in its statistics.

paying a visit to their former homeland, while others have re-affirmed their patriotism, and why Western historiography, in general, does not know how to deal with Hungary's wartime behaviour.

The Age of Hope

Where did it all begin? Historians agree that the unfolding of the intensive Hungarian–Jewish relationship must be sought in early nineteenth century history. Jews had long been living in what is today's Hungary when the conquering Magyar tribes arrived from the east in the ninth century, but originally theirs was a traditionalist and isolated existence. When persecution did occur, it was generally milder than in medieval and early modern Western Europe. The story becomes more exciting, and more complex, with the step-by-step integration of Jews into Hungarian society that began late in the eighteenth century as an integral part of a nation-wide drive for modernisation. Because the landowning nobility that, until the mid-nineteenth century, counted as the embodiment of the nation, was loath to engage in commerce and industry, it needed the services of the Jews. Also, once the ideas of nation and nationality took root, the same nobility became painfully aware that the Hungarian-speakers formed a minority in the country. All the more reason for them to foster the acceptance of the Jews who combined their economic usefulness with a willingness to become patriots and to exchange their German or Yiddish speech for Hungarian.

Understandably, the story was not simple, and one meets with as many signs of anti-Semitism among the reforming nobility as one meets with signs of reluctance on the part of Jews to give up their ancient way of life. Still, one can state with confidence that, in nineteenth century Europe, no country was more hospitable to Jewish immigration and assimilation, and no country won more enthusiastic support from its Jews than the Hungarian kingdom. One might say even that there existed, at least since the liberal, nationalist revolutions of 1848–1849, a tacit agreement between the ruling gentry and the enlightened, educated and patriotic segment of Jewry for a division of labour in modernising Hungary. The Jews would contribute the investment capital, supplied by some great Western banking houses, and their own business acumen, dynamism and diligence. The non-Jewish political elite would provide the legislative and administrative assistance necessary for economic expansion.[4] The resulting success of Jews was dazzling. Although they constituted less than five per cent of the pre-First World War population, Jews created, owned and managed the majority of Hungarian heavy industry and mining, and nearly every one of the great banks. They were hardly less successful in commerce, small entrepreneurship, crafts, the liberal professions and all aspects of culture and the arts. By the beginning of the twentieth century, they had also appeared in state service, the judiciary, the officer corps and large landownership. Assimilation for the Jewish elite increasingly took the form of intermarriage.

Hungarian Jews were, as a whole, very patriotic; they supported both the Emperor-King Francis Joseph and the governing conservative-liberal parties in Hungary. Of course, not all Christian inhabitants of the country were happy with these developments; those who did not profit from the economic boom, or profited less than the others, for instance members of the ethnic minorities, impoverished gentry, the clergy, small shopkeepers, artisans, peasants, etc. tended to blame the Jews for their misfortune. In 1882–1883, there was a wave of wild anti-Semitic outbursts in connection with the so-called Tiszaeszlár blood libel trial, but the government and the dominant liberal press firmly rejected what they considered a return to medieval obscurantism.[5] The anti-Semitic political party that was set up at that time disappeared from the scene within a few years. Meanwhile, the Jewish elite would not even consider creating a separate Jewish political organization. Although Theodor Herzl was born in Budapest, his calls for a Jewish state met with categorical rejection among Hungarian Jewish leaders and in the press. For educated Jews, Judaism was but a religious denomination; therefore, Zionist nationalism amounted to treason. Few people paid attention to Herzl's warning, in 1903, to a Hungarian Jewish politician:

---

4 The best history of Hungarian Jews in English is Raphael Patai, *The Jews of Hungary: History, Culture and Psychology* (Detroit: Wayne State University Press, 1996).
5 See Andrew Handler, *Blood Libel at Tiszaeszlár* (East European Monographs; Distributed by Columbia University Press, 1980).

The hand of fate shall also seize Hungarian Jewry. And the later this occurs, and the stronger this Jewry becomes, the more cruel and hard shall be the blow, which shall be delivered with greater savagery. There is no escape.[6]

If Zionism made no inroads in Hungarian Jewish life, political radicalism and socialist ideology did, mostly among the sons and daughters of assimilated and successful bourgeois, who turned with messianic zeal against the Hungarian ruling elite, which they identified with both retrograde feudalism and oppressive capitalism.[7] Truly, for a young intellectual imbued with the ideas of Marx, Nietzsche and Kautsky, it must have been hard to stomach such a surreal spectacle as the celebration of the 1000th anniversary of Hungary at the new and beautiful Dohány Street synagogue in Budapest. Here is the scene as described in a Neolog Jewish newspaper.

> In front of the temple, which was decorated with flags, there stood... an entire barricade of coaches that had brought the ladies and the gentlemen in white tie. In some of the more decorative private coaches arrived [Jewish] co-religionaries sporting splendid Hungarian national gala costumes, complete with sword, clasps, egret feathers [on their high fur hats], cocky, with pelisses thrown on one shoulder, frogs and loops laden with jewels, as well as gold or silver spurs attached to long and dashing cordovan boots... The most dazzling Hungarian national gala costumes were worn by Berthold Weiss, Sándor Deutsch de Hatvan and Lajos Krausz de Megyer.[8]

---

6   Theodor Herzl to Ernő Mezei, who was a member of the Hungarian parliament, on March 10, 1903. Quoted in T. D. Kramer, op. cit. p. xii.
7   On the much debated subject of Jewish participation in the Hungarian radical movements before the First World War see, for instance, John Lukacs, *Budapest 1900: A Historical Portrait of a City and Its Culture* (New York: Weidenfels and Nicolson, 1988), especially chapter 6.
8   Egyenlőség (Budapest), May 15, 1896. Quoted in Gábor Schweitzer, "Miért (nem) kellett Herzl a magyar zsidóknak? A politikai cionizmus kezdetei és a magyarországi zsidó közvélemény," [Why the Hungarian Jews did (not) want Herzl. The beginnings of Hungarian Zionism and Jewish public opinion in Hungary], Budapesti Negyed, Summer 1994, p. 42. Note that the splendid and frightfully expensive national gala costumes were the creation of the nineteenth century Hungarian nationalist imagination. Their wearers, all members of the highest Hungarian political, social, economic and cultural elite, dressed the way they thought the ninth-century Chieftain Árpád and/or the sixteenth-century Hungarian aristocratic warriors were dressed. Needless to say, the great tailors who created the rather theatrical outfits were mostly of Czech, Austrian or Jewish origin.

The Holocaust in Hungary

Then came the First World War, in which Jews participated en masse, providing, among other things, more than one fifth of the Dual Monarchy's reserve officer corps.[9] But whereas in the armed forces anti-Semitism was not tolerated, in politics, the press and public opinion, it experienced a quick revival. Very simply, scapegoats had to be found for the suffering of the population and the death of half a million Hungarian citizen-soldiers. The defeat of the Central Powers in the fall of 1918 came as a terrible shock to a misinformed public, yet also as a welcome relief from what was perceived to be Habsburg/Austrian oppression. The fact that, in the eyes of the other peoples of the Monarchy, the Hungarians were the quintessentially dominant nationality did not in the least influence the Hungarians' perception of themselves as oppressed victims. Thus the end of the war was celebrated as the beginning of an independent and more progressive Hungary; celebration turned to despair, however, when the terrible costs of war became more visible, and when the armies of Hungary's old and new neighbours occupied much of what in pre-war times had been officially known as the "Hungarian Empire" within Austria-Hungary. For the Jews, the First World War had marked the apogee of their success; in 1944, nothing would symbolise more their fall from grace than the war-time decorations they had to leave on the walls of the houses and flats from which they were deported.

Counter-revolution and the end of the Christian-Jewish symbiosis

The military collapse brought two successive revolutions, one democratic, the other Bolshevik: in both, the youngish Jewish reformers and social critics played a crucial role. In fact, they made up almost the entire leadership of the Soviet Republic, which functioned for 133 days in 1919.[10] This regime

---

9   On Jews in the Habsburg Army before and after the First World War, see István Deák, *Beyond Nationalism: A Social and Political History of the Habsburg Officer Corps, 1848– 1918* (New York: Princeton University Press, 1990), pp. 172– 178 et passim, and Erwin A. Schmidl, *Jews in the Habsburg Armed Forces, 1788–1918* (Studia Judaica Austriaca, XI; Eisenstadt: Österreichisches Jüdisches Museum, 1989).

10 On the role of Jews in the Hungarian Soviet Republic, see Charles Gati, *Hungary and the Soviet Bloc* (Durham, N.C.: University of North Carolina Press, 1986), pp. 100–107, and Rudolf L. Tőkés, *Béla Kun and the Hungarian Soviet Republic; The Origins and Role of the Communist Party of Hungary in the Revolutions of 1918–1919* (Stanford, Cal.: F. A. Praeger, 1967).

was put an end to by the invading Romanian army acting under French guidance; the ensuing power vacuum allowed a small band of White counter-revolutionary officers to seize power in the same year. For this, they enjoyed the support of the French and British governments.

Post-First World War Hungary was not only impoverished but was inundated by refugees from the newly lost territories. Many of the refugees were civil servants and professionals, who now engaged in a desperate competition with the Jews for even the lowliest positions in commerce and the professions. This, combined with the country's dismemberment and the frightening experience with the revolutionary Soviet Republic, led to a deepening of middle-class antiSemitism.[11]

Interwar Hungary stood for a mass of contradictions and so did its Jewish policy. The country was a kingdom without a king; its head of state was Regent Miklós Horthy, a former Austro-Hungarian admiral, of course without a fleet. The system of government was constitutional, but the counter-revolutionary movement that had brought Horthy to power was characterised by violence and terror. Hungary had a parliament in which, as late as March 1944, sat a few Social Democratic and other progressive deputies, but the majority of deputies proclaimed fascist ideas. Both the Lower House and the Upper House were obsessed with the "Jewish question." In fact, pre-occupation with the Jews was akin to a sickness that afflicted all strata of society, but especially the educated classes.[12]

In 1920, the Hungarian parliament adopted a law meant to reduce the presence of Jewish students at the universities to something approximating their presence in the general population, which was a little less than six per cent, but this law was suspended eight years later. What counts is that the old

---

11 On the over-production or better, the under-employment of the Hungarian intelligentsia in the interwar period, see Mária M. Kovács, *Liberal Professions and Illiberal Politics: Hungary from the Habsburgs to the Holocaust* (New York: Oxford University Press, 1994).

12 A very fine work on Regent Miklós Horthy is Thomas Sakmyster, *Hungary's Admiral on Horseback: Miklós Horthy, 1918–1944* (East European Monographs 396; Distributed by Columbia University Press, 1994). For an essay on Sakmyster's book, see István Deák, Essays on Hitler's Europe (Lincoln: University of Nebraska Press, 2001), pp. 148–158. On twentieth-century Hungarian politics and society, in English, see László Kontler, *A History of Hungary: Millenium in Central Europe* (New York: Palgrave, 2003), chapter VII; Paul Lendvai, *The Hungarians: 1000 Years of Victory in Defeat* (Princeton, N.J.: Princeton University Press, 2003), chapters 30–33 and, especially, Ignác Romsics, *Hungary in the Twentieth Century* (Budapest: Corvina, 1999).

silent contract between gentry and Jews had come to an end. Now even the most moderate counter-revolutionaries expected the majority of Jews to leave the country eventually.

The Horthy regime was desperate to open jobs, especially in industry, commerce, and the liberal professions to Gentiles, yet as late as 1935, the proportion in Hungary of Jewish lawyers, medical doctors, journalists and engineers was higher than even in the pre-First World War period, often approximating fifty per cent. The proportion of Jews among the professionals practising in the capital and among those with the biggest income was higher still.[13] And now just one more data: as late as 1941, the absolute majority of the biggest taxpayers and those with the greatest personal wealth were Jews or baptised Jews.[14] These and similar statistics were constantly harped upon up by the press and the politicians but what they failed to say was that the absolute number of Jews was steadily declining because of emigration, a low birth rate and conversions, and that once the economy began to improve, as it did in the late 1930s, there would be ample space in lucrative positions for the newly educated Christian middle class as well.

The counter-revolutionary regime advocated a militant Christian ideology, which meant that it was opposed to free masonry, liberalism, democracy, atheism, secularism, Jewish influence, Marxism, Bolshevism, cosmopolitanism, modernity, abortion, homosexuality, divorce and avant-garde art, yet many of these sinful activities and ideologies flourished in Horthy's Hungary, creating, among other things, a new golden age of literature and the arts. Despite the government's incessant anti-urban and peasantist propaganda, Budapest remained a most sophisticated place in a much poorer and much less developed countryside. In the capital, Jews made up nearly one fourth of the inhabitants and nearly one half of those with the right to vote. The press was infinitely freer than in the Soviet Union, Nazi Germany and fascist Ita-

---

13 For all further information on the role of Jews in the professions, business and industry as well as on the wartime spoliation of the Jews, the reader is referred to Gábor Kádár–Zoltán Vági, "Rationality or Irrationality? The Annihilation of Hungarian Jews," The Hungarian Quarterly, vol. 45, 174, Summer 2004, pp. 32–54. Please note that converts to Christianity, often the best educated among the Jews, were heavily represented in business and the liberal professions, adding substantially to the proportion of unconverted Jews.

14 Dezső Zentay, *Beszélő számok [Eloquent numbers]* (Budapest: Globus, 1941), pp. 102–103.

ly, and the judiciary, although certainly class-based, often ruled in defiance of government interests. The ruling elite was badly divided between those who cultivated old- fashioned conservative values and those with fascistic inclinations, between defenders and critics of the rigid social hierarchy, between moderate and radical anti-Semites, between Anglophiles and the admirers of Nazi Germany. Nor are history books correct which claim that, in the late 1930s and early 1940s, the radical right was steadily gaining ground at the expense of the moderate rightists. Rather, things changed all the time; the fascist Arrow Cross Party, for instance, had three times as many members in 1939 than in the fall of 1944 when the Germans put it in power. Also, to give another example, the conservative, Anglophile elite operating under the guidance of former prime minister Count István Bethlen almost completely regained power in 1943 as well as in the weeks preceding the Arrow Cross takeover in October 1944.[15]

The Horthy regime's main domestic policy goal was to avoid such fundamental social reforms as the distribution of the enormous landed estates among the millions of landless; its main foreign political goal was to recover some, if not all the territories that Hungary had lost after the First World War. At stake were two thirds of the old kingdom and over three million Magyar-speakers now living under foreign rule. The government's policy goals were tightly intertwined with the "Jewish question"; after all, the anti-Jewish economic measures were the beginnings of a most unfair but still genuine redistribution of wealth.[16] Also, the recovery of the lost territories required the support of Nazi Germany; Hitler's insistence on drastic anti-Jewish measures was one reason for a series of Hungarian anti-Jewish laws that began in 1938. However, ideology and greed played their part as well.

---

15 On Bethlen see, Ignác Romsics, *István Bethlen: A Great Conservative Statesman of Hungary, 1874–1946*, translated from the Hungarian by Mario D. Fenyo (New York: Distributed by Columbia University Press, 1995)

16 It has been calculated that, in 1938, Jews owned up to one-fourth of the national wealth. For all further details, see again, Kádár–Vági, "Rationality or Irrationality?" The Hungarian Quarterly, No. 174, Summer 2004, pp. 32–54.

The Holocaust in Hungary

Again at war

The adoption of the first anti-Jewish law coincided with the recovery, thanks to Hitler and Mussolini, of a part of what used to be northern and northeast Hungary.

From then on territorial recovery and anti-Jewish measures intertwined until nearly one half of the lost lands had been regained and the country's antiSemitic laws had become at least as drastic in their definition of race as those of Germany. But, unlike in Germany, these laws were often respected in their breach and, strange as it may sound, until March 1944, most Jews still worked in their professions, if often at a reduced salary.

In June 1941, Hungary entered the military campaign against the Soviet Union, which gradually brought it into war with Great Britain and the United States. But while the Soviet Union and Bolshevism were seen as true enemies, the conservative Horthy regime went out of its way to show admiration and friendship toward the British and the Americans.[17] In the winter of 1942–1943, a great Soviet offensive destroyed the Hungarian army at the front; among the dead, the frozen and the POWs were thousands of Jews whom the army high command had drafted for labour service. By then even highly decorated Jewish reserve officers had been deprived of their ranks and those who had been drafted had to dig ditches or clear minefields in the firing line. It was as if the army found a particular delight in torturing and killing the decorated heroes as well as the intellectuals among the Jewish labour-service men. One of the victims tortured to death in Ukraine was the Olympic gold medalist and reserve officer Attila Petschauer, whose cruel death inspired a horrifying scene in István Szabó's celebrated film, Sunshine. But, again, by far not all Jewish labour-service men were mistreated by their guards, and the Jewish forced labourers suffered fewer casualties due to combat, the atrocious winter weather, and the sadism of their Hungarian guards than as a result of hunger and epidemics in the Soviet PoW camps. The Red

---

17 A characteristic victim of this charm attack was the US minister to Hungary, John Flournoy Montgomery, whose *Hungary: The Unwilling Satellite* (New York: Devin-Adair, 1947), exculpates the Regent and his advisers for collaboration with Nazi Germany and for the anti-Jewish laws. See also Horthy's self-apologetic *Memoirs* (New York: R. Speller, 1957).

Army treated the captured labour-service men no better than it treated the captured Hungarian military.[18]

The government of Miklós Kállay that Regent Horthy installed in March 1942, with the mission of cautiously counterbalancing the German and local fascist influence, at first adopted a few more anti-Semitic measures but, following the defeat of the Hungarian Second Army at the Don River and the German defeat at Stalingrad, changed its policy toward the Jews. The lot of the Jewish labour-service men was considerably alleviated, and the anti-Jewish laws were not always put into effect. Moreover, British and American bombers flying over the country were not fired upon, and Prime Minister Kállay attempted to reach a secret agreement with the Western Allies. But the British and US land forces were nowhere to be seen.[19] Fully informed through his spies of Hungarian machinations and alarmed by the approach of the Red Army, Hitler ordered the German armed forces into Hungary on March 19, 1944. There was no resistance and, within a few days, Regent Horthy was caused to appoint a new, strongly pro-Nazi government.

From March to October

Because the German occupation of Hungary was followed by the Holocaust of Hungarian Jewry, the mobilisation of the non-Jewish population for total war, the Soviet invasion and the country's destruction, Hungarians have been asking themselves ever since what could have been done to avoid it. During the first thirty years after the war, the unanimous judgment of both Communist and democratic authors was that Horthy and Prime Minister Kállay should have turned against the Germans and ordered armed resistance, at least on the day of the German invasion. Yet such a move was scarcely possible in a country whose pro-German elements, especially within the military, wielded enormous influ-

---

18 On the Jewish labour-service system, see Braham, The Politics of Genocide, chapter 10; the tragic fate of the captured labour-service men is well analysed in George Barany, "*Jewish Prisoners of War in the Soviet Union During World War II,*" Jahrbücher für Geschichte Osteuropas 31 (1983), pp. 161–209. Accrding to the author eighty per cent of the Jewish POWs did not survive Soviet captivity.
19 On all this, see Nicholas Kállay's *Hungarian Premier: a Personal Account of a Nation's Struggle in the Second World War* (Westport, Conn.: Greenwood Press, 1954), as well as Mario D. Fenyo, *Hitler, Horthy and Hungary: German-Hungarian Relations, 1941–1944* (New Haven: Yale University Press, 1972).

The Holocaust in Hungary

ence and power. A more sophisticated view is that of Randolph L. Braham, the foremost historian of the Hungarian Jewish Holocaust, who writes:

> Ironically, it appears in retrospect that had Hungary continued to remain a militarily passive but politically vocal ally of the Third Reich instead of provocatively engaging in essentially fruitless, if not merely alibi-establishing, diplomatic maneuvers, the Jews of Hungary might possibly have survived the war relatively unscathed.[20]

Unfortunately, it is highly unlikely that had the Kállay government collaborated more vocally, the Hungarian Jews would have escaped relatively unscathed. The Final Solution was too important for the Germans to let nearly a million Jews stay alive in Central Europe. Still, Braham's argument makes clear that, in 1944 at least, Jews and non-Jews did not have the same immediate interests, and that the meaning and consequences of resistance and collaboration cannot be given a uniform interpretation. For the Jews, every day gained improved their chances of ultimate survival; therefore, it was not in their interest for the government to provoke German aggression. But it was very much in the interest of Hungary as a whole to show, no matter how symbolically, that it was not a German satellite.[21]

When General Döme Sztójay's puppet government took over, late in March 1944, 60,000 odd Hungarian Jews were already dead. Among them, 15–20,000 had been killed by the SS and the Ukrainian militia in the spring of 1942, following the deportation of these Jews from northeastern Hungary to Galicia who were unable to provide evidence of their Hungarian citizenship. Another one thousand were massacred by the Hungarian military during a "cleansing" operation in northern Yugoslavia, and the rest died, as already shown, either in a theatre of war, in 1942–1943, or in Soviet PoW

---

20 Braham, *The Politics of Genocide*, p. 265.
21 On the question of Hungarian behaviour toward the Germans see, among others, István Deák, "A Fatal Compromise? The Debate Over Collaboration and Resistance in Hungary," in István Deák, Jan T. Gross, and Tony Judt., eds., *The Politics of Retribution in Europe: World War II and Its Aftermath* (Princeton, N.J.: Princeton University Press, 2000), pp. 39–73. For an overall view of European behavior during the war, see István Deák, *Europe on Trial: The Story of Collaboration, Resistance, and Retribution During World War II* (Westview Press, 2015).

camps. Now the operation began in earnest against the remaining 760,000, about one hundred thousand of whom were Christians by religion. Within a few weeks, those whom the law regarded as Jews were excluded from all skilled employment and their food and clothing rations were drastically cut. They were subjected to the authority of the newly created Jewish Councils, who were then ordered to help confiscate Jewish telephones, radios, dogs, horses, stamp collections, art works, jewelry and bank accounts. In addition, huge bribes had to be paid to Eichmann's Gestapo detachment, who arrived in Hungary with the German troops.

On April 5, all Jews were made to wear a yellow star and two days later the first secret directives were issued concerning the ghettoisation of Hungarian Jewry. The transfer of Jews into the newly created ghettoes began late in April; systematic mass deportation started on May 15 and ended only in July; in that short period 437,000 persons were dispatched to Auschwitz of whom the great majority were gassed immediately without anyone bothering to register their names. The suffering of the deportees has been described innumerable times: the sudden departure from home, the move from a small ghetto to a larger ghetto and from there to some brick works outside a city with no shelter, hardly any food or drinkable water, and no sanitary facilities. There was the incredible brutality of the gendarmes and many of the city police who, in their ravenous hunger for silver and gold, indiscriminately tortured men, women and children. Finally came the march to the railroad station and the slow, tortured voyage in frightfully overcrowded cattle cars to the ramp in Auschwitz-Birkenau. Note, however, that some 20,000 of the deportees were diverted for industrial and agricultural labour at Strasshof in Austria, where the great majority of them survived. Note also that those who were not gassed immediately at Auschwitz-Birkenau, meaning the relatively healthy of working age, had a fair chance of surviving the periodic "selections" as well as slave labour in German factories and mines.[22] One of the

---

22 There are only a few memoirs, in English, on the process of deportation as, for instance, Judith Magyar Isaacson, *Seed of Sarah: Memoirs of a Survivor* (Urbana: University of Illinois Press, 1990). Christian Gerlach and Götz Aly, *Das letzte Kapitel. Der Mord an den ungarischen Juden 1944/1945* (Stuttgart: Deutsche Verlags-Anstalt, 2002) analyses the Final Solution on the basis of German documentary sources.

The Holocaust in Hungary

many insoluble dilemmas of these mind-boggling events is why Regent Horthy allowed them to happen. True, he was a confessed anti-Semite but he also had some close Jewish friends; he often claimed to prefer the patriotic and assimilated sector of the Jews to the Arrow Cross "hoodlums and traitors," and a year before the German invasion he categorically rejected Nazi demands for the deportation of the Jews.

The event occurred in April 1943, at a meeting at Klessheim, where Hitler demanded that Hungary finally solve the Jewish question. According to a German report on the meeting, Horthy's reply to Hitler's comment on the matter was,

> "What, then, should [I] do with the Jews after they have essentially been denied almost every opportunity to earn a living. Why, [I] couldn't kill them."

Thereupon Goebbels wrote in his diary on May 8, 1943:

> The Jewish question is solved least satisfactorily by the Hungarians. The Hungarian state is permeated by Jews, and the Fuhrer did not succeed during his talk with Horthy to convince the latter of the necessity of more stringent measures....He [Horthy] gave a number of humanitarian counterarguments which of course do not apply at all to this situation."[23]

And now the same old-fashioned gentleman who claimed to follow in the footsteps of Francis Joseph, his famously tolerant former master, informed the council of ministers that he was leaving Jewish matters entirely in their hands. Horthy also quietly assured his visitors that the Jews were simply taken to Germany for useful labour; as a humanitarian gesture, the Germans allowed their families to go with them. He said this knowing full well that, aside from the Jews of Budapest, the only other Jews not deported abroad were men of working age; by June 1944, all Jewish men between the ages of 18

---

23 The Horthy statement is cited in, among others, Lani Yahil, *The Holocaust: The Fate of European Jewry* (New York: Oxford University Press, 1992), p. 501. The Goebbels Diary entry is in Louis Lochner, ed., *The Goebbels Diaries, 1942–1943* (Garden City, N.J., 1948), p. 357.

and 48 had been drafted into Hungarian military labour service, and therefore those who went to the gas chambers were mostly women, children, the old and the infirm. There is really no other answer to the Horthy dilemma than that he was weak and easily influenced, a type of behaviour with which he certainly did not stand alone in Europe.

And what about those serving under the Regent? It has been calculated that 200,000 persons in public service participated in the swift and amazingly efficient execution of the deportations. They included, from Prime Minister Sztójay, through Andor Jaross, László Endre and László Baky, that trio in the cabinet who were directly in charge of the Hungarian Final Solution, down to county prefects, and sub-prefects, the mayors, the entire administrative machinery, including the gendarmes, the police, the railroad men and such teachers who had been drafted into assisting the bureaucrats. Even doctors and midwives were called upon to search the intimate parts of Jewish women for hidden jewelry. History does not record a single instance of a public servant openly refusing to co-operate, yet the punishment would have been minimal. It is true, however, that dozens were dismissed from the higher echelons of service and dozens of others chose retirement. Their deputies took over immediately and completed the process of deportations.

In many places people cried when watching the sorry parade of their former neighbours but then the lure of abandoned goods proved to be irresistible, and there was wholesale looting.[24] A few church leaders tried to intervene in order to alleviate the condition of the baptised Jews in the camps, but basically no one publicly protested the deportations. Nor did anyone attempt to sabotage the trains.

It was indeed a smooth operation, in which the Jewish councils, too, performed their assigned role. The Central Council in Budapest and the local councils have been the subject of much debate with, for instance, both Hannah Arendt and Randolph Braham strongly condemning the councils' collaborationist attitudes.[25] And it is true that these Jewish dignitaries, formerly

---

24 On the wasteful dissipation of Jewish goods and, in general, on the catastrophic economic effect of the anti-Jewish measures, see Kádár– Vági, The Hungarian Quarterly, No. 174, Summer 2004.
25 Hannah Arendt, *Eichmann in Jerusalem: On the Banality of Evil* (New York: Viking, 1963, p. 104 et passim, and Randolph L. Braham, "The Holocaust in Hungary: A Retrospective Analysis," in David

The Holocaust in Hungary

with good governmental connections and often highly decorated by the Horthy regime, could think of no other action but dutiful obedience. They were patriots who remained confident that the Regent and their other Gentile patrons would not abandon them and their flock. There is no doubt, however, that some Council leaders and many Council employees were overzealous in trying to please the Germans and the Hungarian authorities. Witness the contemporary anecdote:

> There is violent banging on the door of a Jewish family early in the morning. All are terrified; finally, the wife gathers enough courage to open the door. She returns much relieved and smiling: "Relax, it is not the Jewish Council, only the Gestapo."

What would have happened if the Councils had refused to obey orders and instead tried to encourage their flock to flee for their lives? It is not clear how such a message could have been communicated and where the hundreds of thousands would have been able to hide. Also, the chaos created by massive disobedience would have benefited primarily the most enterprising, the wealthy, the secularised and the assimilated who were, in any case, often able to fend for themselves. Finally, to ask the Council members to engage in a massive disobedience or to commit suicide, as Hannah Arendt has suggested, is to demand that they get out of their skin.

But why did the Hungarian authorities obey Eichmann and his minuscule crew of a few dozen specialists? Clearly, there remained only a few months before the arrival of the Red Army when those who had collaborated with the Germans were likely to be punished. The answer can only be that those who participated in the Final Solution found the threat of eventual punishment less compelling than the immediate satisfaction of seeing the Jews go away and of being able to acquire houses, apartments, shops and well-paying positions—or for a shoeless poor peasant to acquire a pair of good boots. One thing is certain: even those who bemoaned the fate of the Jews did not ex-

---

Cesarani, ed., *Genocide and Rescue: The Holocaust in Hungary 1944* (Oxford: Berg, 1997), pp. 42–43. For a review of this book, see Deák, *Essays on Hitler's Europe*, pp. 159–162.

pect them ever to return. There is a shattering passage in Imre Kertész's Nobel-Prize-winning novel, *Fateless,* on the last encounter between the deported Jews and a Gentile Hungarian. Kertész's hero, the boy George Köves, reaches the Polish border in a crowded railroad car when a Hungarian gendarme appears at the entrance, offering to relieve the suffocating passengers of their hidden jewels, gold and money:

> "Men," he said to us, "you've reached the Hungarian border." He wanted to use this occasion to make an appeal to us... it was his opinion that we had no need of these where we were going... everything we might still hold on to would be taken from us by the Germans anyway... why shouldn't these things find their final resting place in Hungarian, rather than German, hands?

The gendarme's appeal got him nowhere because the inmates of the car demanded water first and only then would they give up their valuables; he, on the other hand, insisted on a reverse order of proceedings. "After all, you are still Hungarians," the gendarme exclaimed.

> Finally the furious military policeman concluded: "Stinking Jews, you make a business out of even the holiest of things!" And in a voice choking with outrage and disgust, he added this wish: "Die of thirst, then!"[26]

The deportations did not remain a secret and Horthy soon began to receive messages from István Bethlen, who was in hiding, as well from other such conservative, mostly aristocratic politicians whom the Gestapo had not been able to arrest. Now, at last, Pope Pius XII, King Gustav VII of Sweden, President Roosevelt, and other world leaders also began to send messages, urging the Regent to act to protect the remaining Jews in Hungary. Deeply impressed by Allied successes in Normandy, Horthy on July 7, 1944, forbade further deportations. The interdiction came when the gendarmes gathered in

---

26 Imre Kertész, *Fateless,* translated from the Hungarian by Christopher C. Wilson and Katharina M. Wilson (Evanston, Ill.: Northwestern University Press, 1992), pp. 54–55. On Kertész, see István Deák, "Stranger in Hell," The New York Review of Books, Sept. 25, 2003, pp. 65–68.

Budapest to begin deporting the 200,000 odd Jews in the capital. Persuaded by his conservative friends that the gendarmes and some far right politicians were planning a coup d'état against him, the Regent ordered an armoured unit to Budapest.

The smoothness and speed of the deportation of the Hungarian Jews from the provinces was unique in the history of the Holocaust; but so was Horthy's decision to order military forces to prevent the deportation of Jews. Although Eichmann subsequently managed literally to smuggle a few thousand more Jews to Auschwitz, in July the deportations came to an end, not to be renewed until after Horthy's overthrow in October.[27]

Now came another surreal period in wartime Jewish history when those in Budapest were quartered in so-called Yellow-Star houses and suffered from many humiliating restrictions but were also able to make plans for the opening of schools for Jewish children in September, and when it was relatively easy to obtain a certificate from the Regent's office exempting one from the anti-Jewish laws. Also, the Swedish, Swiss, Portuguese and Vatican representatives began to hand out papers, which offered a degree of personal protection with the vague promise of post-war immigration to their country or else emigration to Palestine. Moreover, those in labour service were generally decently fed and could feel quite safe; at the time of the deportations to Auschwitz, many of the men of military age had been literally saved in the last minute by the military authorities. Considering that, before March 1944, the army was notoriously more anti-Semitic and more pro-German than the ci-

---

27 It must be stated that some other Jews, besides those in Budapest and those in labour service, also escaped deportation. One small but important group consisted of the members of the Baron Jenő Weiss, and related great capitalist families who, behind the back of the Sztójay government, negotiated their transportation to Portugal with representatives of the SS. In exchange, they handed over much of Hungary's heavy and armaments industry to the SS. A much larger group, consisting of 1,684 individuals, was allowed by Himmler to be transported out of Hungary, and all eventually reached Switzerland. The release of the group was negotiated by Rudolf (Rezső) Kasztner and other Hungarian Zionists in exchange for money and for the vague promise of Himmler and other SS leaders ultimately escaping the hangman's noose in the case of the Allies winning the War. Both the Weiss and the Kasztner cases provoked an enormous literature, which would constitute the basis for another essay. For an introduction to the subject, see Yehuda Bauer, *Jews for Sale? Nazi–Jewish Negotiations, 1933–1945* (New Haven, Conn.: Yale University Press, 1994), pp. 145–251, as well as Gábor Kádár and Zoltán Vági, *Self-financing Genocide: The Gold Train, the Becher Case and the Wealth of Hungarian Jews* (Budapest–New York: Central European University Press, 2004), especially pp. 175–278, which discuss the case of the SS officer Kurt Becher, who was deeply involved in negotiations regarding the fate of the great capitalist families and the so-called Kasztner train.

vilian leadership, its relatively lenient behaviour in the spring and summer of 1944 belongs to the many unsolved mysteries of the period.

Early in September 1944, following Romania's sudden defection to the Allied side, the Red Army invaded Hungary. Horthy had already dismissed his pro-Nazi prime minister and he now began to negotiate an armistice with the Soviet Union —hoping for an agreement which would allow the German troops to withdraw unmolested—but discussions proceeded slowly. The Germans knew about these plans; they began to prepare for a coup d'état and, as a first step, on October 15 they kidnapped Miklós Horthy, Jr., the Regent's surviving son, whose older brother had been killed when his plane crashed on the Russian front. Horthy announced his intention to surrender to the Red Army that same day, but the army high command, imbued with the fanatical anti-communism which Horthy himself had encouraged, refused to follow his instructions and the surrender attempt failed. German SS and paratroopers arrested Horthy and, in order to secure his son's safety, the old man signed a piece of paper which made his archrival, the Arrow Cross leader Ferenc Szálasi, his successor. Horthy and his family were then put on a train to Bavaria where they were held under house arrest. A few military commanders went over to the Soviets; the army as a whole, however, swore loyalty to Szálasi—not that its fighting ability was of high quality.

Arrow Cross rule

The pre-March and post-March 1944 political leadership did not differ socially from one another; they were all products of the counter-revolution and had their origins in the old aristocracy, gentry and the civil service; only in that they held differing views on Hungary, its Jews and the war. Even the conservative and liberal critics of the Horthy regime originated from the same counter-revolutionary elite. But those whom the SS now entrusted with mobilising the country for a last-ditch defence were different, not because they had no titled aristocrats and old gentry among them (in Hungary nothing ever happened without a few counts and other noblemen) but because they included many people drawn from other classes of society, even from the Lumpenproletariat.

The Holocaust in Hungary

The Arrow Cross has been judged harshly; for instance, while the people's courts tried members of the Horthy regime as individuals, members of the Szálasi regime were branded collectively as traitors and war criminals. The politics of the group was described as of hare-brained ideas and extreme violence; today, Hungarian nationalist circles routinely blame the Arrow Cross for all the crimes of the period; indeed, Szálasi has become the supreme alibi of Regent Horthy and his cohorts. It is currently quite common to hear a younger generation of Hungarians, nay even some confused Jewish survivors, stating that Szálasi had come to power in March 1944 and that the Arrow Cross militia was at least partly responsible for the brutalities of the deportation to Auschwitz. In reality, the latter was the work exclusively of the old administration under Regent Horthy.[28]

Following Horthy's overthrow, Eichmann came back to Hungary to complete his deportation project, but things had changed substantially. The SS Führer Heinrich Himmler no longer allowed deportations to Auschwitz and, in any case, the Red Army was approaching. So late in November, 50,000 Budapest Jews, mostly women, as well as nearly the same number of labour-service men were marched off to the Austrian border, there to build fortifications. The monstrosity of the Arrow Cross militia and the soldiers who guarded the deportees was surpassed only by the monstrosity of the Austrian Hitler-Jugend and other local uniformed formations that took over the deportees at the border.[29] The behaviour of the peasant population ranged from the helpful through the indifferent to the murderously hostile in both countries.

Amazingly, thousands of Jews, especially among the old, were turned around and brought back to Budapest through the decision of Himmler and through the efforts, especially, of Raoul Wallenberg, who was a delegate of the American War Refugee Board, acting under the protection of the Swedish Legation in Hungary. The activities of Wallenberg, the Swiss Consul Carl

---

28 Nicholas Nagy-Talavera, *The Green Shirts and Others: A History of Fascism in Hungary and Romania* (2nd edition; Portland, Oregon: Center for Romanian Studies, 2001), usefully compares the Hungarian Arrow Cross movement with the Romanian Iron Guard.
29 Note that after the War, most of the Austrian people's court trials dealt with the case of such Austrian soldiers and Hitlerjugend who had beaten Hungarian Jews to death. Several of the defendants were executed.

Lutz, the Papal Nuncio Angelo Rotta, the pseudo-Spanish Consul (in reality an Italian anti-Nazi) Giorgio (Jorge) Perlasca, and the International Red Cross representative Friedrich Born constitute perhaps the best-known chapter of the Hungarian Holocaust.[30] These courageous men used mainly the promise of diplomatic recognition by their own governments to impress the Arrow Cross leaders; as a result, they were able to distribute protective passes to thousands of Jews as well as to bring back others from the road to Austria. Most importantly, the consuls caused the creation of a number of so-called Protected Buildings in a once heavily Jewish upper-middle class area of Budapest. But before we accept the claims of the enthusiasts that Wallenberg, for instance, saved the lives of one hundred thousand Jews, we have to consider that were all the claims true, the consuls would have saved more lives than there were Jews left in Budapest. We must also consider that Wallenberg and Co. owned at best a few pistols among them, and that they would have been powerless to save any lives had some Arrow Cross leaders, as for instance the Foreign Minister Baron Gábor Kemény, not been willing to cooperate with them. Ultimately, the decision not to have all the Jews of Budapest killed was that of the Szálasi government. Of course, there is no particular merit in not committing even more murders, but the fact of Arrow Cross co-operation with the consuls must be registered.[31]

The most important of the regime's decisions was to set up a Ghetto in Budapest, late in November, which ended up housing nearly a hundred thousand Jews. This was at that time a unique institution in Europe.[32] Conditions inside the wooden-board fence were atrocious, but the Budapest municipal-

---

30 Of the many works on Wallenberg, see especially Kati Marton, *Wallenberg* (New York: Random House, 1982) and Danny Smith, *Lost Hero: Raoul Wallenberg's Dramatic Quest to Save the Jews of Hungary* (London: HarperCollins, 2001) as well as Per Anger, *With Raoul Wallenberg in Budapest*, translated by David Paul and Margareta Paul (New York: Holocaust Library, 1981). The Swiss consul's extraordinary achievements are lovingly presented in Theo Tschuy, *Dangerous Diplomacy: The Story of Carl Lutz, Rescuer of 62,000 Jews* (Grand Rapids, Mich.: William B. Eerdmans, 2000).

31 The activities of the neutral consuls are convincingly discussed in Robert Rozett, "International Intervention: the Role of Diplomats in Attempts to Rescue Jews in Hungary," in Randolph L. Braham and Scott Miller, eds., *The Nazis' Last Victims; the Holocaust in Hungary* (Detroit, Mich.: Wayne State University Press, 1998), pp. 137–152.

32 On the Jewish policy of the Szálasi regime see, among others, László Karsai, "The Last Phase of the Hungarian Holocaust: the Szálasi Regime and the Jews," in Braham and Miller, *The Nazis' Last Victims*, pp. 105–116.

The Holocaust in Hungary

ity and the International Red Cross fed the inhabitants so long as any food could be found. Also, a mixed crew of Budapest policemen and Arrow Cross militiamen offered some degree of protection against roving bands of other Arrow Cross militiamen and SS men. Such protection was something sorely missing at the Swedish, Swiss and other Protected Buildings. As conditions in Budapest worsened and the Szálasi government took off to Western Hungary towards the end of December, the capital remained in the hands of local Arrow Cross leaders, who terrorized the entire population and, among other things, regularly took out inhabitants of the Protected Buildings to shoot them into the nearby Danube River. Meanwhile, however, small units belonging to Zionist organizations had installed themselves under the protection of especially the Swiss Consulate and forged thousands of papers, birth certificates and whatever one needed to hide in the city. This, of course, often devalued the real documents, and Arrow Cross authorities tore up such papers as often as they accepted them. The Zionists had long concluded that there was no point in trying to offer armed resistance; this was left to a handful of Communists and other armed partisans; nevertheless, the Zionists' efforts were invaluable.[33]

The Red Army reached the southeastern outskirts of Budapest at the end of November 1944 and, on December 24, in a dashing move, Soviet tanks surrounded the entire capital. The chaos and the hardships in the place are impossible to describe in a few sentences. Before the siege began, the Arrow Cross regime attempted to mobilise the entire population, or at least to force everyone to move to the West. Ever more bloodthirsty proclamations threatened recalcitrants with immediate execution. Because almost no one obeyed the mad orders, the city was now hiding thousands of deserters and draft dodgers, which meant that the population at large had become accomplices, in a way, with the Jews in the ghetto and, even more, with those in hiding. It seems that about 25,000 Jews and baptized Jews survived the war and the siege disguised as Gentiles. Considering, however, that in Budapest almost

---

33 On Zionist activities in Budapest see, among others, Asher Cohen, "The Dilemma of Rescue and Revolt," in Braham and Miller, *The Nazis' Last Victims*, pp. 117–136. Also, by the same author, *The Halutz Resistance in Hungary, 1942–1944* (Social Science Monographs; distributed by Columbia University Press, 1986).

everyone was capable of detecting a Jew and also that most of those in hiding were not denounced, it is likely that at least a hundred thousand Gentiles gave active assistance to the Jews, while many more simply looked the other way.[34] The tragedy is that such popular solidarity was all but inconceivable in the spring when the deportations to Auschwitz took place.

Because of the furious madness of roving Arrow Cross bands, it was now truly risky to hide a Jew. In this connection, let me name only three of the saviours, the Catholic Grey Sister Margit Schlachta, the Lutheran minister Gábor Sztechlo and the journalist Béla Stollár. The first repeatedly intervened on behalf of the Slovak Jews during the war as well as journeying to see the Pope on their behalf; in 1944, she mobilised her entire order to assist the Hungarian Jews. The second harboured hundreds of Jewish children in different homes. The third hid many Jews as well as providing others with forged papers; he also set up a small resistance group made up of deserters and Jewish escapees from labour-service. On Christmas Day of 1944, Béla Stollár and his companions were killed in a gunfight with the Arrow Cross militia. That there were many others equally brave is shown by the hundreds of Hungarian names among the Righteous Gentiles listed at the Yad Vashem Institute in Jerusalem.

Liberation and post-war trauma

The siege of Budapest led to enormous destruction and the death of about 20,000 civilians, maybe half of whom were Jews. The Red Army freed the starving Jews in the Ghetto and in the Protected Buildings between January 16 and 18, 1945. Many of those hiding on the Buda side of the city had to

---

34 A characteristic case of a Jewish family in hiding is that of the financier and philanthropist George Soros, who was then fourteen. Their adventures in Budapest in 1944–1945 are entertainingly described in the memoirs of his father, Tivadar Soros, in *Masquerade: Dancing Around Death in Nazi-Occupied Hungary* (New York: Arcade Publishing, 2000). The book was translated into English from the original 1965 edition in Esperanto. Not uncharacteristically, the Soros family in disguise had regular access to swimming pools, restaurants, and opera performances in Budapest and, not uncharacteristically, the author fails to recognise how many Gentiles had assisted him or, at least, how many had failed to denounce him, his mother, his wife, his sons, and other relatives in hiding. For a critique of the Soros memoirs, see István Deák, "Artful Dodger," The New York Review of Books, November 15, 2001.

wait until February 13 to be free. No doubt, most were painfully aware that what was liberation for them, appeared as enemy occupation to their Gentile neighbours. In any case, both Jews and Gentiles suffered from the rapaciousness and unpredictability of the Red Army. The classic picture is that of the recently freed Jewish survivor being taken into a Soviet PoW camp and ending up in Siberia simply because the Soviets needed workers to help rebuild their country.

The Jews who had been dragged to the West from Budapest in Arrow Cross times were liberated only in the last days of the war in places like Dachau and Mauthausen, where they often met with the survivors of the death marches from Auschwitz and other concentration camps in the east. The death rate among the deportees was enormous both before and following liberation by the US army; many died because of the sudden availability of nourishing food. Soon, the majority of survivors made their way home, often in the company of Hungarian soldiers, right-wing refugees, students and others who had been ordered abroad by the Arrow Cross regime. Many among these people returned not to Hungary but to areas that now again belonged, respectively, to Romania, Yugoslavia and Czechoslovakia, or to a land that had been part of Czechoslovakia then became Hungary but was now part of the Soviet Ukraine. Thousands of Jewish survivors as well as fugitive war criminals and other Gentile refugees remained in Germany, many Jews hoping to get to Palestine, others, whether Jewish or nonJewish, eventually moving to the USA, Canada, Australia and in the case of the war criminals, mainly to Argentina.

The postwar fate of the survivors and of the perpetrators, the memory of the Holocaust or rather, how both Communists and nationalists attempted to play down its memory, deserve a separate essay. Here it should be enough to say that retribution under the aegis of a democratic coalition regime was more severe than in most other countries and that, despite many grave shortcomings, the proceedings of the newly constituted people's courts were adequate. Certainly, these were no show trials, and every defendant had his day in court. Many of the guilty escaped justice, especially those who had fled west with the German troops, but over three hundred of the principal war criminals were sent back by the US Army in 1945–1946. As a result, four prime ministers, including, of course, Döme Sztójay and Ferenc Szálasi, were executed, together with nearly two hundred other generals, politicians, high-ranking civil servants as well as ordinary sadists and the murderers of Jews. Prime minister László Bárdossy was shot for the debatable crime of having waged war on the Soviet Union, but crimes against the Jews figured in almost every trial. Regent Horthy was never tried, in part because the Americans refused to send him back from his German exile, and in part because Stalin appreciated Horthy's effort, in October 1944, to secede from the war. He died in Portugal in 1957, having been supported, as a penniless refugee, by a few American diplomats and by his Jewish friends. If anyone should ever have been both decorated for valour and executed for the vilest of crimes against humanity, it was this dignified, charming, rather dim-witted former Austro-Hungarian admiral.[35] The reconstruction of a Hungary in ruins proceeded at an amazing pace in which Jewish entrepreneurs and engineers played a crucial role. Moreover, because the Jews alone were absolutely reliable and untainted by fascist crimes, the Soviet occupation authorities, and the first democratic coalition governments, entrusted the Jewish survivors with key positions in the police and administration. In 1947–1949, the Communist leaders, returning from Moscow, gradually established a totalitarian dictatorship; the infamous Bolshevik "Quadriga," consisting of Mátyás Rákosi, Ernő Gerő, Mihály Farkas and József Révai, were all of Jewish origin and so was the head, as well as many commanders, of the powerful political police. Thus it came that, following the massacre of most of the Hungarian Jews, individual Jews assumed control, for the first time since 1919, not only of much of the economy but also of politics and the administration. Ironically, it was as if the right-wing regimes had made sure that only the most vigorous, the most talented, and the most revengeful of the Jewish population should survive: the rich, the assimilated and the labour-service men who came home to find their homes pillaged and their families forever gone. The most mind-boggling aspect of these developments was that all the Communists firmly hid their Jewish origins, and that Jewish political policemen unhesitatingly

---

35 Retribution in post-Second World War Hungary is well discussed in László Karsai's essay, „The People's Courts and Revolutionary Justice in Hungary, 1945–1946", in Deák, Gross and Judt, eds, *The Politics of Retribution in Europe* pp. 233–251.

tortured their Jewish—and Gentile—victims, more and more of whom were themselves Communists.

All this lasted only a few years. In the late 1940s and early 1950s, many of the Second World War expropriators of Jewish goods were themselves expropriated and very soon a new elite arose, often of peasant and working-class stock; meanwhile, most of the Jews, whether Communists, non-Communists, or antiCommunists, left the country. Today, there exists only a very small community of maybe 15,000 practising Jews, although there are many other Hungarians of Jewish or partly Jewish origin. Happily, the feared anti-Semitic scapegoating for Communist rule never took place, although there were some local cases in 1946, with maybe a half a dozen victims.

After the war, as a form of collective punishment, much of Hungary's Germanspeaking minority, nearly 200,000 persons, was expelled from the country. The great historic ethnic cleansing that marked the twentieth century was now almost complete, a procedure that seems to have taken place everywhere in Eastern and Central Europe at great cost in suffering, in economic crises and in declining public morality. Only slowly are the leaders of these countries coming to the recognition that the expulsions, deportations and killings were self-defeating madness.

Chapter 6
Facts about the Number of Shoah Victims in Hungary[1]

Tamás Stark

When we study a historical event or series of events that had a major influence on the size of a population, it usually turns out quickly that the source considered to be the most accurate, i.e., statistical census, does not provide exact data of the kind that could serve as solid grounds for further analysis. This is especially the case with population statistics in relation to the World War II. As a result of the war, the passage of the front, and the disintegration of public administration, statistical data provision was also disrupted. Data on the dramatic changes in the number and composition of the population that occurred in the last months of the war are scarce and fragmented. Therefore, we will never learn exactly how many Hungarian soldiers were killed in World War II, what the number of civil casualties was, or how many fell into Soviet captivity as prisoners of war, and how many of the latter never returned home.

It is especially difficult to determine the number of Holocaust victims; and the reason for that is not only the general lack of figures in relation to the last months of the war. The difficulties due to the lack of data supply are capped by decades of uncertainty regarding the statistical census of the Jewish population.

For about half a century, censuses carried out every ten years from 1869 on gave a thorough insight into the population data of the Hungarian Jewry. Uncertainties regarding their numbers begin in 1920. After 1919 the spread

---

[1] First published as: Tamás Stark, "Adatok a holocaust magyarországi áldozatainak számáról", in *Visszatérés, újrakezdés*, edited by János Botos, and Tamás Kovács (Budapest: Holocaust Dokumentációs Központ és Emlékgyűjtemény Közalapítvány, 2007).

of anti-Semitism triggered a surge of conversion to Christianity among a significant proportion of the Jewish population. Hungarian censuses traditionally did not register ethnic belonging – religion, however, figured among the first questions on the census sheets. As a result of apostasy, the registered number of "Israelites" comprised less and less of the total size of the Hungarian Jewish population. In 1920 Israelites numbered 473,310 – 454 persons fewer than in 1910.[2] In 1930 the number of Israelites dropped to 444,567, then by 1941 to 403,614.[3] Thus a growing part of Hungary's Jewry – or to be more precise, of the former Israelite community – was disappearing from the statistics from 1920.

Despite these insecure and defective sources, a detailed and seemingly reliable set of data was produced about the number of Hungarian Shoah victims as early as in spring 1946, which has since then come to be adopted by nearly all historical works on the subject. The calculations made by the Statistical Department of the Hungarian Section of the World Jewish Congress were published, together with explanations, by Jenő Lévai in his book *Fekete könyv a magyar zsidóság szenvedéseiről* (Black book about the sufferings of Hungarian Jews).[4] The calculations, carried out in two different ways, came down to 560,000 victims.[5]

This figure and the related series of data were incorporated into numerous historical monographs, while a rounded off version of 600,000 was picked up mostly by journalists. That figure covers the victims on the territory of Hungary enlarged between 1938 and 1941.

We can understand the weight and the size of the calculated loss as it became common knowledge if we review the estimates made before spring 1946.

The first detailed loss calculations appeared on April 26, 1945, in a magazine of modest format published by the Borochov Circle, *Az Út* (Haderech – The road). The anonymous compilers of the data set estimated the number of those struck by the "Jewish laws" at one million. From that, they deducted 40,000 and 60,000 persons – those killed during deportations in 1941

---

2 *A zsidó népesség száma településenként, 1840–1941* (Budapest: Központi Statisztikai Hivatal, 1993), 26.
3 Ibid.
4 Jenő Lévai, *Fekete könyv a magyar zsidóság szenvedéseiről* (Budapest: Officina, 1946), 313–316.
5 Several works cite 565,000 instead of 560,000.

Facts about the Number of Shoah Victims in Hungary

and in forced labor service, respectively – as well as the 720,000 victims of the German occupation and the Hungarian Arrow Cross era. After these deductions, they estimated the number of survivors at 100,000 to 120,000 people. In reality, the latter figure applied only to the Jews of Budapest, because those deported or taken into labor service from the countryside were all considered to have perished. The compilers of the data set did not deem it likely that anyone would return from deportation or labor service. According to their calculations, the total loss was approximately 880,000 to 900,000 people.

The May 18, 1945, number of the daily *Mai Nap* published an article with the title "Az első hivatalos statisztika" (The first official statistics). The figures published were supplied by the Israelite Community of Pest. According to the stocktaking, the number of those having fallen victim to deportation in fall 1941 and to labor service before 1944 was 110,000. In these calculations, to the loss of 720,000 Jews after the German occupation was added the approximately 12,000 victims of the Arrow Cross terror in Budapest. Nonetheless, the total loss was still lower than the previous sum total (842,000 persons). The reason for that is that when determining the number of survivors, the authors of the figures counted on the return of 30,000 people from deportation, and they also set a Jewish population for 1941 that was somewhat smaller than 1,000,000.

In his *Sárga könyv* (Yellow book), published in summer 1945, Béla Vihar estimated the number of those affected by the racist laws at around 900,000. According to his calculations, 80,000 lost their lives before March 19, 1944;[6] 680,000 Jews were deported in summer 1944, and the victims of the Arrow Cross terror numbered 35,000. Similarly to the statistics published earlier, he also estimated the number of the Jews liberated in Budapest at around 110,000. But Béla Vihar also took into consideration 20,000 registered returnees, mentioning that another 40,000 survivors were expected to come home. Due to the fact that he adopted a population figure for 1941 smaller than the earlier estimates and a relatively high estimated number of returnees, the total loss was 720,000 persons.

---

6   Béla Vihar, *Sárga könyv* (Sao Paulo, 1945), 223–224.

Although the Statistical Department of the Hungarian Section of the World Jewish Congress had most likely participated in the elaboration of the above data set, the first summary definitely issued by this institution came out in December 1945.[7] According to the account prepared by Zsigmond Pál Pach and Szigfried Róth, two senior fellows of the Statistical Department, the Jewish population numbered 925,000 in 1941, at the onset of the Shoah. The two experts adopted as a benchmark value the population size of Israelites of the 1941 census, i.e., 725,000. They estimated the number of Jews belonging to various Christian denominations at 200,000, thus arriving at the figure of 925,000. As of March 1944, 63,000 persons perished during the deportations of 1941 or in labor service, and 728,000 were deported and killed during the German occupation. There is an important difference, though, in comparison with the previous data set: the Statistical Department determined the number of survivors, including those deportees who eventually returned, to be 243,000 persons. Mainly as a result of the latter statistic, the calculated loss was substantially lower than the previous calculation: 628,000 persons.

The Statistical Department produced its second data set, significantly modified and eventually adopted by historiography, in spring 1946. With reference to the calculations statistician Alajos Dolányi Kovács made during the war, the authors of the new calculation determined the number of Jews having converted to Christianity to be 100,000. The loss before the German occupation is identical to the number that was supplied by the first version prepared a few months earlier (i.e., 63,000). The number of those deported and killed in 1944 was modified from 728,000 to 618, 000, mainly due to the reduction of the total number of the Jewish population by 100,000. The authors of this data set arrived at this result with the help of two different calculation methods that confirmed each other.

According to them, there were 231,453 Jews living in Budapest when the German troops marched in. Since they estimated the number of survivors in Budapest at 124,000 – based on sources of information about the ghetto population and the number of those in hiding – the missing population consists of 105,435 people, in consideration of the 2,000 who had fled abroad. In the

---

7   MOL Jelenkortörténeti Gyűjtemény, XIX-J-1-a-II.21.t. 29/Be/1946.

Facts about the Number of Shoah Victims in Hungary

view of the staff of the Statistical Department, the accuracy of this calculation by subtraction was also demonstrated by factual data. During the deportation of the Jews living in the countryside, 7,500 people were deported from the outskirts of the capital. In addition, 76,209 Jews were deported from the capital during the Arrow Cross era, while 21,744 people lost their lives in acts of terror. The total number of those deported and killed was 105,455, which is almost identical to the previous end result.

In March 1944 there were 530,544 Jews living in the countryside: from there the entire Jewish population was deported. The number of those serving in labor battalions liberated at the end of the war "reached barely 15,000 people within the increased territory of the country," the Statistical Department claims in its analysis. It goes on to write: "If we add to that those 3,000 Jews who had originally lived in the countryside, but fled abroad, and deduct that sum from the size of the countryside Jewry as of March 19, 1944, it transpires that during the German occupation 512,554 people were deported from the rural areas of the increased Hungary." The authors declared that the correctness of the figures was also confirmed by factual data. Based on gendarme Lieutenant Colonel László Ferenczy's report and other sources cited in the compilation, altogether 453,551 people were deported from the countryside up until the Arrow Cross coup d'état. During Szálasi's rule, 74,000 men in labor service were turned over to the Germans. This figure should be added to the number of those deported in summer 1944, and then after deducting the number of those in labor service who were eventually liberated (15,000), we arrive exactly at the figure calculated with the help of the subtraction method: 512,554.

From 618,000 – the number of deportees and persons killed in the capital and in the countryside (105,455 + 512,554) – the experts of the Statistical Department deducted the number of those who had returned from deportation, i.e., 121,000 people to their knowledge. The number of the victims of deportations and massacres thus turned out to be 497,000. To the latter they added the number of those annihilated before 1944 (63,000), which yielded a total loss of 560,000.

The end result and the key details of the calculations were first published by Zsigmond Pál Pach on March 26, 1946 in *Új Élet*, the journal of Hungarian Israelites. A few months later Jenő Lévai published the data set in its entirety, along with explanations.

If we go over the calculations carried out right after the war, we can declare that in every case the loss was determined by deducting the number of survivors, known or assumed, from the estimated population size of 1941 – an essentially correct method. Thus the loss was the difference between the initial figure and the total number of those liberated in the capital and in the countryside, plus those who had come back. Since, however, the number of those who had returned varied from 30,000 to 100,000 in the calculations presented above, and the extreme values of the size of the Jewish population in 1941 differed from each other by about 160,000, the size of the loss depended crucially on the initial figure, i.e., on the assumed size of the population prior to the Shoah. Based on the above, it seems that the compilers of the various data sets used the end result of the difference between the population size before and after the Shoah to determine and sort out the intermediate figures, that is, the number of those deported and those murdered by the Arrow Cross regime.

What supports this assumption is primarily the analysis published by the Statistical Department in March 1946. The fact that the end results calculated to six digits with the help of two different methods are identical could be proof of the accuracy of the calculations; but such an exact correspondence in the figures also raises a shadow of doubt, for there were not and could not have been such verifiable facts at the experts' disposal. Several pieces of the factual data were not upheld by historical research in the long run. During Szálasi's rule the number of labor servicemen turned over to the Germans was not 74,000; and 76,000 Jews were not deported from the capital. After the Arrow Cross coup, Szálasi agreed to "lend" 50,000 Hungarian Jews. However, the number of the Jews driven towards the German border in death marches and those transported by train cannot be defined precisely. There were 35,000 Jews who arrived in the area of the Südostwall that was being constructed on the German (Austrian)–Hungarian border, but no aggregate data survived about those deported to Dachau, Bergen-Belsen and other concentration camps.[8] The fate of labor force battalions cannot be traced back precisely, either. One list was preserved regard-

---

8   The document marked "Unterlagen BAM Freiburg-RM 11111/289" of the Military Archives of Freiburg is quoted by Leopold Banny, *Schild im Osten. Der Südostwall zwischen Donau und Untersteiermarkt 1944/45* (Eisenstadt, 1985), 89. See also Szabolcs Szita, "Történelmi áttekintés a munkaszolgálatról 1942–1945", in *Holocaust Füzetek* 2 (1993): 33.

ing the battalions handed over to the Germans, according to which 70 companies (15,000–17,000 people) were ordered to take part in fortification works in November 1944. There are no sources available about subsequent handovers. From November 1944 domestic troops were already disintegrating, and the fragmented data that came down to us imply that thousands of labor servicemen fled from their troops, or surrendered to the Soviet army with its superior numbers. Nonetheless, several retreating companies reached Germany and finished the war in a concentration camp. We do not have adequate data about the victims of the massacres carried out by the Arrow Cross in Budapest, either. Based on the trials held by people's courts and on funeral statistics, about 15,000 people perished as a result of murder and inhuman living conditions.[9] However, since the summary was prepared about eight months after the end of the war, the figures supplied regarding the number of those who had returned were inevitably fragmented.

It is unfortunate that the inaccuracies and inconsistencies of the data set compiled by the Statistical Department of the Hungarian Section of the World Jewish Congress usually go unnoticed by the researchers of this era, who adopt the figures, calculated in rudimentary conditions and with a lack of adequate sources, unaltered and without criticism.

The dimensions of the total loss of lives may be deduced from the difference of headcounts before and after the war, but we should not expect to receive accurate results from this operation because both the population size of 1941 and the number of survivors can be determined only as widely varying figures.

The census of 1941 registered 725,007 Israelites. This figure, however, does not include those who were considered as Jews according to the anti-Semitic Jewish laws. At the earlier censuses in Hungary only religion was registered, but this time statisticians manifested a sudden surge of curiosity about the "origin" of the respondents as well.[10] Some of the census sheets had already

---

9 On the victims of the Cross Arrow terror, see Tamás Stark, *Zsidóság a vészkorszakban és a felszabadulás után, 1939–1955* (Budapest: MTA Történettudományi Intézete, 1995), 29.
10 The "Jewish question" and the "Swabian question" were raised simultaneously during the preparation and implementation of the 1941 census. Since 1880, censuses in Hungary had contained no question related to ethnicity, therefore the ethnic background of the population could only be inferred from the mother tongue and the spoken language. During the census of February 1941, the interviewers

been printed when the original list of questions was completed with two additional ones in order to identify the number of those Christians who were of Jewish origin. In the month of the census, the relevant legislation was Act IV of 1939, approved as of May 4, 1939.[11] According to that, a person would be considered a Jew, regardless of his or her religious affiliation, if at least one of his or her parents or two of his or her grandparents were members of the Israelite faith. The additional questions on the census sheets thus inquired whether any ancestors of the respondent belonged to the Israelite faith, and whether the respondent should be considered a Jew or not on the basis of the above mentioned article. During the census 61,548 Christians said that at least one of their grandparents was or had been an Israelite. Based on their own declarations, 34,435 of these Christians came within the scope of Act IV of 1939; whereas 27,113 of these data providers did not qualify as Jews.[12]

At the same time, there were a number of distorting factors to take into consideration with regard to the results of the 1941 census. Although the census law stipulated that supplying false data was to be punished by a fine and also that the data provided had to be substantiated by authentic documents, in reality, many – sensing the dangers inherent in conscription – tried to conceal their origin. It should also be noted that Act IV of 1939, which was in force at the time of the census, was followed soon after the census by another act that further expanded the definition of who should be considered Jews. The so-called "racialist" Act XV of 1941 went further than the second Jewish law: it abolished all the exemptions of the earlier law. The disenfranchising measures were capped by the legal prohibition of mixed marriages, and sexual relationships between Jews and non-Jews were regarded as "a racial disgrace" for the latter. Out of the 61,548 census responders belonging to Christian denominations but having Jewish ancestors,

---

inquired not only about mother tongue but also about ethnicity. With the help of the census, the Hungarian government wished to be informed regarding two important "racial" issues. On the one hand, they wanted to see how many people identified themselves as ethnic Germans regardless of the mother tongue in the expanded national territory. The Hungarian government was curious to know how many Hungarian citizens could be affected in theory by the German "repatriation" program initiated by Hitler. On the other hand, the census provided an opportunity to define the number of those affected by the "Jewish laws".

11 That was the so-called Second Jewish Law. The first was passed in 1938 and it restricted the percentage of Israelites in various occupations. (The editor.)

12 About the census of 1941 see Alajos Dolányi Kovács, "A keresztény vallású, de zsidó származású népesség a népszámlálás szerint", *Magyar Statisztikai Szemle* 4–5 (1944).

Facts about the Number of Shoah Victims in Hungary

57,477 declared having two or more Israelite grandparents. They were all categorized as Jews according to Act XV of 1941. Thus the Jewish laws concerned at least 782,000 Hungarian citizens at the outset of the Shoah.

With reference to the "unreliability" of the data providers, the results of the 1941 census were regarded as only an approximation by many anti-Semitic statisticians. From 1938, with the creation of the first Jewish law, the daily press often published exaggerated estimates of the number of Christians with "Jewish blood". Alajos Dolányi Kovács, a senior fellow of the Central Statistical Office, who was regarded as an expert on the matter, estimated "the number of Christians more or less mixed with Jews" at 100,000.[13] This estimate was adopted by the Statistical Department of the Hungarian Section of the World Jewish Congress when making its own calculations in early spring 1946. According to Dolányi Kovács, the upper limit of the number of the persecuted was 820,000. Based on that estimate and the census data of 1941, the number of Israelites and Hungarians categorized as Jews was most likely somewhere in the range of 780,000–820,000 at the beginning of the Shoah.

The number of survivors, however, can be determined only within a wide margin on the basis of the historical sources. The greatest number of people were liberated from the ghetto of Budapest, but sources disagree about the number of residents and deportees there. Miksa Domokos, a member of the Jewish Council from October 28, 1944, and one of the leaders of the ghetto in Pest, estimated the number of those living in the ghetto at 69,000 in his testimony given in the Szálasi trial.[14] Edmund Veesenmayer, Germany's plenipotentiary in Hungary after March 19, wrote about 80,000 people in his report of November 20.[15] This figure was also confirmed by Sweden's minister in Budapest, Carl Ivan Danielsson in his report of November 26.[16] At the same time, in a mid-November memorandum, Friedrich Born, the Budapest representative of the International Committee of the Red Cross, mentioned about 100,000 people living in the ghetto.[17] On December 25 Born repeated

---

13 Ibid., 100.
14 Elek Karsai and László Karsai, *A Szálasi-per* (Budapest: Reform, 1988), 605–606.
15 *Eichmann in Hungary*, ed. Jenő Lévai (Budapest: Pannónia Press, 1961), 160.
16 Lani Yahil, "Raoul Wallenberg – His Mission", *Yad Vashem Studies* XV, Jerusalem: Note 67, 43.
17 See Arieh Ben-Tov, *Facing the Holocaust in Budapest* (Geneva: Henry Dunant Institute, 1988), 323.

his figure of 100,000, adding that there could be even more people inside the ghetto. In his memoirs, Rezső Kasztner, one of the heads of the Zionist rescue team of Budapest, also wrote about 100,000 individuals when recalling the population size of the ghetto.[18] In consideration of all of the above sources, the number of those liberated from the ghetto was most probably between 70,000 and 100,000.

At least 20,000 people survived the war in safe houses.[19] An additional 20,000 to 30,000 people went into hiding with forged documents.[20] In light of the above, 120,000 to 140,000 Jews can be assumed to have survived the Shoah in Budapest.[21] According to the data of the National Committee for Attending Deportees (DEGOB), 83,331 deportees returned to Hungary from April 1945 to September 1946,[22] 63,000 of whom were originally from the country's present-day territory. The Government Agency for Repatriation registered an additional 4,765 persons during 1946–47.[23] To the number of the Jews liberated in Budapest and of those having returned from deportation (a total of 180,000–200,000 persons) should be added the headcount of liberated labor servicemen and Jews hiding in the countryside.

The data set compiled by the Statistical Department in early spring 1946 calculated with 11,000 labor servicemen, liberated mostly in the countryside.

---

18 *Der Kastner-Bericht über Eichmanns Menschenhandel in Ungarn* (München: Kindler Verlag, 1961), 241.
19 Gábor Vajna and Gábor Kemény, ministers of Szálasi's government, testified in the Szálasi trial that in November 1944 there were about 40,000 people in the safe houses. In early December, however, about half of the people hiding in the safe houses were taken to the ghetto of Pest. See Elek Karsai and László Karsai, *A Szálasi-per* (Budapest: Reform, 1988), 248, 421.
20 Lévai, *Fekete könyv* , 315. Lévai cites one of the reports of the Hungarian Section of the World Jewish Congress. See also Alexander Grossmann, *Nur das Gewissen. Carl Lutz* (Wald: Waldgut, 1986), 260–270.
21 The Budapest Municipal Statistical Office carried out a census on the theoretical date of March 25, 1945. A separate account was taken of Israelites upon the commission of the Israelite Community of Pest. Thus, a little more than a month after the liberation of the capital, 86,910 Jews were registered. Since more than one third of Budapest's Jewry belonged to Christian denominations, this figure implies at least 130,000 survivors. About the census see "Népmozgalmi események a főváros ostroma idején", *Városi Szemle* (1945): 54–56.
22 DEGOB registered precisely 74,331 returning Jews between May 1945 and September 1946, while the number of those having returned in April 1945 was estimated at 9,000. Source: Hungarian Jewish Museum and Archives (Magyar Zsidó Múzeum és Levéltár), Budapest; National Committee for Attending Deportees (Deportáltakat Gondozó Országos Bizottság), L.4/6.; József Pásztor's legacy. The figures were first published by Rita Horváth, "A Deportáltakat Gondozó Országos Bizottság története", *Magyar Zsidó Levéltári Füzetek* 1 Budapest (1997): 25.
23 Military Archives, Budapest, 1947 eln. 1333.

Facts about the Number of Shoah Victims in Hungary

As far as the authors of that report knew, there were no survivors outside the capital other than those returning from labor service. At the same time, in a letter to Miklós Béla Dálnoki, prime minister of the interim [provisional] government, dated April 20, 1945, the Israelite Community of Pest wrote about 20,000 Jews hiding in the countryside and 20,000 to 30,000 liberated labor servicemen who had returned or were returning to their former domicile.[24] Numerous memoirs and contemporary documents make mention of labor servicemen liberated all over the countryside, but there is no comprehensive and authentic figure about their number at our disposal (for Hungary's present territory). Nonetheless, the rapid report released by the Central Statistical Office in June 1945 provides a hint at the number of survivors in the countryside, mostly from among labor servicemen, in that it cites the number of those returning to their country homes as 39,729.[25] Unfortunately, the rapid report did not clarify whether this figure referred to the entire rural Jewish population, to liberated labor servicemen who had come home, or only to returned deportees. The DEGOB figures facilitate interpreting the result of the survey carried out by the Central Statistical Office. From April to June 30, 1945, DEGOB registered a total of about 47,000 deportees who were originally from Budapest, the countryside, or beyond the national borders. However, about half of those who had returned were from the areas again detached from Hungary or from Budapest. Thus, based on the DEGOB figures, it is reasonable to assume that the bulk of the rural population of about 40,000 Jews, was comprised of labor servicemen who had been liberated in various corners of the country and had returned to their homes, along with a limited number of survivors who had been hiding in the countryside.

Therefore, historical sources –depending in part on whether or not we accept the report of the Israelite Community of Pest as reliable – allow us to go only so far as to affirm that the number of survivors within the current national borders was certainly greater than 190,000 but most likely fewer than 260,000. The estimates of two leading statisticians, Árpád Snyder and Lajos Thirring, support this claim. Snyder estimated the number of the

---

24 *A magyarországi zsidóság holocaustja, 1944*, ed. Ágnes Ságvári (Budapest: Jewish Agency, 1994), 23.
25 "Tájékoztató gyorsfelvétel a községek és városok közérdekű viszonyairól", *Magyar Statisztikai Szemle* 1–6 (1946).

remaining Hungarian Jewry at 220,000 in his paper published in 1946 in *Magyar Statisztikai Szemle*, entitled "Becslés Magyarországnak a második világháború következtében elszenvedett emberveszteségeiről" (Estimates of the human losses suffered by Hungary as a result of World War II). In his memorandum written upon the request of the Ministry of Foreign Affairs in preparation for the Paris peace conference, Lajos Thirring set the number of survivors at 260,000.[26]

In contrast, we have detailed information about the number of people liberated in, or having returned to, the territories lost by Hungary in the 1947 peace treaty.

According to a report drafted in November 1944 by Ernő Marton, who was delegated to Northern Transylvania on behalf of the Joint Representation of Bucharest, the Jewish Agency and the International Red Cross, there were 7,200 survivors in the area that had belonged to Hungary two months earlier.[27] The Romanian Section of the World Jewish Conference gathered data about the Jewish population living in Northern Transylvania in September 1945, in 1946 and in January 1947. Based on that information, the number of Jews living there rose from 22,909 in fall 1945 to 44,706 by early 1947.[28] The sources reveal that basically the population increase was due not to immigration from various other Romanian regions but to the return of deportees.

In summer 1945 the International Red Cross also collected data in Subcarpathia, which had been annexed to the Soviet Union. According to the census, sluggish and partial, the number of those having returned from deportation and those locally liberated was about 12,000 to 13,000 people.[29] However, the total number of Subcarpathian survivors was much higher than that. In Czechoslovakia more than 8,000 Jews originating from Subcarpathia were registered

---

26 Lajos Thirring, *Megjegyzések a Zsidó Világkongresszus Magyarországi Képviseletének a magyarországi zsidók helyzetére vonatkozó adataihoz* (MOL Jelenkortörténeti Gyűjtemény XIX-J-1-a-II. 21.t. 29/Be/1946).
27 Yad Vashem Archives, Ernő Marton Archives I.M. 2624/I.
28 La population juive de la Transylvanie du Nord, Congrès Juif Mondial Section Roumanie, Bucarest, 1945; Les résidences des Juifs de Roumanie, Bucarest, 1947. See also Tamás Stark, *Hungarian Jews during the Holocaust and after the Second World War, 1939–1949, A Statistical Review*, East European Monographs (New York: Boulder-Columbia University Press, 2000), 101–103.
29 Yad Vashem Archives, Ernő Marton Archives I.M. 2625/4.

Facts about the Number of Shoah Victims in Hungary

in fall 1945.³⁰ A substantial part of them had gone straight to Czechoslovakia from the camps because they did not want to live in the Soviet Union. Numerous Subcarpathian Jews settled in Hungary, too, if only temporarily. The partial data lead us to conclude that of a Jewish community once numbering more than 100,000 people, only about 20,000 lived to see the day of their liberation.³¹

In Slovakia survivors were enumerated with the help of the American Jewish Joint Distribution Committee (the Joint) at the beginning of 1946. Of the 27,000 Slovakian Jews, 6,000 were living on the strip of land annexed to Hungary in 1938.³² However, the sum total of Jews having returned from labor service and deportation surpassed the number of those registered. In its report sent to the World Jewish Congress on November 14, 1947, the Israelite Community of Bratislava spoke of 4,000 survivors in relation to Košice only.³³ A memorandum of February 1946 issued by the Central Organization of Slovakian Jewish Communities stated the number of survivors of the Hungarian Shoah as the round number of 10,000.³⁴

In Délvidék (i.e., lands to the south of Hungary) the Vojvodinian Regional Committee registered 3,532 survivors in 1946.³⁵

In the stocktaking report repeatedly cited above, the Statistical Department of the Hungarian Section of the World Jewish Congress determined the number of the Jews liberated in the areas formerly re-annexed by Hungary and of those returning there to be 65,000 people. Based on sources that were not yet available in spring 1946 when the data set related to the loss of Jewish lives was compiled, and also on later research, the number of survivors in the territories re-annexed, then again detached from Hungary was close to 80,000. Thus, with regards to Hungary's territory during the war, the sum total of survivors was between 270,000 and 340,000.

---

30   Yad Vashem Archives, Ernő Marton Archives I.M. 2624/I, also American Jewish Archives, Cincinnati, WJC, H96, A14/3/93.
31   Subcarpathian researcher András S. Benedek, however, estimates the number of Jewish survivors of the Shoah at more than 30,000. András S. Benedek, *Kárpátalja története és kultúrtörténete* (Budapest: Bereményi Kiadó, 1995), 47.
32   Register of All Persons Saved from Anti-Jewish Persecution in Slovakia, World Jewish Congress, Bratislava, 1946.
33   American Jewish Archives, Cincinnati, WJC, H96, A14/3/92.
34   Yad Vashem Archives, Ernő Marton Archives I.M. 2625/4.
35   Museum of History of Vojvodina, Novi Sad, Ák. 23410, 35–38.

Based on the population census data of 1941, there were about 780,000 to 820,000 Hungarians who fell under the scope of the Jewish laws. Taking into consideration the widely varying number of survivors, the only reasonable claim that can be made regarding the losses is that in Hungary the death toll in the war against Jewry was certainly smaller than 550,000 but larger than 440,000.[36]

The Statistical Department of the Hungarian Section of the World Jewish Congress was not involved solely in taking stock of the losses. Under the direction of Zsigmond Pál Pach and Vilmos Sándor, and with external help, the staff of that department began to identify the survivors in July 1945. Most of the data collection was performed in summer and fall 1945 in Budapest, but the stocktaking in the countryside lasted till November 1946. In Budapest 117,363 personal forms were completed; in the countryside, there were 47,967 of them.[37] Of the 165,330 registered survivors, 143,924 people, i.e., 87 percent, identified themselves as Israelites.

In the framework of the research led by sociologist András Kovács, published in *Zsidók a mai Magyarországon* (Jews in Hungary today), I recently attempted to identify and trace the size of the Jewish population from the Shoah till 2000.[38] I used two essential data sets. One of them was the number of Israelites registered by the Statistical Department in 1945–46 by sex and age cohort. The second figure taken as a benchmark value was the potential maximum of the estimated 260,000 survivors, also broken down by sex and age cohort. Applying the statistically elaborated method of population forecast, I modelled the main demographic changes also taking emigration into

---

36   For more on figures, see Stark, *Zsidóság a vészkorszakban*, and Stark, *Hungarian Jews during the Holocaust*, 110–120.
37   National Archives of Hungary, Present-day History Collection (MOL Jelenkortörténeti Gyűjtemény) XXXIII July 1–October 1, 1946. The census was comprehensive only in theory. Questionnaires were not filled in by many survivors. Not even the census methodology allowed for taking stock of the total loss. In Budapest the primary source of information was usually the concierge. The interviewers paid a visit to them and asked them about the Jewish residents of the house that they should visit. In the countryside interviewers inquired of authorities and at Israelite communities about the address of survivors. Besides direct contact, the Statistical Department also requested data from the local public administration authorities by correspondence.
38   About the calculation see Tamás Stark, "Kísérlet a zsidó népesség számának behatárolására 1945 és 2000 között", in *Zsidók a mai Magyarországon*, ed. András Kovács (Budapest: Múlt és Jövő, 2002), 101–127.

Facts about the Number of Shoah Victims in Hungary

account. In order to calculate the Jewish population size, I looked at the live birth rates of the female population of Budapest by cohorts as well as at the mortality rates of men and women of Budapest by cohorts. In other words, I extrapolated the demographic specificities of the total population of Budapest to the Jewish population of the country, since at least two thirds of the remaining Jewry were from Budapest, and in the post-war decades the majority of the rural Jewish population also settled in the capital.

The results reflect the continuous diminution of the Hungarian Jewry. The final figures derived from the data set in relation to the Israelite population registered during 1945–46 (143,624 people) suppose the existence of 67,000 Jews by 1995 and 64,000 Jews by 2000. In theory, these figures indicate the lower threshold of the Hungarian Jewish population. The second series of calculations, which took the presumed maximum number of survivors (260,000) as a starting point, lead to 124,000 Jews by 1995 and 118,000 by 2000. Theoretically, these results designate the upper limit of the Hungarian Jewish population.[39]

There were 18,634 persons in the registry of the Hungarian Jewish Heritage Public Foundation as of January 19, 1999. Since all who were persecuted during the war are entitled to receive an annuity, this figure represents those Jews who were born in 1945 or earlier, i.e., those people who were at least 54 years of age in 1999. Based on the calculation taking the assumed maximum number of the surviving population (260,000) as a starting point, the number of those belonging to the age cohort above 54 is 21,073 in 2000. Although the small difference between the calculated and the actual result does not prove the accuracy of the calculations, it is an indication that the trend presented above is correct and the initial data are well founded.

---

39 It should be noted, however, that while the number of persons born from Jewish parents steadily decreased in the past decade (as a result of the disadvantageous age structure due primarily to the losses in the Shoah), the circle of the Jewish population has expanded significantly thanks to mixed marriages.

Chapter 7
The Role of Colonel Ferenc Koszorús in the Prevention of the Deportation of the Jews of Budapest

Attila Bonhardt

The roots of the operation led by Colonel Ferenc Koszorús – which took place on 6 July 1944 and involved the removal from Budapest of the gendarmes who had been brought to the capital to implement the deportation of the city's Jewish population – stretched back to the occupation of Hungary by the German army in March 1944.

By the summer of 1943, Germany was facing an increasingly dire situation across Europe, and given the military, political and economic exigencies faced by the Third Reich, Hitler could not permit Hungary to follow Italy's example and withdraw from the war. He was prepared to take even the most drastic steps in order to ensure that this not happen, and so he ordered a plan of operations to be drawn up for the military occupation of Hungary, which was given the name Operation Margarethe.

In February 1944, concerned because of the increasingly intense attempts by the Hungarian government to make a separate peace with the Western allied powers, Hitler ordered that the necessary troops be made available and the plans for Operation Margarethe be finalized. The day chosen for the attack was 19 March 1944.

However, in the first half of March, before Operation Margarethe was launched, a memorandum based on a report by the agents of the Reich Main Security Office (Reichssicherheitshauptamt) in Hungary was presented to

Hitler.[1] According to the memorandum, it would be more effective and more practical to take power in Hungary with the collaboration of pro-German elements in Hungarian political and military circles. The authors of the memorandum felt that aggressive intervention in Hungary, with the participation of Romanian and Slovak troops, would be technically feasible, but might have the following consequences:

1. a unified resistance would emerge, comprised of both left-wing and right-wing elements;
2. Regent Miklós Horthy would step down;
3. it would only be possible to form a government consisting of individuals who did not have the support or acceptance of the general population;
4. complete political, military, and economic chaos;
5. the supervision or disarmament of the Hungarian military would place significant demands on the German and Romanian military.

The authors of the memorandum proposed an alternative "evolutionary" solution. This solution was based on the assumption that most of the Hungarian political elite, having lost all hope of ever receiving help from the British after the failure of Allied troops to land in the Balkans and increasingly fearful of the spread of Bolshevism, would be willing to continue cooperating with Germany. Horthy was a key figure in this plan. It would be necessary, according to the memorandum, to negotiate with Horthy in order to ensure that German troops would be able to occupy the country without any armed resistance. Were the regent to remain in power, it would be possible to ensure a

---

1 The Memorandum, drawn up by Wilhelm Höttl, acting head of Counter Espionage in Central and South East Europe of the Reich Main Security Office (Reichssicherheitshauptamt or RSHA), was put on Hitler's night table. It argued against using Romanian and Slovak troops in occupying Hungary. See: http://www.bibl.u-szeged.hu/bibl/mil/ww2/doksi/d679.html . Cf. Péter Bokor, *Végjáték a Duna mentén: ausztriai beszélgetés* [End-game along the Danube: conversation in Austria with Wilhelm Höttl] (Budapest: 1982), 187. For the details of Hitler's decision to occupy Hungary see C.A. Macartney, *October Fifteenth: a history of modern Hungary, 1929–1945* (Edinburgh: Edinburgh University Press, 1956–1957) Vol. II, 225; Deborah C. Cornelius, *Hungary in World War II. Caught in the Cauldron* (New York: Fordham University Press, 2011), 270–71, reproduced in the present volume. (Editor's note)

"legal" framework for the occupation, which potentially would have the following consequences:

1. it would be possible to create a new government consisting of pro-German politicians;
2. Hungary would remain pro-German and consolidated from the perspective of domestic politics;
3. the Hungarian army and the Hungarian police and gendarmerie would remain in a state of readiness and would be at the disposal of the Reich;
4. the territory of Hungary would be completely accessible to economic exploitation;
5. the Reich would be able to add pro-German Romanian and Hungarian troops to its forces and thus would not have to pull German units away from the front for a long period of time in order to tend to affairs in Hungary.

Hitler and his inner circle agreed with the ideas in the memorandum. They decided to invite Horthy to Klessheim on 18 March, but they nonetheless gave the order to launch Operation Margarethe, regardless of the results of the negotiations.

The results of the Klessheim negotiations have been familiar to historians for some time: essentially, the German occupation of Hungary took place without any armed resistance from the Hungarian army.

What goals were the two parties able to achieve?

The Germans achieved the military objectives of Operation Margarethe. Namely, they prevented Hungary from withdrawing from the war. They also reinforced the southern part of the Eastern front, gained control of what was effectively the hinterland for the German troops who were fighting in the Balkans, and ensured the continued delivery of oil from Romania to Germany. Furthermore, with the appointment of Edmund Veesenmayer as Reich plenipotentiary in Hungary and the rise to power of an unambiguously pro-

German government, they gained complete control over the domestic situation in Hungary. Finally, this form of occupation left significant Hungarian, Romanian and German military forces free to fight on the front.

What could Horthy have hoped to achieve when he decided to remain in power and essentially permit German troops to enter and occupy Hungary without having to face any armed resistance? He may well have hoped, first and foremost, to ensure that a person would remain at the helm of the country with whom the Allied powers would be willing to negotiate when and if the military situation shifted. Another important issue was the preservation of the Hungarian army. According Miklós Kállay, who was compelled to resign as prime minister on 19 March 1944, under the circumstances it was not the government but the army that was important.[2] Both Kállay and Horthy believed (as time would tell, mistakenly) that the army would obey unconditionally the orders of the supreme commander in chief. They cherished the hope that the country might be saved from utter destruction when, at the right moment, the army switched sides and fought with the Allies. The explanation for why this did not take place is complex and would go beyond the framework of this modest inquiry, but it is quite clear that had the Hungarian army been disarmed following the occupation of the country on 19 March, all hope of any such turn of events would have been lost.

Colonel Ferenc Koszorús offered the following characterization of the situation:

> The part of the officer corps which was, given its birth and upbringing, Hungarian in its sentiment, watched the German occupation of the country on 19 March 1944 and everything that took place in its wake with tremendous despair. Their despair notwithstanding, they could do nothing to stop it. Or they did not dare do anything to stop it. For the country was under military occupation. In the leading military posts, elements were in place which leaned at all costs towards the Germans, and the part of the officer corps that was pro-German would have nipped any

---

[2] *The Confidential Papers of Admiral Horthy*. Prepared for the press and introduced by M. Szinai and L. Szűcs, (Budapest: Corvina Press, 1965), 287. Cf. *Nicholas Kállay, Hungarian Premier. A Personal Account of a Nation's Struggle in the Second World War* (Westport, CT: 1954).

The Role of Colonel Ferenc Koszorús in the Prevention of the Deportation of the Jews of Budapest

movement in the bud. But the paralysis was strengthened in large part by the fact that the officer corps had been raised in an anti-Bolshevik spirit, and Bolshevism was on the other side, since the Western powers were not terribly concerned with Hungary's fate. So if someone dared act, he could only do so at his own risk and responsibility.[3]

Since, with Horthy's sanction, the occupation of Hungary took place without any armed resistance, as far as most of the population of the country was concerned, there had merely been a change of government in the course of which politicians "more acceptable" to the German Reich had assumed control of some of the ministries. As no other substantial measures were taken, the army continued training as usual and soon began to move into the theater of military operations in order to do battle, under close German supervision and control, against the Red Army, which in the meantime was approaching the Carpathian Mountains from the east.

The German occupation had "only" two repercussions that were immediately noticeable to everyone: the harassment and arrest of people who were considered anti-war and anti-German (acts that were carried out under the oversight and with the active participation of the German security forces), and the rapid enactment of a series of government decrees that had devastating consequences for the Jewish citizens of Hungary.

Since 1938, Hungary had passed three laws and issued numerous decrees that infringed drastically on the civic and human rights of people who were legally defined as Jewish. In addition, often the individuals responsible for the enforcement of these measures went well beyond the actual framework of the laws at their own initiative. However, as a whole the Jewry of Hungary (between 760,000 and 780,000 people) had not faced any immediate direct threat. Indeed, on more than one occasion Germany had criticized Hungary's government and Horthy himself for the comparatively mild treatment of the Hungarian Jewry.

---

3   *Koszorús Ferenc emlékiratai és tanulmányainak gyűjteménye.* [The Memoirs and the collected essays of Ferenc Koszorús], ed. Mrs. István Varsa [Koszorús's widow] (New York: Universe Publishing Company, 1987), 56.

However, in March 1944 the implementation of the so-called Final Solution began in Hungary. Adolf Eichmann, the architect since 1942 of the deportations, was brought to Budapest and put at the head of an SS Sonderkommando unit of only some 200 men. His task was to organize the deportation of the Hungarian Jewry to the Nazi extermination camps under the pretext of removing them to labor camps, where allegedly they would work to contribute to the German war effort. Eichmann divided the country into six zones. His plan, much of which was efficiently implemented, was to begin with the rural Jewish communities in the eastern part of the country, specifically Sub-Carpathia, and proceed westward, concluding with the deportation in one swift and devastating stroke of the Jewish communities of Budapest and any Jews who had fled to the capital.

The German officers and military forces in Hungary were small in number and hardly well-armed; they obviously never would have been able to execute Eichmann's plan. However, it began to become clear that the "more acceptable" politicians might well offer significant assistance in the implementation of the deportations. Minister of the Interior Andor Jaross and his two undersecretaries, László Endre and László Baky, put the Hungarian administrative apparatus at the disposal of the Germans, along with the gendarmerie, a well-organized force with a military sense of discipline under the authority of the Interior Ministry. With the help of the gendarmerie, which was responsible for ensuring order in the rural towns and villages of Hungary, registries were rapidly compiled of the Jews in rural Hungary, who were then compelled to move to the designated ghettos. On 15 May 1944, the deportation began of Jews from the first zone in Hungary to the territory controlled by the Third Reich.

According to Eichmann's plan, deportations from the sixth and final zone, which included Budapest and its surroundings, were to be completed by the middle of July, and they also would be implemented with the assistance of the gendarmerie.[4] In order to ensure that the arrival and presence

---

4 The systematic deportation of the Hungarian Jews to the territory occupied by the Third Reich began in Sub-Carpathia and northern Transylvania on 15 May 1944 – the ultimate destination was the concentration camp at Auschwitz in occupied Poland. The first deportation and massacre of Hungarian Jews had taken place in late August 1941 in Kamenec-Podolsk, Ukraine; an estimated 23,000 people

The Role of Colonel Ferenc Koszorús in the Prevention of the Deportation of the Jews of Budapest

of the gendarmerie in Budapest not be met with surprise or suspicion (since the gendarmerie in principle had no jurisdiction in the capital), a celebratory dedication of the flag of the gendarmerie of Galánta (today, Galanta, a small town in Southern Slovakia) was planned for 2 July at Heroes Square. Horthy's wife was to serve as the so-called "flag mother" (a lady who acted as a patron at such ceremonies). The procession would include another three or four gendarmerie battalions, as well as the Budapest police regiment. After the celebration, the men were to be given three days' leave in Budapest, the essential goal of which was to enable them to familiarize themselves with the city. This was to be followed by the implementation of the process of deportation.[5]

By June, however, the situation had changed fundamentally. In the intervening period, the deportation of the rural Jewish communities of Hungary had proceeded according to plan,[6] but in the meantime the information contained in the so-called Vrba-Wetzler report, also known as the Auschwitz notebook, had begun to circulate in Budapest.[7] The report dispelled any doubt con-

---

who allegedly could not document their citizenship were murdered by German soldiers.) Eichmann's plan was to deport the roughly 250,000–300,000 Jews of Budapest last. By the end of July 1944, Under-Secretary Baky of the Ministry of the Interior had summoned several thousand gendarmes to the city. See: *A magyar Quisling-kormány. Sztójay Döme és társai a népbíróság előtt* [The Hungarian Quisling government: Döme Sztójay and his accomplices before the People's Court], ed. and with an introduction by László Karsai and Judit Molnár (Budapest: 1956-os KHT., 2004), 222–223.

5   *Csendőrtiszt a Markóban. Ferenczy László csendőr alezredes a népbíróság előtt* [Gendarme officer in Markó Street: Lieutenant Colonel Gendarme László Ferenczy before the People's Court], ed. and with an introduction and prepared for press with the inclusion of indices by Judit Molnár (Budapest: Scolar Kiadó, 2014), 111–112; (The record of the interrogation of the accused, László Ferenczy, by the political police, 9 November 1945), 192–193; (Gábor Faragho's interrogation of witnesses on the fourth day of the hearing concerning László Ferenczy, 6 April 1946), 241–245; (the interrogation of László Ferenczy in the open hearing of the Endre – Baky – Jaross trial, 22 December 1945). Cf. "The trial of Gendarme Colonel István Láday" in the Budapest Archives, Nb 4995/1946.

6   See: *Csendőrtiszt a Markóban*, the reports of László Ferenczy; *A Wilhelmstrasse és Magyarország* [Wilhelmstrasse and Hungary; henceforth *Wilhelmstrasse*], coll., ed. and introduced. by György Ránki et al. (Budapest: Kossuth Könyvkiadó, 1968), documents 673, 683 and 685.

7   The so-called Vrba-Wetzler report was compiled at the end of April 1944 in Zsolna (today Žilina in Slovakia) by Walter Rosenberg (who in 1944, after his escape from Auschwitz, took the name Rudolf Vrba) and Alfréd Wetzler, two Slovak Jews. With the help of a resistance organization in Auschwitz, both men managed to escape from the camp tasked with informing the world and, first and foremost, the Jewish communities of Hungary of what was taking place in Auschwitz, where preparations were already underway for the arrival of the Hungarian Jews. On 21 April, Wetzler and Rosenberg made it to the territory of Slovakia. By 26 April, they had put together a detailed account (written in German) in which they described the layout of Auschwitz-Birkenau, the system according to which it functioned, the process by which the deportees were sorted (some sent immediately to the gas chambers, others sent to the work camp) and tattooed, and the gas chambers and crematoria. The report also contained data concerning the number of Jews who had been gassed between April 1942 and April 1944, as well as their countries of origin.

cerning the camps' function as the sites of the systematic mass extermination of European Jewry, including the Jews of Hungary. Horthy and the Hungarian government were inundated with telegrams, demands and threats motivated by fears concerning the fate of the Jewish communities of Hungary. The Swedish king and the Pope, for instance, sent several telegrams on the subject. Several times a day the papal nuncio sought audiences with Horthy and Döme Sztójay (the unambiguously pro-German and deeply anti-Semitic politician who had been made prime minister on 23 March), as did representatives of the Swiss and Turkish governments, leading figures in political life in Spain, and (last but not least) numerous representatives of the Churches in Hungary and figures in public life. Hungary and Horthy himself were harshly attacked in the organs of the press in the Allied and neutral countries for essentially having handed over the Jewish population of the country to the Germans (and for allowing the full cooperation of the Hungarian police forces and administrative infrastructure). The U.S. State Department announced in the name of the Allies that if Horthy did not bring an end to the deportations, after the war he would be held personally responsible for having participated in the crime of genocide. This announcement, however, also made clear that were Horthy to bring an end to the deportations, he would not be held accountable for Hungary's contribution to the extermination of the Hungarian Jewry.[8]

In the meantime, it had also become clear, despite German claims to the contrary, that the German forces had failed to drive the Allied troops who had landed at Normandy back into the sea. On the Eastern Front, the Soviet army had launched an offensive and was slowly but surely making its way westward. Thus, the war on two fronts was placing increasing strains on the Wehrmacht. Horthy and members of his circle began to hope that they would be able to enter into direct communication with the Allied powers and possibly even form a new government that would be acceptable to them. They also knew, however, that this would only be possible if they promptly put an end to the deportations.[9]

---

8   *Wilhelmstrasse*, documents 691, 692; *Magyar Quisling-kormány*, 770–780 (notes of Deputy Foreign Minister Mihály Jungerth-Arnóthy on the so-called Jewish Question); *Csendőrtiszt a Markóban*, 156 (interrogation of Ernő Pető on the first day of the hearing concerning László Ferenczy, 1 April 1946).
9   *Horthy Miklós titkos iratai* [The secret papers of Miklós Horthy], prepared for press and with added ex-

The Role of Colonel Ferenc Koszorús in the Prevention of the Deportation of the Jews of Budapest

For this reason, on 26 June 1944, at a session of the Crown Council, Horthy ordered a halt to the deportation of Jews who had converted, Jews who were capable of working in the Labor Service Battalions, and their family members. He also called for the dismissal of Baky and Endre, the two undersecretaries in the Ministry of the Interior responsible for Jewish affairs, and forbade the gendarmerie from participating in the deportations.[10]

By that time, however, the gendarmerie units that had been given orders to come to Budapest in preparation for the deportation of the city's Jewish population had already begun to arrive. On the basis of the appearance in the capital of the gendarmes (who officially were under the authority of Baky) and the intense negotiations between Baky, Endre and the Germans, Horthy and those immediately surrounding him concluded that Baky and the members of his circle were prepared, with German support, to defy Horthy's orders and continue the deportations. Essentially, this would be tantamount to an open rejection of Horthy's authority as regent and indeed an utter dismissal of Horthy himself as the head of state. Rumors were circulating in the city according to which Baky and his circle were planning to launch a coup and remove Horthy from power.[11] These rumors were strengthened by the failed assassination attempt on 28 June against István Bárczy, permanent under-secretary of the prime minister's office, who was a known anglophile and one of Horthy's trusted men. The trail of the attempt against his life led back to Baky's circles.[12]

---

planatory notes by Miklós Szinai and László Szűcs (Budapest: Kossuth Könyvkiadó, 1972), documents 85, 87; *Wilhelmstrasse*, document 687; *The Confidential Papers of Admiral Horthy*, prepared for press and introduced by M. Szinai and L. Szűcs (Budapest: Corvina Press, 1965), documents 62 and 64.

10 *Vádirat a nácizmus ellen* [Bill of Indictment against Nazism], vol. 3, 26 June–15 October 1944, edited with an introduction by Elek Karsai (Budapest: Magyar Izraeliták Országos Képviselete, 1967); "Nyilatkozat-tervezet Horthy Miklós kormányzó részére a Koronatanács 1944. június 26-i ülésére" [Draft proclamation for Regent Miklós Horthy for the session of the Crown Council on 26 June 1944]; *Magyar Quisling-kormány*, 779–780 (notes of Deputy Foreign Minister Mihály Jungerth-Arnóthy on the so-called Jewish Question).

11 The trial of Gendarmerie Colonel István Láday, Budapest Archives, Nb 4995/1946; *Szálasi naplója* [Szálasi's diary; henceforth *Szálasi naplója*], written and compiled by Elek Karsai (Kossuth: 1978), 253–254; *Wilhelmstrasse*, documents 691, 692, 694 and 695; "Vitéz Vörös János m. kir. vezérezredes vezérkari főnök naplója 1944. ápr. 7-től – 1944. okt. 15-ig" [Diary of Colonel 'Vitéz' János Vörös, Chief of the General Staff, 7 April 1944–15 October 1944], *A Magyar Történeti Kutató Társaság* [The Hungarian Historical Researcher Society], 3 (1979) USA. (Henceforth: "Vörös napló"). See the entry from 29 June 1944.

12 Péter Bokor "Merénylet magyar módra" [Assassination attempt Hungarian style] in *Zsákutca* [Dead-end street] (Budapest: RTV-Minerva, 1985), 7–37; *Szálasi naplója*, 258–259; "Vörös napló", entry from 30 June 1944.

Horthy took the threat of a right-wing coup seriously. He knew that a coup not only would affect him personally but also might well extinguish all hope of forming a government that the Allied powers would regard as a possible negotiating partner.

On 28 June, Horthy informed János Vörös, the head of the general staff, of his fear of a putsch led by pro-German elements in which the gendarmerie might well take part. He asked Vörös to bring military forces to the city. Vörös informed the First Army Corps of Budapest and the commanding officer of the Budapest military of Horthy's concerns, but he took no practical steps in response to Horthy's request.[13] Horthy was made increasingly uneasy by a proclamation made by Ferenc Szálasi on 2 July, according to which the Arrow Cross Party-Hungarist Movement, a national socialist party under Szálasi's leadership, had nothing to do with a possible coup led by Baky.[14] At the same time, on 2 July the gendarmerie units that had been summoned to the capital began to gather together and deport the Jews from the outskirts of Budapest – according to plan and against Horthy's wishes.[15]

Vörös, however, continued to show no sign of mobilizing the armed forces,[16] so instead members of Horthy's circle began to look to Colonel Ferenc Koszorús, the chief of staff of the First Armored Division, which was stationed in and around Budapest. The division was equipped with tanks and other armored vehicles, so in the event of resistance, it would have a decisive advantage over the gendarmes, who were equipped only with small arms.

Who was Ferenc Koszorús? He was the son of a Calvinist family from Debrecen. Like his father, he pursued a career in the military. On 18 August 1918, he was made second lieutenant at the Ludovika Military Academy in Budapest. At the academy, he developed a strong sense of loyalty to his nation and to his oath as a member of the Hungarian army, which he regarded as the cornerstone of an officer's honor. He wrote in his memoir, "An honorable soldier can only be freed of what he has undertaken before God in his oath as a Hun-

---

13 "Vörös napló", entry from 29 June 1944.
14 *Szálasi napló*, 253–254.
15 The trial of Gendarmerie Colonel István Láday in the Budapest Archives, Nb 4995/1946; *Csendőrtiszt a Markóban*, 111–112 (the record of the interrogation by the political police of the accused, László Ferenczy, November 9, 1945. *Wilhelmstrasse*, documents 693, and 696.
16 "Vörös napló", entry from July 5 and 6, 1944.

The Role of Colonel Ferenc Koszorús in the Prevention of the Deportation of the Jews of Budapest

garian soldier by death or by the person to whom he took the oath; anyone who for any other reason goes back on what he has undertaken by oath has broken his oath and is dishonorable."[17] He was too young to play a role of any particular significance in World War I. Following the creation of the Hungarian "National Army" in 1920, he served as a cavalry officer in Debrecen and Nyíregyháza. In the autumn of 1926, having earned positive assessments for his service and distinguished himself as an officer of remarkable talent, he was admitted to the program for further officer training at the Ludovika Academy, which in the 1920s was the cover name for what was essentially the secret military academy. When he completed the program, he was made part of the general staff, and from then on he served in various leadership positions, first and foremost as a commander of cavalry divisions. In 1940, he received the Officers' Cross of the Order of Merit of the Kingdom of Hungary in recognition of his service.

Beginning in June 1941, he took part in the military operations in Ukraine as the head of the rapid deployment force that had been mobilized. In 1941, he was awarded the Knight's Cross of the Order of Merit. (The cross that was given in recognition of military distinction had crossed swords and a ribbon that was mostly red, in contrast with the green ribbon that was given in recognition of civil merits.)

On 1 October 1941, he was made chief of staff of the Second Armored Division, which had recently been reestablished in the city of Munkács (today, Mukacheve in Ukraine).

In May 1942, he was again put back into military operations. As the chief of staff of the First Field Armored Division, he served on the front until October 1942 in the theater of military operations along the banks of the Don River, where he took active part in the bridgehead battles in August and September 1942. In recognition of his service, he was awarded the Officers' Cross of the Order of Merit of the Kingdom of Hungary.

On 1 October 1942, he was elevated to the rank of colonel and transferred to Budapest, where he was made the chief of staff of the First Armored Army Corps.[18]

---

17 *Koszorús*, 59.
18 Military History Archives, Military History Records (AKVI) 1107/1899.

In the years he spent in Debrecen, Koszorús served alongside General Károly Lázár, later the commander of the Home Guards and one of Horthy's most trusted military advisors. They remained in contact with each other, thus it is perhaps not surprising that Horthy sought out Lázár and, through Lázár, asked Colonel Koszorús to prevent Baky from staging a potential coup with the assistance of the gendarmerie. Koszorús wrote about this in his memoir:

> The next day, on 3 July, Major General Lázár gave me the Regent's command to prepare to execute the operation within a few days. ... In the late afternoon, I went to where the soldiers in the First Armored Division were stationed, first and foremost to Esztergom, where I spoke with the officer corps of the tank division and the reconnaissance battalion. I informed the officer corps, on the basis of Lázár's assessment of the situation, that we would force those who were rejecting supreme orders to fulfill them.[19]

That night, he completed and put in writing plans for a rapid occupation of Budapest with the aim of closing off the city. The plans were taken in a sealed envelope by a patrol armed with handguns and traveling by motorcycle to the commanders of the tank division and the reconnaissance battalion. Koszorús told the officer carrying the plans that if anyone were to try to stop them, they should immediately open fire.[20] On 4 July, Koszorús took measures to ensure that the units be provisioned with the necessary ammunition and fuel, and he informed Horthy, using Lázár as an intermediary, that they were prepared to execute his order.

On the evening of 5 July, he was ordered to Horthy's residence, where Horthy informed him in Lázár's presence that Baky and his circle wanted to begin the deportation of the Jews of Budapest on 6 July. He gave them the order by word of mouth to expel the gendarmerie battalions from the city as quickly as possible, using the armored divisions that were in waiting, if necessary by force.

---

19 *Koszorús*, 58–59.
20 *Zsákutca*, 38–49.

The Role of Colonel Ferenc Koszorús in the Prevention of the Deportation of the Jews of Budapest

At 11:30 PM, Koszorús gave the order by radio for the units of the armored division to enter the city. He then rushed to Óbuda, where he waited for them. The units arrived on the outskirts of the city on 6 July at 5:00 AM.[21]

In the early morning of 6 July, General Lázár, who had been made commander of the Budapest armed forces by Horthy, summoned Tibor Paksy-Kiss and Győző Tölgyessy, the gendarmerie colonels who had been put in charge of the deportations from Budapest and its surroundings, and gave them the written order concerning the immediate withdrawal of their units from the territory of the capital.[22]

In his diary, Ferenc Szálasi wrote the following concerning the events of 6 July: "Armored units arrived in the area around Óbuda and took up places on the streets and squares, concealed with green branches. In some of the streets, the guns were put in a firing position, and news spread that Major General Lázár, the commander of the Home Guards, had taken over command of the armed forces."[23]

According to his own memoir, at 7:00 AM General Koszorús sent an officers' patrol to inform Baky that he and his troops were prepared to execute Horthy's order concerning the withdrawal of the gendarmerie from Budapest.[24]

On 6 July, Horthy ordered the commanders of the gendarmerie units to appear before him at 11:00 AM. One of the officers of the Galánta Gendarmerie Battalion offered the following retrospective account of the meeting to his commander, gendarmerie Colonel István Láday:

> Lieutenant General Faragho, the supervisor of the gendarmerie, and the commanders of all of the gendarmerie units in Budapest were standing in a line waiting for the Regent, who in a manner that was raw and nervous and bore no trace of courteousness gave a short briefing. "You have betrayed my confidence and become political playthings. Perhaps against

---

21 *Koszorús*, 60–61.
22 The People's Court trial of Tibor Paksy-Kiss, in the Budapest Archives, Nb 5045/1945; *Csendőrtiszt a Markóban*, 111–112 (the record of the interrogation of the accused, László Ferenczy, by the political police, 9 November 1945).
23 *Szálasi napló*, 254.
24 *Koszorús*, 61.

your will. I order all gendarmerie units to leave the capital today by 4:00 PM. I do not wish to see a gendarme in Budapest. In order to ensure calm, I have summoned army units to the capital."[25]

Since the gendarmerie units had only small arms and the gendarmes themselves did not wish to defy Horthy, Baky, knowing that he could not count on assistance from the Germans, ordered the units to withdraw. The aforementioned officer of the Galántai Battalion wrote the following about the subsequent events:

> The battalion set out on foot in the direction of Vác in order to board train cars in Göd, just outside the borders of Budapest. The decorative sickle-feathers were removed from the Bocskai caps.[26] The mood was tense and nervous, though the rank and file men and even the sub-officers knew almost nothing of what was going on. The unit proceeded quietly down Hungária Boulevard. In front of the Andrássy army barracks the guns were ready to fire, and the soldiers were in readiness, keeping their eyes on the withdrawing unit. Armored units followed the battalion, a medium distance behind us, neither close nor far. ... By the time the battalion had reached the train station [in Göd], the units of the Esztergom Armored Division had closed off the road leading to Pest, and they made a fairly tight ring around the battalion as it loaded up, dropping this state of readiness for battle and returning to Pest only after the train had left the station.[27]

By 8 July, the gendarmes had left Budapest, and on 9 July the units under Koszorús's command returned to their garrisons.

Because Horthy succeeded – by calling on the soldiers of the first armored unit – in compelling the gendarmes to leave the capital, there were no armed

---

25 Béla Lám, "Emlékek gyertyafénynél" [Memories by candlelight], Military History Archives, Essays and Memoirs Collection (Henceforth *HL Tgy*) 3406.
26 The sickle-feathers (*kakastoll*) were a distinctive feature of the uniforms of the gendarmerie, as was the so-called Bocskai cap.
27 Lám Béla: "Emlékek gyertyafénynél", *HL* [Military Archives, Budapest], *Tgy*, 3406.

forces available in Budapest with which to implement the deportation of the city's Jews. As the individual most responsible for the execution of this operation, Koszorús prevented the transport of most of the Jewish population of Budapest to Auschwitz. Thus, he played a significant role in giving some 250,000 people at least a chance of survival.

Koszorús' actions, furthermore, made clear that, where there was resolute political will, the Hungarian army was capable of acting in defiance of the Germans' wishes.

However, neither the Germans nor their Hungarian adherents abandoned their plans, as is illustrated with tragic clarity by the fact that on 9 July, Jaross informed Veesenmayer that he had carried out an operation involving the Jews on the outskirts of the capital in the course of which some 24,128 Jews had been deported, Horthy's order notwithstanding. Jaross also confirmed that he was willing to deport all of the Jews of Budapest, even if he had to do so in defiance of Horthy.[28]

In July 1944, however, the Germans did not have at their disposal the armed forces necessary to carry out the deportation of the Budapest Jews against Horthy's wishes. Furthermore, they did not want the issue to cause a complete rift in their relationship with the regent. Horthy's resignation, whether at his own initiative or under compulsion, would have shaken the very foundations of the image that had been carefully maintained since March 1944, namely that Hungary was an independent ally of the Third Reich. This would have caused political, military and economic complications that Germany could not have afforded.[29]

Instead of force, the Germans used flattery, promises and threats in their attempts to persuade Horthy to permit the deportation of the Budapest Jews or at least to allow them to be relocated to areas outside the capital. They wanted to complete the modified deportation plan by the end of August.[30]

In the end, the vast majority of Budapest's Jewry was not deported. Following the decision by Romania to switch sides in the war and join the Allies on 23 August 1944, Germany had to devote all of its forces, weaponry and

---

28 *Wilhelmstrasse*, document 696.
29 Ibid., documents 694 and 696.
30 Ibid., document 709.

transport capacities to stabilizing the southern part of the Eastern Front. On the Western Front, the Allies were already on the outskirts of Paris.

By then, even Himmler had realized that it would be possible to avoid a complete collapse and the occupation of Germany only if negotiations were begun with the Western allied powers in the interests of securing a separate peace; and a minimal precondition of any negotiations was the immediate halt of the deportations. Indeed, this had already taken place in the rest of the countries of Europe, including Hungary, where only the Jewish communities of Budapest remained comparatively intact. On 25 August 1944, Himmler ordered that preparations be made for the permanent cessation of the deportations from Budapest, and Eichmann was ordered to return to the Third Reich.[31]

With this order, the significance of the operation led by Koszorús on 6 July became clear. Roughly 250,000 people were saved from deportation to the extermination camps. After 15 October, when Eichmann returned to Hungary, it was no longer possible to deport these people with the kind of devastating efficiency that had characterized the deportations of late spring and early summer 1944. Nonetheless, many thousands of Jews subsequently perished in the course of the forced marches towards the territory of the Third Reich or at the hands of the Arrow Cross. This is historical fact, and as such lies beyond the realm of expiation. However, had Eichmann and Baky succeeded in launching the deportations of the Jews of Budapest in July, as they had sought to do, many more tens- or hundreds of thousands would have died. The military operation organized and implemented by Ferenc Koszorús was the essential key in preventing this. Thus, Koszorús deserves to be remembered among those who defied the will of the Reich and, in doing so, helped to save many, if tragically not all, of the Jews of Budapest.

---

31 Péter Bokor, *Végjáték a Duna mentén* [End play alongside the Danube] (Budapest: RTV-Minerva-Kossuth, 1982), 192 (Dr. Wilhelm Höttl, responsible for the affairs in Hungary of the Reich Main Security Office); *Wilhelmstrasse*, document 710.

Chapter 8
Raoul Wallenberg – Not an Accidental Choice for Hungary in 1944

Susanne Berger and Vadim Birstein[1]

On July 8, 1944, a young Swedish businessman, Raoul Wallenberg, a member of an influential Swedish family of bankers and industrialists, arrived in Budapest, having been appointed secretary to the Royal Swedish Legation (Embassy).[2] In his work in Budapest, he also represented the American War Refugee Board (WRB), an organization established by President Franklin D. Roosevelt in January 1944.[3] The WRB's task was to provide active aid to civilian victims of the Nazi and Axis powers.

Although Hungary had been formally allied with Nazi Germany since 1940, on March 19, 1944, Germany had nevertheless moved to occupy the country. In just a few months, almost 500,000 Jews who had been residing in the Hungarian countryside were deported to extermination camps in Poland and Czechoslovakia. At the time of Wallenberg's arrival in Budapest, only

---

1   This is an expanded, updated version of an article, "Not a 'Nobody': Choice of Raoul Wallenberg in 1944 Not Accidental" (2012), previously published on the Internet (see http://www.vadimbirstein.com/wallenberg.html). An excerpt from the Internet version appeared in Swedish in *Dagens Nyheter*, April 12, 2012. See also Louise Nordstrom, "Researchers: Wallenberg Budapest mission no fluke", Associated Press, March 19, 2012.
2   On the appointment of Raoul Wallenberg (1910–1947) to the Swedish Legation and Wallenberg's activity in Budapest see, for instance, Jeno Levai, *Raoul Wallenberg: His Remarkable Life, Heroic Battles and the Secret of His Mysterious Disappearance*, translated into English by Frank Vajda (Melbourne: The University of Melbourne, 1989); Bengt Jangfeldt, *The Hero of Budapest: The Triumph and Tragedy of Raoul Wallenberg*, translated by Harry D. Watson and Bengt Jangfeldt (London & New York: I.B. Tauris & Co., Ltd., 2012); Ingrid Carlberg., *Raoul Wallenberg: The Heroic Life and Mysterious Disappearance of the Man Who Saved Thousands of Hungarian Jews from the Holocaust*, translated from the Swedish by Ebba Segerberg (New York: MacLehose Press, 2015).
3   Rebecca Erbeling, "The United States War Refugee Board, the Neutral Nations, and the Holocaust in Hungary", in: *Bystanders, Rescuers, or Perpetrators? The Neutral Countries and the Shoah*, edited by Corry Guttstadt et al. (*Berlin*: Metropol Verlag & IHRA, 2016), 183–197.

approximately 200,000 Jews remained living in the capital. Wallenberg's initial task in Budapest was to protect a few hundred families of Jewish-Hungarian industrialists and businessmen who were important to the Hungarian economy. Soon, however, his mission expanded as Wallenberg tried to save as many of Budapest's Jews as possible. In doing so, he overstepped his official instructions, which led to serious tensions with both his diplomatic colleagues and Swedish superiors.

From the very beginning Wallenberg made it clear that he did not want simply to protect only those individuals with close business or family ties to Sweden but intended to use the system he and his colleagues were putting in place to save as many people as possible. "In my opinion, the aid project should continue on the highest scale", Wallenberg wrote in late July 1944.[4] To accomplish this, in August 1944 he strongly urged the Swedish Foreign Office "to sacrifice the sacred institution of the provisional passport and to grant [us] the full right to hand them out". His request was not granted, forcing him to rely on an alternate document, the by now famous Swedish "Schutzpass" (protective passport).

On January 15, 1945, Raoul Wallenberg was detained by Soviet military authorities and transferred to Moscow, where he was imprisoned and investigated by Soviet military counterintelligence, SMERSH.[5] The full reasons for Wallenberg's arrest have never been disclosed. There are some indications, among others, that Soviet dictator Joseph Stalin possibly wished to use Raoul Wallenberg as a "bargaining chip" in order to obtain post-war concessions from the Swedish government.[6] Presumably, Wallenberg died in Lubyanka, Moscow's notorious prison for conducting investigations, on July 17, 1947, or shortly thereafter – most likely, he was killed on the direct order of the Soviet leadership.

---

4   The Swedish National Archives, Kálmán Lauer Personal Papers, letter from Raoul Wallenberg to Kálmán Lauer, July 24, 1944. See also letter of July 18, 1944. For Wallenberg's request to be allowed to hand out Swedish Provisional Passports, see "P.M. für Gesandschaftssekretär Anger", dated August 6, 1944.

5   SMERSH (Смерть шпионам [SMERt' SHpionam], Russian acronym of "death to spies") was an umbrella organization for three counter-intelligence agencies in the Soviet Red Army formed in late 1942. On SMERSH and its activity, including the arrests of Wallenberg and other foreign officials, see Vadim Birstein, *SMERSH, Stalin's Secret Weapon* (London: Biteback Publishing, 2012).

6   See, for instance, Vadim Birstein, "Raoul Wallenberg and Ivan Serov's Memoir 'Notes from a Suitcase'" (September 2016), at http://www.vbirstein.com.

Raoul Wallenberg – Not an Accidental Choice for Hungary in 1944

A major challenge for researchers in the Raoul Wallenberg case has always been that very little original documentation about him has survived from his adult life before 1944. Only several personal letters and a few other documents have been preserved.

For decades the idea has prevailed that the choice of Raoul Wallenberg for his dangerous assignment was largely accidental, the result of a fortuitous set of circumstances that settled on a smart young businessman just weeks before he left Sweden for Budapest. Only 31 years old at the time, Wallenberg has been routinely portrayed as highly intelligent, yet stuck on a rather average career path as director of a small import-export foodstuff company, Mellaneuropeiska, generally cut off from his powerful second cousins, the banker/industrialists Marcus and Jacob Wallenberg, and eager for a chance to make his own mark in the world.

While much of this description is accurate, new documentation recently discovered in Hungary and Sweden suggests that Wallenberg's background story may be more complex than previously thought. For one, as early as 1943, his personal network of contacts ran deeper and broader than researchers have realized.[7] This raises new questions not only about Raoul Wallenberg's relationship with the Wallenberg business group, but also what exactly prompted his selection for the Budapest assignment. In addition, the documents add important pieces to the puzzle of why Soviet authorities may have been so interested in detaining him.

In 2012, Lovice Maria Ullein-Reviczky, the daughter of the former Hungarian minister in Stockholm, Dr. Antal Ullein-Reviczky, contacted the authors of this essay. Before his stay in Sweden from 1943–45, Ullein-Reviczky had been a high ranking member of the Hungarian Foreign Ministry, heading its powerful and influential Press Department and Cultural Section.[8]

---

7   Susanne Berger, C.G. Mckay and Vadim Birstein, "Raoul Wallenberg's Secret German Contacts" (January 14, 2015), http://www.raoul-wallenberg.eu/articles/ludolph-christensen/; Susanne Berger and Vadim Birstein. "Blasieholmsgatan 3" (2015), https://www.academia.edu/11973759/Blasieholmsgatan_3_-_N
8   Dr. Antal Ullein-Reviczky (1894–1955) was a prominent Hungarian lawyer and diplomat. He received his doctorate in 1927 from the István Tisza Royal Hungarian University in Debrecen. Since 1919 he worked in the Ministry of Foreign Affairs. Appointed secretary of the Hungarian Legation in Paris, he participated as well in the work of the Societé des Nations. In 1929, he was decorated with the "Légion d'honneur", the first of his many decorations. Dispatched as consul to Turkey from 1929

More importantly, he was a well-known opponent of Nazism and a key figure in the Hungarian resistance movement that included leading diplomatic and political figures around the Hungarian prime minister, Miklós Kállay. Since 1942, Ullein-Reviczky had been instrumental in numerous efforts to contact the Western Allies, especially Britain, to discuss a way for Hungary to leave its alliance with Nazi Germany.[9]

Lovice Maria Ullein-Reviczky provided us with some materials from her personal archive – notes from the diary of her mother, Mrs. Ullein-Reviczky, British-born Lovice Louisa Grace Ullein-Reviczky, née Cumberbatch, who married Antal Ullein-Reviczky in 1929.[10] Her father, Cyril James Cumberbatch (1873–1944), was for many years British Consul in Constantinople (Istanbul), Turkey. The Cumberbatches were well acquainted with Raoul Wallenberg's grandfather, Gustaf Oscar Wallenberg (1863–1937), the Swedish minister to Turkey from 1920 until 1936, who also lived in Constantinople.[11]

---

to 1935, he was then consul in Zagreb, Croatia, from 1935 to 1938. An expert in international law, Dr. Ullein-Reviczky published several important academic texts and books, including *La nature juridique des clauses territoriales du traité de Trianon* (Paris: A. Pedone, 1929). In 1941, he was named an Honorary Professor at the University of Debrecen. From 1938 to 1943, Dr. Ullein-Reviczky headed the Foreign Press and Culture Department of the Hungarian Foreign Affairs Ministry. By 1941, it merged with the Press Department of the Hungarian prime minister's office, elevating Ullein-Reviczky to an even more powerful position. From 1943 to October 1944, he was Hungarian minister to Stockholm, Sweden. Before that, he participated in a number of secret discussions between representatives of the Western Allies and Hungarian/German officials regarding the conclusion of a separate peace agreement. These discussions continued in Sweden and involved members of the Wallenberg family. After the German occupation of Hungary on March 19, 1944, Ullein-Reviczky was ousted. However, the Swedish government formally allowed him to retain his official diplomatic status as minister, and he stayed with his family in Sweden. At the end of the war, the Ullein-Reviczkys moved to Turkey, Switzerland, France, and, finally, came to Britain in 1950. See Tibor Frank. "Antal Ullein-Reviczky: A Tribute", in: Antal Ullein-Reviczky, *German War – Russian Peace: The Hungarian Tragedy* (Saint Helena, CA: Helena History Press, 2014), xvii–xxxvi. In this "Tribute" Prof. Frank mentions that we wrote our article "Not a 'Nobody'" for the International Raoul Wallenberg Foundation; in fact, we never worked for or with that foundation.

9   See, for instance, Deborah S. Cornelius, *Hungary in World War II: Caught in the Cauldron* (New York: Fordham University Press, 2011), 236–39.

10 In 1993, Lovice Maria Ullein-Reviczky established the Antal Ullein-Reviczky Foundation at an estate in northeastern Hungary. In 2014, she translated into English one of Ullein-Reviczky's main works, *German War – Russian Peace: The Hungarian Tragedy*, originally published in French in Switzerland in 1947, and translated into Hungarian in 1993. *We are extremely grateful to Lovice Ullein-Reviczky for sharing her personal archival materials with us.*

11 Since Raoul's father died before Raoul was born, Gustaf Wallenberg became a sort of father figure for Raoul. See numerous correspondence between Raoul and his grandfather in: Raoul Wallenberg, *Letters and Dispatches: 1924–1944* (New York: Arcade Publishing, 1995).

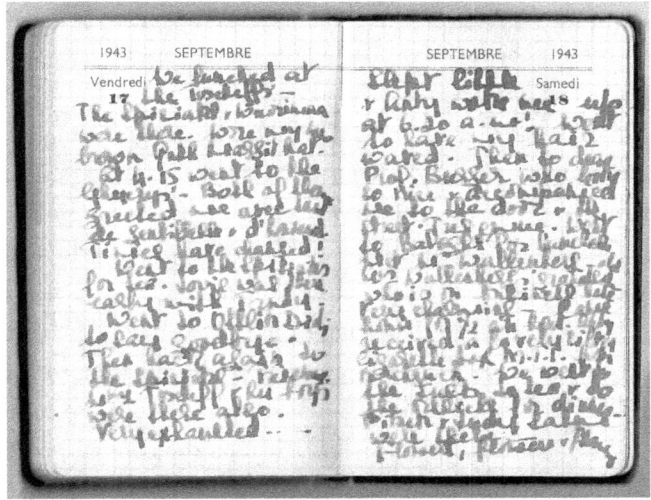

Fig. 1. Excerpt of a social diary kept by Mrs. Ullein-Reviczky for September 18, 1943.
Courtesy of the Antal Ullein-Reviczky Foundation, Hungary.

Mrs. Ullein-Reviczky's records show that Raoul Wallenberg was personally acquainted with Antal Ullein-Reviczky as early as September 1943, when he visited Budapest on business for his company, Mellaneuropeiska. Both men attended a private lunch given by József Balogh, the famous editor of several influential Hungarian periodicals and a close friend of the Ullein-Reviczky couple.[12] Mrs. Ullein-Reviczky's diary notes allow us to discuss this important circle of the Hungarian political and business elite with which Raoul Wallenberg was acquainted and assess how these relationships might have positively influenced the decision to send him to Budapest in 1944.

---

12   József Balogh (1893–1944) was a literary scholar and journalist. From 1927–1934 he served as chief secretary of the Society of the Hungarian Review *(Magyar Szemle Társaság)*, which was founded in 1927 by Prime Minister István Bethlen (1874–1946) and Baron Móric Kornfeld (1882–1967). The central issue of discussion in the Society's main periodical, *Magyar Szemle (The Hungarian Review)*, was a revision of the Hungarian borders according to the Treaty of Trianon (1920). Basically, the Society considered the necessity of re-establishing Hungary within the borders of the historical Kingdom of Hungary. Balogh was also the editor-in-chief of two periodicals associated with the Society and published in French and English, *La Nouvelle Revue de Hongrie* (1932–1944) and *The Hungarian Quarterly* (1936–1944). See details in Matthew Caples, "Et in Hungaria Ego: Trianon, Revisions and the Journal *Magyar Szemle* (1927–1944)", *Hungarian Studies* 19/1 (2005): 51–104. See also Tibor Frank: "Editing as Politics. József Balogh and the Hungarian Quarterly", *Hungarian Quarterly* 34, Nr. 129 (1993): 5–13. Reprinted with notes added: *Ethnicity, Propaganda, Myth-Making: Studies on Hungarian connections to Britain and America, 1848–1945*, Budapest: Akadémiai Kiadó, 1999. (Editor's note.)

On September 18, 1943, Mrs. Ullein-Reviczky wrote in her diary, "Went to Balogh's for luncheon. Met Mr. Wallenberg – old Mrs. Wallenberg's grandson who is on business here. Very charming."[13]

As for József Balogh, he moved in a highly exclusive group of people, a mix of aristocrats, industrialists, politicians, diplomats and writers. They included the Hungarian prime minister from 1921 to 1931, István Bethlen; Baron Móric Kornfeld and the extended family of Hungary's powerful industrialist Manfred Weiss; Lipót (Leopold) Aschner, the managing director of Hungary's largest electrical concern, Tungsram (the United Incandescent Light and Electricity Company); the former Hungarian prime minister, in 1917, Count Móric Esterházy; Marquis György Pallavicini Jr., a lawyer and businessman; and many others.[14] All these individuals formed the core group of anti-Nazi sentiment around Hungarian Regent Miklós (Nicholas) Horthy.[15] The anti-German resistance group also included the regent's son, Miklós Jr., called Nicky, whom Ullein-Reviczky knew well.

The group had very strong ties to Britain, as well as close personal and business contacts with Sweden. The enormous Manfred Weiss industrial empire, which produced everything from airplanes, trucks and bicycles to tinned goods and needles, had numerous subsidiaries and associations in Sweden, especially with the business group of Swedish shipping magnate Sven Salén (who owned Raoul Wallenberg's firm Mellaneuropeiska) and Salén's close associates, the Wallenberg brothers.

The Wallenberg family, in turn, had a powerful presence in Hungary, with both their Swedish Match company and the ball bearing trust Svenska Kullagerfabriken AB (SKF) enjoying monopoly status. During the war, Hungary constituted an important market for Sweden for a variety of goods,

---

13 "Old Mrs. Wallenberg" refers to Raoul's paternal grandmother, Annie (nee Annie Adelsköld).
14 Like Raoul Wallenberg, in April 1945 István Bethlen was arrested by Soviet military authorities and transferred to Moscow. He died on October 5, 1946, in Butyrka Prison Hospital in Moscow. See Ignác Romsics, *István Bethlen: A Great Conservative Statesman of Hungary, 1874–1946* (New York: Columbia University Press, 1995), 386–88. During World War II, György Pallavicini (1912–1949) participated in the Hungarian resistance against the German occupation. After the war, he was arrested by the Hungarian secret police AVO, transferred to the Soviets, and, apparently, died in a labor camp in 1949. Details of his arrest and death remain unknown.
15 See details in: Thomas L. Sakmyster, *Hungary's Admiral on Horseback: Miklós Horthy, 1918–1944* (Columbia Univ. Press, 1993); *Admiral Nicholas Horthy: Memoirs*, annotated by Andrew L. Simon (Safety Harbor (FL): Simon Publications LLC, 2000).

Raoul Wallenberg – Not an Accidental Choice for Hungary in 1944

Fig. 2. Hungarian minister Dr. Antal Ullein-Reviczky, shown here at a banquet in Stockholm's Grand Hotel, March 15, 1944.
Courtesy of the Antal Ullein-Reviczky Foundation, Hungary.

especially for the import of foodstuffs, textiles and critical raw materials, including bauxite, flax and oil.

The introduction of the so-called "Jewish laws" in Hungary in 1938 and 1939 increasingly restricted the roles Jewish citizens could play in public life. In September 1940, Jacob Wallenberg, CEO of the family's Stockholms Enskilda Bank (SEB), received a message from Jewish business owners who were worried about further restrictions of their activities. Some of these Jewish businessmen were looking to Sweden for "the purpose of the [temporary] 'aryanization' of their businesses".[16] Should Jacob be interested, the message stated, he should send a representative to Budapest.

---

16 The request came from Philip Weiss (Archives of the Stockholm Enskilda Bank (SEB), Stockholm. Dossier 65, April 1, 1940–October 31, 1940, correspondence of Jacob Wallenberg), cited in "Sverige och Judarnas Tillgånger: Slutrapport från Kommissionen om Judiska Tillgångar i Sverige vid Tiden för Andra Världskriget". *Statens offentliga utredningar* (SOU) 1999:20 (in Swedish). Weiss was a member of the Upper House of the Hungarian Parliament and president of the Commercial Bank of Pest. There is no information about Jacob Wallenberg's response to the petition.

Attached to the request Jacob Wallenberg had received was the card of Tungsram CEO Lipót Aschner. Most of Raoul Wallenberg's closest aides in 1944 would come from the management ranks of this firm.[17] It is quite possible that Aschner's approach to Jacob and the deteriorating conditions in Hungary both played a substantial role in the creation of Mellaneuropeiska. Raoul Wallenberg had ostensibly joined Mellaneuropeiska in order to learn the intricacies of international business, especially during the war. But aside from his regular business activity dealing with the importation of foodstuffs such as Hungarian wine and geese, Wallenberg would also have been well suited to take on the role of a confidential representative, as Lipót Aschner had requested.

There are indications that Raoul may have been working for Jacob Wallenberg in some confidential capacity even before he joined Mellaneuropeiska. On September 26, 1939, when German and Soviet troops were marching through Poland, he wrote to Jacob: "At our last meeting you told me that the war would perhaps lead to a number of problems and that you possibly would want to use my services in connection with the solving of these problems."[18] After the war, Raoul Wallenberg's business partner in Mellaneuropeiska, Dr. Kálmán Lauer – a Hungarian Jew with good business contacts in Budapest and Germany – claimed that Raoul had worked for some time as Jacob's personal secretary.

Mellaneuropeiska was founded in 1941, mainly as a response to the severe restrictions of transatlantic trade with the United States., South America and the Far East after the outbreak of the war. The company was part of the Banankompaniet business group, owned by the Norwegian entrepre-

---

17 By that time, Leopold Aschner had already been deported to the Mauthausen concentration camp. In September 1944, John Pehle of the US WRB asked Raoul Wallenberg to check in Hungary to learn with whom the German ransom request for Aschner had originated (Franklin D. Roosevelt Presidential Library, Hyde Park, USA. Cable to Minister Johnson at Stockholm for Olsen, September 29, 1944; Records of the US War Refugee Board). Tungsram's Swedish contacts were longstanding: since 1928, a subsidiary called Svenska Orion had operated in Sweden. British and American interests in Tungsram were represented by many companies, including General Electric and British Thomson Houston. Additionally, the German Osram GMBH and the Dutch concern Philips held minority shares. In the spring of 1944, the SS kidnapped Leopold Aschner and moved him to Mauthausen. After payment of a large ransom, he was released to Switzerland in December 1944. Negotiations with the Germans about the payment were handled by Swedish representatives from ASEA and Svenska Orion in Stockholm, as well as Tungsram's Swiss subsidiary in Zurich.

18 Gert Nylander and Anders Perlinge, *Raoul Wallenberg in Documents, 1927–1947* (Stockholm: The Foundation for Economic History Research within Banking and Enterprise, 2000), 57.

neur Carl Matthiessen and the Swedish businessman Sven Salén. Under the Banankompaniet umbrella, Salén ran a network of smaller firms, including Mellaneuropeiska. While the company nominally belonged to Sven Salén, it operated fully in the Wallenberg business sphere.

Mellaneuropeiska was clearly created with the idea that it could fulfill an important economic role for Sweden by providing crucial foodstuffs and raw materials, in particular from Hungary. In just three years, from 1941 to 1943, Mellaneuropeiska managed to import foodstuffs and other goods worth about 10,000,000 Swedish crowns (SEK) (approximately $25,000,000 today). Because Lauer was Jewish, he himself was unable to travel to Hungary and Germany at the time. Most of transactions were facilitated with the help of German intermediaries, such as the import-export firm J. Nootbaar, which was headed by one of Lauer's old acquaintances from his time in Hamburg during the 1930s, Ludolph Christensen.[19]

However, Mellaneuropeiska did not deal exclusively in foodstuffs but also functioned as an important agent for other business matters. In 1941, one of Mellaneuropeiska's first official orders came from the Swedish National Agency for Reserve Goods. It requested that Mellaneuropeiska arrange a purchase of 160 tons of fuel from Hungary.[20] In January 1943, Wallenberg and Lauer received permission to deliver high-speed drilling equipment (then worth about 22,000 SEK or approximately $55,000 today) from the Swedish electrical concern ASEA to the Hungarian Manfred Weiss Flugzeug und Motorenfabrik AG (Duna Aircraft Manufacturing Plant).[21]

Raoul Wallenberg's visa application for his September 1943 trip to Hungary specifically states that he intended to visit Manfred Weiss AG and To-

---

19   Ludolph Christensen was one of Mellaneuropeiska's most important business associates. In 1943, his sister Ingrid Christensen married SS General Karl Wolff, in a second marriage. Ludolph Christensen was never a member of the German Nazi Party. In August 1944, Christensen traveled to Budapest to assist Raoul Wallenberg with the search for Kalman Lauer's relatives. After the war, Christensen lived permanently in Sweden and became a Swedish citizen. See Berger et al, "Raoul Wallenberg's Secret German Contacts".
20   At the time, gasoline was already severely rationed in both Sweden and Hungary. In September 1941 Mellaneuropeiska also helped to arrange a shipment of fur coats from Hungary for the Swedish Army. See http://mnl.gov.hu/a_het_dokumentuma/ismeretlen_wallenbergiratok.html.
21   ASEA operated in the Wallenberg business sphere. At the time, the Duna plant produced planes for the German Luftwaffe. See Berger et al, "Raoul Wallenberg's Secret German Contacts".

ledo Stahl AG, a steel company in Budapest.²² The trip's sponsors were Jacob Wallenberg, Sven Salén and Erik Björkman, director of the Skandinaviska Banken (and head of the Swedish-Hungarian Chamber of Commerce). According to the official Hungarian/Swedish trade register for October 1943, the main Swedish trading partner of Toledo Stahl was Hellefors Bruk AB, a large iron and steel manufacturing concern, then owned by the Skandinaviska Banken's investment arm, AB Custos.²³

As for the Manfred Weiss AG, it encompassed the Globus canning factory (trading partner of the Svenska Konserv AB Globus and Mellaneuropeiska), but at the time it also did business with a variety of Swedish firms dealing in steel products, including the ball bearing concern SKF, which was controlled by the Wallenberg family. It appears, therefore, that while visiting Hungary on behalf of Mellaneuropeiska, Raoul Wallenberg also may have handled other business matters that were not strictly limited to the importation of foodstuffs, at least on this particular trip.²⁴ Carl Matthiessen and Banankompaniet had longstanding ties to Hungary and the Manfred Weiss business group.²⁵

After the outbreak of the war, the Weiss family transferred some of their assets to smaller foreign entities such as Svenska Konserv AB Globus. In other words, Salén's businesses – and by extension the Wallenberg sphere – provided important "cover" for key Hungarian business interests in Sweden and in Hungary.²⁶ As the historian C.G. McKay has pointed

---

22 Raoul Wallenberg's 1943 visa application filed with the Hungarian Legation in Stockholm. Presented on the Hungarian National Archives website: http://www.mol.gov.hu/a_het_dokumentuma/raoul_wallenberg_vizumkerelme.html. Toledo Stahl AG. (Toledo Acél Rt.) was a producer of a wide variety of steel products. In 1943 it was located in central Budapest, at Visegradi utca 47/A. The majority of the company shares were owned by the Szalkai and Kadelburger families, who were Jewish. Later, in 1944, some members of these families were protected by the Swedish Legation and Raoul Wallenberg's offices (see http://www.raoul-wallenberg.eu/testimony/kate-and-gustav-kadelburger/).
23 The Hungarian–Swedish trade register for October 1943. Swedish National Archive, HP2860, Files of the Swedish Legation, Budapest.
24 On several occasions Marcus Wallenberg stated that he had discussed Hungarian business affairs with Raoul Wallenberg, including in a speech he made at the Raoul Wallenberg Hearings in Stockholm in 1981.
25 Susanne Berger's correspondence with Lilian Matthiessen, 2010.
26 During the war years, Mellaneuropeiska functioned in a largely anglophile, anti-Nazi environment. Carl Matthiessen was a staunch supporter of the Norwegian resistance and was close friends with several key British diplomats and intelligence representatives in Stockholm. Salén's mindset, too, was

Fig. 3. Heinrich (Heinz) von Wahl.
Courtesy of Peter Zwack, Hungary.

out, Kálmán Lauer was an expert at such arrangements, which proved profitable for both sides.[27]

In his visa application Wallenberg listed Ritter [Baronet] von Wahl as one of his main contacts in Hungary. This was certainly Henrik de Wahl, the managing director of the Manfred Weiss AG who – like Salén and Björkman – in 1944 would play a key role in ensuring Raoul Wallenberg's selection for the humanitarian mission to Budapest. Heinz von Wahl, as he was known in Budapest, was a nephew of Manfred Weiss's wife, Alice von Wahl. He was

---

definitely pro-Allied. He served as vice president of the Swedish-American Society for many years. Yet, both men had a very pragmatic attitude when it came to business. The all-important goal for them was to help and protect fellow business associates and, in the process, secure a favorable position for Swedish companies in the post-war economy. To this end, Matthiessen and Salén, as well their bankers – chief among them the powerful Wallenberg brothers – extended considerable assistance to numerous persons throughout the war, across a broad political and ideological spectrum. Jacob and Marcus Wallenberg played a key role in helping German companies and individuals cloak their assets abroad, for which they stood accused by US authorities for aiding the enemy.

27 The claim that Svenska Globus held Weiss family assets is supported by a letter Baroness Weiss received from Sweden on February 22, 1945, as reported by Britain's Economic Warfare Department on March 28, 1945. The letter was written by Elisabeth Uggla, wife of Heinrich von Wahl, the former managing director of the Manfred Weiss AG; see C.G. McKay, "Notes on the Case of Raoul Wallenberg", http://www.raoul-wallenberg.eu/wp-content/uploads/2011/11/20111001McKays-Notes.pdf)

```
F r e u n d e .
Unsere Freunde werden mit den untenstehenden Namen bezeichnet:

Per Anger                    Helena
Der Minister                 meine Freundin
v. Balasz                    Aurel
Isso Büchler                 Istvan
General Coffin               Kistner
Deak                         von Denkovitz
Fodor Lajos                  Lajos
Hollo                        der Kleine
Dr. Germanus                 der Grosse
Dir. Iller                   Irma
Jakobovits                   Johan
Kelemen                      XXXXX der Agent
Judith Koch                  Klara
Endre Milos                  Endre
Georg von Pogany             Dr. Georg
Orssich                      Nandor
Sauer                        der Doktor
Dr. Wrangel                  Bo
Zwack Janos               )  Janos
Frau Zwack                )  Janos Frau
Alfons Weiss                 Alfred
Dr. ....                     ... Zyllberg
Dr. ....                     .. Grünfeld
Familie Peichwald            Rolf
Familie La....f              Ludwig
```

Fig. 4. Raoul Wallenberg's private code list.
Courtesy of Dr. Guy von Dardel, Private Archive.

closely involved in the founding of the Svenska Konserv Globus AB.[28] This raises the question of how much Raoul Wallenberg knew about the Salén/Wallenberg sphere's sheltering of the Weiss family business assets and whether he had any role in these transactions.[29]

As early as 1937, Raoul Wallenberg was engaged in providing economic assistance to Jewish refugees in Sweden, and he almost certainly had knowledge of a number of different projects for supporting foreign busi-

---

28 McKay, "Notes on the Case of Raoul Wallenberg". By 1944, the Manfred Weiss Works had been "aryanized" (51% of the company shares were in the hands of the Catholic members of the Weiss family). In April 1944, the family was forced to transfer the company to the SS in exchange for a transfer of the entire Weiss-Chorin family to neutral Portugal.

29 Heinz von Wahl's sister, Vera von Wahl, was married to the beverage magnate János Zwack. Both he and his wife are listed as "Friends" in a private code list that Raoul Wallenberg created for his humanitarian work in Budapest in 1944. Before his departure, Wallenberg and Lauer worked out a list of code names to hide people's identities in their correspondence.

ness associates.[30] For instance, since 1942, Sven Salén and the director of the Royal Hungarian Free Port, Félix Bornemissza – a close friend of Miklos Horthy Jr., the son of Hungarian Regent Nicholas Horthy – were involved in a joint Swedish-Hungarian shipping venture that aimed to facilitate trade between Hungary and South America.[31] In 1943, the discussions – carried out with the help of Mellaneuropeiska – focused on three ships Bornemissza had commissioned to be built in Hungary that were to be designated as Swedish property, due to the precarious wartime conditions. In September 1943, Raoul Wallenberg was to take the necessary legal papers with him to Budapest.[32]

Possibly, Marcus Wallenberg was also involved in these plans. He had numerous longstanding business contacts in Hungary, one of whom was Felix Bornemissza. Bornemissza's name also later appears in Raoul Wallenberg's address book, which he took with him to Budapest in 1944, and the two met on several occasions.[33]

The Wallenberg family also found other ways to quietly help the beleaguered members of the Hungarian elite to protect their holdings. A good example is Count Móric Esterházy, who happened to be a good friend of Antal Ullein-Reviczky. Some of Esterházy's funds were held during the war years by the Wallenbergs' SEB in a so-called Special Account "U".[34]

---

30 Already in 1939, Raoul Wallenberg helped a prominent Jewish businessman and refugee from Germany, Dr. Erich Philippi, to establish a business in Sweden (Special-Metall Förening, u.p.a.). See Susanne Berger, "Prologue to Budapest: Raoul Wallenberg and Special-Metall Förening" (June 10, 2008), http://www.raoul-wallenberg.eu/articles/prologue-to-budapest-raoul-wallenberg-and-special-metall-forening/.
31 In 1941, Sven Salen and Félix Bornmissza formed the joint Csepel Hungaro-Swedish Shipping Company Ltd. (Csepel Magyar-Svéd Hajózási RT). See Carlberg, *Raoul Wallenberg*, 316–317.
32 See http://mnl.gov.hu/a_het_dokumentuma/ismeretlen_wallenbergiratok.html.
33 Félix Bornemisza's name appears in Raoul Wallenberg's address book in 1944, as does another of Marcus Wallenberg's old contacts, Joseph Bartha. Raoul Wallenberg rented Bartha's house in Budapest in late 1944. See Paul Levine's report from May 13, 1998, of his review of Marcus Wallenberg's correspondence, hich is archived at the Foundation for Economic History Research within Banking and Enterprise, the private Wallenberg family archive (EI, Vol. 51, 1 March 1942–30 June 1942. Levine's review was carried out in preparation for the final report of the official Swedish commission that investigated lost Jewish property during World War II, "Sverige och judarnas tillganger" (13 May 1998), SOU 1999, 20. A copy of Levine's notes is in the possession of the authors.
34 Special Account "U" was maintained in the United States by the investment firm Brown Brothers Harriman & Co. National Archives, Department of Justice Records, Records of the Office of Alien Property (RG 131), APC File No. F-62-472. Vesting Order for accounts maintained in the name of Stockholms Enskilda Bank, issued by Harold I. Baynton, Assistant Attorney General and director of the Office of Alien Property, April 11, 1951.

While his last name alone would have opened doors, these facts make Raoul Wallenberg's attendance at a private lunch at József Balogh's house in September 1943 all the more understandable. The timing of the gathering, too, is noteworthy. The meeting took place on September 18, two days before Antal Ullein-Reviczky was to depart for Stockholm to take up his new post as Hungarian minister to Sweden.

At that very moment the Hungarian diplomat was involved in highly secret and sensitive separate peace discussions via Turkey (Ullein-Reviczky's in-laws were British diplomats living in Istanbul).[35] These discussions involved representatives of the Special Operations Executive (SOE), Britain's foreign sabotage organization, which at the time was headed by the British banker Charles Hambro, who happened to be married to Marcus Wallenberg's first wife.[36] Both Marcus Wallenberg and Hambro were in regular contact concerning efforts to broker an end to the war. Additionally, Ullein-Reviczky's close friend Tibor Eckhardt, the Hungarian Smallholders Party leader, travelled (with the government's approval) to the United States in October 1941 in order to represent the anti-Nazi elements of Hungary. Not surprisingly, while in Budapest, the Ullein-Reviczkys maintained regular contact with the Swedish Legation, inviting both Sweden's minister, Ivan Danielsson, and First Secretary Per Anger to frequent lunches, dinners or bridge parties. Due to Sweden's neutrality, Swedish channels became one of the few reliable routes by which to deliver news about Hungary to the outside world.

The Ullein-Reviczkys' social contacts with Swedish diplomats intensified in Stockholm. Regular guests at private dinner parties hosted by minister and Mrs. Ullein-Reviczky at the Hungarian Legation building at Strandvägen 63 included high-ranking officials such as Swedish foreign minister Christian Günther; the head of the Foreign Ministry's Political Department, Sven Grafström; Undersecretary of State Erik Boheman; the head of the Swedish Foreign Ministry's Bureau of Foreign Trade, Gunnar Hägglöf; Östen Undén, who headed the Swedish Parliament's Foreign Relations Committee during

---

35 A brief description of the negotiations in Turkey is given in Barry Rubin, *Istanbul Intrigues* (New York: Pgaros Books, 1991), 142–144; and in Cornelius, *Hungary in World War II*, 236–239.
36 David Bartal, *The Empire: The Rise of the House of Wallenberg* (Stockholm: Dagens Industri, 1996), 128.

Raoul Wallenberg – Not an Accidental Choice for Hungary in 1944

Fig. 5. Antal Ullein-Reviczky and his wife, Lovice Louisa Grace, in the Hungarian Legation, Stockholm, September 30 1943 (before a Royal audience). Courtesy of the Antal Ullein-Reviczky Foundation, Hungary.

the war; and the chief of the Swedish Foreign Ministry's Legal Department, Gösta Engzell, among others. And on several occasions, Raoul Wallenberg is listed as someone who attended these gatherings.

The entry in Mrs. Ullein-Reviczky's diary for November 6, 1943, states: "Had Bohemans, Gripenberg, Exstrand [sic], Angelica Bunde [sic], young Raoul Wallenberg to lunch." In this group of guests, Eric Boheman had just been appointed Swedish ambassador to France and had been involved in trade negotiations with Britain, as well as with the Soviet Union. "Gripenberg" was obviously the Finnish minister to Stockholm, Georg Gripenberg, while Angelica Bonde (not Bunde) was the daughter of Baron Knut Bonde and, apparently, Raoul Wallenberg's girlfriend at the time. "Exstrand" was most likely Envoy Einar Ekstrand, who was involved in refugee assistance matters.

Wallenberg reciprocated by inviting the Hungarian minister and his wife to a cocktail party at his home on December 2, 1943. Then, on December 18, Raoul Wallenberg attended an exclusive dinner party at the Hungarian Legation. On that day, Mrs. Ullein-Reviczky wrote about the gathering organized by her and her husband:

> Foreign Minister and Mrs. Günther, Ramels, Thybergs [Swedish minister to Greece], Grippenberg [sic – [Gripenberg, Finnish minister], Nicolaeffs [Bulgarian minister and his wife], de Riba-Tamega [Portuguese minister], Dinicherts [Swiss minister and his wife], Haggelhoffs [sic – most likely Hägglöf, the above-mentioned head of the Swedish Bureau of Foreign Trade, and his wife], [Harry] Sombor, Facht, Ihres, Kesceru [sic], Nordwalls, etc. 44 guests. Great success!

"Ihres" apparently refers to a key official in the Swedish Foreign Ministry's Foreign Trade Section, Nils Ihre, and his wife. This name points again at the high level of Raoul's contacts in Swedish society.

As Mrs. Ullein-Reviczky noted, two days later she received a polite letter from Raoul Wallenberg in which he "congratulat[ed] me on everything, for arranging the [Hungarian] Legation so beautifully".

Wallenberg's inclusion in this exclusive circle is somewhat surprising to anyone familiar with the strict Swedish social rules and general diplomatic etiquette of the time. It is perhaps a sign of the relative importance Ullein-Reviczky attached to him as a representative of a business sphere vital to Hungarian economic interests.

Both Ullein-Reviczky and his wife attended Raoul Wallenberg's farewell dinner at his parents' house on July 6, 1944. Mrs. Ullein-Reviczky wrote in her diary: "We dined at the Dardels with Raoul Wallenberg, who is leaving for Budapest tomorrow, and couple Lauer."

Interestingly, Ullein-Reviczky's name does not appear in Raoul Wallenberg's calendar on that day.[37] Raoul was not a careful note taker and often omitted sensitive data, but he also might have been careful not to write down the name of the rebellion Hungarian diplomat. In his memoirs, Ullein-Revitczky explained his situation in Stockholm at that time:

---

37 This is the calendar that the Soviet authorities released to Raoul Wallenberg's family from the KGB Archive in 1989.

Raoul Wallenberg – Not an Accidental Choice for Hungary in 1944

The first real news about the occupation of Hungary by the Germans, which took place on March 19, 1944, reached me on the evening of the 21st, when I received a coded telegram from the Ministry of Foreign Affairs ...

On the basis of the first telegram, I immediately sent a note to Mr. Christian Günther, Swedish minister of foreign affairs, to make the official announcement Hungary had fallen victim to German aggression and, consequently, the so-called government installed in Budapest by the aggressors could not be called legal. I therefore asked the government of His Swedish Majesty not to recognize this government and to continue to consider me as the representative of the constitutional Hungarian State.

As for the second and third telegrams [stripping Ullein-Revitczky of his citizenship], I kept them as souvenirs without attaching the slightest importance to them.[38]

Ullein-Reviczky remained minister, and the Swedish government allowed him to maintain a "free legation" in Stockholm. The minister's presence underscores both the official importance of the mission and the personal rapport that apparently had developed between the two men.

During his stay in Sweden, Ullein-Reviczky's focus remained the fate of his home country and the plight of its Jewish population. On April 8, 1944, Ullein-Reviczky sent an urgent appeal to Swedish foreign minister Christian Günther outlining the suffering of the Hungarian Jews and urging active Swedish assistance:

What appears to me to be of general interest ... is the undeniable fact that in the center of Europe, 800,000 human beings are doomed to martyrdom. May I, Mr. Minister, express the hope that the fate of these unfortunate people will not be indifferent to the Government of Sweden...? ... May I solicit

---

38   Ullein-Reviczky, *German War – Russian Peace*, 142, 145. After the German occupation in March 1944, the Hungarian government functioned essentially as a "Quisling" regime. SS-Obersturmbannführer Adolf Eichmann and his staff took control of mass deportations of Hungary's Jews to concentration camps in Poland and Czechoslovakia. The deportations were carried out with frightening speed and efficiency and received significant assistance from the Hungarian governmental and civil authorities. See Krisztián Ungváry, "Robbing the Dead: The Hungarian Contribution to the Holocaust", in *Facing the Nazi Genozide: Non-Jews and Jews in Europe*, edited by Beate Kosmala and Feliks Tych (Berlin: Metropol, 2004), 231–262.

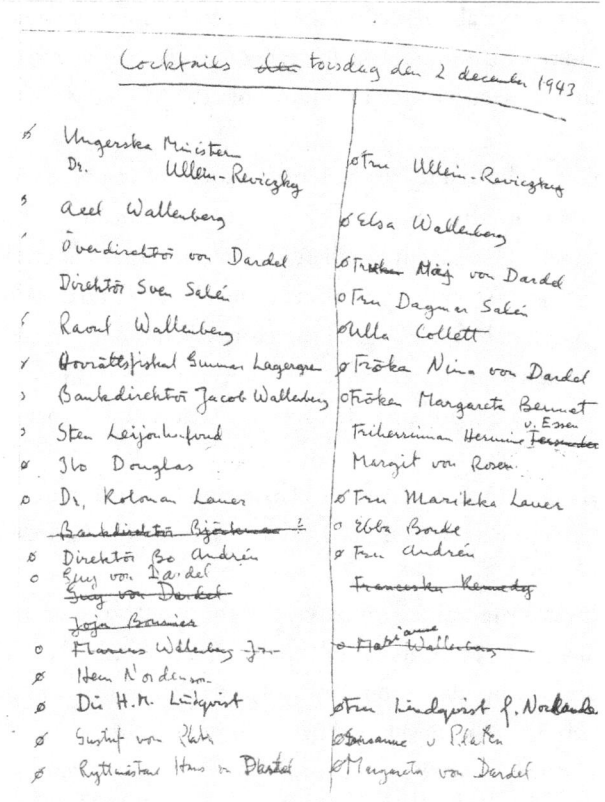

Fig. 6. List of guests invited by Raoul Wallenberg to his party on December 2, 1943. The Ullein-Reviczkys are first on the list. Courtesy of Dr. Guy von Dardel, Private Archive.

your government to take all measures it considers appropriate in order to improve the situation of my Jewish compatriots? [39]

This appeal was no doubt prompted by the increasingly horrific reports of mass deportations of Hungarian Jews, and, possibly, by the creation of the WRB in the United States in January 1944. The same day, Ullein-Reviczky forwarded copies of the appeal to the American and British governments

---

39 Dr. Ullein-Reviczky's letter to Swedish foreign cabinetinister Christian Günther, dated April 8, 1944, appeared on March 5, 1946, in *Le Journal d'Orient*, a daily newspaper in French published in Istanbul. Later, Dr. Ullein-Reviczky included it in his memoir in French, "Guerre allemande – paix russe" (1947).

Fig. 7. Dr. Antal Ullein-Reviczky's letter, dated April 8, 1944, to Swedish foreign minister Christian Günther, published in Le Journal d'Orient on March 5, 1946. Courtesy of the Antal Ullein-Reviczky Foundation, Hungary.

via the American minister in Stockholm, Herschel V. Johnson, and the British minister, Victor Mallet. Both ministers expressed their sympathy for and strong support of the appeal. Reviczky continued to be in touch with the Allied missions, as well as with numerous important contacts in Hungary, including Miklós Horthy Jr.[40]

---

40 In August 1944, Ullein-Reviczky asked Per Anger (1913–2002), first secretary at the Swedish Legation in Budapest, who worked with Raoul Wallenberg, to give his letter to a "personal friend, Horthy's son Miklos" in which he asked Horthy Jr. "to persuade his father ... to depose Sztojay [the prime minister after Kallay's ouster] with the help of the Hungarian military". Per Anger, *With Raoul Wal-*

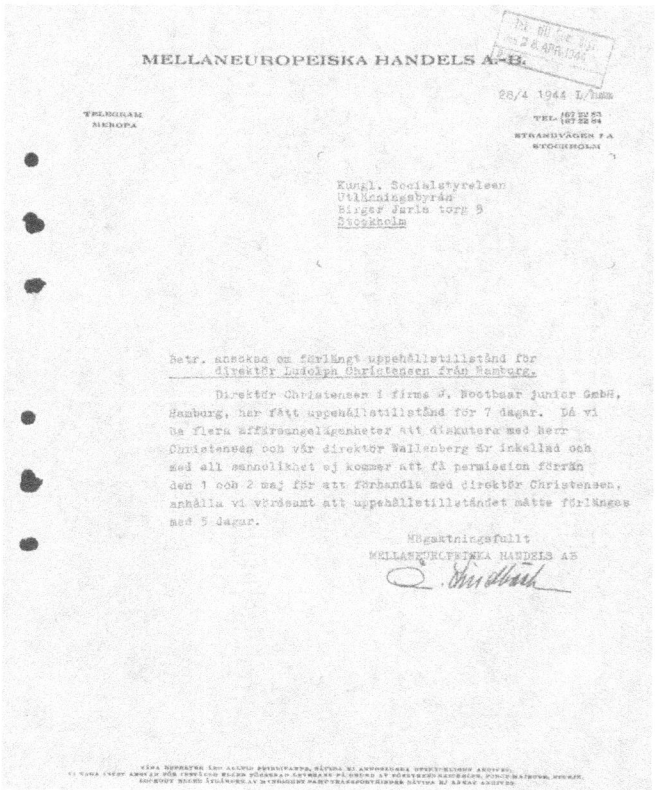

Fig. 8. Letter from Mellaneuropeiska in April 1944 requesting an extension of Ludolph Christensen's visa so that he could meet with Raoul Wallenberg on May 1–2, 1944. (Riksarkivet, Stockholm)

It is now possible to trace in even greater detail when exactly the idea was conceived to send a special Swedish representative to Hungary to save the Jews and how Raoul Wallenberg was chosen for the assignment.

lenberg in Budapest: Memoirs of the War Years in Hungary, translated from the Swedish by David Mel Paul and Margareta Paul (New York: Waldom Press Inc., 1981), 52. Unfortunately, on October 15, 1944, the Germans launched Operation Mickey Mouse; Miklós Jr. (1907–1993) was abducted by German commandos under the command of Otto Skorzeny and threatened with death unless his father surrendered and agreed to appoint the Arrow Cross Party as the new government. Regent Horthy complied and was placed under house arrest in Bavaria, while Miklós Jr. was sent to the Dachau concentration camp. He survived imprisonment and eventually was liberated by the Fifth US Army on May 5, 1945. After the war the Horthys lived in Portugal. See Sakmyster, *Hungary's Admiral on Horseback*, and *Admiral Nicholas Horthy Memoirs*.

Raoul Wallenberg – Not an Accidental Choice for Hungary in 1944

With the German occupation of Hungary on March 19, 1944, all Jewish citizens in the country faced deportation and death. Kálmán Lauer immediately realized that urgent measures should be taken to protect his sister Irén, her husband and their daughter, as well as relatives of Lauer's wife Marika; all of them were at the time living in Hungary.[41] Rudolph Philipp, the author of the first book on Wallenberg's mission to Budapest, wrote that Lauer immediately phoned his "close friend in Hamburg" for help –[42] this was the aforementioned Ludolph Christensen.

According to Philipp, initially, the idea was discussed that a special business deal should be concluded between Hungary and Sweden that would provide an "advantage" for Germany if it permitted the departure of certain Jewish citizens from Hungary.[43] Philipp claims that these discussions occurred in June 1944, and that they at some point included the American official Iver Olsen. Olsen was the financial attaché at the American Legation also representing the WRB in Stockholm and worked for the Office of Strategic Services (OSS, the predecessor of the CIA).

However, it is likely that some deliberations had already begun a month or so earlier, when Ludolph Christensen came to Sweden for a short visit from April 24–May 5, 1944. During this trip, he and Lauer undoubtedly discussed the crisis in Hungary caused by the German occupation. Regardless of whether or not Raoul Wallenberg and Christensen's meeting scheduled for May 1–2, 1944, took place (Wallenberg was on military service), a plan for how to help Lauer's family was almost certainly discussed by all three.[44]

Ullein-Reviczky's letter probably further intensified the already widespread discussions of how to aid Hungary's Jews. Already in April 1944, members of the Swedish Jewish Community proposed sending a special envoy to Budapest

---

41 These included her elderly parents, Lajos and Irene Stein, and their only son, Julius Stein.
42 Rudolph Philipp, *Raoul Wallenberg: Diplomat, kämpe, samarit – och martyr* (Höganäs: Wiken, 1981), 76–77.
43 Ibid.
44 In Sweden, all men 18 to 47 years of age were eligible to serve with the armed forces for from 80 to 450 days. At the time, Raoul Wallenberg was away from Stockholm on duty with the Swedish Home Guard. However, most likely he was informed about the discussions, because he was expected to consult with Christensen around May 1 or 2, 1944. Swedish National Archive, Files of the National Alien Commission (Statens utlänningskommission), 1944–1969, Ludolph Christensen, Personal Dossier.

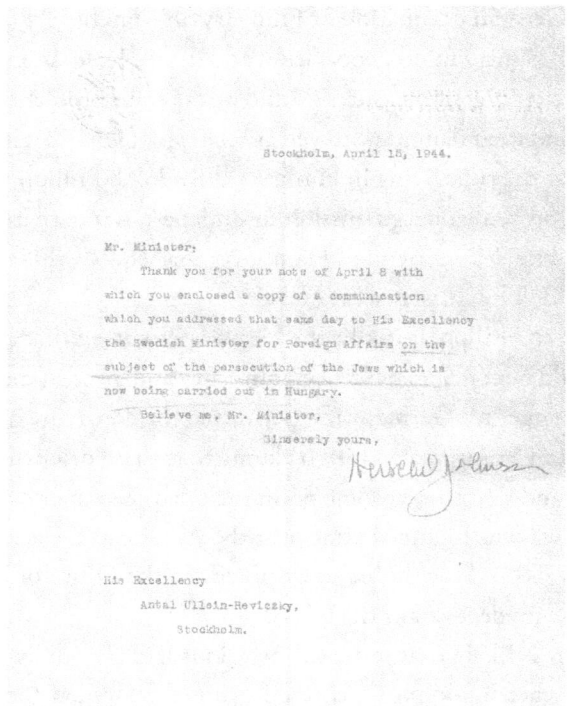

Fig. 9. Reply sent by the US minister to Stockholm, Herschel V. Johnson, to an appeal authored on behalf of the Hungarian Jewish population by Dr. Antal Ullein-Reviczky on April 8, 1944. Courtesy of the Antal Ullein-Reviczky Foundation, Hungary.

with official Swedish diplomatic status and sufficient funds to conduct limited rescue operations.[45] From the beginning, many of these and similar deliberations surely involved Raoul Wallenberg. In addition to Lauer, Wallenberg and Christensen's efforts, there was also a plan to create an aid committee that would function in an official capacity under the auspices of the Swedish Legation in Budapest.[46] Among the main initiators of this plan were Kálmán Lauer and Raoul Wallenberg's aunt, Countess Ebba Bonde, who conducted dis-

---

45 See the letter from Norbert Masur to Chief Rabbi Marcus Ehrenpreis, dated April 18, 1944. Document 54, in Steven Koblik, *The Stones Cry Out: Sweden's Response to the Persecution of Jews 1933–1945* (New York: Holocaust Library, 1988), 227. Masur served as a Swedish representative to the World Jewish Congress.
46 Jangfeldt, *The Hero of Budapest*, 137.

cussions with Swedish foreign minister Christian Günther. Countess Bonde was famous for her anti-Nazi views and support of refugees.[47]

On May 14, 1944, in connection with all these events, Raoul Wallenberg applied for an extended leave from his military service. As a reason for this request, Wallenberg stated his plans to go to Hungary "to buy foodstuffs, partially for export to Sweden, partially for distribution among Hungarian Jews through the Committee that shall be formed for this purpose".[48]

A few weeks later, the Swedish undersecretary of state, Erik Boheman, informed US minister Johnson that he favored the American requests to increase the official Swedish representation in Budapest and pointed out that Sweden "is already considering the possibility of sending food to [the Hungarian Jews] in concentration camps, to be distributed under supervision".[49]

Very likely Wallenberg referred to this project when he requested an official leave from military service, and Boheman, in his turn, almost certainly knew of Wallenberg's intentions regarding Hungary. Boheman's sister was married to Gunnar Josephson, a leading figure in the Stockholm Jewish community (Mosaiska Församling), and Boheman must have been aware of the ongoing discussions to aid Hungary's Jews. As for Minister Johnson, he was well acquainted with Sven Salén who, among other positions, was a vice president of the Swedish-American Society and whose business offices were located in the same building as the American Legation, Stockholm.

In early June 1944, Ullein-Reviczky sent a second round of official appeals to both Swedish and Allied representatives, which were met with the same assurances of support. This was the exact time when the actual choice to send Raoul Wallenberg to Budapest was made.[50] On the evening of June 9,

---

[47] Peter Tennant, *Touchlines of War* (Hull: University of Hull Press, 1992), 76. After the war, Countess Bonde brought hundreds of German children to Sweden. Wallenberg definitely was in close contact with his aunt. His diary contain notes that he visited her on January 20 and 30, 1944.

[48] Letter from Raoul Wallenberg to the chief of the Swedish Army, May 14, 1944. The letter was first published by Swedish author Lars Brink. See Lars Brink, *När hoten var starka. Uppkomsten av en väpnad folkrörelse* (Göteborg: Text & Bild Konsult, 2009).

[49] Hershel Johnson to US Secretary of State, June 9, 1944, US National Archives and Records Administration (NARA), RG 59, 840.48/6139.

[50] According to Lauer, Professor Marcus (Mordecai) Ehrenpreis, chief rabbi of Stockholm, was the first person to talk to Raoul Wallenberg about the necessity of going to Budapest to investigate the conditions of the Jews. Lauer's letter to Marcus Wallenberg, dated April 20, 1945, published in: Nylander and Perlinge, *Raoul Wallenberg in Documents*, 68–69.

Wallenberg and Kálmán Lauer met with Iver Olsen – apparently in his capacity as a WRB representative.[51] Olsen promised to try to obtain the full support of the US State Department for Wallenberg's future mission to Budapest; while Lauer informed Sven Salén about the possibility that Wallenberg would go to Budapest.

Both Salén and Olsen informed Minister Johnson, and the next meeting was between Wallenberg, Salén and Johnson. After this meeting, Johnson had an appointment with Sweden's foreign minister Günther and recommended Wallenberg for the job. Most likely, Minister Johnson's appreciation of Raoul as a candidate for the Budapest mission was partly because Raoul had spent several years in the United States – he was a graduate of the University of Michigan, Ann Arbor.[52]

On June 12, Wallenberg had one more meeting with Olsen.[53] The approval of Raoul's powerful relative, Jacob Wallenberg, was also obtained before Raoul agreed to go to Hungary.[54] On June 14 and 15, Raoul met with Jacob Wallenberg at the Wallenberg family bank, SEB.[55] Jacob subsequently provided a personal reference for Raoul Wallenberg's application for a diplomatic passport. The discussions may have also dealt with important technical details of the mission that needed to be resolved, such as the involvement of SEB in the planned transfer of monies that Raoul required for his humanitarian work in Budapest. In a Europe divided by the war, international

---

51   Levai, *Raoul Wallenberg*, 38. On April 12, 1944, John W. Pehle, WRB executive director, appointed Olsen "as the Board's special representative in Stockholm, Sweden, assigned as special attaché to the Legation on War Refugee matters". WRB's release no. 8 for morning newspapers, dated April 12, 1944 (Franklin D. Roosevelt Presidential Library, Hyde Park, USA. WRB Papers). In this capacity, later Olsen was Wallenberg's WRB "boss".

52   As Lauer wrote later, at another meeting Günther and Undersecretary of State Boheman asked Wallenberg "whether he was willing to take up duty with the Minister... After a few days of thinking the matter over, Raoul accepted the Foreign Ministry's proposal." Lauer's letter to Marcus Wallenberg, dated April 20, 1945.

53   The above-cited letter from Lauer to Marcus Wallenberg, dated April 20, 1945. Probably, Olsen handed Wallenberg 10,000 SEK for the beginning of his work in Budapest.

54   Letter from World Jewish Congress, Stockholm to Tage Erlander, November 23, 1946. Archives of the Swedish Ministry for Foreign Affairs (Riksarkivet), P2 Eu 1, Raoul Wallenberg case file. Jacob Wallenberg had already assisted Raoul with his previous foreign trips. In 1941, Jacob helped Raoul to obtain a *Kabinettspass* (cabinet passport) — a special passport that indicated that the bearer was traveling on official business for the Swedish government.

55   Notes in Wallenberg's diary and Nylander and Perlinge, *Raoul Wallenberg in Documents*, 80.

banking actions were a serious problem and the money could be obtained via Swiss banks.[56]

Finally, by the end of June, Wallenberg had resigned from Mellaneuropeiska and received an official diplomatic appointment as first secretary to the Swedish Legation, Budapest.[57]

Numerous names listed in Antal Ullein-Reviczky's personal address book match Wallenberg's own contact list in Budapest. First, there was Dr. Géza Soós, a close colleague of Ullein-Reviczky's in the Hungarian Foreign Ministry's Press Department. He was one of the people who Raoul Wallenberg met immediately after he arrived in Hungary in July 1944. Soós was the leader of a Hungarian resistance group, the MFM (Magyar Függetlenségi Mozgalom – Hungarian Independence Movement). He also had important ties to US and Swedish intelligence operations. Many details of these operations remain unknown.[58]

Additional matches included the politician and newspaper owner Count Gyula Dessewffy, whom Raoul Wallenberg hid in his private residence in Budapest; the already mentioned Nicky Horthy Jr., with whom Wallenberg met on several occasions; the wealthy and influential Countess Hetta von Wenckheim, one of Raoul Wallenberg's earliest contacts; Heinz von Wahl, to whom Mrs. Ullein-Reviczky affectionately referred in her diary as Heinzi von Wahl; as well as Count Ferdinand Orssich, whose son Ferdinand Jr., nicknamed

---

56 Regarding the complexity of Raoul Wallenberg's payments in Budapest see Leni Yahil, "Raul Wallenberg—His Mission and His Activities in Hungary", *Yad Vashem Studies* 15 (1983): 7–54.
57 Letter from Raoul Wallenberg to Cabinet Secretary Erik Boheman, June 19, 1944. He formally applied for a Swedish diplomatic passport on June 30, 1944. Swedish Foreign Ministry Archive, HP 21 EU.
58 For instance, the name of Géza Soós appears in a cable sent by the American wartime intelligence organization, the Office of Strategic Services (OSS), in November 1944, from Stockholm to Caserta, Italy (NARA, Raoul Wallenberg File, OSS cable from Stockholm to Caserta, Italy, dated November 7, 1944). The sender is "Crispin", which was Iver Olsen's OSS pseudonym. The text states that Soós can be contacted only through the first secretary of the Swedish Legation in Budapest, Per Anger, and that Raoul Wallenberg will know if he, Soós, is not in Budapest. The cable also points to the involvement of Swedish intelligence, including C-Bureau (C-byrån) and its deputy chief, Helmut Thernberg, in the preparation of the so-called "Swedish Signal Plan". It was designed to signal to the MFM supporters the moment of a planned national Hungarian uprising. Olsen states that "the whole affair was administered by the Swedes". Swedish archival records indicate that Helmut Thernberg traveled to Hungary at least twice during 1943–44. See Susanne Berger, *Swedish Aspects of the Raoul Wallenberg Case* (2001), 38, http://www.raoul-wallenberg.eu/researcher/susanne-berger/. After the war, Soós fled the country with his family, and in 1951, he settled in North Carolina, USA; he lectured at the Theological Seminary. In 1953, 41-year-old Soós was killed in a suspicious road accident.

Pizek, was Ullein-Reviczky's close associate.[59] Apparently, Raoul Wallenberg and Ullein-Reviczky also both were acquainted with Peter Matuska-Komáromy, the Hungarian minister to Sweden before Ullein-Reviczky.[60]

Some of these names indicate that Raoul Wallenberg's mission, while primarily humanitarian, may have also included other aspects. Throughout his stay in Sweden Ullein-Reviczky continued his clandestine discussions with US and British intelligence representatives about possible Allied military intervention in Hungary and the possibilities of limiting future Soviet influence in the region. These talks included the very same individuals who were involved in the preparation of Wallenberg's mission, such as Andor Gellert, a Hungarian journalist and diplomat who worked for the OSS; Vilmos Böhm, former minister of war in the short-lived 1919 Hungarian Communist government, who was employed as a consultant by the British Legation in Stockholm and who shared his network of valuable contacts in Hungary with Raoul Wallenberg; R. Taylor Cole, head of the OSS Secret Intelligence Branch in Stockholm (OSS Deputy Chief of Stockholm Station), who discussed US intelligence aims in Hungary with Raoul before Raoul's departure; and, of course, Iver Olsen.[61]

Clearly, the official Swedish–American selection of Raoul Wallenberg for the delicate and dangerous mission of saving Jewish lives in Budapest was not accidental. Instead, it was in many ways a logical choice. Raoul was a member

---

59 Count Ferdinand Orssich de Slavetich (1916–2013). Orssich's name appears on Raoul Wallenberg's coded list of names as a "friend". In late 1943, "Pizek" Orssich traveled to Stockholm, apparently on a confidential mission to contact British intelligence representatives on behalf of Professor Albert Szent-Györgyi, the 1937 Nobel Prize Laureate (Berger's telephone interview with Count Orssich, 2012). Later, Prof. Szent-Györgyi headed the "Taurus" resistance group in Budapest, which was formed in 1943. He was protected by the Swedish Legation and hid for a while in Raoul Wallenberg's personal apartment. See Gellért Kovacs, *Skymning över Budapest* (Stockholm: Carlssons, 2014), 197–207.

60 Before Sweden, Petér Matuska-Komáromy was the Hungarian minister to Poland. Matuska-Komáromy's wife was the sister of László Bárdossy, the pro-German Hungarian prime minister (in 1941–42) executed after the war as a war criminal. However, Matuska-Komáromy had the reputation of a diplomat very sympathetic to the plight of the Jews. He was a good friend of Ivan Danielsson, Swedish minister to Hungary from 1943–45 and Raoul Wallenberg's superior. See http://www2.arts.u-szeged.hu/legegyt/oktatok/Karsai_Laszlo/FatefulYear1942.pdf. He was also a distant relative of Lieutenant Colonel Peter Matuska, who worked for the Toledo Stahl AG and invited Raoul to Budapest in 1943 – it was his name that Raoul put on the visa application as his contact in the Toledo Stahl AG.

61 Robert Taylor Cole, *The Recollections of R. Taylor Cole, Educator, Emissary, Development Planner* (Durham (NC): Duke University Press, 1983), 84–85.

of an extremely influential Swedish family, and he was a businessman with excellent connections to the highest economic, diplomatic and intelligence circles in Stockholm. Just as importantly, he also had many important ties to members of Hungarian high society – far more than previously understood.

Interestingly, none of Raoul Wallenberg's diplomatic colleagues in Budapest, including Per Anger, Ivan Danielsson, Lars Berg and Kálmán Lauer, who knew of Wallenberg's personal contact with Ullein-Reviczky and his circle mentioned this connection in later accounts of the case. Anger merely refers to his own discussions with the Hungarian minister in 1944.[62]

Dr. Antal Ullein-Reviczky's role in originating the Swedish humanitarian mission in 1944 deserves closer examination than it has received so far. Aside from in Hungary, helpful additional sources for this research could possibly be found in archival collections in Sweden, Great Britain, the USA and also Russia. In spite of Dr. Ullein-Reviczky's obvious affection for Raoul Wallenberg, like other former Hungarian diplomats, he was rendered essentially powerless after the war. He died in exile in London in June 1955.

Selected Bibliography

Aalders, Gerard and Cees Wiebes. *The Art of Cloaking Ownership: The Secret Collaboration and Protection of the German War Industry by the Neutrals. The Case of Sweden.* Amsterdam: Amsterdam University Press, 1996.

Admiral Nicholas Horthy: Memoirs. Annotated by Andrew L. Simon. Safety Harbor (FL): Simon Publications LLC, 2000.

Agrell, Wilhelm. *Skuggor runt Wallenberg: Uppdrag I Unger 1943–1945.* Lund: Historiska Media, 2006.

Anger, Per. *With Raoul Wallenberg in Budapest: Memoirs of the War Years in Hungary.* Translated from the Swedish by David Mel Paul and Margareta Paul. New York: Waldom Press Inc., 1981.

Bartal, David. *The Empire: The Rise of the House of Wallenberg.* Stockholm: Dagens Industry, 1996.

Bauer, Yehuda. *Jews for Sale? Nazi–Jewish Negotiations, 1933–1945.* New Haven (CT): Yale University Press, 1996.

Berg, Lars G. *The Book That Disappeared: What Happened in Budapest.* New York: Vantage Press Inc., 1990.

---

62   Anger, *With Raoul Wallenberg in Budapest*, 52.

Berger, Susanne. "Swedish Aspects of the Raoul Wallenberg Case" (2001), http://www.raoul-wallenberg.eu/researcher/susanne-berger/

———. "Stuck in Neutral: The Reasons behind Sweden's Passivity in the Raoul Wallenberg Case" (2005), http://www.raoul-wallenberg.eu/articles/stuck-in-neutral-susanne-berger/

———. "Prologue to Budapest: Raoul Wallenberg and Special-Metall Förening" (June 10, 2008), http://www.raoul-wallenberg.eu/articles/prologue-to-budapest-raoul-wallenberg-and-special-metall-forening/

Berger, Susanne and Vadim Birstein. "Not a 'Nobody' – Choice of Raoul Wallenberg in 1944 Not Accidental" (2012), http://www.vadimbirstein.com/wallenberg.html

———. " A Memorial More Durable than Marble" (2013), Guy_von_Dardel_A-Memorial_More_Durable_T.pdf.

———. "Blasieholmsgatan 3" (2015) https://www.academia.edu/11973759/Blasieholmsgatan_3__New_Questions_About_Raoul_Wallenberg_And_The_Wallenberg_Family.

Berger, Susanne, C.G. McKay and Vadim Birstein. "Raoul Wallenberg's Secret German Contacts" (January 14, 2015), http://www.raoul-wallenberg.eu/articles/ludolph-christensen/

Bierman, John. *Righteous Gentile: The Story of Raoul Wallenberg, Missing Hero of the Holocaust*. New York: Penguin Books, 1996.

Birstein, Vadim. "The Secret of Cell Number Seven: The Mysterious Fate of an 'Extremely Important Prisoner'". *Nezamisimaya gazeta*. April 25, 1991 (in Russian, translated into English by the author), http://www.vadimbirstein.com/wallenberg.html.

———. "The Mystery of Raoul Wallenberg's Death". *Evreiskie novosti*. No. 2 (2002) (in Russian, translated by the author), http://www.vadimbirstein.com/wallenberg.html.

———. *The Perversion of Knowledge: The True Story of Soviet Science*. Boulder (CO): Westview Press, 2001.

———. *SMERSH, Stalin's Secret Weapon*. London: Biteback Publishing, 2012.

Birstein, Vadim and Susanne Berger. "Surprised Again – New Documentation about Raoul Wallenberg's Cellmate Surfaces" (August 1, 2011), http://www.vadimbirstein.com/wallenberg.html

———. "Das Schicksal Raoul Wallenbergs – Die Wissenslücken". In: *Auf den Spuren Wallenbergs*, Stefan Karner (Hg.), 117–140. Innsbruck: Studien Verlag, 2015.

———. "The Fate of Raoul Wallenberg – Gaps in the Official Record" (2016). Submitted.

Braham, Randolph L. *The Politics of Genocide: The Holocaust in Hungary*. 2 vols. Revised and Enlarged Edition. New York: Columbia University Press, 1994.

Brink, Lars. *När hoten var starka. Uppkomsten av en väpnad folkrörelse*. Göteborg: Text & Bild Konsult, 2009.

Carlberg, Ingrid. *Raoul Wallenberg: The Heroic Life and Mysterious Disappearance of the Man Who Saved Thousands of Hungarian Jews from the Holocaust*. Translated from the Swedish by Ebba Segerberg. New York: MacLehose Press, 2015.

Caples, Matthew. "Et in Hungaria Ego: Trianon, Revisions and the Journal Magyar Szemle (1927–1944)". *Hungarian Studies* 19/1 (July 2005): 51–104.

Cole, Robert Taylor. *The recollections of R. Taylor Cole, Educator, Emissary, Development Planner.* Durham (NC): Duke University Press, 1983.

Cornelius, Deborah S. *Hungary in World War II: Caught in the Cauldron.* New York: Fordham University Press, 2011.

Dardel, Fredrik von. *Raoul Wallenberg: Facts around a Fate.* Stockholm: Proprius Förlag, 1970.

Erbeling, Rebecca. "The United States War Refugee Board, the Neutral Nations, and the Holocaust in Hungary". In: Bystanders, Rescuers, or Perpetrators? The Neutral Countries and the Shoah, edited by Corry Guttstadt et al., 183–197. Berlin: Metropol Verlag & IHRA, 2016.

Fenyo, Mario D. *Hitler, Horthy, Hungary: German–Hungarian Relations 1941–1944.* New Haven (CT): Yale University, 1972.

Frank, Tibor. "Patronage and Networking: The Society of The Hungarian Quarterly 1935–1944". *The Hungarian Quarterly* 50/196 (Winter 2009): 3–12.

Frank, Tibor. "Antal Ullein-Reviczky: A Tribute", in: Antal Ullein-Reviczky. *German War–Russian Peace: The Hungarian Tragedy,* xvii-xxxvi. Saint Helena, CA: Helena History Press, 2014.

Freed, G. B. "Humanitarianism vs. Totalitarianism: The Strange Case of Wallenberg". *Papers of the Michigan Academy of Sciences, Arts and Letters* 46 (1961): 503–528.

Gilmor, John. *Sweden, the Swastika and Stalin: The Swedish Experience in the Second World War.* Edinburgh: Edinburgh University Press, 2011.

Handler, Andrew. *A Man for All Connections: Raoul Wallenberg and the Hungarian State Apparatus, 1944–1945.* Westport (CT): Praeger, 1996.

Jangfeldt, Bengt. *The Hero of Budapest. The Triumph and Tragedy of Raoul Wallenberg.* Translated by Harry D. Watson and Bengt Jangfeldt. London & New York: I.B. Tauris & Co., Ltd., 2012.

Kallay, Nicholas. *Hungarian Premier: A Personal Account of a Nation's Struggle in the Second World War*; foreword by C. A. Macartney. New York: Columbia University Press, 1954.

Ken, Oleg, Aleksandr Rupasov, and Lennart Samuelson. *Sweden in Moscow Policy, the 1930s–1950s.* Moscow: ROSSPEN, 2005 (in Russian).

Koblik, Steven. *The Stones Cry Out: Sweden's Response to the Persecution of the Jews 1933–1945.* New York: Holocaust Library, 1988.

Kornfeld, Baron Móric. *Reflections of Twentieth Century Hungary: A Hungarian Magnate's View,* edited by Ágnes Széchenyi. Boulder (CO): Social Science Monographs, 2008.

Kovacs, Gellert. *Skymning över Budapest.* Stockholm: Carlssons, 2014.

Levai, Jeno. *Raoul Wallenberg. His Remarkable Life, Heroic Battles and the Secret of His Mysterious Disappearance.* Translated into English by Frank Vajda. Melbourne: The University of Melbourne, 1989.

Levine, Paul A. Raoul Wallenberg in Budapest: Myth, History and Holocaust. London: Vallentine Mitchell, 2010.

Macartney, C. A. *October Fifteenth: A History of Modern Hungary 1929–1945.* 2 parts. Edinburgh: Edinburgh University Press, 1956 and 1957.

Matz, Johan. "Cables in Cipher: The Raoul Wallenberg Case and Swedish-Soviet Diplomatic Communication 1944–1947". *Scandinavian Journal of History* 38/3 (2013): 344–366.
McKay, C.G. "Notes on the Case of Raoul Wallenberg", http://www.raoul-wallenberg.eu/wp-content/uploads/2011/11/20111001McKays-Notes.pdf.
Nylander, Gert, and Anders Perlinge. *Raoul Wallenberg in Documents 1927–1947*. Stockholm: The Foundation for Economic History Research within Banking and Enterprise, 2000.
Oberführer SA Willi Rödel: Documents from the FSB Archives, Russia. Edited by V. S. Khristoforov. Moscow: Glavnoe arkhivnoe upravlenie goroda Moskvy, 2012 (in Russian).
Ormos, Mária. "Kállay Miklós (1887–1967)". *Korunk* (March 2004): 68–94 (in Hungarian).
Petrov, Nikita. "Was wissen wir wirklich über Wallenbergs Schicksal?" In: *Auf den Spuren Wallenbergs*, Stefan Karner (Hg.), 107–116. Innsbruck: Studien Verlag, 2015.
Philipp, Rudolph. *Raoul Wallenberg. Diplomat, kä mpe, samarit – och martyr.* Höganäs: Wiken, 1981.
Raoul Wallenberg: Report of the Swedish–Russian Working Group. Stockholm, 2000. http://www.government.se/information-material/2000/01/raoul-wallenberg---report-of-the-swedish-russian-working-group-copy/.
Romsics, Ignác. *István Bethlen: A Great Conservative Statesman of Hungary, 1874–1946.* New York: Columbia University Press, 1995.
―――. *Hungary in the Twentieth Century.* Budapest: Corvina–Osiris, 1999.
Rosenfeld, Harvey. *Raoul Wallenberg – Angel of Rescue* (revised version). London: Universe, Inc., 2005.
Sakmyster, Thomas L. *Hungary's Admiral on Horseback: Miklós Horthy, 1918–1944.* New York: Columbia Univ. Press, 1993.
Szegedy-Maszak, Marianne. *I Kiss Your Hands Many Times: Hearts, Souls, and Wars in Hungary.* Budapest: East European Monographs, 2013.
Szita, Szabolcs. "Langfelder Vilmos, Raoul Wallenberg budapesti segítöje". *Magyar ellenállók* 1 (2008): 150–177.
―――. *Trading in Lives? Operations of the Jewish Relief and Rescue Committee in Budapest, 1944–1945.* Budapest: Central European University Press, 2005.
Tennant, Peter. *Touchlines of War.* Hull: The University of Hull Press, 1992.
Ullein-Reviczky, Antal. *German War – Russian Peace: The Hungarian Tragedy.* Translated from the French by Lovice Ullein-Reviczky. Saint Helena (CA): Helena History Press, 2014.
Ungváry, Krisztián. "Robbing the Dead: The Hungarian Contribution to the Holocaust". In *Facing the Nazi Genocide: Non-Jews and Jews in* Europe. Edited by Beate Kosmala and Feliks Tych, 231–262. Berlin: Metropol, 2004.
Wallenberg, Raoul. *Letters and Dispatches.* 1924–1944. New York: Arcade Publishing, 1995.
Yahil, Leni. "Raoul Wallenberg — His Mission and His Activities in Hungary". *Yad Vashem Studies* 15 (1983): 7–53.

Chapter 9
Colonel Ferenc Koszorús: Witness and Paragon
Frank Koszorús, Jr.

Background

> *"We swear that we will fight every domestic or foreign enemy of our sacred country at all times, everywhere and in all circumstances valiantly in a manly fashion even at the cost of our lives."*
>
> (Oath of Hungary's Honvéd[1] soldiers)

Being aware of Hungary's planned defection from the Axis, Hitler occupied Hungary on 19 March 1944, drastically changing the situation of Hungary and its 800,000-strong Jewish population.[2] Nazi occupation resulted in the destruction of the majority of Hungary's Jewry, which had survived

---

1 Hungarian term, literally "homeland defender" – *the name of the Hungarian Army since the 1848 Hungarian War for Independence.*
2 Joseph Rothschild and Nancy M. Wingfield describe pre-19 March 1944 Hungary by noting that "to the chagrin and rage of the Radical Rightists, domestic social and institutional coordination with the Nazi model was also diluted by the ruling conservatives. Parliamentary debate was vigorous, opposition parties were active, trade unions remained free, the press was lively – though overt criticism of Germany was taboo. Civil liberties endured. Escaping Poles and Allied war prisoners received shelter, and the Jews though economically and socially molested, were shielded from extermination. Finally, the exasperated Hitler occupied Hungary in mid-March 1944 and forced the replacement of the foot-dragging and peace-seeking conservative government with a more pro-German one, though still not with an all-out Radical Right one." Joseph Rothschild and Nancy M. Wingfield, *Return to Diversity: A Political History of East Central Europe since World War II*, 3rd ed. (New York: Oxford University Press, 2000), 40. As succinctly noted by Randolph Braham, a specialist of that period, "[it] was primarily to safeguard their security interests that the Germans decided to invade Hungary. The destruction of Hungarian Jewry, the last surviving large bloc of European Jewry, was to a large extent a concomitant of this German military decision." Randolph L. Braham, "The Uniqueness of the Holocaust in Hungary", *The Holocaust in Hungary Forty Years Later,* Randolph L Braham and Bela Vago, eds. (New York: Columbia University Press, 1985), 185.

under the pre-invasion conservative governments. Adolf Eichmann arrived to direct the deportation of Hungary's Jews so that by the end of June and with the active involvement of the Hungarian authorities, virtually the entire Jewish population of the provinces had been deported. Between May and the beginning of July, approximately 430,000 Jews were deported, mainly to Auschwitz, where most of them were murdered.

In July, the more than 250,000 Jews still living in Budapest, including refugees from surrounding countries, were targeted for deportation. László Baky, a rabidly anti-Semitic under-secretary in the Ministry of the Interior,[3] planned to complete their deportation from the capital using the armed gendarmerie[4] that he ordered to Budapest to execute a putsch-like lightning strike and carry out the deportations by the middle of July. Colonel Ferenc Koszorús intervened militarily in an operation known as the Koszorús Action, which saved *countless lives*.

Being a modest individual, he hesitated to publicize his involvement in this singular initiative. Only after his action was mischaracterized and after being urged by friends to recount the events for posterity did he explain the decision he made in a dark, chaotic and dangerous period in Hungary's history. He explained why it was important for him to recount the history of his action as follows:

> From the beginning it has been my unequivocal feeling that I owe our Hungarian future a description of this brief historical period. It is my duty to describe this episode because it is characteristic of that historical period and serves to refute accusations that have been used to bury Hungary. I also had to record this account as some extremist political parties have misappropriated and mischaracterized the facts and attempted to turn them to their advantage. Distorted accounts are worthless from a historical perspective and hence cannot serve the objectives noted above.

---

[3] László Baky (1898–1946). A military officer and politician, he was a member of Hungary's parliament from 1939, serially representing various radical, pro-Nazi parties. As Under-secretary of the Interior from March to September 1944, he was responsible for the deportation of the Jews. Sentenced to death by a Hungarian court and hanged in 1946. (Editor's note.)

[4] Until 1945 the gendarmerie was responsible for maintaining public order in rural Hungary; while in the towns this function was performed by the police force. (Editor's note.)

Colonel Ferenc Koszorús: Witness and Paragon

... By publishing this account, my sole goal is to serve Hungarian public interest. I need to make my writing available to the public to read, since public opinion in the West is still largely misled in this regard.[5]

Not surprisingly, the historians of the communist regimes of the Stalinist Mátyás Rákosi[6] and János Kádár[7] periods ignored this valiant episode in Nazi German-occupied Hungary. The existence of heroic action on the part of Colonel Koszorús, especially from someone they considered a representative of the *ancien regime* spanning the inter-war and war period, was anathema to them. Nevertheless, by the 1980s the story was too enticing to ignore, and a few courageous, curious and intellectually honest individuals, e.g., Károly Vígh and Péter Bokor, uncovered and began writing about this incident that had such far-reaching consequences for tens of thousands of individuals.

Since then, a growing number of documents, reminiscences and historical research, not least of which are Colonel Koszorús's own recollections, have shed light on the events that unfolded in those few but fateful July days. As Colonel Koszorús's son, having had access to archival materials and personal papers, and having had the privilege of listening to my father's oral reminisces, I have attempted in this essay to summarize the Koszorús Action, my father's world view, facts that characterize and define him – the person – and why he volunteered for a seemingly hopeless task assumed at considerable personal risk.

---

5   Koszorús Ferenc, *Emlékiratai* és *Tanulmányinak Gyűjteménye* [Memoirs and a collection of his articles]. Magyar Történelmi Kutató Társaság Kiadványa. (New York: Universe Publishing Company, 1987), 53. (Henceforward *Emlékiratai*.) All translations from the Hungarian are by the author.
6   Mátyás Rákosi (1892–1971). Communist politician. After his imprisonment in Hungary and exile in the Soviet Union he became the leader of Hungary's communist Hungarian Workers Party, a ruthless and hated Stalinist dictator. Replaced in June 1956, he left Hungary for the Soviet Union, from where he was never permitted to return. (Editor's note.)
7   János Kádár (1912–1989). Communist politician. Minister of the Interior from 1948–1950, he was imprisoned on trumped-up charges (1951–1954), then was a member of the revolutionary Nagy government (30 October–4 November 1956), but under Soviet pressure he betrayed it and formed a puppet government. He had about 300 political prisoners executed, including Nagy and other leaders of the Revolution. After 1963 he eased the oppression with his "goulash communism" and made Hungary "the jolliest barrack in the Communist bloc". (Editor's note.)

Frank Koszorús, Jr.

The Koszorús Action

> *"Absence trustworthiness there is no 'soldier' – absence complete adherence to the soldier's oath, there is no trustworthiness."* (Colonel Koszorús)

On 2 July 1944 Colonel Ferenc Koszorús, colonel on the general staff and commander of the First Armored Division, had a chance meeting with Lt. General Lázár, commander of Regent Horthy's bodyguard. General Lázár complained that the situation had deteriorated to the point where even Regent Horthy's commands were ignored and disobeyed, as evidenced by László Baky moving armed gendarmerie to Budapest to deport the capital's Jewish population, thus countermanding Regent Horthy's directive to halt the deportations. Upon hearing Lt. General Lázár's account of the chaos reigning in Budapest, Colonel Koszorús offered his services to block Baky on the condition that he receive a lawful order. He received the order from Regent Horthy himself. Colonel Koszorús then proceeded to occupy strategic points with his armored division, prepared to use force to rid Budapest of Baky's armed gendarmerie. Baky had no choice but to capitulate and to retreat from the capital.

Witnesses and participants in the Action corroborate Colonel Koszorús's recollection of the event, which he shared with our family when prodded by us to do so. Former U.S. congressman Tom Lantos, himself a survivor of the Hungarian Holocaust, paid tribute to the memory of Colonel Koszorús on the 50th anniversary of the Hungarian Holocaust.[8] In his 1945 statement, Lt. General Lázár characterized Colonel Koszorús as follows: "[he] was anti-German [Nazi] and a democrat. In July 1944 with his division he carried out my orders with exceptional speed, energy and resolution… As a result of his action he precluded the deportation of approximately a quarter of a million Jews. He also participated in the resistance movement and guided his officers in that direction." This statement by Lt. General Lázár before the post-

---

8 Hon. Tom Lantos in the U.S. House of Representatives, Thursday, 26 May 1994. [Congressional Record Volume 140, Number 68)][Extensions of Remarks][Page E1109] https://www.gpo.gov/fdsys/pkg/CREC-1994-05-26/html/CREC-1994-05-26-pt1-PgE94.htm. The complete text from the Congressional Record is reproduced as Chapter 1 in this volume.

Colonel Ferenc Koszorús: Witness and Paragon

war screening committee[9] is particularly significant given that he was in a position to witness and participate in the frustration of Baky's plan. As noted by Péter Bokor, "Colonel Koszorús presumably was unaware of the fact that General Lázár executed a quick action simultaneously with Koszorús's move: he summoned the gendarmerie's senior officers to the [royal] palace and compelled them to issue an order by phone to their gendarmerie units to leave the capital. But clearly Baky would have paid little heed had Colonel Koszorús's tanks not threatened him."[10] Indeed, Baky ignored the Regent's directive and continued to make the necessary preparations to complete the deportations on or around 10 July. His total disregard for the order halting deportations is also demonstrated by the fact that thousands of individuals from towns and regions outside of Budapest were deported even as Colonel Koszorús's armored division rumbled into Budapest.

Colonel Koszorús: His World View and Principles

A Glimpse of His Character. In order to understand what motivated Colonel Koszorús to volunteer to confront Eichmann and the Hungarian rightists, one needs to consider his values, world view and deeply held principles.

Colonel Koszorús was born on 3 February 1899 in Debrecen into a military family that originally hailed from Transylvania. According to him,

> The Koszorús family ... has not used its family predicate since 1848. It has professed the same classical liberal values that regard every individual as being endowed with the same rights and obligations in accordance with the laws of 1848 ... On the other hand, under no circumstances would I like to provide a pretext for anyone to be arrogant, act in a superior manner or without empathy toward their fellow human beings ... Only the ignorant can be haughty and conceited. Moreover, accomplishments of our

---

9   Károly Lázár, statement, Budapest, 23 August 1945. Statement is in the author's possession. With the expulsion of the Germans and their Hungarian hirelings, all civil servants and professionals were vetted, their statements were taken and their previous political conduct was investigated by a screening committee composed of delegates from the five major political parties and a colleague. This process ended in 1948. [Editor's note]

10 Péter Bokor, *Zsákutca: A Századunk sorozat interjúi* [Dead end. Interviews of the TV-series "Our Century"] (Budapest" RTV-Minerva, 1985), 54.

ancestors do not authorize anyone to act in any special way and particularly do not bestow any privileges. Our forebears have already received their rewards for their accomplishments; therewith their case is closed. Their successors have no other rights and obligations other than to simply know, acknowledge and honor the valuable contributions and heroic acts of their ancestors and to follow their example.[11]

A letter to a friend sheds further light on his character: "Please refrain from addressing me as 'Vitéz'.[12] Even though I have more than enough combat service decorations to qualify for this order, and although the Deputy Commander of the Order has twice asked me to submit my application, I requested a delay until every qualified member of our troops has received the Order, as I have inherited an estate."[13]

This humanitarianism manifested itself in other far more difficult circumstances. For example, a fellow prisoner of war recalls Colonel Koszorús's bearing when "during the most difficult days of captivity he labored elegantly to maintain order among the other officers, who often shed their dignity and honor. No one put faith in this approach, yet he was able to preserve a certain measure of order. At the height of our starvation, he gave his rations to others who did not get their share. It took considerable effort by me to convince him to take half of my portion."[14]

Colonel Koszorús Did Not Embrace Any Political Extremism.

A background report dated 6 December 1951 concluded that this "man [Colonel Koszorús] is one of the very few high ranking Hungarian ex-officers with a clean past, untainted by either Nazism or Communism, who commands the respect of the better element of Hungarian veterans."[15]

---

11 *Emlékiratai*, 7.
12 The Vitéz Order was created after World War I in recognition of bravery on the battlefield. The honoree was also entitled to a land grant. Members of the Order represented individuals from all walks of life, from Defense Minister Vilmos Nagy de Nagybaczon (who was awarded the title Righteous Among the Nations) to farmers and occasionally to right-wing radicals.
13 Ferenc Koszorús's 26 June 1971 letter to János Nádas. Koszorús Family Archives.
14 *Emlékiratai*, 14–15, quotes Dr. Egon Nezsényi's letter.
15 Report, 6 December 1951. https://archive.org/stream/KoszorusFerenc/KOSZORUS%2C%20FERENC_0004#page/no/mode/1up

Not only was he untainted by these two murderous isms, Colonel Koszorús condemned them and considered both Communism and Nazism to be lethal enemies of Hungary. He considered Hitler to be among the most treacherous enemies of Hungary for several reasons, not least of which were Hitler's ambitions and his political leadership based on "racial discrimination" and "living space", which posed grave threats to Hungary. Colonel Koszorús clearly recognized that Hitler revealed himself not as a friend but as one of the most dangerous enemies of independent Hungary. Even prior to the war, Hitler "declared Hungary to be 'German living space', which meant that in case of victory, he wanted to eliminate an independent Hungary."[16] Colonel Koszorús stressed that as a Hungarian he could not approve of Hitler, who "intended to tread on our country and destroy Christian values in order to freely lie, rob and murder at will."[17]

Colonel Koszorús also severely condemned those Hungarians who placed their loyalty to Hitler above their duty to their country. In his words, "other than Hitler, the most harm was done to Hungary by his own followers in Hungary, who did everything possible outside the realm of the law during the war to enable Hitler's will to prevail in Hungary to the detriment of their country. The subsequent harsh treatment of Hungary by the victorious powers can be mainly attributed to the behavior of these Hitler devotees."[18]

Colonel Koszorús equally detested Communism:

> The Hitler-like tyranny that was taken to the extreme has been replaced by another bloody chapter of history and age of terror in Central and Eastern Europe. This Asiatic barbaric despotism … is blackmailing humanity that is otherwise yearning to have lasting peace with the specter of a third world war. In order to maintain its own tyrannical power, it has extended its boundaries to the heart of Europe; annihilated the ancient culture and civilization of countries that it invaded and occupied; relegated its peoples to inhuman slavery; robbed them of their wealth

---

16 *Emlékiratai*, 216.
17 Ibid., 171.
18 Ibid., 172.

... moreover, millions were exiled, taken away to forced labor camps, starved and stripped of their freedom.[19]

In other words, he saw no difference between Hitler and Stalin. He also personified the dilemma tragically and uniquely confronting Hungary (and other loyal and patriotic Hungarian military personnel), which was caught in an untenable middle, facing a life-threatening Hobson's choice, with Hitler on one side and Stalin on the other.

Colonel Koszorús often expressed his convictions about the two isms – Nazism and Communism – around the dinner table when the conversation drifted to World War II or the Soviet domination of Hungary and Central and Eastern Europe. It was also fascinating for me to listen to the conversations he had with former colleagues who shared his views, such as General Lajos Veress[20] and General Kálmán Hardy[21] or former Prime Minister Miklós Kállay[22] or historians, including C.A. Macartney,[23] or members of the resistance movement, such as his good friend Géza Soós.[24] Sitting in, questioning, debating and listening to the discussions among these individuals was a virtual oral library for me.

As I absorbed these discussions I realized that although Colonel Koszorús held conservative views and values, he did not think in terms of "party pol-

---

19 Ibid., 456–457.
20 Lajos Veress de Dálnok (1889–1976). General, Commander of the 2nd Hungarian Army (1944). Following Hungary's failed attempt at an armistice, he was arrested by his pro-Nazi officers, sentenced, but managed to escape. Sentenced to life imprisonment by the Communist government in 1947, he fled the country in 1956 and died in London. (Editor's note.)
21 Kálmán Hardy (1892–1980). Naval officer of the Austro-Hungarian Navy, Commander of the Hungarian River Fleet in 1942–1944. Involved in the attempted armistice, he was sentenced to death by the pro-Nazi regime, liberated by the U.S. Army and died in exile in the United States. (Editor's note.)
22 Miklós Kállay de Nagykálló (1887–1967). Prime Minister from 9 March 1942 to 22 March 1944. While in office he did his best to extricate Hungary from the war. Following the German occupation he was given asylum at the Turkish Legation, but was subsequently captured by the Gestapo and sent first to Dachau, then to the Mauthausen concentration camp, where he was liberated by the U.S. Army. Kállay died in exile in the United States. (Editor's note.)
23 C.A. Macartney (1895–1978). British historian specializing in the history of Central Europe. During the war he was in charge of the Hungarian section of the Foreign Office Research Department and regularly spoke on the BBC to Hungary. (Editor's note.)
24 Géza Soós (1912–1953). Head of the Soli Deo Gloria Calvinist youth movement and a prominent member of Hungary's anti-Nazi resistance. He helped to circulate the Auschwitz Protocols in high Hungarian circles, including the Regent. He worked with Wallenberg and saved many Jews. In 1946, to avoid arrest by the Communist secret police, he escaped from Hungary and became a leader in the democratic Hungarian emigration. (Editor's note.)

Colonel Ferenc Koszorús: Witness and Paragon

itics" or describe himself as a "liberal" or "conservative". He often expressed his opinion on the relationship between the military and party politics thus: "Because a soldier who is engaged in party politics is everywhere considered to be untrustworthy, he is not to be armed."[25] And after the war he continued to speak out against both right wing and left wing former military personnel. As he noted in his resignation from the Magyar Harcosok Bajtársi Közössége (MHBK), a Hungarian veterans organization in whose leadership the right wing, which Colonel Koszorús opposed, became dominant:

> Contrary to previous agreements, the small group that effectively controls the central command [of the MHBK] includes people whom I consider untrustworthy (unless proven otherwise) due to their past involvement in the shameful sedition of 15 October 1944. Moreover, it is these very same individuals who have the most influence within the central command. I don't see any assurances that MHBK's leadership would not lead the numerous, naive but misinformed people during these fateful times when it's easier to stray from the right path then it was in 1944 and with the currently prevailing pressures, into a coup-like adventure similar to that of 15 October 1944, which again would cause immeasurable harm to the entire Hungarian nation. This would go completely against my outlook and deep-seated beliefs, and I want to avoid being any part of it, even if inadvertently as an individual bereft of any official responsibility.[26]

He was a soldier, not a politician.

But what kind of soldier was Colonel Koszorús? Even though he did not boast about his military exploits, as he also did not about the Koszorús Action, one can draw the conclusion that he was a brave, loyal and fearless warrior from the medals that adorned his chest. Andrew Erdélyi, a subordinate of Colonel Koszorús, has given a graphic eyewitness account of one of Colonel Koszorús's engagements:

---

25 *Emlékiratai*, 456–457.
26 Letter from Colonel Koszorús to Major-General Endre Zákó, 22 April 1951. Koszorús Family Archives.

> My commander [Colonel Koszorús] left a deep impression on me during a difficult battle in the Arad vicinity ... I have the most vivid memory of the armored battle between us and the Russian–Romanian forces ... . The battle was well underway with both sides firing at will. The Colonel stopped under a tree in a wide field and jumped out of his tank as if he were strolling toward a promenade. With a riding crop in his hand he proceeded toward the middle of the battle. Pisti and I, frightened out of our wits, followed him as shells fell around us like hailstones in a darkening storm. He just continued on and on! Head raised, he marched! His tanks followed. The outcome of the battle symbolized his personality and courage.[27]

The result: 23 T-34 tanks lost with not a single Hungarian tank casualty. At the same time, he clearly saw the mortal danger threatening Hungary if it continued to participate in the war:

> By this time [1944] Hungary's continuation of the war became a suicide exercise, because the country was turned into a "Festung Deutschland" battlefield. Thus, in addition to the senseless military sacrifice of the entire country, the capital was also completely destroyed. Being the last one [country] to remain with Hitler resulted in Hungary receiving the harshest treatment by the victorious Powers, losing Transylvania and the previously regained Hungarian-inhabited regions, with Hungary's very independence called into serious question. Although all of these consequences were foreshadowed; excepting the country's Regent, the political and military leadership of Hungary simply ignored them.[28]

Witnesses confirm that Colonel Koszorús consistently held and articulated these views both in private discussions I was privy to and in the considerable volume of correspondence in my possession. A sworn statement by Lieutenant Jánossy from 1945 states:

---

27 Letter from Andrew J. Erdély, Ph.D., to Gabriella F. Koszorus-Varsa, , 6 October 1993. Koszorús Family Archives.
28 *Emlékiratai,* 290–291.

Colonel Ferenc Koszorús: Witness and Paragon

I have known Colonel Ferenc Koszorús's anti-German [Nazi] attitude, which he often publicly declared. As a sensible and thoughtful Hungarian he was a democrat by conviction ... He expressed his opinion to me that the final moment had arrived for Hungary to seek a ceasefire and leave the war, even if via military means! I know that he met with the Regent, who involved him in certain aspects of the already ongoing ceasefire negotiations.[29]

Colonel Koszorús's Views about the Anti-Baky Action

Considering his world view, deeply held principles, character and actions, it was natural that Colonel Koszorús would volunteer to confront and thwart Baky. In his words:

> The consequences to me as a result of my volunteering for the action were obvious to me ..... *I was aware that if this seemingly futile initiative was successful, I would be frustrating the most coveted desire of Nazi Germany's highest leadership, for which they would not hesitate to take any steps to liquidate me. I also had to anticipate that I would be forced into armed conflict with occupying German forces. Yet my inner conviction and sense of honor and responsibility unequivocally compelled me to act. I had to assume this most thankless task because I knew that there were hardly others who would do so, because of the prevailing circumstances (German occupation, the state of affairs immediately preceding the lost war), but most importantly because there was hardly anyone whose troops (even if they existed) would have participated in such an endeavor under the circumstances noted above. What made my assuming the task possible was that I had troops who were willing to follow me on the path of honor.*[30]

Rescuing Jews. There is no question that the Koszorús Action was also intended to block the deportation of the Jewish population to the German

---

29 Lt. Janossy, statement, Budapest, 17 August 1945. Koszorús Family Archives
30 *Emlékiratai,* 58.

death camps. Immediately prior to launching the military intervention against Baky, Colonel Koszorús addressed his officers as follows:

> Based on Lt. General Lázár's report, we will compel obedience to orders from our highest superior .... I reminded them that only death of those superiors to whom they swore loyalty could excuse their obligations assumed by them before God in the Honvéd oath. Anyone who disobeys the Honvéd oath under different circumstances is a dishonorable traitor. I further reminded them that the Honvéd oath mandated unconditional obedience from us to defend Hungary's borders, independence and constitution against all enemies whoever they may be. I said there were some who were ignoring these commitments and attempting to defeat Hungary's constitution and legal order in Hungary with the assistance of an oppressive foreign power and were ready to expose and betray hundreds of thousands of Hungarian citizens and leave them to the mercy of this alien power. Our Honvéd oath and Hungarian soldier's honor, I said, require us to block these disgracefully treasonous acts. I considered this to be the honorable path on which I would embark. Who is willing to follow me, I asked, along the path of honor?[31]

Without hesitation they all followed, which speaks volumes of his leadership skills and the respect his troops held him in. When this topic came up at home, Colonel Koszorús expressed his great appreciation and respect for his troops who followed him "on the path of honor". Loyalty, trustworthiness and honor were the three words that most often crossed his lips.

In the final analysis, there is no doubt that Adolf Eichmann and Baky planned to deport the Jewish population of Budapest in July 1944. This is why they brought the armed gendarmerie to Budapest. As Colonel Koszorús observed, his "armored division had to intervene precisely because Baky ... and the gendarmerie under him refused to obey the Regent's directive to leave Budapest, but instead intended to arrest the deportation-forbidding Regent so that they could implement their deportation plans."[32]

---

31 Ibid., 59.
32 Ibid., 71.

Colonel Ferenc Koszorús: Witness and Paragon

This is what is known as the Baky gendarmerie putsch. By forcing Baky's armed gendarmerie out of Budapest, Colonel Koszorús prevented them from deporting the Jewish population of Budapest to the German death camps in July 1944, which would have occurred but for the Koszorús Action. And this conclusion is supported by survivors, participants, witnesses, documents and objective historians.

Other consequences. Colonel Koszorús knew what awaited him. Separating him from his troops was a prerequisite to his becoming a prey of the Gestapo. As he bitterly recalled, "I had to leave Budapest and my gravely ill mother. I found temporary refuge in Transdanubia, where my former subordinate officers cared for me … . I could not even attend my mother's funeral. This was the most bitter consequence of my sacrifice. I became stateless in my own home because, remaining true to my soldier's oath, I enforced Hungarian laws in occupied Hungary."[33] Along with losing his country, the loss of his mother under these circumstances was the most painful personal consequence for him. To his chagrin, in order to maintain the U.S. security clearance required for his employment, he was never able to return to his beloved Hungary, not even after the Rákosi period.

From Hungary's perspective there was a serious consequence which should not be forgotten. In his sworn statement, Lt. Jánossy mentions that according to his best knowledge "the [First] Armored Division was ordered out of Budapest because it was loyal to the Regent. In my opinion our effort to withdraw from the war [in October 1944], even with the cost of lives lost, would have succeeded if the armored division had been able to stay in Budapest."[34]

Extremists and Revisionists Belittle the Koszorús Action

While the mobilization of the First Armored Division and its deployment in Budapest by Colonel Koszorús to confront and frustrate Baky is an unassail-

---

33 Ibid., 67. A Gestapo patrol looked for Colonel Koszorús and field chaplain Ferenc Kálló in the officer's hospital in Budapest. They found Kálló and killed him. Colonel Koszorús was not in his room but visiting his gravely ill mother in another room. The head nurse mislead the Gestapo, telling them that Colonel Koszorus was in town. He immediately left Budapest.
34 Jánossy, statement of 1945. Koszorús Family Archives

able fact, as there is far too much credible evidence confirming the military intervention, both the extreme Left and Right have sought to belittle the Koszorús Action.[35] Such blackening of history is nothing more than the denial of facts, revisionism that has no relevance to what actually transpired. Judging the events of July 1944 and the Koszorús Action in today's political and ideological terms is especially ironic because Colonel Koszorús did not consider it to be a political act. In his words: "I requested and received a lawful order for the implementation of the Action from my superior, in a lawful manner; thus, there was no politics in the implementation of a military operation."

Recalling the negative consequences to him personally, Colonel Koszorús nevertheless once again revealed his character when he wrote in 1964 that "from the perspective of 17 years and upon calmly and objectively considering the memorialization of the episode, all I can say is that in similar circumstances I would do exactly what I did 17 years ago. This conviction means more to me than anything else."[36]

---

35 For example, a far right extremist publication circulated by the Hungarist Movement in Argentina in 1960 complained that in 1944 while the "horrible hordes of the new Ogata Khan, Stalin, are at the Carpathian borders, Hungarian armored units are protecting the Jews of Budapest. If one enemy is attacking the Carpathians, let the other enemy stay in the capital ... The Jewry is still more important than the Hungarian nation." Kálmán Koós, *Voltunk, Vagyunk, Leszünk*, (A Hungarista Mozgalom Kiadása, Argentina, 1960) 237.
36 *Emlékiratai*, 68.

Appendix

Source of Documents: Public Record Office, London
German Foreign Ministry: Inland II geheim, Bundle 58/3
Collection Titled: Juden in Ungarn - Sonderaktion
Date: 1944–1945
Class/Serial No.5795 H.

Appendix

I

Memorandum from LUTHER[1] to RIBBENTROP[2]
Concerning a Discussion with SZTÓJAY[3] on the Treatment of Jews in Hungary

I/K213351   NG-1800; NG-5086; NG-5562

U.ST.S.-D.-Nr.6932   Berlin, the 6th of October 1942

For presentation,
via Mr. State Secretary *[Staatssekretär]*   JJ 6/70
To Mr. Reich's Foreign Minister *[Reichsaussenminister]*

Discussion Transcript

On the occasion of his visit on 2 October, I informed the Hungarian Minister *[Gesandter]* that I would like to speak with him again about the question of the treatment of the Hungarian Jews living in the occupied territories, in Germany and in Hungary. Accordingly, Mr. Sztojay visited me yesterday. I resumed my discussion with him of 11 August, the transcripts of which I am again attaching hereto,[4] and presented the following to him:

1) Hungarian Jews in the occupied territories.

Our concern about the safety of the German troops does not allow Jews of any nationality to be excluded from the measures ordered by the Military Commanders or the State Commissioners *[Reichskommissaren]* (introduction of the Jewish badge *[Judenstern - yellow star]*, internment and later evacuation). We therefore have approached all governments in question, including the Hungarian government, with the

---

1   Martin Franz Julius Luther (1895–1945). Nazi party activist; 1941–1942, Head of Division (*Ministerialdirektor*); 1942–1943, Deputy State Secretary [*Unterstaatssekretär*] in the German Foreign Office.
2   Joachim von Ribbentrop (1893–1946), was Foreign Minister of Nazi Germany from 1938 until 1945. He was sentenced to death at the Nuremberg Trials and hanged.
3   Döme Sztójay (1893–1946) Hungarian military officer of Serbian origin. Hungary's Minister to Germany 1936–1944. Prime Minister following the German occupation (April–August 1944). Hungary's Quisling was tried by a Hungarian court and sentenced to death.
4   No attachment was found with the paper.

request that by 31 December 1942 they approve the measures ordered or <u>take back the Jews of their nationality by that date. Otherwise, after that date, the evacuation of all Jews would be initiated.</u>

Concerning the treatment of the assets of the Hungarian Jews in the occupied territories, we are prepared for negotiations and would <u>agree to fiduciary participation</u> [*treuhänderischen Beteiligung*] <u>by the Hungarian Government in the proprietary</u> [*vermögensrechtlichen*] <u>measures</u>, if the Hungarian Government were to make an application to that extent.

Minister Sztojay inquired whether the same measures had been taken regarding the Italian Jews in the occupied territories, which I confirmed with the addition that because of the reasons stated above, exceptions could no longer be allowed. Mr. Sztojay noted this and opined that <u>under these circumstances, his government would not raise objections, that it would likely only request the repatriation</u> [*Rückführung*] <u>of some few Jews to Hungary, but that it definitely would request fiduciary participation in the proprietary measures. With regards to the evacuation</u> of the greatest share of the Hungarian Jews from the occupied territories, agreement would be given, because, of course, "Hungary does not intent to be second [*zurückstehen*] to the other countries."

2) <u>Hungarian Jews in Germany.</u>

<u>I informed Mr. Sztojay that it is now time to include the Hungarian Jews in Germany in the general measures affecting Jewry</u> [*Judenmassnahmen*] (<u>marking</u> [with the yellow star] <u>and later evacuation),</u> because it is really <u>no longer acceptable</u> that, for the understood reasons, we evacuate all German Jews as well as the foreign Jews from Germany, leaving only the <u>Hungarian Jews behind</u> to invoke their Hungarian citizenship and act in a more provocative manner every day. We would intend to approach his government about this, with a request to agree to this measure or to take the Jews back to Hungary, also by 31 December 1942. Regarding the <u>handling of the assets,</u> we suggest applying the <u>territorial</u> principle [*Territorialprinzip*], i.e., we keep the assets of the Hungarian Jews in Germany, and Hungary [keeps] those of the formerly German Jews [*ehemals reichsdeutschen Juden*] in Hungary. Regarding this matter there should still be separate negotiations with the Hungarian Government, just as with the other countries.

Mr. Sztojay immediately asked the question again about the treatment of the Italian Jews, to which I replied that there would be the same negations about this with Italy. Mr. Sztojay opined that if the Italian Government would issue the same approvals regarding the Italian Jews, his government would not present any difficulties on this point either. It only places importance on Hungary being treated according to the most-favored principle *[Meistbegünstigung]* regarding the Jewish question *[Judenfrage]*.

3) Treatment of the Jewish question in Hungary.

I explained to Mr. Sztojay in detail the reasons that move us to ask the Hungarian Government to, in turn, move forward the resolution of the Jewish question in Hungary themselves and to bring it to a conclusion as soon as possible. The following measures seem desirable to us:

> Proceeding with legislation with the goal of the elimination of all Jews from cultural and business life,
> Marking *[Kennzeichnung]* the Jews for identification,
> Resettlement to the East in agreement *[Benehmen]* with us, with the end goal of complete resolution *[restlosen Erledigung]* of the Jewish question in Hungary, Consultation *[Absprache]* with us regarding the handling of assets of the former German and Hungarian Jews with the goal that these assets will be confiscated by the state in whose territories it is located (territorial principle).

Mr. Sztojay again asked whether we had the intention of taking similar steps with the Italian government, which I affirmed. He further asked me if my statements to him were already to be viewed as an official step by the German Government towards the Hungarian Government, which I denied regarding points 2 and 3. I replied that we would undertake this step through Minister *[Gesandter]* v. Jagow, whereupon Mr. Sztojay requested of me that we present our suggestions or wishes before 18 October, because he would be in Budapest on that date and intended to discuss this entire matter with the Prime Minister[5] and possibly also with the Regent.[6] He has al-

---

5 Miklós Kállay de Nagykálló (1887–1967), Prime Minister from 9 March 1942 to 22 March 1944. While in office he did his best to extricate Hungary from the war. Following the German occupation he was given asylum at the Turkish Legation, but was subsequently captured by the Gestapo and sent first to the Dachau concentration camp, then to Mauthausen, where he was liberated by the U.S. Army. Kállay died in exile in the United States

6 Miklós [Nicholas] Horthy de Nagybánya (1868–1957), naval officer in the Austro-Hungarian Fleet,

ready conducted such conversations, especially with the Regent, several times, and we could definitely count on the fact that the Regent in particular, based on <u>his experiences with Bela Kun[7] in the year 1919, would have [the] utmost understanding of our wishes</u>. Hungary has indeed suffered especially greatly under the Jews, but unfortunately the fact is that the Jews, as a consequence of the proximity to Galicia, settled in Hungary in greater numbers *[besonderen Umfang]* and to an especially great extent took on influential positions in all important branches of the economy. <u>Therefore it would not be easy to approach a final rectification</u> *[Bereinigung]* <u>of this question and to implement it at a very fast pace</u>. It would involve <u>excluding</u> *[auszuschalten]* <u>8 – 900,000 Jews from all branches of the economy, and that would of course take a certain amount of time</u>. From his previous discussions, he knows that the <u>Prime Minister</u> is especially interested in the question of whether the Jews, following their evacuation, would be <u>given the opportunity for continued livelihood</u> in the East. There were some rumors going around in that regard, which he personally did not believe of course, but Prime Minister Kallay was somewhat concerned about them. He did not want to be accused of being responsible for leaving the Hungarian Jews, after their evacuation, in misery or even worse. My answer, that all evacuated Jews, including of course the Hungarian Jews, <u>would initially be put to use</u> *[Verwendung fänden]* <u>for building roads and later would be housed in a Jewish reservation</u> *[Judenreservat]*, calmed him visibly, and he opined that this message would have an especially calming and encouraging effect on the Prime Minister. I also reminded Mr. Sztojay about Prime Minister Kallay's remarks on the occasion of his inaugural address to Parliament. These remarks had shown that Prime Minister Kallay had a special understanding *[Verständnis]* for a resolution of the Jewish question in accordance with our wishes *[in Sinne]* and apparently *[augenscheinlich]* also seemed willing to resolve this question for Hungary soon. When taking his leave, Mr. Sztojay explained to me personally and with special emphasis that he very much welcomed our suggestions, because he had experienced, not only in Hungary but especially in Germany, the dev-

---

Rear Admiral and Commander of the Fleet (1918). Elected by the National Assembly Regent of the Kingdom of Hungary on 1 March 1920, a post he filled until 16 October 1944, when he was forced to abdicate. Was held under house arrest in Germany until liberated by the U.S. Army. At Nuremberg no charges were raised against him; he died in exile in Portugal.

7   Béla Kun (1886–1939), leader of the 1919 Hungarian Soviet Republic, responsible for the so-called Red Terror. In August 1919 he fled to Austria and then to the Soviet Union, where he became one of the innumerable victims of Stalin's purges, around 1939. Although of Jewish origin, Kun never considered himself anything but a Bolshevik internationalist.

astating *[verheerend]*, subversive *[zersetzend]* impact *[Einfluss]* that the Jews elicited *[hervorriefen]* everywhere.

I ask Mr. Reich's Foreign Minister *[Reichsaussenminister]* for the authorization to forward the instructions intended for 2) and 3) to Minister v. Jagow.

It seems to me to be of special significance <u>that we prompt the Italian government to also finally bring the Jewish question to a definitive *[engültig]* solution</u>. This matter would be most expediently discussed personally by Mr. Reich's Foreign Minister with <u>Count</u> Ciano.[8]

I will submit in the next few days a <u>memorandum about the status of the Jewish question</u> in Italy and the expedient suggestions or wishes to be presented by us to the Italian government.

[signature]

(Luther)

JJ 6/77

---

8   Count Galeazzo Ciano (1903–1944), Italy's Foreign Minister 1936–1943, Mussolini's son-in-law. He voted for the latter's removal in 1943, and was executed by order of Il Duce in 1944. He was a strong friend of Hungary.

Appendix

2

Telegram from LUTHER to the German Legation in Budapest
Concerning the Treatment of Hungarian Jews in German-Occupied Western Europe

I/K213370-372

File Nr. *[Akt.Z. = Aktenzeichen]* D III 792 g

Berlin, the 8th October 1942

    To the
    German Legation
    Budapest

    Nr. 2402

Referent: Under State Secretary *[U.St.S.=Unterstaatssekretär]* Luther
          Minister *[Gesandter]* Klingenfuß
Subject: Jews with Hungarian Citizenship

Three months ago an order was issued that in the occupied Western Territories, Jews with Hungarian citizenship can be included in the measures being implemented there (marking for identification *[Kennzeichnung]*, internment for later deportation). These measures have led to various protests by Hungarian representatives and an intervention by the Hungarian Minister. Hungary asks that [the] measures taken be reversed and requests that their Jews be treated as exceptions *[Ausnahmenbehandlung]* in accordance with the principle of most-favored status *[Meistbegünstigung]* and [requests] fiduciary participation *[treuhänderische Beteiligung]* in the proprietary *[vermögensrechtlichen]* measures.

Please inform [the] government there that [these] measures [are], for reasons of military security, necessary in the Western Territories. However, in order to accommodate [the] Hungarian Government, it should be given the opportunity to withdraw Hungarian Jews from the specified territories by year's end. After 1 January

1943, treatment as exceptions *[Ausnahmebehandlung]* is no longer possible, [and] Jews will then have to be deported with others.

In any case, securing the assets will take place to Hungary's benefit. There are no objections here to Hungarian offices being involved and being given the opportunity to state their wishes *[geltend zu machen]* regarding the implementation of Aryanizations *[Arisierungen]*.

Regarding Hungary's demand for most-favored *[Meistbegünstigung]* status, it can be said that these measures are not intended to be against individual nations but against [the] international Jews. Italy [was][1] approached with the same request *[Ansinnen]*.

Also notable is that Rumania as well as Slowakia[2] and Croatia not only agree with the subjugation of their Jews to German measures, but with German support have also started or completed the deportation *[Aussiedlung]* of Jews in their own countries.

In this context, it can be pointed out that also in the Reich, exceptional treatment *[Ausnahmebehandlung]* is no longer possible in the long run and that the question of taking [Jews] back *[Zurücknahme]* before being subjugated to our measures must be investigated. It would be desirable to also reach an agreement with Hungary whereby each state can have control over the assets of the Jews that are located in their sovereign territory *[Hoheitsgebiet]*, even if that affects citizens of other countries. This territorial solution, which will be of benefit *[gut stellen]* to Hungary, offers [the] only opportunity for [a] quick and final resolution given [the] complexity of proprietary disputes *[vermögensrechtlicher Auseinandersetzungen]*.

Luther

---

1   In the German original the word "wurde" = "was" is struck out. Perhaps the approach to Italy had not yet happened. (Translator's note)
2   We retained the contemporary German spelling for Romania and Slovakia. Rumania or Roumania was customary in English.

Appendix

3

Note from SZTÓJAY to the German Foreign Office
Transmitting the Answer of the Hungarian Government Concerning the German Request
for the "Solution of the Jewish Question" in Hungary

I/K213262-269

TRANSCRIPT

On 17 October of this year, the German Minister *[Gesandte]* in Budapest, Mr. von Jagow, handed to the permanent deputy of the Royal Hungarian Minister of Foreign Affairs[1] a note *[Aufzeichnung]* containing three points about the solution to the Jewish question.[2]

The Royal Hungarian Minister *[Königlich Ungarische Gesandte]* in Berlin,[3] in line with his instructions *[auftragsgemäss]*, has the honor to deliver the response of his government, as follows:

In Reference to Point I.

The Royal Hungarian Government continues to insist on the position that the principle of most-favored status *[Meistbegünstigung]* must be applied to Jews holding Hungarian citizenship who reside in the occupied Western Territories. It can therefore only endorse a provision that will be applied uniformly to all Jews of foreign citizenship.

The Hungarian Government is prepared, in principle, to accept the resolution of the assets questions proposed by the German side; provided, of course, that the removal of all Jews of foreign citizenship is carried out. In that case, it therefore asserts its claim to all the assets of Hungarian Jews, but would like to inform itself about these assets and their status beforehand. It is therefore requested that it be made possible for a Hungarian commission to conduct an examination of the assets *[Vermögensobjekte]* locally.

---

1   Jenő Ghyczy (1893–1982), Deputy Minister of Foreign Affairs (1941–1943), Minister of Foreign Affairs (1943–March 1944).
2   The document referred to could not be found among the papers.
3   Döme Sztójay.

The Hungarian Government also agrees in principle to the formation of a trusteeship *[Treuhändergesellschaft]*. However, it requests that, as a courtesy, it be informed about the laws on which this trusteeship is intended to be based, and about the intended manner of participation.

In Reference to Point II:

In this matter, the Royal Hungarian Government also insists on the application of the most-favored-status principle.

A circumstance that also must be pointed out is that the majority of Jews whose Hungarian citizenship was recognized have already left the German Reich. In regards to the assets of these Jews who have already returned home *[heimgekehrten]*, it is well known that negotiations that took place in 1938 and 1939 between the two governments led to certain mutual agreements.

The Hungarian Government is therefore not in a position to agree to a new provision that is based on territorial principles. The Hungarian Government continues to be of the opinion that these assets form a part of the Hungarian national wealth *[Nationalvermögens]*. This opinion was also recognized by the German side in 1938.

In Reference to Point III.

The Hungarian Government never doubted the pan-European *[gesamteuropäischen]* character of the Jewish question. It is, however, of the opinion that, as in the case of other questions of universal significance, the individual sovereign states must each find the most applicable forms of the solution. Up until now, the Hungarian Government has, itself, found these solutions in a timely manner – indeed, Hungary was the first State, in 1920, to restrict the free development *[Entfaltung]* of Jewish influence.[4]

Surely in Germany one can still remember the public aversion *[Abneigung]* with which world public opinion *[Weltöffentlichkeit]* received this first step on the path

---

4   Law XXV (1920) stipulated that the national/ethnic composition of the university student population should reflect the national proportion of the various nationalities. The aim was to reduce the number of Jews entering the universities, and thus eventually to reduce the high proportion of Jews in the professions.

toward institutional anti-Semitism and that under the influence of international worker organizations and economic powers, almost all of Europe's states wanted to rebuke Hungary, which stood alone, by means of a well-organized boycott. Even this pressure could not move Hungary to abandon its stance, and since then, Hungary continues to proceed consistently on the path toward moving the Jewish question to a solution, using its own methods, which it views as an internal matter.

Reference is especially made to the speech given by the Royal Hungarian Prime Minister before the governing party on 22 October of the current year, the text of which is attached hereto.[5] As is known, the speech was also published widely in the German press and was received sympathetically. This speech most clearly and unequivocally expresses the standpoint of the Hungarian Government.[6]

Given that the note *[Aufzeichnung]* in question also raises some questions of detail, the Royal Hungarian Government would like to make the following statement to courteously inform the Government of the Reich:

It is known that the so-called Jewish Laws *[Judengesetze]* (Act XV. of the year 1938, Act IV. of the year 1939) limit the participation of the Jews in intellectual life *[geistigen Leben]*, in the press and in the performing arts *[Schauspielkunst]* to their proportional numbers. The actual participation of the Jews in these areas today is already lower than their [proportional] percentage and is declining further because a Jewish succession *[Sukkreszenz]* is not allowed. The few remaining [professional] Jews will eventually die out *[Aussterbétat]*. A further modification of this situation would be possible only through protracted new legislative measures. It concerns only a few persons, whose exclusion would likely not be worth the implementation of new legislative measures, even less so because strict supervision makes it impossible for them to have a negative influence anyway. Further, it should be noted that the chambers *[Kammern]* in question here have already long accepted only persons who could invoke reasons of special equity *[Billigkeit]*.

The Jews have thus already been practically excluded from the intellectual professions. This is especially true in the field of education *[Unterrichtswesen]*, where the proportion of Jews has been in constant decline since 1920 and will rapidly reach *Numerus Nullus*. In this context, a reminder that as far back as 1920 Hun-

---

5   The text is not included in the present publication.
6   Kállay did his best to avoid doing further harm to the Jews of Hungary, but he tried to mislead the Germans by using anti-Semitic rhetoric. His deeds showed his true feelings.

gary was the first state to restrict Jews' university studies by means of a *Numerus Clausus* law.

The Hungarian Government cannot avoid pointing out, with the utmost emphasis, the circumstance that the Hungarian Jewry, which is quite numerous in and of itself – (it can be assessed at 800,000 souls) – was able to show a rate of participation in the country's economic life that far exceeded even this very high proportional number. It is generally known that in Hungary the Jewry almost exclusively occupied the positions in business and industry.

In comparison it can be noted that only 600,000 Jews lived in the so-called Old Reich *[Altreich]*. Among the 14,000,000 residents of Hungary, there are 200,000 more Jews than there were among the 60,000,000 Germans in the Old Reich.

Compared to the situation that existed before the Jewish Laws took effect and were implemented, we have already achieved extraordinary results in economic life. Of course, it must be taken into consideration here that the results of many years of undesirable social and economic development *[Fehlentwicklung]* had to be radically redressed in just a few years, and entire layers of Hungarian society had to be retrained to fulfill new tasks. This deep restructuring also had to be implemented during a period of time when the country's sources of economic strength were strained to the maximum for [our] own purposes as well as in the interests of the allies. Under these circumstances, the Jewish question has therefore become a question of production; but maintaining production is a pan-European *[gesamteuropäisches]* interest.

The Hungarian Government, nevertheless, has done everything and will continue to do everything to further speed up the restructuring that has already been rapidly occurring for years. It would however be misguided to force upon it a pace that is not sustainable for our economic apparatus, because its normal functioning is a German, Hungarian and pan-European interest in exactly equal measures.

The extent to which Germany is interested in maintaining the productivity of the Hungarian economy is sufficiently demonstrated by the fact that 80% of Hungarian industry is currently employed in the service of German economic interests. Next to these joint interests, it seems completely unimportant whether the total elimination of Jews from economic life is completed a little sooner or a little later.

The elimination of Jews from key positions has been taking place for quite some time and will be completed soon. Consequently, the Jewry has already lost its leading role in Hungarian economic life, and their work was put in the service *[dienstbar gemacht]* of Hungarian and European economic interests. The yield of Hungary's industrial production, as well as the absence of serious incidents of sabotage, provide reassuring proof that the Hungarian Government is guarding with a firm hand against any damaging activities carried out by the Jewry in this area.

Special marking *[Kennzeichnung]* of Jews in Hungary cannot be considered at the present time, as such a measure would only impede the implementation of all governmental measures that serve the purpose of the elimination of said Jewry. Their proportional numbers in business and in the population of the cities is so extraordinarily high that their increased visibility *[Hervortreten]* would doubtlessly unleash such expressions of passion *[Leidenschaftsäusserungen]* as would result in serious jeopardy to the legal and social order.

In regards to the question of resettlement of the Jewry from Hungary, the Hungarian Government today does not possess the possibility or [the] technical means to enforce practical implementation of such governmental measures. In no way can a partial solution achieve the purpose of such measures, but it could certainly easily offer cause for serious unrest and would in any case create serious disturbances of the country's war economy.

The Hungarian Government can assure the German Government that it continues to be intent on an accelerated solution to the Jewish question and will not fail to undertake anything that a responsible government acting under the extraordinarily difficult conditions of a country at war can reconcile with Hungarian, and consequently, with German and European interests.

Budapest, the 2nd of December 1942.

Appendix

4

Letter from STEENGRACHT[1] Transmitting Copy of HITLER's Decree Appointing VEESENMAYER[2] as German Plenipotentiary and Envoy to Hungary and Defining VEESENMAYER's Authority

NG-2947

Berlin, W4 the 4th of March
Secret Reich Matter *[Geheime Reichssache]*

In the attachment I am sending you [a] transcript of the letter of authorization *[Vollmacht]* issued by the Führer for the Plenipotentiary of the Greater German Reich *[Reichsevollmächtigter]* and Minister *[Gesandte]* to Hungary, Party Comrade *[Pg. = Parteigenosse]* Dr. Edmund Veesenmayer, for your confidential information.

Secret Reich Matter *[Geheime Reichssache]*

The Führer

1) The interests of the Reich in Hungary will from now on be represented by a Plenipotentiary of the Greater German Reich in Hungary, who also carries the official designation *[Amtsbezeichung]* of Minister *[Gesandte; Envoy]*.

2) The Plenipotentiary is responsible for the overall political development *[Entwicklung]* in Hungary and receives his instructions from the Reich Minister of the Exterior *[Reichsminister des Auswärigen*; Foreign Minister*]*.[3] His particular task is to initiate the formation of a new national government that is resolved to fulfill the

---

1 Gustav Adolf Steengracht von Moyland (1902–1969), German diplomat of Dutch descent. Served as Nazi Germany's State Secretary (*Staatssekretär*) at the Foreign Office from 1943 to 1945.
2 Edmund Veesenmayer (1904–1977), German politician and officer (SS-Brigadeführer), plenipotentiary representative to Hungary (19 March–April 1945). Sentenced for 20 years at Nuremberg in 1949, but was already released in 1951.
3 Joachim von Ribbentrop (1893–1946), was Foreign Minister of Nazi Germany from 1938 until 1945, sentenced to death at the Nuremberg Trials and hanged.

obligations of the Tripartite Pact[4] *[Dreimächtepakt]* loyally and to the final victory *[Endsieg]*. The Plenipotentiary is to advise this government authoritatively *[massgebend]* and represent to it all the interests of the Reich.

3) The Plenipotentiary is to assure *[darauf Bedacht zu nehmen]* that the country's entire administration, also as long as German troops are present there, is carried out by the new government under his leadership and is carried out with the goal of taking the utmost advantage of all the country's resources, especially its economic capabilities, for the purpose of joint warfare.

4) Any type of German civilian operational units *[Stellen]* that are to become active in Hungary are to be established only with the agreement of the Plenipotentiary, are subjugated to him, and carry out their activities according to his instructions.

For the tasks of the SS and the police [that are] to be implemented in Hungary with German staff *[Kräften]*, in particular political tasks regarding the Jewish question, a higher-ranking SS and police leader will join the staff of the Plenipotentiary, who will act according to his [the Plenipotentiary's] instructions.

5) As long as German troops are in Hungary, the military's sovereign rights in Hungary are exercised by the Commander *[Befehlshaber]* of those troops. The commander is subordinated to the Leader of the High Command of the Wehrmacht *[Oberkommando der Wehrmacht]* and receives directives from him.

The internal security of the country is the responsibility of the Commander, as are surprise threats from the outside.

He [the Commander] supports the Plenipotentiary in his political and administrative tasks, and consistently presents to him the demands of the Wehrmacht, especially with regard to the utilization *[Ausnutzung]* of the country's resources to supply the German troops.

In the civilian area, the Wehrmacht's demands are enforced by the Plenipotentiary.

In cases of imminent danger, the Commander of the German troops has the right also to order measures in the civilian area that are necessary to carry out the military tasks. He will coordinate and reach agreement with the Plenipotentiary as soon as possible.

---

4   Tripartite Pact was the official name of the Axis, the alliance of Germany, Japan and Italy, signed in Berlin on 27 September 1940.

Wherever their areas of responsibility touch upon one another, the Plenipotentiary and the Commander of the German troops are to cooperate in the closest possible way and to mutually coordinate their actions.

6) I name party comrade Dr. Edmund Veesenmayer as Plenipotentiary of the Greater German Reich and Minister to Hungary.

Führer headquarters [Führerhauptquartier], the 19th March 1944
signed Adolf Hitler

Appendix

5

Telegram from ALTENBURG to VEESENMEYER Relaying RIBBENTROP's Instructions concerning Relations with HORTHY and the New Hungarian Government

NG-5574

Telegram

(G-Schreiber) NG – 5 5 74

RAM 249/44]

Secret Reich Matter! *[Geheime Reichssache]*

Nr. 532 of 2.4. [2 April]

Telegram Control
Diplogerza Budapest
Telegram in Numbers (secret encryption)
Designation Secret for Secret Reich Matter

For the Plenipotentiary personally.

Mr. Foreign Minister of the Reich [*Reichsaussenminister*] asks you that your political approach *[Linienführung]* be to work towards having the Regent kept more and more at a distance from the business of the government, pushed into the background and gradually completely isolated in the castle. The goal is to gradually eliminate [*auszuschalten*] him completely and to conduct the necessary political work solely with the new Hungarian government.

Altenburg

Appendix

6

[Note by Counselor von Thadden[1]
Concerning the Progress in the Deportations]

Secret Reich Matter *[Geheime Reichssache]*

Ref.: LR I.K1. von Thadden

<u>The Jewish question in Hungary is</u>, as I was able to ascertain during my brief stay in Budapest,[2] <u>being driven at urgent speed towards a solution</u> with the vigorous <u>support of Hungarian State Secretaries *[Staatssekretäre]* Endre Laslo [sic][3] and Baky</u>. These are the details:

The Hungarian <u>Government has agreed to the transport to the Eastern territories *[Ostgebiete]* of all Jews who are to be viewed as Hungarian citizens. Only the 80,000 Jews</u> who are <u>destined</u> to be <u>put to work in Hungarian defense factories,</u> under strict guard by the Hungarian Army, are to be held back.

The <u>total number of Jews</u> in Hungary, based on the Hungarian definition of a Jew, <u>is estimated to be 900,000 to 1,000,000</u>. Of those, <u>about 350,000 [live] in Budapest</u>.

First of all, a comprehensive package of anti-Jewish legislation has started to assure the removal of Jews *[Entjudung]* from political life, the economy, etc. This legislation is continuously being expanded.

<u>At the same time, ghettoization was begun in the entire country, with the exception of the city of Budapest</u>. For the most part, these measures have been completed. Budapest itself was secured by a police cordon to prevent, as much as possible, the illegal departure of Jews.

<u>At the southern and southeastern borders, a 30 km-wide strip was</u>[4] <u>cleared of Jews, and the concentration *[Konzentrierung]* of Jews within large collection camps *[Sammellagern]* in the northeast Provinces was begun</u>.

---

1   Ehrental von Thadden was the head of the Internal Department of the German Foreign Office.
2   Von Thadden visited Budapest on 22 May. See International Military Tribunal, N.G. 4089. [Footnote in the Hungarian collection, Wilhelmstrasse, p. 854.]
3   The correct spelling is László.
4   The word überhaupt = "completely" is struck out by hand at this point. (Translator's note)

Appendix

These concentration measures led to the detention *[Erfassung]* of 320,000 Jews, of which, since 15 May, 12- to 14,000 a day are loaded [and transported] to the General Government *[Generalgouvernement⁵]*. By noon on 24 May, 116,000 Jews had been deported.

The onset of the deportations has caused significant unrest among the Jews in the other areas of Hungary, especially in Budapest. Therefore, despite the immediately imminent radical solution *[Radikallösung]*, the legislative machinery is running at full speed, and at the same time one has had the Jewish Council *[Judenrat⁶]* announce in Budapest that these measures would encompass only the Jews in the eastern territories [of Hungary], who had retained their Jewish particularities *[Eigenart]* and, unlike the Jews in the other territories, are not Magyarized *[magyarisiert]*. The legislation would clearly show that the remaining Hungarian territories were to be treated differently, because otherwise, such legislation would be superfluous. Whether as a result of this propaganda or for other reasons remains to be seen, [but] at any rate, the Jewry in the remaining Hungarian territories has remained calm until now. Generally, the SS-Departments are, however, expecting certain difficulties as soon as the concentration and deportation transports start up in the other provinces as well.

Currently, a meeting of the County Governors *[Obergespane]*, Police Commanders *[Gendarmeriekommandeure]*, etc., of the northern provinces is taking place with the Hungarian Minister of the Interior⁷ presiding – who on this occasion is moving for the first time into the foreground on the Jewish question, after hesitating until now – during which the administrative offices are to receive instructions for the concentration work [to be done] in their provinces. On 7 June, concentration in northern and northwestern territories will start. Following that, the same measures will be carried out in the south and southwest.

It is believed that in mid- to end of July the work in Budapest itself can get started. For this purpose, a large, one-day action *[Grossaktion]* is planned, which is to be carried out using a strong Hungarian gendarmerie presence from the provinces, all

---

5   *Generalgouvernement* = German-administered part of Poland during World War II.
6   The Jewish Council was formed from prominent Jews on 21 March by the order of the occupying forces and with the aim of calming – and misleading – the Jewish population.
7   Andor Jaross (1896–1946) was a member of the pro-German puppet governmnent. He was tried by a Hungarian court in 1946 and executed.

special units, and police academies, as well as making use of all Budapest mail carriers and chimney sweeps as guides. All bus and streetcar traffic will be suspended for this one day in order to be able to use all modes of transportation for the transport of the Jews. The concentration is to take place on an island in the Danube *[Donauinsel]* above Budapest.[8] One hopes that sufficient forces will be available to capture *[erfassen]* all Jews if possible and to prevent the disappearance of large factions into illegality. It is believed that by the beginning of September at the latest the removal, with the exception of the above-mentioned 80,000, will have been completed.

The sorting out of foreign Jews is sufficiently assured by [virtue of] the instructions from the Central Office *[Zentralstelle]*. However, the local Hungarian gendarmerie commanders are exhibiting such extreme eagerness that they view it as a matter of honor not to have to report any foreigners, if possible. Hesinger has, within the framework of the instructions he received from Inland II, conducted spot checks *[Stichproben]* in the camps and found a larger number of foreign Jews in the camps and had them sorted out. The further participation of the organs of the Foreign Office in the manner carried out until now by Hesinger is considered important, because the organs of the Reichsführer[9] in northern Hungary and Budapest expect an especially large contingent of foreign Jews and would like to prevent problems, if possible. Due to a manpower shortage, Group Inland II unfortunately cannot leave Hesinger in Budapest. Minister Veesenmayer intends to entrust this task to Legation Councilor *[Legationsrat]* Grell, whose arrival has been announced.

The term Jew is defined somewhat differently in Hungary than according to the Nuremberg Laws. There are no mixed races at all according to the Hungarian legislation, only Jews and Non-Jews. Making a stronger definition of the term Jew, in the sense of the Nuremberg Laws, had to be refrained from because in that case a significant part of the circle of friends of Horthy and the Hungarian country gentry *[Landadels]* would have to be included in the Jewish measures *[Judenmassnahmen]*. This does not seem advisable to all [the] German organs in Budapest, at least not right now. However, for the so-called certificate Jews *[Zertifikatsjuden]* – that is, those Jews who are to be treated as Aryans because of their special merits – an exam-

---

8   The large Szentendre island.
9   Heinrich Himmler (1900–1945), leader of the Schutzstaffel (SS), chief of the German Police and Minister of the Interior, overseeing all police and security forces, including the Gestapo, the Secret State Police.

ination of the certificates has been ordered. Tightest cooperation between State Secretary Endre Laslo, who is the head of the Verification Commission *[Überprüfungskommission]*, and the offices of the SD *[Sicherheitsdienst[10]]* is assuring that misuse of certificates will not happen again.

The anti-Jewish action is receiving propaganda support from a newly-founded anti-Semitic newspaper, *Harc* [Fight], which was published for the first time on Sunday, 21 May in a print run of 50,000 copies. The papers distributed in Budapest were gone within the first hour. It was observed that Jews wearing a star bought up to 30 copies. It is not known to what extent the newspaper also reached the Aryan readers for whom it is actually intended.

According to estimates to date, about 1/3 of the deported Jews are able to work *[arbeitseinsatzfähig]*. Immediately after arrival at the collection camp[11] they are immediately distributed to the offices of Gauleiter Saukel, to the OT *[Organisation Todt[12]],* etc. Numerous organizations have sent representatives to Berlin for the purpose of acquiring Jewish workers. The offices of the Reichsführer in Budapest, however, do not take part in any discussions, and instead send all such representatives away with the sensible statement that the SS Main Economic Office *[SS-Wirtschaftshauptamt; also SS-Wirtschafts- und Verwaltungshauptamt]* in Berlin is responsible for such demands.

Berlin, the 26th May 1944.

---

10 Security Service; Intelligence Agency of the SS and the Nazi Party.
11 The name of the camp is blacked out, but looks like "Auschwitz". (Translator's note)
12 Organisation Todt: civil and military engineering group named after its founder, Fritz Todt; part of the Ministry for Armaments and War Production – Reichsministerium für Rüstung und Kriegsproduktion,

Appendix

7

Telegram from VEESENMAYER to RIBBENTROP
Concerning the Postponement of the Deportations

Telegram

Budapest, the 30th June 1944

Nr. 289 of 30.VI.   Secret Reich Matter

Intended action had to be postponed because Regent *[Reichsverweser]* raised objections vis a vis the responsible Ministers *[Ressortministern]* and withdrew them only after Interior Minister Jaross took a very strong stand against it. With the proviso of exclusion of all practicing Jews *[Glaubensjuden]* in Budapest, the Regent finally agreed to the implementation of the action, with the stipulation that it should not be carried out at this moment but somewhat later, following completion of [action in] last province zone *[Provinzzone]*. Action is therefore postponed by about 10 days, and simultaneously, yesterday concentration [of Jews] in final Province Zone V (area not previously included, west of the Danube, excluding Budapest) [was] begun. Simultaneously, concentration [of Jews] is taking place in Area [of] 1. Police Command *[Gendarmeriekommandos]* in more distant suburbs of Budapest in order to make action in capital easier.

Veesenmayer

Appendix

8

Telegram from VEESENMAYER to RIBBENTROP
Concerning a Discussion with SZTÓJAY on the Cessation of the Deportations

NG-5523

Secret Reich Matter *[Geheime Reichssache]*

T e l e g r a m

From Budapest Nr. 299 of 5 July 1944

Citissime with Priority!¹

For Mr. Reich Foreign Minister *[Reichsaussenminister]* via Ambassador Ritter.

Am just now learning from a telephone call to Sztojay that the Regent *[Reichsverweser]*, apparently with agreement of Hungarian Government, has stopped continuation of Jewry actions *[Juden-Aktionen]*. Sztojay has asked me to see him tomorrow in order to provide me with detailed information about the context that led to this step. Also had longer conversation with Sztojay yesterday evening, which I reported on as instructed in accordance with Drahterlass[2] RAM 788/44 I[3] of 3 July.[4] Sztojay was very much concerned *[betroffen]* about this and again asked me to approach Mr. RAM *[Reichsaussenminister = Reich Foreign Minister]* and to obtain the Reichgovernment's *[Reichsregierung]* consent to the various offers foreign countries [are making] on behalf of the Hungarian Jews. The reasons he cited are:

1. The Hungarian Government has learned that no special measures are being conducted in Rumania against the Jews there and that the Reichsgovernment is tolerating the fact that a relatively generous treatment of the Jewish problem is taking place there.

---

1 Citissime = swiftest, fastest; Latin term used in German diplomatic communications. Citissime refers to the mode of transmission, the fastest possible (technical) mode should be chosen. When, as here, it is followed by "mit Vorrang", the telegram must be processed before other telegrams. (Translator's note)
2 Drahterlass = German diplomatic term for encrypted telegrams from the Reich Foreign Ministry (RAM) to its missions. (Translator's note)
3 The second number in this series is quite blurred in the original typescript and is difficult to decipher. In the Hungarian edition of this document it appears as 708/44.
4 The report is not be found among the German documents.

2. Also in Slovakia, there are still thousands of Jews, mainly converted ones, who with the toleration *[Billigung]* of the Reichsgovernment were under the protection of Tiso.[5]

3. The fact of the arrival of the Jewish-Hungarian millionaires in Lisbon today, which became known via enemy radio broadcast *[Feindrundfunk]*, has caused enormous agitation all over Hungary and has given rise to doubts about a fair and consistent implementation of the Jewish question in Hungary. If Jews like this can get to neutral foreign countries with the help of the SS, then the Regent and also the Hungarian Government have the right to advocate that, for the mitigation *[Abmilderung]* of the Jewish question in Hungary, the special requests of individual neutral countries be taken into account. They [the Hungarian government] would like to take the sting out of *[die Spitze nehmen]* the general agitation against Hungary, especially through such gestures, particularly because these neutral countries are often of importance for Hungary in other areas.

4. The Regent and the Hungarian Government are currently being bombarded by telegrams, appeals and threats because of the Jewish question. For example, the King of Sweden has sent multiple telegrams, as well as the Pope. The papal nuncio[6] is said to visit the Regent and Sztojay several times a day. Further, the Turkish Government, the Swiss Government, important men from Spain, and last but not least numerous Hungarian personages do the same.

5. In strict confidence Sztojay also read to me three secret telegrams, decoded by the Hungarian Security Agency *[Abwehr]*, from the English and American envoys in Bern to their governments. These contain a detailed account of what happens to the Jews who are deported from Hungary. It is mentioned therein that 1½ million Jews have already been annihilated there and that currently and ongoing, the majority of deported Jews suffer the same fate. In these same telegrams, the following suggestion is made: bombardment and destruction of the destination to which the Jews are being taken, further, destruction of railways that connect Hungary with these locations. Targeted bombing of all Hungarian and German offices that are participat-

---

5   Jozef Tiso (1887–1947), Slovak Roman Catholic priest, leader of the Slovak People's Party. Between 1939 and 1945 Tiso was the head of the Slovak satellite state of Nazi Germany.
6   Angelo Rotta (1872–1965) was the Apostolic Nuncio in Budapest from 1930 to 1945. As the Dean of the Diplomatic Corps, he vehemently protested several times to the Hungarian governments against the Jewish deportations. Rotta was recognized as Righteous among the Nations by Yad Vashem in 1997.

ing in this matter, with precise, accurate street names and house numbers in Budapest; and finally, large scale propaganda across the entire world and description of the whole state of affairs. In a further telegram, 70 Hungarian and German personages representing individuals with primary responsibility *[Hauptverantwortliche]* are named.

Sztojay explained to me that these threat[s] cut no ice *[kalt lassen]* with him personally, because in the event of our victory, this matter will have no consequence, and in the other event, his life will end *[mit seinem Leben abgeschlossen]* anyway. Despite this, he was obviously very much impacted by the telegrams, about which I heard in the meantime that they were also presented in the Cabinet *[Ministerrat]* and caused a similar reaction there.

I am assuming that in the meantime, during the night, the Regent has also been informed about this. That, and the points just listed led to the decision mentioned at the beginning [of this telegram]. Further contributing [to this] are the enemy reports about the situation in the East, which have caused a more or less deep depression among all groups *[Lagern]* friendly to us. The good mood created with the use of the "V1"[7] has disappeared as a result of the reports from the East and has turned into its opposite. Here people look primarily only at the Russian front. At the same time, the internal state of affairs has reached a state of crisis *[Lage zugespitzt]* again. The impacts of the most recent, in part apparently quite heavy bombardments, which also hit residential areas, are very unpleasant *[unangenehm]*, and broad segments fear that after the removal of the Jews, Budapest will be opened up for destruction *[der Vernichtung freigegeben]*. A skillful whispering campaign as well as enemy flyers are doing the rest in this regard. Apart from this, the battle of the parties among themselves continues on a more intense level, which is causing the practical work to suffer in all areas. This is being taken advantage of by radical circles on the left and right, primarily Szalazi [sic[8]], who is causing the Castle *[Burg]* and the Government to live in latent fear of a coup *[Putschangst]*. A failed assassination [attempt] against State Secretary Barcsy[9] has created additional great unrest among the middle class

---

7   The *V-I* missile or *V-I* flying bomb was the first of the so-called "Vengeance weapons" (*Vergeltungswaffen*) series designed for terror bombing of London.
8   The correct spelling is Szálasi.
9   István Bárczy de Bárcziháza (1882–1952) was Permanent State Secretary of the Cabinet Office and note taker at all the government and crown council meetings, 1921–1944. Regarding the mismanaged attempt on his life, see the article by Bonhardt in the present volume.

Appendix

[bürgerlichen Kreisen]. Barcsy is in and of himself a harmless political figure, [who] fearlessly, has personally emphasized time and time again that in his role to date he has already served 21 Hungarian Prime Ministers faithfully but is viewed as a spy and a dangerous figure by a certain side. Sztojay also takes this matter very seriously and intimated yesterday that the current investigations are showing some interesting and peculiar results. He equivocated regarding my further inquiry to learn more. I will report immediately following my conversation with Sztojay tomorrow.

Veesenmayer

Appendix

9

Telegram from VEESENMAYER to RIBBENTROP
Concerning a Discussion with HORTHY on 4 July 1944

NG-5684

Secret Reich Matter *[Geheime Reichssache]*

Telegram

From Budapest Nr. 301 of 6 July 1944

Citissime

For Mr. Reich Foreign Minister *[Reichsaussenminister]* via Ambassador Ritter.[1]

At the request of the Regent [I] had a two-hour meeting with him the evening before last. He began immediately by stating that he urgently asks the Führer to carry out the removal *[Abbau]* of the "Gestapo", as he referred to it, for the purpose of reconstituting Hungary's sovereignty. He is in a very difficult position, feels like a puppet who is not the leader of his country, even though, with a view to the military situation, he is prepared to do everything to fight the battle against Bolshevism on the side of Germany. He would also, if supplies and armaments would allow for it, be prepared to establish new divisions to deploy in the battle against Russia.

Transitioning to Hungary's domestic political situation, he emphasized how much the parties' fighting *[Parteienstreit]* disgusted him and that all efforts to create a unity party *[Einheitspartei]* have unfortunately remained unsuccessful. He implied that he was also not satisfied with Sztojay because he had shown himself to be ignorant regarding domestic political questions and was not able to handle the individual parties.

Imredy, and especially his wife, he referred to as very ambitious. He valued his expertise but viewed him as just a party politician who pursued his own special interests. His strongest criticism was directed at State Secretaries Baky and Endre; the latter he referred to as not normal and mentioned in confidence that two of his un-

---

1   Karl Ritter (1883–1968), German diplomat, ambassador to Brazil, during World War II the liaison between the Ribbentrop Foreign Office and the OKW, the High Command.

cles died in an insane asylum. Baky is a political weather vane, who would stand with us today and would also stand with the Bolshevists tomorrow. On the Jewish question, he mentioned that he is daily being bombarded from all sides domestically and internationally with telegrams, such as from the Vatican, the King of Sweden, from Switzerland, from the Red Cross and many more like these.

He said he is not a friend of the Jews but supported the Jewish Christians for political reasons and [supported] retention of the Jewish doctors as well as the retention of the Jewish labor battalions in Hungary, especially to the extent that they are deployed for work that is important for the war. In the end, he <u>frowned</u> on this subject [and] went on with general statements and historical reminiscences from which he wanted to derive proof that Hungary was the only true ally *[Bundesgenosse]* of the Reich. I replied to the Regent that Sztojay had already discussed the question of dismantling the SS and SD[2] offices with the Führer during his last visit, [and] that their retention was absolutely essential as long as the Führer was not certain that Hungary had severed its ties 100 percent with the old politics of betrayal under Kallay. In addition, these organizations operate exclusively in the interests of the conduct of the joint war and contribute towards helping Hungary promote its internal cleansing *[Bereinigung]*. The same was true for the Jewish question, which Hungary could indeed implement but in practice could never be solved without our support. Increasingly, the Hungarian people are starting to understand what monumental risks and what burdens the Jews represented for Hungary. Also, his [Horthy's] name, especially after the World War, is connected with the image of a fighter against Jewry and Bolshevism, and we are not doing anything other than to help to realize his earlier convictions. About the question of parties, I explained that from the beginning I was of the opinion that parties cannot be merged, they can only be overpowered *[überwinden]* by action. This, however, requires a strong, authoritarian government, which is only partially the case with Sztojay's current government. I then sharply criticized Defense Minister Csatay[3] and his deputy Ruszkicay–Rüdiger [sic[4]]

---

2   SS = Schutzstaffel, literally "defense squadron", the internal security force of Nazi Germany, founded in 1930 as Hitler's bodyguard.
    SA = Sturmabteilung, literally "storm detachment", functioned as the original paramilitary wing of the Nazi Party.
3   Lajos Csatay (1886–1944), General, Minister of Defense (June 1943–October 1944). He was arrested by the Gestapo for his involvement in the failed attempt at an armistice. In captivity he, together with his wife, committed suicide.
4   The correct spelling is "Ruszkiczay-Rüdiger". Imre Ruszkiczay-Rüdiger (1889–1957), General, Depu-

and demanded *[verlangen]* their hopefully immediate departure, because in our experience, these two men lived up neither to the requirements of joint warfare nor to Hungary's national interests. Regarding Csatay, he [the Regent] accepted this criticism without objections,[5] while he made very negative remarks with regard to Ruszkicay-Rüdiger, and – as I heard that very night from Colonel-General *[Generaloberst]* Vörös[6] – recommended to him [Vörös] that he remove him [Ruszkiczay-Rüdiger] as soon as possible. I countered his indication *[Hinweis]* that currently he knew of no other solution than to resign by telling him that I did not doubt for a second that he would remain in office. His reaction to that proved to me the importance of my statement *[die Wichtigkeit meiner Behauptung⁷]*.

His worries about the Russians were more in evidence than usual. Obviously, in the clique that controls him, those who are constantly talking to him about England's and America's guarantee[s] *[Garantie]* have lost some of their influence. In this context, the Regent then made some peculiar intimations regarding [the] Hungarian Army's obligation to his person, without going into details. In the meantime, tonight I received messages from two sides that say that the Regent is seriously expecting a coup by Szalasi or Baky.[8] Supposedly, Hungarian officers were on alert; however, neither the higher-level SS- and police leaders *[Polizeiführer]* nor the commanding general of the German Wehrmacht in Hungary was able to confirm any details. Another message says that the environment around the Regent is influencing him in the direction of preparing a military government and military dictatorship. If these messages are confirmed, then the Regent's aforementioned remarks would acquire a certain meaning. Personally, I currently see no serious starting point *[Ansatzpunkt]* for the possibility of a coup. The plan to introduce a military dictatorship is also not to be expected based on the current situation. However, in the case of a successful offensive by the Russians on the southern part of the Eastern Front *[Ostfront]*

---

    ty to the Minister of Defense (1942–October 1944). He was arrested by the Gestapo, then a POW in the Soviet Union (1945–1948), followed by imprisonment and torture by the Hungarian authorities.

5 Since Horthy managed to keep Csatay at his post until 15 October, Veesenmayer must have taken the Regent's silence as acceptance.

6 János Vörös ((1891–1968), military officer, Chief of Hungary's General Staff (March 1944–October 1944), Minister of Defense in the Provisional Government (1945).

7 "Behauptung" can mean statement, assertion, claim or allegation – the correct choice is not clear from the context. (Translator's note)

8 László Baky (1898–1946), military officer, a member of parliament from 1939, serially representing various radical pro-Nazi parties. Under-secretary of the Interior from March to September 1944, responsible for the deportation of the Jews. Sentenced to death and hanged in March 1946.

as well, such a development would be expected. I judge the current situation to be substantially unsettled and tense, but do not at all see any cause for concern. I also am in constant contact with Sztojay through my best middleman, and with a view toward a possible development to his benefit, I have kept open all possibilities to play a joint game with him myself. Sztoay himself is too weak to get into power without support and therefore, in the end, depends on me. His discussions with other parties and groups had a negative outcome [and] in no way reach beyond achieving a truce *[Burgfrieden]*.

Without a doubt, the increasing threat from the East has strengthened the Regent's will for the battle against Bolshevism. One proof of this was his intention a few days ago to drive to his troops on the Eastern Front to strengthen them in their courage to fight and their operational readiness. This journey was only suspended because Sztojay, the War Minister *[Kriegsminister]* and the Chief of General Staff *[Generalsstabschef]* recommended patience, since the opening of the Russian offensive on the Southern Front is expected any day.

Veesenmayer

Appendix

10

Telegram from Plenipotentiary Veesenmayer to Foreign Minister Ribbentrop
Concerning the Stoppage of the Deportations

Secret Reich Matter [*Geheime Reichssache*]
To be treated only as Classified

Telegram
(open)

Budapest, the 7th July 1944
Arrival, the 10th July 1944

Nr. 302 of 7.7.44.

Citissime!
With Priority!
Secret Reich Matter

For Mr. Reich Foreign Minister [*Reichsaussenminister*] via Ambassador Ritter.

Following Drahtbericht Nr. 299 of 6 July.[1]

Reporting that Jewish action [*Judenaktion*] in Zone V was completed yesterday evening as planned and that Suburb Zone-Budapest (Drahtbericht to Berlin Nr. 1838 of 30 June) is continuing as planned and should be completed by tomorrow. City and County [of] Pest[2] stopped however. The police forces that were concentrated in Budapest for this purpose have returned to their locations.

Veesenmayer

---

1 See Document 8 in the present volume.
2 In fact only deportations from Budapest were stopped.

Appendix

II

Telegram from VEESENMAYER to the Foreign Ministry
Concerning a Talk with Sztójay

Secret

Telegram
(open)

To Be Treated Only as Classified

Budapest, the 8th July 1944
Arrival, the 9th July 1944

Nr. 303 of 8.7.44.

From Budapest directly
forwarded to Fuschl[1]

Citissime!

Just had hour and a half talk with Sztojay. He informed me about the concerns of the Regent regarding a coup by State Secretary Baky together with the gendarmerie. He himself did not take these things seriously, but the Regent was alarmed, therefore temporarily ordered alarm status for the Budapest garrison. Meanwhile, this has been lifted. At the same time, the gendarmerie, which were concentrated here in Budapest for the planned Jewish action *[Judenaktion]*, were transported back to their locations. This morning, the Prime Minister, at the behest of the Regent, issued a fierce declaration in front of a gathering of the Ministers and all party leaders stating that the Regent and the Government are willing to counter by force of arms all plans to stage a coup *[Putschabsicht]*. He also warned the parties not to carry their methods of fighting each other *[gegenseitige Kampfmethode]* too far, because otherwise the Government would be forced to implement effective counter measures.

---

1 Fuschl (today Hotel Schloss Fuschl, near Salzburg) was seized by the Nazis in 1938 and converted into a residence for Foreign Minister von Ribbentrop.

In fact, in the meantime, the situation has calmed down substantially and the abundance of circulating rumors has waned. Sztojay is leaving Budapest this evening for two days of rest.

Then Sztojay told me about the information he had received *[zugetragenen Meldungen]* whereby the SS intended to carry out the Jewish action in Budapest using German organizations by bringing in 1,000 SS members from Vienna. I immediately consigned this message to the realm of fantasy but did ask for clarification about [the] status of the Jewish action in general. Sztojay informed [me] that Interior Minister Jaros [sic[2]] had already been charged with carrying out the selection of Jewish Christians in an accelerated manner, that further he again requests that the Reichsgovernment agree to accommodate the various foreign offers (Drahtbericht Nr. 1826 of 29.6.) to benefit Hungarian Jews, a gesture that would assuage the external and internal situation, and in return, he would make efforts to obtain agreement from the Regent as soon as possible to resume the Jewish action in Budapest. I left him no doubt that this date would have to be determined as soon as possible and that the Reich insists that, come what may, the residual Jewish action in Budapest be undertaken soon.

Based on a telephone call this morning from General Bodenschatz,[3] I raised the now urgent question of provisioning 20,000 *Flak*[4] soldiers and helpers. I described to him the seriousness of the situation and referred to the statement made to me by the Regent that he is willing to increase his contribution for fighting Bolshevism. Sztojay held out the prospect of immediate investigation and support.

Then I raised the demand presented to me by General Field Marshal *[Generealfeldmarschall]* Keitel via the commanding general of the German Wehrmacht in Hungary for delivery of 80,000 additional horses. This was already rejected day before yesterday in the Cabinet *[Ministerrat]*. I refrained from representing this demand in full, since due to the current situation in Hungary, it does not seem realizable to me, but [I] did urgently ask Sztojay to hold out the prospect of another tranche of horses as soon as possible. I hope to also achieve partial success on this

---

2 The correct spelling is "Jaross".
3 Karl-Heinrich Bodenschatz (1890–1979) was a German general, the liaison officer between Adolf Hitler and Hermann Göring (1893–1946), pilot, Hitler's deputy in all matters until 22 April 1945, when Hitler ordered his arrest. Göring was tried and sentenced to death at the Nuremberg Trials, but committed suicide before the sentence could be carried out.
4 *Fliegerabwehrkanonen* or *Flugabwehrkommando*, a division of the Luftwaffe. (Translator's note)

question in the course of the next week. The last point I touched upon was the question of the release of the three officers.[5] I called his attention to the fact that this conduct is a breach of good faith and insisted on re-arrest *[Wiederverhaftung]* and additionally on the arrest of Szombathelyi and Bajnoozy [sic].[6]

Sztojay requested time for consideration.

In reference to Drahtbericht Nr. 299 of 6.7.,[7] would like for tactical reasons to suggest being accommodating towards the Hungarians' wishes in regards to Drahtbericht 1826 of 29.6. The deciding factor is that this will make it possible to implement the residual Jewish question as quickly as possible, whereby the question of Jewish Christians could be taken care of later without notice *[auf kaltem Wege]*, without great difficulties and without creating a stir.

Veesenmayer

---

5   Ferenc Szombathelyi (1887–1946), General, Chief of the General Staff until the German occupation, prepared Hungary's break with Germany. Following an unfair trial in Yugoslavia was executed as a war criminal.
    Gyula Kádár (1898–1982), Colonal, as head of counter-intellgence from 1943 until the German occupation he communicated with the Allies to receive their hoped-for expeditionary force. He was arrested by the Gestapo, liberated in Germnay by the U.S. Army. Upon his return to Hungary he was arrested by the Soviet authorities and imprisoned in the Soviet Union until 1955, then sent home and imprisoned in Hungary until the 1956 Revolution.
    István Ujszászy (1894–1948?), General, as head of state security he was closely involved with the planned break with Germany. Arrested by the Gestapo, then again in 1945 by the Sovier NKVD. It is not known when and how he died in Hungarian communist captivity.
6   József Bajnóczy (1888–1977) was the Deputy Chief of the General Staff until May 1944.
7   Document 8 in this collection.

Appendix

12

Telegram from VEESENMAYER to RIBBENTROP
Concerning a Discussion with HORTHY

VI/91-92

Secret Reich Matter *[Geheime Reichssache]*
(To be treated only as Classified)

Telegram
(G.Schreiber) *[Secret Teleprinter]*

Foreign Ministry *[Auswärtiges Amt]*
Inland II *407*
Received 11 July 1944
Attachment (single or multiple) Copy of Received

Budapest, the 8th July 1944

Note:

From Budapest directly forwarded to Fuschl.
Tel.Ktr.10.7.44
[Telegrammkontor=Office or Telegrammkontrolle=Control]

Distribution:

1. 1a Office of the Foreign Minister *[BRAM=Büro des Aussenministers]*
2. State Secretary
3. Under State Secretary Political Affairs
4. Ambassador Ritter
5. Department Head Political Affairs *[Dg. Pol=(Ministerial-) Dirigent Politsche Angelegenheiten]*
6. Political Department IV *[Pol IV=Politische Abteilung IV]*
7. Inland II
8. Ambassador v. Rintelen
9. Envoy Schmidt – Press
10. Envoy Frohwein
11. Legation Councilor v. Grote

This is copy nr. *11*

Citissime!
=========

For Mr. Reich Foreign Minister *[Reichsaussenminister]*

Regent surprisingly asked me to see him today at 21 hours. Meeting lasted 45 minutes. He explained the following:

During the past 48 hours he received unequivocal messages that State Secretary Baky together with the gendarmerie intended to carry out a coup. He then alerted the Budapest garrisons, had the gendarmerie returned to their locations, and instructed the Prime Minister to issue the statement that was already reported in Drahtbericht nr. 303 of 7 July.[1]

These precautionary measures are a purely local matter and are not the least bit related to the multi-

---

1 See Document 11.

faceted rumors that have been connected with this in Budapest and were also believed by various German offices. He is still resolutely determined to carry the battle on the side of Germany through to the end, for better or for worse, but is now finally fed up with having to watch the parties bicker for any longer and was seriously thinking about cleaning up, if necessary, the current, unsatisfactory government affairs. Regarding the Jewish question, he has ordered the segregation of the Jewish Christians, and he is prepared to agree to further deportation – with the exception of the Jewish labor battalions – of Budapest Jews in the near future. However, he attaches great importance to avoiding the harsh treatment of the past, because this was inconsistent with his entire nature.

The reason for this meeting was likely a call from Sztojay to the Regent, because the former was concerned about creating a false impression based on the way I made fun of all the alarm measures, while at the same time pointing out the bad impression that, in my opinion, these had to have made on the Reichsgovernment. The Regent was also already informed about my demands regarding the 20,000 Flak [air defense] helpers and regarding additional delivery of horses, and commented on both points that he would like to help regarding the first question, provided that the prerequisites allowed for it, and that he would also arrange for increased delivery of horses after the harvest. However, during the harvest [season] (being a farmer *[Landwirt]* himself), it would be impossible, given the shortage of tractors and fuel, to bring the harvest in on time if at the same time horses were removed on a larger scale.

I expressed my regret to the Regent that he did not personally inform me early enough about the precautionary measures that were implemented, because that would have made it possible for me to counter the rumors and false conclusions in a timely manner. Among other things, I intimated that the issuance of a party ban and the proclamation of a military dictatorship were generally expected for today at 11 AM. He replied that these would not be the worst [things], [and] later he returned to this topic and told me in strict confidence that he had not yet discussed this topic with anyone but was thinking about it seriously and would call me again if he himself had reached clarity in this regard, especially concerning the choice of the person. Finally, I again made some very unequivocal statements regarding the Jewish question, pointed out to him the dangers that several hundred thousand Jews represented in a country's capital during the fifth year of war and urgently asked him to call for the resumption of the halted Jewish action as soon as possible.

Appendix

It's the same old song with the Regent, whoever visits him last is right. Since, however, 75% of his visitors have to be rated as negative, my work is countered again and again. Also this whole story about Baky and a coup, which the Regent obviously honestly believes, was just talked into him by malicious people who have an interest in creating difficulties for Germany. The true background and the dominant momentum are the fear that Germany loses the war. This also explains the desperate efforts in these circles to create an alibi for themselves for the future.

Despite all this, I again emphasize that in my opinion, there is no cause for serious concern regarding further developments in Hungary in the near future. The continued hardening *[Versteifung]* is primarily a result of the current difficult situation on the fronts.

Veesenmayer

Appendix

13

Telegram from Plenipotentiary VEESENMAYER to Foreign Minister RIBBENTROP Concerning the Resumption of the Deportations

(To be treated only as Classified)

Foreign Ministry *[Auswärtiges Amt]*
Inland II *1402*
Received 11 July 1944
Attachment (single or multiple) Copy of Received

Budapest, the 9th July 1944 15.05 Hour
Arrival, the 9th July 1944 16.20 Hour

Fuschl, Nr. 308 of 9.7.44. *[9 July 44]*

Cito!
Secret!

For Mr. Reich Foreign Minister *[Reichsaussenminister]* via Ambassador Ritter.

Just now Interior Minister Jaross visited me and informed me that he received messages from German and Hungarian border stations, especially from Hegyeshalom, that SS units were advancing on the German side, presumably to be channeled into *[einschleusen]* Hungary. He placed this in the context of the supposition that Sztojay had already expressed to me that – as reported in Drahtbericht 303[1] – the Jewish action in Budapest was to be continued solely under German direction with the help of these SS men. I calmed Jaross down [and] told him that I am not aware of an intended enlistment of SS units and that we continued to maintain the principle that the further elimination of the Jews *[Entjudung]* of Budapest had to be carried out by the Hungarians themselves.

Jaross took this opportunity to report to me that, against the Regent's directive, he had the Jewish action in Zone V and Suburb-Action-Budapest carried out.

---

1   See Document 11.

This [action] was in fact, for all practical purposes, completed smoothly last night. [A] Drahtbericht about this will follow. During the next few days, segregation of the Jewish Christians is to be completed. Jaross estimates the number to be 15–20,000.

He is also willing, also against the Regent, to carry out the further elimination of the Jews in Budapest without prior notification *[auf kaltem Weg]*.

To avoid substantial difficulties, he is thinking about initially concentrating them in a few camps – presumably in the current Zone V – and then releasing them for deportation to the Reich on a case by case basis, whenever 30–40,000 Jews have been accumulated. Even though this procedure is significantly more inconvenient and takes substantially more time, it nevertheless assures continuation of the action, and I will do everything I can to support Jaross in speeding up and implementing his plans as smoothly as possible. Towards this purpose, I propose to bring Attaché *[Gesandtschaftsrat]* Grell, who has been handling the Jewish question at the embassy very well for the past 6 weeks, into closer contact with Jaross, which is not meant to preclude his continuing to work together closely with the Eichmann office. I further report that based on my detailed knowledge of the situation, there continues to be no reason at all for any kind of concern. During this past week, the German embassy has shown itself to be a calming presence even during the most tense days. This did not fail to impress the Hungarians especially. I continue to view any kind of security measure as superfluous and even misguided, because it would only be viewed as a sign of weakness. The embassy is firmly in charge of all political connections and therefore [has] the means to deal with all eventualities in purely political ways.

The Führer therefore does not need to direct units to Hungary that are deployed to much better purpose elsewhere right now, even if such suggestions were to be made by the military or the police.

Veesenmayer

Appendix

14

Telegram from Plenipotentiary Veesenmayer to the German Foreign Ministry Concerning the Result of the Deportations

To be treated only as Classified

Budapest, the 11th July 1944 15.15 Hour
Arrival, the 11th July 1944 19.30 Hour

Nr. 1927 of 11.7.44. *[11 July 44]*

Secret!

Follow up to telegram nr. 1838+) of 30 June.[1]

I. Concentration and removal [of] Jews in Zone V [and] including Suburb Action-Budapest, totaling 55,741, completed on 9 July as planned. Total number to date from Zones I to V including Suburb Action, 437,402.

II. Progress on action against Budapest has been reported on separately to Fuschl.

Veesenmayer

---

[1] Not available.

Appendix

15

Telegram from Plenipotentiary Veesenmayer to the German Foreign Ministry
Concerning Horthy's Mood

Secret Reich Matter
To be treated only as Classified

(Secret Encryption)

Budapest, the 13th July 1944 17.20 Hour
Arrival, the 13th " " 23.15 Hour

Nr. 1948 of 13.7.44.

Secret Reich Matter!
=============

As reported to me by a confidant, the Regent is said to have spoken in an extraordinarily bleak and despondent manner last night about the political situation in Hungary. He himself no longer has any influence at all, which can be deduced from the fact that he was not even able to enforce the removal from office of the two under-secretaries, Baky and Endre.[1] He has now decided to put in place [a] military government. However, he did not state the names of the persons in question.

The Regent further stated that, regarding the Jewish question, he was being inundated with correspondence warning him against continuing on the current course. In this context, he is [said] to have mentioned not only letters from the Pope and the King of Sweden, but allegedly also a letter from the King of England. Finally, he declared that he had turned to the Führer himself in a personal letter regarding the Jewish question.[2]

Veesenmayer.

---

1   Although Minister Jaross, in compliance with the will of the Regent, on 30 June 1944 relieved both of them of their departmental responsibilities as heads of the Office of Public Security and the Office of Jewish Affairs respectively, they still remained under-secretaries. They were removed from their posts in the Ministry of Home Affairs only after the fall of the Sztójay administration at the end of August 1944.
2   Horthy to Adolf Hitler, 17 July 1944. *The Confidential Papers of Admiral Horthy*, Prepared for the press and introd. by M. Szinai and L. Szűcs (Budapest: Corvina Press, 1965), 317. Cf. G. Jeszenszky's Introduction to the present volume, p...

Appendix

16

Telegram from VEESENMAYER to RIBBENTROP
Reporting on a Discussion with Sztójay.

IV/K213961-962

Secret Reich Matter
To be treated only as Classified

Telegram
(Secret Encryption)

Budapest, the 17th July 1944 23.30 Hours
Arrival, the 18th " " 1.05 Hours
Nr. 1984 of 17.7.

Citissime!
Secret Reich Matter
============

For Mr. Reich Foreign Minister *[Reichsaussenminister]*

Just visited Sztojay, who was gratifyingly positive today. He informed me about the following:

1.) He had a longer conversation with Bardossy,[1] who approached him on his own initiative and explained to him that it is now time to take all measures to cleanse the Regent's entourage *[Umgebung]*. Bardossy took the position that one must make a clear distinction between the Regent and his entourage. The former can be guided and influenced, the latter must, under any circumstances, disappear. He is prepared to participate in this [endeavor] with all his strength. Sztojay suggested either including him in the Cabinet as Foreign Minister, since he expected this to be of significant benefit not only to that department but also to the Government's striking power in general, or to attempt to position him in place of the current head of the Cabinet, Ambrosi,[2] thereby to effect an incursion into the Castle Clique *[Burg-Klique]*.

---

1 László Bárdossy (1890–1946). Professional diplomat (Minister of Foreign Affairs February 1941 to March 1942, and also Prime Minister 4 April 1941 to 9 March 1942) who agreed to join in the war against the Soviet Union and to declare war on the United States. He was tried by a Hungarian court and shot in January 1946.
2 Gyula Ambrózy (1884–1954), jurist, a confidant of Horthy. As head of the Regent's Cabinet Office from 1943 to 15 October 1944, he was a key person in the attempts to leave the war. Arrested by the Germans and kept at the Mauthausen concentration camp. In 1951 the communist authorities of Hungary exiled him to a remote farm.

I view this last suggestion as a very welcome one, all the more so because I hear from different sides that Bardossy is increasingly less reserved and in a gratifying way is taking a clear position on our common cause.

2.) Sztojay explained that – assuming that he and his government remained – he would demand that the Regent's entourage be cleansed of all damaging elements, come what may. He and his government, with which he had an internal briefing at mid-day today, are in complete agreement on this, and if necessary, he will carry out arrests on his own initiative. He views this as a prerequisite for carrying out fruitful work with his government in the future. He will no longer tolerate another repetition of the events of Saturday.[3] He merely wants to wait until the Regent has <u>distanced</u> himself <u>for good</u> from <u>implementing</u> his plans regarding military and bureaucratic rule. I corroborated his position <u>and</u> assured him of my full support with all the means available to me.

3.) Sztojay led me to the next room and showed me his Foreign Ministry's diplomatic pouch, which was to have departed for Switzerland yesterday and which he had confiscated at the border. Together with a commission, he will investigate it personally tonight, because he harbors a suspicion that individuals in his Foreign Office have connections to the enemy side. Should this be confirmed, he will have the <u>corresponding</u> arrests carried out this same night and take uncompromising action. He also will no longer consult the Regent in such matters.

4.) This morning the Swiss envoy, Jäger, visited him, raised the Jewish question with him and prepared him for the fact that public opinion in Switzerland was outraged about the Hungarian Government's measures in this area and that Hungary needed to be prepared for Switzerland to consider severing its ties with Hungary. Sztojay <u>rejected</u> this announcement and expressed his strongest indignation to him and also pointed out to him that certain mitigation measures are being provided but that the Hungarian Government was not inclined to succumb to such extortionate pressure and needed to reserve all options for now.

Veesenmayer

---

3 On Saturday, 15 July 1944, Horthy had decided to dismiss the Sztójay Government, but an ultimatum from Hitler compelled him to drop the idea – temporarily.

Index

Aly, Götz, 17
Ambrózy, Gyula, 305n2
Anger, Per, 232, 237n40, 243n58, 245
Antal, István, 124n62, 142
Antall, József, 16n15, 18
Antonescu, Ion, 61–63, 88, 107, 160
Apor, Vilmos, 143, 144
Arendt, Hannah, 174, 175
Aschner, Lipót (Leopold), 224, 226
Auer, Pál, 72

Bajcsy-Zsilinszky, Endre, 81, 98
Bajnóczy, József, 116, 297n6
Baky, László, 8, 24–28, 34, 135–137, 145, 148, 152–154, 174, 208, 209n4–n5, 211, 212, 214–216, 218, 250, 252, 253, 259–261, 281, 290–292, 295, 298, 300, 304
Balogh, József, 223, 224
Bánffy, Miklós, 97
Barcza, György, 72, 76, 88n48, 103, 104, 108, 155
Bárczy, István, 152, 211, 288n9
Bárdossy, László, 29, 53, 78–85, 184, 244n60, 305, 306
Bartha, Károly, 79
Bartók, Béla, 78
Bauer, Yehuda, 138
Becher, Kurt, 133, 177n27
Beneš, Edvard, 60, 76, 79, 89, 104
Berecz, Endre, 139
Bereggfy, Károly, 115, 116
Berg, Lars, 245
Bethlen, István (count), 25–27, 29, 45, 76, 120, 122, 147, 155, 168, 176, 223n12, 224

Bibó, István, 16
Björkman, Erik, 228, 229
Bodenschatz, Karl-Heinrich, 296
Boheman, Erik, 232, 233, 241, 242n52
Bokor, Péter, 251
Bonde, Angelica, 233
Bonde, Ebba (countess), 240, 241
Bonde, Knut (baron), 233
Bonhardt, Attila, 32
Born, Friedrich, 180, 195
Bornemissza, Félix, 231
Braham, Randolph, 7n1, 14, 23, 28n42, 138, 150n130, 154n141, 161n3, 171, 174, 249n2

Chorin, Ferenc, 119, 121, 122, 133
Christensen, Ludolph, 227, 239
Christian X (King of Denmark), 120, 126, 159
Churchill, Winston, 69, 72, 77, 78, 93, 94, 97, 98, 104, 106
Ciano, Galeazzo (count), 49n24, 269
Cole, R. Taylor, 244
Cornelius, Deborah, 96
Cumberbatch, Cyril James, 222
Czapik, Gyula, 149
Csáky, István, 48, 49, 53

Danielsson, Carl Ivan, 195, 232, 245
Darányi, Kálmán, 48
Deák, István, 26, 32, 150, 154
Dessewffy, Gyula (count), 243
Hatvany-Deutsch, Sándor, 164
Dolányi-Kovács, Alajos, 190, 195
Dreisziger, Kálmán, 139, 140
Dulles, Allen W., 109

Index

Dulles, John Foster, 3

Eckhardt, Tibor, 47, 72, 78, 232
Eden, Anthony, 84, 86, 96, 98, 148
Eichmann, Adolf, 8, 14, 17, 27, 66, 128, 130, 131, 134, 136, 139, 142, 147, 150, 154, 172, 175, 177, 179, 208, 209n4, 218, 235n38, 250, 253, 260, 302
Ekstrand, Einar, 233
Endre, László, 24–26, 135, 137, 142, 145, 148, 154, 174, 208, 209n5, 211, 281, 284, 290, 304
Engzell, Gösta, 233
Erdélyi, Andrew, 257
Erez, Tsvi, 146
Esterházy, Móric (count), 224, 231

Faraghó, Gábor, 153, 209n5, 215
Farkas, Mihály, 184
Fenyvesi, Charles, 32, 91, 92
Ferenczy, László, 191, 209n5, 215n22
Francis Joseph (emperor-king), 20, 21, 68, 163, 173
Freudiger, Fülöp, 146
Fülöp, Gabriella, 4

Gellért, Andor, 244
Gambetta, Léon, 44
Gerlach, Christian, 17
Gerő, Ernő, 184
Ghyczy, Jenő, 110, 111, 115, 272n1
Gömbös, Gyula, 41–46, 48
Grafström, Sven, 232
Greiffenberg, Hans von, 116
Gripenberg, Georg, 233, 234
Gustav VII (King of Sweden), 2, 20, 26, 148, 176, 287, 291, 304
Günther, Christian, 232, 235, 236n39, 241, 242

Habsburg, Otto von, 94
Hägglöf, Gunnar, 232, 234
Hambro, Charles, 232

Hanák, Péter, 75
Hardy, Kálmán, 256
Hatz, Ottó, 91
Herzl, Theodor, 163, 164n6
Himmler, Heinrich, 17, 107, 128, 133, 134, 157, 177n27, 179, 218, 283n9
Hitler, Adolf, 1, 2, 11–13, 15, 17, 20–23, 26, 28, 29, 31, 33, 38, 40–42, 45, 47n16, 48, 49, 52n28, 53, 55–58, 60–62, 66–73, 75–78, 80, 83, 84, 86–90, 94, 96–100, 104–113, 118, 119, 122, 123, 126, 135, 143, 145, 150n130, 152, 156, 159, 168–170, 173, 179, 194n10, 203–205, 249, 255, 256, 258, 279, 296n3, 306n3
Horn, Gyula, 19
Horthy (Edelsheim Gyulai), Ilona, 119, 151
Horthy, István, 85, 100, 119
Horthy, Magda, 109, 151, 209
Horthy, Miklós, 2–5, 8, 9, 13, 18, 20–31, 37, 51, 52n28, 52nn29, 57–59, 61–64, 67, 70, 71, 77, 80, 81, 84–89, 91–93, 98–100, 104–115, 119, 120, 123–127, 129, 133–137, 142, 144–157, 166–170, 173, 174, 176–179, 184, 204–207, 209–212, 214–217, 224, 238n40, 252, 267n6, 283, 291, 292n5, 304, 305n2, 306n3
Horthy, Miklós (Nicky), Jr., 25, 100, 105, 147, 178, 224, 231, 237, 243
Höttl, Wilhelm, 106, 107, 204n1
Hull, Cordell, 53

Ihre, Nils, 234
Imrédy, Béla, 51, 112, 120, 123, 124, 133, 134, 143n110, 149, 290

Jagow, Gottlieb von, 58, 110, 267, 269, 272
Jaross, Andor, 24, 124n62, 132, 142, 154, 174, 208, 209n5, 217, 282n7, 285, 286, 301, 302, 304n1

Index

Jodl, Alfred, 58
Johnson, Herschel V., 226n17, 237, 241, 242
Joó, András, 96
Jurcsek, Béla, 124

Kádár, Gábor, 17
Kádár, Gyula, 91, 127, 297n5
Kádár, János, 251
Kállay, Miklós, 12, 21, 22, 38, 52–62, 85–89, 91, 94–99, 103, 104, 109, 110, 113, 115, 116, 118–123, 127, 170, 171, 206, 222, 237n40, 256, 267n5, 268, 274n6, 291
Kaltenbrunner, Ernst, 17
Kánya, Kálmán, 42, 46, 48
Kapi, Béla, 141
Károlyi, Mihály, 78, 89
Karsai, László, 17
Kautsky, Karl, 164
Keitel, Wilhelm, 52, 60, 105, 111, 116, 296
Kemény, Gábor (baron), 180, 196n19
Kennan, George, 74
Keresztes-Fischer, Ferenc, 110, 115, 119
Kern, Károly, 127
Kéthly, Anna, 122
Kiss, Sándor, 114
Kollontay, Alexandra, 96
Kornfeld, Móric (baron), 119, 133, 223n12, 224
Kossuth, Lajos, 38, 109, 122
Koszorús (also: Koszorus), Ferenc, 1–5, 8, 28, 32–35, 153, 154, 203, 206, 212, 214, 215, 217, 218, 250–262
Kovács, András, 17, 200
Közi-Horváth, József, 120
Krausz de Megyer, Lajos, 164
Kristóffy, József, 74, 79
Kunder, Antal, 124n62

Láday, István, 215
Lakatos, Géza, 30, 100, 155, 156
Lantos, Tom, 32, 252
Lauer, Kálmán, 226, 227, 229, 230n29, 234, 239, 240, 241n50, 242, 245
Lázár, Károly, 3, 153, 214, 215, 252, 253, 260
Lévai, Jenő, 188, 191
Lieszkovszky, Pál, 110
Listowel, Judy, 54
Lloyd George, David, 69
Luther, Franz Julius, 265, 269, 270
Lutz, Carl, 20, 180

Macartney, C.A., 38, 93, 96, 101, 111, 136, 256
Mackensen, Eberhard von, 41
Major, Jenő, 117
Mallet, Victor, 237
Márton, Áron, 24, 144
Marton, Ernő, 198
Marx, Karl, 164
Matthiessen, Carl, 227,–229
Matuska-Komáromy, Péter, 244
Mikes, János (count), 143
Miklós, Béla, dálnoki, 29, 197
Molnár, Judit, 138
Molotov, Vyacheslav, 74, 79, 83, 98
Mussolini, Benito, 55–57, 66, 69, 87, 90, 98, 169

Náday, István, 115, 116, 127
Namier, Lewis, 16, 95
Neurath, Konstantin von, 42
Nietzsche, Friedrich, 164

O'Malley, Owen, 72
Olsen, Iver, 226n17, 239, 242, 243n58, 244
Orbán, Viktor, 8, 9, 19
Orssich, Ferdinand (count), 243, 244n59

Pach, Zsigmond Pál, 190, 191, 200
Paksy-Kiss, Tibor, 215
Pallavicini, György., Jr. (marquis), 224

Index

Pelényi, János, 78
Pell, Herbert Claiborne, Jr., 81, 82
Perlasca, Giorgio (Jorge), 180
Pető, Ernő, 142n108, 144, 210n8
Petrusz, Tibor, 117
Petschauer, Attila, 169
Philipp, Rudolph, 239
Pius XII (Pope), 20, 26, 27, 81, 143, 148, 176, 182, 210, 287, 304

Rákosi, Mártyás, 184, 251n6, 261
Ránki, György, 16, 32, 97
Rassay, Károly, 121
Rátz, Jenő, 112, 124n62
Ravasz, László, 141, 142, 149, 150
Reményi-Schneller, Lajos, 124, 142n108
Révai, József, 184
Ribbentrop, Joachim von, 21, 25, 28, 29, 52, 107, 111, 112, 126, 127, 156, 256n2, 277n3, 285, 286, 290, 294, 295n1, 298, 301, 305
Roosevelt, Franklin D., 20, 26, 27, 83, 90, 93, 94, 98, 104, 106, 148, 176, 219
Róth, Szigfried, 190
Rotta, Angelo, 24, 144, 149, 180, 287n6
Ruszkiczay-Rüdiger, Imre, 291, 292

Sakmyster, Thomas, 29
Salén, Sven, 224, 227–231, 241, 242
Sándor, Vilmos, 200
Sargent, Orme, 71, 86
Schellenberg, Walter, 107
Schlachta, Margit, 182
Schreker, Károly, 89
Schwerin von Krosigk, Ludwig, 42
Serédi, Jusztinián, 24, 141–144, 149
Snyder, Árpád, 197
Soós, Géza, 243, 256
Stalin, Joseph, 31, 74, 84, 93, 95, 98, 100, 103, 106, 184, 220, 256, 262n35
Stark, Tamás, 154, 155n144,
Steengracht von Moyland, Gustav Adolf, 277

Stern, Samuel, 30, 130, 131n76, 137
Stollár, Béla, 182
Stúr, Judit, 125
Szabó, István, 169
Szakasits, Árpád, 122
Szálasi, Ferenc, 50n27, 126, 178–181, 184, 192, 195, 196n19, 212, 215, 288, 292
Szász, Lajos, 124
Szegedy-Maszák, Aladár, 88n49, 89
Szent-Györgyi, Albert, 57, 84, 244n59
Szent-Iványi, Domokos, 81, 88n48
Szombathelyi, Ferenc, 56, 91, 92, 97, 105, 109, 110–112, 116, 117, 126, 127, 297
Sztéhló, Gábor, 182
Sztójay, Döme, 13, 14, 23–26, 28–30, 50n26, 100, 119, 123–125, 135, 141–143, 145, 148, 151, 153, 155, 156, 174, 177, 184, 210, 237n40, 265–268, 272, 286–289, 290, 291, 293, 295–297, 299, 301, 304n1, 305, 306

Thadden, Ehrental von, 281
Teleki, Pál (also: Paul), 49n22, 50, 70, 74, 76–78
Thirring, Lajos, 197, 198
Tildy, Ferenc, 122
Tito, Josip, 31, 93, 104
Tölgyessy, Győző, 215
Török, Sándor, 146, 151

Újszászy, István, 127, 297n5
Ullein-Reviczky, Antal, 79n25, 81, 96, 104, 221–¬225, 231–237, 240–245
Ullein-Reviczky, Lovice Louisa Grace, née Cumberbatch, 222
Ullein-Reviczky, Lovice Maria, 221, 222
Undén, Östen, 232
Ungváry, Krisztián, 1781??

Vági, Zoltán, 17
Vámbéry, Rusztem, 78
Vansittart, Robert (lord), 70–71

Veesenmayer, Edmund, 12, 13, 15, 23–25, 27–31, 118, 119, 123, 127, 129, 135–137, 154, 155n146, 156, 195, 205, 217, 277, 279, 283, 285, 289, 292n5, 293
Veress, Lajos, 90, 122, 256
Vígh, Károly, 251
Vihar, Béla, 189
Vörös, János, 115, 116, 126, 153, 155n146, 156, 212, 292
Vrba, Rudolf, 146, 147, 209n7

Wahl, Alice von (baronet), 229
Wahl, Heinz von, 229, 243
Wahl, Vera von, 230n29
Wallenberg, Gustaf Oscar, 222
Wallenberg, Jacob, 221, 225, 226, 242
Wallenberg, Marcus, 221, 228n24, 229n26, 231, 232, 241n50
Wallenberg, Raoul, 9, 20, 29, 32, 34, 179, 180, 219–245, 256n24
Weichs, Maximilian von (baron), 118, 119, 123, 124
Weiner, Kati, 140
Weiss, Berthold, 164
Weiss, Jenő (baron), 133, 177n27
Weiss, Manfréd, 224, 227–229
Werth, Henrik, 79, 81n29
Wetzler, Alfred, 146, 209n7
Wiesel, Elie, 29

Zwack, János, 230n29
Zsilinszky, Antal, 78

Contributors

Géza Jeszenszky (b. 1941) is a retired professor of history at Corvinus University of Budapest, as well a politician and diplomat. Instrumental in the transition of Hungary into a democracy in 1989, he served as Minister of Foreign Affairs in the first freely elected government (1990-94) after the fall of communism. From 1998 to 2002 he served as the Hungarian ambassador to the United and States and to Norway and Iceland from 2011 to 2014.
He was visiting professor at the University of California, Santa Barbara, as well as the University of Michigan, Ann Arbor, in Warsaw, Poland, and in Cluj/Kolozsvár in Romania. He is the author of a large number of scholarly publications, his latest book in English is *Post-Communist Europe and Its National/Ethnic Problems* (Budapest, 2009). His memoir and analysis of Hungary's relations with its neighbors during the years of the regime change (in Hungarian) came out in 2016.

Charles Fenyvesi. A student of Central European history, Charles Fenyvesi was born in Debrecen in 1937. Joined the revolution of 1956, then fled to Austria in December of 1956. He won a full scholarship to Harvard and received a BA (cum laude) in 1960 and won a graduate fellowship to study philosophy at the University of Madras, India and received an MA (first class) in 1962. From 1970 to 1979 he served as editor of the National Jewish Monthly. In 1979 he joined the Washington Post as a staff writer, later garden columnist and frequent contributor to the Op-Ed page and Outlook section. From 1985 to 1997 he was a columnist for the U.S. News & World Report. Since then he has been a free-lance wrier, in 2000 he spent a year as writer and editor for the U.S. Presidential Advisory Commission on Holocaust Assets in the U.S. He has authored seven books on history and botany including *When Angels Fooled the World: Rescuers of Jews in Wartime Hungary* (University of Wisconsin/Dryad Press, 2003).

Contributors

Deborah S. Cornelius is a historian of East Central Europe. Her research focuses on the formation of a new political order after the Treaty of Trianon and movements for social and political reform. Her book, *Hungary in World War II: Caught in the Cauldron*, examines efforts of the truncated Hungarian state to restore governance, institutions, and the economy after World War I, and the path by which it agreed to an alliance with Nazi Germany during World War II in hopes of restoring its lost lands. The book, translated and expanded, was published with the title: *Kutyaszorítóban: Magyarország és a II. világháború*. Among other topics she has also written on questions of national identity, radical youth movements, the folk college movement and education for a new peasant leadership. She is currently researching the collapse of the traditional social order in Hungary after 1945. She received her PhD in History from Rutgers University.

Susanne Berger b. 1963 in Hannover, Germany, (B.A. International Relations, American University, Washington D.C.). Her research addresses the political and economic aspects of Swedish diplomat Raoul Wallenberg's humanitarian mission to Budapest during WWII, as well as his disappearance in the Soviet Union in 1945. Ms. Berger's studies have also focused on the fate of other disappeared Swedish citizens during the Cold War period.
Since 2001, Ms. Berger, together with historian Dr. Vadim Birstein, has conducted a detailed correspondence with Russian archivists and officials about the Raoul Wallenberg case. Their research confirmed that important additional documentation with direct relevance for the Wallenberg case remains available in key Russian archival collections, especially those of the former Soviet State Security and Intelligence Services.
Ms Berger's reports and more than one hundred articles about the Wallenberg case and related issues have appeared in various international publications. She is the founder and coordinator of the Raoul Wallenberg Research Initiative (RWI-70) and the Raoul Wallenberg International Roundtable.

Dr. Vadim J. Birstein is a geneticist and historian, born in Moscow and educated at Moscow State University. Since coming to New York in 1991, he has been a Visiting Scientist at the American Museum of Natural History, NY, and an Adjunct Professor of Biology at the University of Massachusetts, Amherst. In 2001, Dr. Birstein published his first history book, *The Perversion of Knowledge: The True Story of Soviet Science* (Westview Press). In 2012, his second history book, *SMERSH: Stalin's Secret Weapon, Military Counterintelligence in WWII*, was published in London (Biteback Books). It received the inaugural St. Ermin's Intelligence Book Award, beating out 33 other nominated books. In 2013, *SMERSH* was published in Poland. Dr. Birstein is also the author of over 150 scientific papers and three scientific books and papers on the Raoul Wallenberg case and Soviet military counterintelligence. He is a member of the American writers' Authors Guild.

Frank Koszorus, Jr., is an attorney and a life-long student of Central and Eastern Europe (CEE).
Mr. Koszorus has lectured at various universities; debated foreign policy issues on radio; testified before congressional committees; and briefed government officials concerning CEE. Mr. Koszorus has written letters to the editor; chapters; and articles relating to that region, including *Reflections on March 19, 1944 and Its Aftermath: A Perfect Storm of Tragedy and Folly*. He co-authored *Group Rights Defuse Tensions,* The Fletcher Forum of World Affairs. He also participated in a Carnegie Endowment for International Peace self-determination project.
In 1997, Mr. Koszorus traveled to NATO headquarters and CEE as a member of a government fact-finding mission on NATO enlargement. He was also appointed a public member of the U.S. delegation to the Paris meeting of the Conference on Security and Cooperation in Europe on the Human Dimension.
Mr. Koszorus is the recipient of several awards, including the The Commanders' Cross of the Order of Merit of Hungary. Mr. Koszorus graduated from The American University and from DePaul University College of Law *cum laude*.

István Deák, who is an emeritus professor at Columbia University in New York City, was born in Hungary and studied history in Budapest, Paris, Munich, and at Columbia University where he obtained his PhD degree in 1964.

For numerous years he was the director of Columbia's Institute on East Central Europe. His publications include, *Weimar Germany's Left-wing Intellectuals* (California, 1968); *The Lawful Revolution: Louis Kossuth and the Hungarians, 1848-1849* (Columbia, 1979); *Beyond Nationalism: A Social and Political History of the Habsburg Officer Corps, 1848-1918* (Oxford, 1990); *Essays on Hitler's Europe* (Nebraska, 2001), and *Europe on Trial: The Story of Collaboration, Resistance and Retribution During World War II* (Westview Press, 2015). Almost all the books appeared in several languages. He has been a frequent contributor to *The New York Review of Books* and *The New Republic*. István Deák is an external member of the Hungarian Academy of Sciences and has received other awards and honors.

György Ránki (1930 –1988) was Professor of History at Debrecen University and Director of the Institute of History, Hungarian Academy of Science. He was elected member of the Hungarian Academy of Sciences (1976). Having survived the Auschwitz concentration camp studied economics and history in Budapest. His interest and his many publications covered the economic history of Central Europe, international relations, the Second World War, and Hungary's political history in the 20th century. He was the first vice chairman of the International Committee of Historical Sciences, and member of the editorial board of several scholarly publications.

Thomas Lantos was an American politician who served as a Democratic member of the United States House of Representatives from California, serving from 1981 until his death in 2008 as the representative from a district that included the northern two-thirds of San Mateo County and a portion of southwestern San Francisco. A Hungarian-American, Lantos was the only Holocaust survivor to have served in the United States Congress.
In 2008, after his death, the Congressional Human Rights Caucus, which he founded in 1983, was renamed the Tom Lantos Human Rights Commission. Its mission is partly "to promote, defend and advocate internationally recognized human rights". In 2011, the Tom Lantos Institute was set up in Budapest to promote tolerance and support minority issues in Central and Eastern Europe and in the world.

Tamás Stark received his PhD from the Eötvös Lóránd University of Budapest in 1993. From 1983 he was a researcher at the Institute of History, Research Centre for the Humanities of the Hungarian Academy of Sciences, and in 2000 he was appointed a senior research fellow. His specialization is forced population movements in East-Central Europe in the period 1938-56, with special regard to the history of the Holocaust, fate of prisoners of war and civilian internees, and the post war migrations. He was involved in numerous international research projects. In 1995/96 he was Pearl Resnick Post-Doctoral fellow at the United States Holocaust Memorial Museum. In 2014 he was Fulbright professor at Nazareth College, Rochester, NY. USA. His main publications include *Hungary's Human Losses in World War II* (Uppsala, 1995), *Hungarian Jews during the Holocaust and after the Second World War, 1939-1949: A Statistical Review* (Boulder, CO 2000), *Magyarok szovjet fogságban [Hungarians in Soviet Captivity]* (Budapest, 2006), *A magyar polgári lakosság elhurcolása a Szovjetunióba a korabeli dokumentumok tükrében. [Deportation of Hungarian civilians to the Soviet Union. Documentary Collection]* (Budapest, 2017).

Attila Bonhardt (b. 1954). Studied history, geography and archival studies at Eötvös Lóránd University in Budapest, graduating in 1979. In the same year he joined the Military History Archives as an archivist. He received a Ph.D. in 1984 with a dissertation on the return of Hungarian POW's to their homeland after World War I. In 1989 he was appointed deputy director of the Military History Archives. From 1997 he served as the archivist in the Hungarian collection at the *Kriegsarchiv* in Vienna. Soon after his return, in 2004, he was appointed Director of the Military History Archives with the rank of colonel. Recently his area of scholarship focuses on the history of the Hungarian artillery in the period 1938–1945.

Photo Gallery

HUNGARY DURING WWII

Admiral Miklós Horthy de Nagybánya, Regent of Hungary – March 1920–October 16, 1944.
CREDIT: GETTY IMAGES

Viewing of a new tank. Regent Miklós Horthy climbing into a tank, From left, Lt. General Keresztes-Fischer, Lt. General (later) Szombathelyi Ferenc, Major Ferenc Koszorús fourth from left. Spring 1938.
CREDIT: KOSZORÚS FAMILY ARCHIVES

From left to right: Major Károly Chemez, Lt. Colonel Ferenc Koszorús and Major István Beleznay, circa 1941

Credit: Koszorús Family Archives

Lt. Colonel Ferenc Koszorús (third from right) and fellow tank officers left to right Károly Chemez, unknown, István Beleznay. Circa 1941

Credit: Koszorús Family Archives

Colonel Ferenc Koszorús at a gala dinner at the Ludovika Military Academy. Circa 1942–1943
CREDIT: KOSZORÚS FAMILY ARCHIVES

Minister of Defense General Vilmos Nagybaczoni Nagy and Prime Minister Miklós Kállay. 1942
CREDIT: NAGYBACZONI FAMILY ARCHIVES

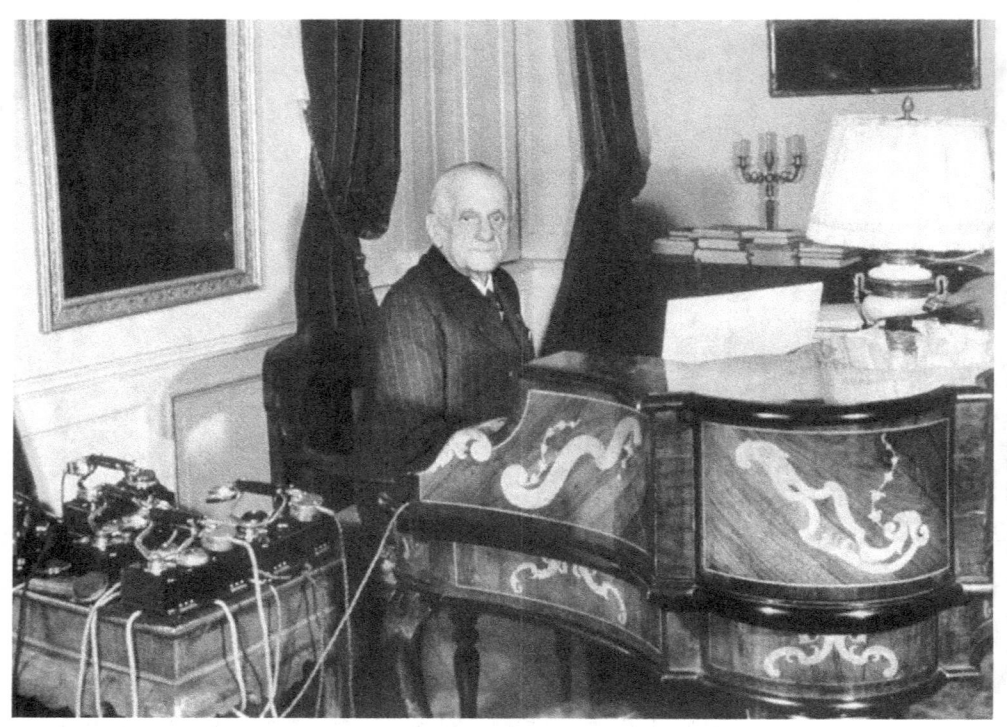

Kálman Kánya, Hungarian Foreign Minister from 1933–1938.
CREDIT: GETTY IMAGES: PHOTOGRAPHER – MARGARET BOURKE WHITE

AFTER GERMAN OCCUPATION OF HUNGARY MARCH 15, 1944

Edmund Veesenmayer: SS Brigadenfuehrer and Reich plenipotentiary in Hungary March 1944

CREDIT: HUNGARIAN NATIONAL MUSEUM PHOTO ARCHIVE

Veesenmayer giving Nazi salute at an event at the Uránia Theater, Budapest.

CREDIT: HUNGARIAN NATIONAL MUSEUM PHOTO ARCHIVE

Döme Sztójay, Prime Minister of Hungary under the German occupation, March 22, 1944–August 29, 1944.
Credit: Hungarian National Museum Photo Archive

Adolf Eichmann German Nazi SS Obersturmbannführer. Oversaw deportation of much of Hungary's German population after German occupation of Hungary in March of 1944.
Credit: Hungarian National Museum Photo Archive

The new prime minister of Hungary, Arrow Cross party leader Ferenc Szálasi , greets his troop commander in front of the Ministry of Defense in Budapest. Pictured left to right: Jenő Szöllősi (Deputy Prime Minister) Emil Kovarcz (minister in charge of mobilization and war readiness) Ferenc Kassai-Schallmayer (Minister of Propaganda and National Defense), Gábor Vajna (Minister of the Interior), a German SS photographer, a member of the Hungarian Military Police; an Hungarian police official and Károly Beregfy (Minister of Defense)
CREDIT: UNITED STATES HOLOCAUST MEMORIAL MUSEUM, COURTESY OF EVA HEVESI EHRLICH.

1944 View of wartime Budapest after the American bombings
CREDIT: UNITED STATES HOLOCAUST MUSEUM: COURTESY OF ENRICO MANDEL- MANTELLO

The British legation like many others of the diplomatic community in Budapest flew the flag of the neutral Switzerland as a safe house.
Credit: United States Holocaust Memorial Museum: Eric Saul

Police attempt to control the crowd of Jews, who are waiting outside a branch of the Swiss legation located in the Glass House on Vadász Street hoping to obtain a *Schutzbriefe* that would protect them from deportation. The Glass House ultimately became the refuge for over four thousand Jews. In the foreground is the car used by Vice Consul Carl Lutz.
Credit: United States Holocaust Memorial Museum, courtesy of Agnes Lutz Hirschi

Consul Charles (Carl) Lutz, the Swiss Vice Consul in Budapest poses at the gate of the "evacuation quarters" of the Swiss legation in Bicske, about a half hour from Budapest. Lutz is credited with saving more than 62,000 Jews who were living in Budapest between 1942–1945. He established 76 safe houses in Budapest St. Stephen's ghetto and put them under his diplomatic protection. The Safe houses sheltered over thirty thousand Jews, nearly all survived the war. In 1965 he was recognized by Yad Vashem as one of the Righteous Among the Nations.

CREDIT: UNITED STATES HOLOCAUST MEMORIAL MUSEUM, COURTESY OF ERIC SAUL.

Swedish Schutzpass issued to Éva Balog signed by Carl Ivan Danielsson

CREDIT: UNITED STATES HOLOCAUST MEMORIAL MUSEUM: COURTESY OF ERIC SAUL

Carl Ivan Danielsson, Head of Swedish Legation Budapest, named Righteous Among the Nations by Yad Vashem for his rescue of Budapest Jews during the last year of WWII

CREDIT: UNITED STATES HOLOCAUST MEMORIAL MUSEUM: COURTESY OF ERIC SAUL

Entrance to a yellow star house Orsós Street 35 in Budapest's II district.

CREDIT: UNITED STATES HOLOCAUST MEMORIAL MUSEUM; FORTEPAN TIVADAR LISSAK

George Mandel-Montello – Salvadoran Diplomatic rescuer. Born György Mandl in Transylvania, served as First Secretary of the El Salvadoran consulate in Geneva where he used his position to issue thousands of Salvadoran citizenship papers to Jewish refugees in Nazi occupied Europe between 1942–1944. He initiated a publicity campaign to inform the world about the deportation of Hungarian Jews and the mass murders taking place Auschwitz.

CREDIT: UNITED STATES HOLOCAUST MEMORIAL MUSEUM: COURTESY OF ERIC SAUL

Decree in Kassa restricting movement of its Jewish population. 27 April 1944.

CREDIT: FORTEPAN

Jewish deportees 1944. Credit: Fortepan

Jewish Children being deported 1944. Credit: Fortepan

Jewish Children in the Budapest Ghetto
CREDIT: FORTEPAN, PHOTOGRAPHER: TIVADAR LISSÁK

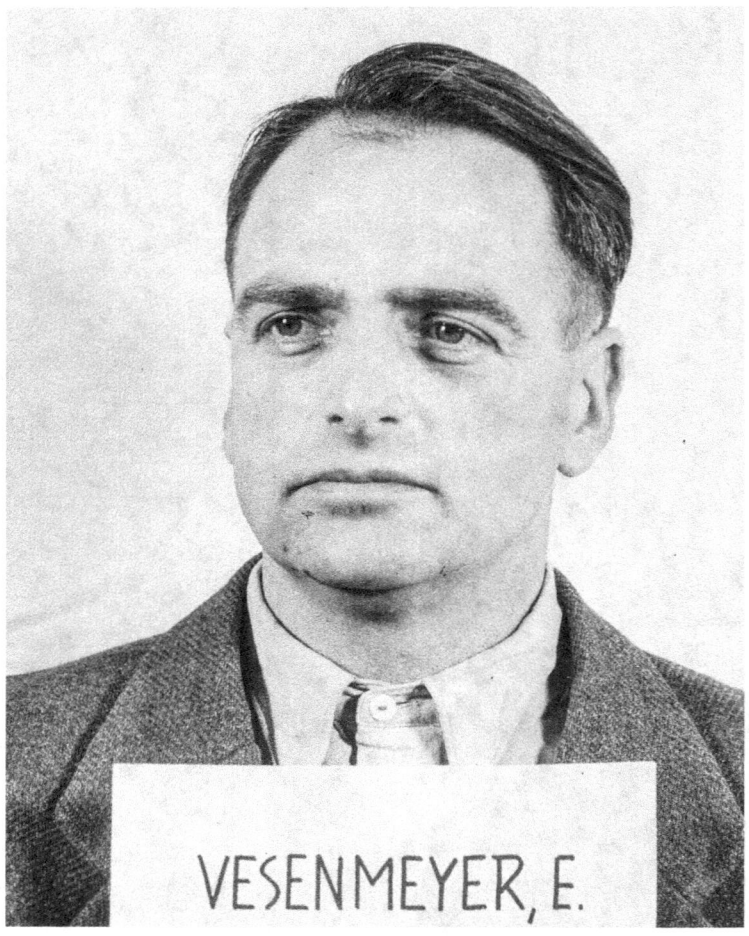

Mug shot of Edmund Veesenmayer (name spelled incorrectly as Vesenmeyer, the former Nazi governor of Hungary) taken at the Nuremberg trials 1948

CREDIT: UNITED STATES HOLOCAUST MEMORIAL MUSEUM, COURTESY OF ROBERT KEMPNER

Hungarian soldiers prepare former Prime Minister Döme Sztójay for execution in the courtyard of the Academy of Music Budapest.
CREDIT: UNITED STATES HOLOCAUST MEMORIAL MUSEUM, COURTESY OF HERBERT C. KAPLAN

Hungarian soldiers execute former Prime Minister Béla Imrédy convicted of war crimes February 28, 1946.
CREDIT: UNITED STATES HOLOCAUST MEMORIAL MUSEUM, COURTESY OF HERBERT C. KAPLAN

Thomas Peter Lantos (born Tamás Péter Lantos; February 1, 1928–February 11, 2008) was an American politician who served as a Democratic member of the United States House of Representatives from California, serving from 1981 until his death in 2008. A Hungarian-American, Lantos was the only Holocaust survivor to have served in the United States Congress.

In 2008, after his death, the Congressional Human Rights Caucus, which he founded in 1983, was renamed the Tom Lantos Human Rights Commission. Its mission is partly "to promote, defend and advocate internationally recognized human rights". In 2011, the Tom Lantos Institute was set up in Budapest to promote tolerance and support minority issues in Central and Eastern Europe and in the world.

PHOTO CREDIT: GETTY IMAGES. PHOTOGRAPHER: FREDERIC J. BROWN

www.ingramcontent.com/pod-product-compliance
Lightning Source LLC
Chambersburg PA
CBHW070041230426
43661CB00034B/1453/J